TESI GREGORIANA

Serie Teologia

57

JOHN CHIJIOKE IWE

JESUS IN THE SYNAGOGUE OF CAPERNAUM: THE PERICOPE AND ITS PROGRAMMATIC CHARACTER FOR THE GOSPEL OF MARK

And Exegetico-Theological Study of Mk 1:21-28

EDITRICE PONTIFICIA UNIVERSITÀ GREGORIANA

Roma 1999

Vidimus et approbamus ad normam Statutorum Universitatis

Romae, ex Pontificia Universitate Gregoriana
die 18 junii anni 1999

R.P. Prof. KLEMENS STOCK, S.J.
R. Prof. MASSIMO GRILLI

ISBN 88-7652-846-6
PRINTED IN ITALY

GREGORIAN UNIVERSITY PRESS
Piazza della Pilotta, 35 - 00187 Rome, Italy

Riproduzione anastatica: 28 dicembre 1999
Stab. Tipolit. Ugo Quintily S.p.A. - Roma
Finito di stampare nel mese di Dicembre 1999

ACKNOWLEDGEMENTS

I am obliged to acknowledge and thank those who helped me to bring this dissertation to a successful end. I must give glory and thanks to God, whose divine providence sustained me throughout the period of this work and my studies in Rome. My heartfelt gratitude goes to the director of this Thesis, Rev. Prof. Klemens Stock, S.J., whose scrupulous and invaluable guidance, rigorous and constructive criticism, fatherly patience and consideration made it a reality. I sincerely thank Rev. Prof. Massimo Grilli for accepting to read this work and for his constructive suggestions that improved its quality. I am greatly indebted to Pfr. Karl-Anton Kornes, Don Luigi Bandera, Don Leonello Birettoni, P. Johannes Wenning, C.M.M., P. Gilbert Wieners, O.F.M., Fam. Francescaglia, Diana, Colavita, Sig. Gianni Campagnoli, Fam. Zangrossi, Heinen, Huchwajda, Frau Linda Kittlaus, and a host of others I cannot exhaust here, whose support and encouragement sustained me in this Thesis. Likewise my gratitude goes to Very Rev. Fr. Rudolph Smit, the Rector of Pontifical College Olandese, for his concern and support, and for the condusive atmosphere, which I enjoyed in my studies in this College. I am also grateful to the Congregation for the Propagation of Faith for their scholarship award for my studies during my Licentiate in Biblicum.

I want to express my deep appreciation to Rev. Prof. James Swetnam, S.J., Rev. Dr. John I. Okoye and Rev. Dr. Fortunatus Nwachukwu for their insightful contribution to this work. I am very grateful to Rev. Dr. Augustine Akubeze and Rev. Fr. John I. Amuji for reading some parts of this Thesis, and to Sig. Carlo Valentino, Rev. Frs. Andreas L. Atawolo, Agustinus Kunarwoko and Antonius H. Kustono for their assistance in the Computer setting of this work. I will also extend my thanks to the Universities of Würzburg and Eichstätt, for allowing me to use their Libraries. My special thanks go to all the Parishes in Italy, Germany and

America, where I did my pastoral work during this period for making me feel at home among them, and for their generosity.

I must thank my Bishop, Most Rev. Dr. Anthony E. Ilonu, for his fatherly care and for sending me to Rome for this specialization. My profound gratitude goes to the members of my family, especially my parents, Mr. & Mrs. Martin and Veronica Iwe, whose love and affection have supported my priesthood and studies. Finally, to all my Professors, Rectors, Benefactors and Benefactresses, Collegues, Friends and wellwishers in Nigeria, Italy, Germany, Malta, America, I say from my whole heart: Many Thanks!

GENERAL INTRODUCTION

1. The Theme and its Limits

The Theme of our dissertation, which is limited to the pericope (1:21-28), considers Jesus' first public appearance and activity in Galilee. Jesus' presence in the synagogue of Capernaum effectively initiated his public ministry. Here Jesus taught and cast out an unclean spirit from a possessed man in the synagogue. Although the unclean spirit resisted him crying out Jesus' identity, yet Jesus' peremptory command silenced and drove it out of the man. The people were greatly amazed at this new teaching with authority (not like the scribes), that even unclean spirits obey his command. And immediately the news of Jesus' word and deed in the synagogue spread everywhere in Galilee.

It is our central affirmation (thesis) that this text has a programmatic character for the Gospel of Mark. When we say that this pericope is «programmatic», we mean that it contains major features or many of the main themes of Jesus' activity in the Gospel story. However, the programmatic character in Mark is structurally different from what one could experience in Matthew or Luke. Indeed, in Luke, this programmatic character is seen in the pericope, 4:16-30, which presents in summary form the theme of fulfillment and rejection that will mark Jesus' ministry as a whole; and in Matthew, 5:1-7:29 (the Sermon on the Mount) gives an important place to Jesus' teaching activity in his whole ministry; while in Mark, the pericope (1:21-28) is regarded as programmatic, because the themes/motives present in it are found throughout the ministry of Jesus, and are both repetitive and verifiable in the Gospel. In fact, this pericope is dense and contains, not all Markan themes, but rather, many of the fundamental or very important themes of Jesus' ministry in Mark's Gospel. Its placement at the beginning of the account of Jesus' ministry introduces the reader to what is going to happen in the story of Jesus' public activity, and affects his understanding of the entire narrative. Therefore, it will be our task in this dissertation: to analyze and discover, in the first part, the important words and themes/motives in this pericope; and to demonstrate systematically, in the second part, that these themes/motives in Mk 1:21-28 are present throughout Jesus' ministry in Mark's Gospel.

2. Status Quaestionis

We observed from our investigation that there are no books or monographs specifically dedicated to this pericope, but rather there are some monographs on some of the themes within the text[1]. However, we saw two articles devoted to the systematic study of this pericope. These are the articles of R. Pesch[2] and P. Guillemette[3]. Pesch observes the overemphasis on teaching without content, and thus sees «exorcism» as Jesus' first miracle, which has an important role to play in his ministry[4], and acts as the illustration of Jesus' teaching with authority[5]. While Guillemette, in his article (a critique of Pesch's), sees the link established between teaching and exorcism in 1:21-28 by Mark, as influencing his whole gospel because this story is «programmatic»[6].

Many scholars affirmed the important function of this pericope in Mark's Gospel, and observed that it has a *programmatic character*. And this means that the pericope contains major features or many of the main themes of Jesus' ministry in Mark's Gospel. However, some attribute this programmatic character to the Teaching: Osborne opines,

> As the content of the temptation narrative in 1:12-13 may have been omitted partly because it is programmatic for the cosmic conflict theme of the rest of Mark's Gospel, so the content of Jesus' teaching may have been omitted

---

[1] These are some of the themes and their monographs: Jesus' being with his disciples: K. STOCK, *Boten*; the people's motif of wonder: T. DWYER, *Motif of Wonder*; Jesus' authority: K. SCHOLTISSEK, *Vollmacht Jesu*; Jesus' identity: C.R. KAZMIERSKI, *Jesus, the Son of God*; and Jesus' exorcism: G.H. TWELFTREE, *Jesus the Exorcist*.

[2] R. PESCH, «Eine neue Lehre».

[3] P. GUILLEMETTE, «Un enseignement nouveau».

[4] Cf. R. PESCH, «Eine neue Lehre», 266-267.

[5] R. PESCH, «Eine neue Lehre», 269-272.

[6] P. GUILLEMETTE, «Un enseignement nouveau», 243.

here partly because it is *programmatic* of Jesus' ongoing teaching in the rest of the Gospel[7].

Some others see this function in the Exorcism: Lane states that «this initial act of exorcism in the ministry of Jesus is *programmatic* of the sustained conflict with the demons which is a marked characteristic in the Marcan presentation of the gospel»[8]. This programmatic function of this pericope is also seen by some others in the combination of Teaching and Exorcism: Okoye affirms,

> That Mark portrays this combination of teaching and exorcism as *programmatic* is evident from 1:39 where his style in proclaiming the rule throughout Galilee was characterized as «preaching in their synagogues and driving out devils», just as in our story Jesus preached in the synagogue and cast out a demon[9].

While some others consider the pericope as a unit playing this role: Ambrozic observes that

> the pericope ought, undoubtedly, to be looked upon as a *programmatic* and, in a sense, paradigmatic statement in regard to the rest of the ministry of Jesus, for it introduces the reader to a number of themes dear to Mark's heart: Jesus' teaching and casting out of demons, his divine sonship, the amazement aroused in the witnesses of his teaching and mighty work, the universal echo produced by his ministry and, possibly, the theme of the Messianic secret[10].

Based on this last group, I want to note that although they affirmed the function of this pericope, yet they noticed only some but not all the programmatic aspects, for example: Jesus in company; the concept of

---

[7] G.R. Osborne, «Structure and Christology», 149.

[8] W.L. Lane, *Mark*, 75; Cf. D. Trunk, «Jesus, der Exorzist», 9; J. Lagrand, «First of the Miracle Stories», 480; R.A. Guelich, *Mark*, 55, 60; E. Bianchi, «Esci da costui»,116.

[9] J.C. Okoye, «Mark 1:21-28», 241; Cf. K. Scholtissek, *Vollmacht Jesu*, 122-123, 137; P. Guillemette, «Un enseignement nouveau», 243; K. Tagawa, *Miracles et Évangile*, 88.

[10] A. M. Ambrozic, «New Teaching, 114; G.H. Twelftree, *Jesus the Exorcist*, 57; R.T. France, «Teaching of Jesus»,106, 110; K. Stock, *Boten*, 25, 27, adds that this pericope should not be there by chance, but rather it programmatically introduces Jesus' ministry in Mark, and therefore must have the same meaning in the Gospel as Mt 5-7 and Lk 4:16-30. The *italics* of «programmatic» in the above quotations are mine.

sabbath, or of synagogue; Jesus' authority; Jesus' mission; Jesus' contrast with the scribes; and Galilee in Jesus' mission; and moreover, they didn't prove this character. Hence it is precisely the aim of our Thesis, to discover all these aspects and to prove or demonstrate systematically that this pericope as a unit, with its themes and motives, has a *programmatic character* in Mark's Gospel.

3. Method

The exegetical method that will be adopted in our work will be *synchronic*. It «concentrates on the text as it now presents itself in written form and as a complex whole of text signals»[11], and considers this text as a structured and coherent unit in which the elements are combined in a manner to determine a unitary body[12]. The significance of the text is therefore found in relationships created by organizational patterns within this common framework. Thus, the text becomes an autonomous system which creates meaning within a singular frame of reference[13]. In other words, our pericope will find its significance or meaningful interpretation within its textual unit, and above all, within the wider context of Mark's Gospel. In our analysis we shall also benefit from the results of other critical studies of our pericope.

4. Division of Work

This Thesis will be divided into two parts: the first will be exegetical and analytical; while the second will be theological and synthetical. The first part will analyze our pericope in four different ways: Linguistic-Syntactic, Semantic, Narrative and Pragmatic (Reader-Response) Analysis. On the other hand, the second part will aim at verifying whether these theological themes/motives that emerged from the exegetical analysis, can be seen throughout Mark's Gospel.

Our Thesis will consist of *seven chapters* and a *general conclusion*. The *first* chapter begins with preliminary observations of the pericope, in which the textual unit is established through its delimitation, textual

---

[11] B.M.F. VAN IERSEL, *Reader-Response Commentary*, 17; J.G. COOK, *Structure and Persuasive Power*, 2, adds that it looks at the meaning of the text as it stands without asking questions about its historical development.

[12] Cf. W. EGGER, *Methodenlehre zum Neuen Testament*, 74.

[13] Cf. E.K. BROADHEAD, *Teaching with Authority*, 26.

criticism, structure and synoptic comparison. The importance of the position of this pericope is very much highlighted in the comparison with *Matthew* and *Luke*. The Linguistic-Syntactic Analysis immediately follows by examining the lexical, grammatical, syntactical and stylistic elements of the text which reveal the first appearance of the key-words and the peculiarity of *Mark*. The Semantic Analysis is seen in the *second* chapter, where the meaning of the text is sought through verse by verse analysis of the key-words, phrases and expressions of the pericope. It is also through this analysis that the main themes/motives of the pericope are put in relief. In the *third* chapter, the Narrative Analysis shows how the author/narrator transmits his message to his readers/hearers. Here Jesus is characterized as the main character of the story, through the development of the plot, narrator's point of view, narrative patterns, and above all, through the words and actions of the main characters. While the *fourth* chapter examines the function and effect of the Gospel message on the reader/hearer. This analysis shows how active and creative the reader is in the process of reading a text, and the dialectical relationship between the text and the reader in the product of meaning. At this juncture, the Part I ends with a summary of the themes/motives highlighted through the exegetical analyses, which will be taken up in Part II.

In Part II, the verification of these themes throughout Mark's Gospel begins. In fact, these themes/motives are limited to those relating to Jesus. Thus, the *fifth* chapter takes up the question about Jesus' identity, his authority and his mission. This investigation reveals that the dominant designation of Jesus' identity is the «Son of God»; that Jesus' authority is most evident in his words and deeds, a cause of wonder among the people and offence and conflict among his antagonists; and that Jesus' mission leads him to the inauguration of God's kingdom, destruction of demonic/evil powers, salvation of man, and crowns it with a total self-giving of himself. In the *sixth* chapter, we shall meet Jesus' main activity in the synagogue of Capernaum, Teaching and Exorcism. Indeed these are also Jesus' main activities in Mark's Gospel, because «teaching» is the habitual activity of Jesus (10:1), which attracts the crowd always to gather around him; while «exorcism» is the dominant and largest single healing story, in which Jesus manifests his superior power over the cosmic forces. However, in the *seventh* chapter Jesus' relationship with the main characters in the story will be considered, especially with his disciples, the crowd and the scribes. Here Jesus is always in the company of his disciples, both in his movements and ministry; the crowd (people) reacts often with wonder at Jesus' words and deeds; while the scribes' contrast with Jesus is constant from the beginning to the end of his ministry. The *general conclusion* will bring this proof to an end.

Therefore, it is through the discovery of the concentration of Mark's principal and dominant themes in our pericope, its verification within the larger context of the whole of Mark's Gospel, the position of this pericope in the Gospel, the first appearance of some important words in this pericope, and the centrality of Jesus in the story, that I want to demonstrate that *Mk 1:21-28 has a programmatic character* for Jesus' ministry in the Gospel of Mark.

PART ONE

EXEGETICAL ANALYSIS OF MARK 1:21-28

INTRODUCTION

The main purpose of this first part of our Thesis is to analyze exegetically and discover the principal elements, key-words, and themes in our pericope (Mk 1:21-28). In the first chapter we shall concentrate on the establishment of the text, and its linguistic-syntactic content. The second chapter attempts to investigate into the meaning of the text, and to highlight the themes/motives in the pericope. In the third chapter attention will be focused on the author/narrator, especially on how he communicates his message to his readers/hearers and characterizes the actors in the story. Lastly, the fourth chapter will reflect on the reader's role in the process of reading and product of the meaning of the text.

CHAPTER I

Linguistic-Syntactic Analysis

In this chapter we shall try to situate our pericope within its larger context. It will be divided into two sections: Preliminary Observations and Linguistic-Syntactic Analysis. In the preliminary observations, we shall not only establish the text in its context, but also its position in Mark's Gospel. While in linguistic-syntactic analysis, we shall concentrate in examining Markan key-words or favourite terms.

1. Preliminary Observations

In this section we shall place the text in its context, examine and establish the textual unit through its delimitation, textual criticism, structure and synoptic comparison. We shall attempt to discover the significance of the pericope's position in Mark's Gospel, by comparing it with other synoptic evangelists, Matthew and Luke.

1.1 *The Text in its Context*

As our pericope belongs to a larger text, it will be necessary to place it within the global structure of the Gospel of Mark. The problem of deciding what the structure of the Gospel under discussion is, has engaged many scholars for many years now. This will not be our concern here, suffice it to indicate the generally accepted working structure for our task. Earlier it was the geographical structure, or the topographical and the like, but today the structure mostly accepted is that based on literary and theological criteria.

According to this literary and theological structure, Mark's Gospel begins with an introduction (1:1-13), and then is divided into two principal parts: 1:14-8:26 and 8:27-16:8. The first part is further subdivided into three sections: 1:14-3:6; 3:7-6:6a; 6:6b-8:26; while the second part is also subdivided into three sections: 8:27-10:52; 11:1-13:37; 14:1-16:8[1].

This first part of the Gospel (1:14-8:26) is *characterized* by the problem of Jesus' identity on the part of the people; while on Jesus' part, there is a progressive revelation of his messianic identity through his public activity. The second part of the Gospel is *characterized* by the passion of Jesus. Here Jesus' identity is revealed through the mystery of the suffering Son of Man. Based on the literary and theological structure of the Gospel, one sees the role of 8:27-30, in revealing Jesus' messianic identity through Peter's confession (8:29): Σὺ εἶ ὁ Χριστός. As this is at the centre of the Gospel it constitutes the transition from the first to the second part. Therefore, Peter's Confession, as De La Potterie affirms, is the *terminus-ad-quem* of the first part (of what precedes) and the *terminus-a-quo* of the rest (of what follows)[2].

Hence, our pericope falls within the first part (1:14-8:26) of the Gospel, and within its first section (1:14-3:6). Jesus' ministry in this section is characterized by an authority that is extraordinary and unique (cf. 1:22,27; 2:7,28)[3]. In fact, Jesus exhibited his authority by calling his first disciples, who followed him immediately (1:16-20), and with them he came to Capernaum (1:21-28), where he exercised this divine authority in word and deed through his teaching and exorcism in the synagogue. Here in the synagogue of Capernaum, Jesus begins his first public activity in his Galilean ministry. Having established the text in its context, we shall now go to the text itself.

1.2 *The Delimitation of the Text*

In order to delimit our pericope from its context and establish the unity of the text, we shall examine the literary (verbs, as the motor of action), locational (geographical or topographical), thematic, temporal or stylistic factors, and above all, the characters (*dramatis personae*) in the story.

---

[1] I. DE. LA POTTERIE, «De Compositione», 138-141; Cf. E. SCHWEIZER, «Theologische Leistung», 337-355; ID., *Markus*, 214; K. STOCK, *Boten*, 54; S. KUTHIRAKKATTEL, *The Beginning*, 45-60; J.G. COOK, *Structure and Persuasive Power*, 13-52 (a summary of different structures in Mark's Gospel).

[2] Cf. I. DE LA POTTERIE, «De Compositione», 137; S. KUTHIRAKKATTEL, *The Beginning*, 37.

[3] Cf. S. KUTHIRAKKATTEL, *The Beginning*, 263.

Jesus came from Nazareth to Galilee (ἦλθεν, 1:9,14), passing the sea of Galilee (παράγων, v.16) he called his disciples, and they came to Capernaum (εἰσπορεύονται, v.21), and then they came into the house of Simon and Andrew (ἦλθον, v.29). One can observe a continuous movement in Jesus' ministry. That v.20 ends with ἀπῆλθον ὀπίσω αὐτοῦ and v.21 begins with εἰσπορεύονται, shows the beginning of a new pericope[4]. As a matter of fact, v.21 has two indications of entry: entry into Capernaum and into the synagogue (εἰσελθὼν εἰς τὴν συναγωγήν). This entry into the synagogue and going out of it, ἐκ τῆς συναγωγῆς ἐξελθόντες (v.29), highlights the unity of our text. Moreover, v.29 does a double job, of closing the pericope that began in v.21 and opening a new one. Thus, the opening and closing of our pericope is clearly stated. On the other hand, the literary connection between v.27 and v.22, and the stylistic expression in vv.21b and 23, καὶ εὐθύς, strengthen the unity of our text[5].

On the locational (geographical or topographical) setting, our pericope also forms a unit: in v.16: the Sea of Galilee; v. 21: Capernaum/ synagogue[6]; v.29: the house of Simon and Andrew. Likewise the main themes differ for these three pericopes: Call of the first disciples; teaching and exorcism; and healing of the sick. Our text has also a definite temporal setting «on the sabbath» - τοῖς σάββασιν, unlike the preceding or following pericopes. With regard to the characters in the story of the pericopes: Jesus and the four disciples (vv.16-20); Jesus, the disciples and those in the synagogue (vv.21-28); Jesus, the disciples and the household of Simon (vv.29-31). Thus, we see here what seems like «Private-Public-Private». From what we have seen so far, it is quite clear that the unity of our text constitutes no problem to identify or establish. Now we turn to the textual criticism of our pericope.

---

[4] Cf. R. PESCH, «Eine neue Lehre», 245, confirms that v.21a begins a new pericope but in no way ends the preceding one (1:16-20).

[5] Cf. R. PESCH, «Eine neue Lehre», 245; R.A. GUELICH, Mark, 55, affirms that, «the crowd's response to Jesus' "new teaching with authority" in 1:27 forms an inclusion with their response to his teaching "with authority" in 1:22 and makes 1:21-22, 23-28 into a single literary complex». Cf. D. DIDEBERG – P.M. BEERNAERT, «Jésus vint en Galilée», 317, 323.

[6] Cf. R. PESCH, «Eine neue Lehre», 245; E. MANICARDI, Il Cammino di Gesù, 26, observes that the fact that the synagogue is explicitly mentioned (cf. v.29), indicates that the location in a building changes with regard to vv.21b-28, and the location at Caperanum (v.21a) instead still remains valid.

1.3 *Textual Criticism*

In our pericope there are no serious textual problems to discredit the authenticity of the text, however, there are some minor indications of insertions, omissions, transpositions and parallels that do not constitute obstacles to establishing our text. We shall try to examine some four textual problems.

Our attention will go first to v.21. It is interesting to note that the *GNT³*, the *Nestle-Aland²⁶* and the *SQE¹³* all identified this problem, but for the latest *GNT* (4th revised edition), such a problem does not exist anymore. However, here there is a problem of either insertion which tries to correct a seemingly awkward construction or an accidental omission of the participle. For this study I will base myself on the *Synopsis* since it has more variants[7]. Now let us look at the variant witnesses:

1) ἐδίδασκεν εἰς τὴν συναγωγήν ℵ L f¹³ 565 pc (syˢ); Or
2) εἰς τὴν συναγωγὴν αὐτῶν ἐδίδασκεν Δ (892, syᵖ)
3) εἰσελθὼν εἰς τὴν συναγωγὴν ἐδίδασκεν αὐτούς D Θ 700. 1342 lat syʰ** boᵐˢˢ
4) εἰσελθὼν ἐδίδασκεν εἰς τὴν συναγωγήν 33
5) εἰσελθὼν εἰς τὴν συναγωγὴν ἐδίδασκεν A B W f¹ 1006. 1342.1506.2427 M (t) syʰ

Looking at the five variant readings numbers 2, 3 and 4 are inclined to the improvement of the text for a smoother reading: with the insertion of αὐτῶν; αὐτούς and the transposing of ἐδίδασκεν respectively. The problem rests with numbers 1 and 5. It is really not so easy to decide especially with external and internal evidences, and also the critical editions or commentators have divided opinions on the matter[8]. Nevertheless, there is a way out: no. 5 is, on the one hand, supported by the predominant weight of external evidence (A B D W Θ f¹ (33) 700 al)[9] for εἰσελθών; on the other hand, Mark has stylistic preference for compound verbs and especially participles. «He likes to use circumstantial

---

[7] Cf. K. ALAND, *Synopsis,* IX.

[8] The number 1 is supported by Tischendorf and Von Soden, and some authors like Cranfield, Taylor, etc; while number 5 is backed by GNT/Nestle-Aland, Merk, Westcott-Hort, and others like Lagrange and Swete, etc.

[9] Cf. B.M. METZGER, *Textual Commentary,* 75.

participles like εἰσελθών, in fact, he likes this one in particular»[10]. May be the preposition εἰς may have created the confusion for its accidental omission. With the above reasons in mind, we retain our text without any omission or transposition.

Another minor problem is that created by v.23 whereby some witnesses wish to omit εὐθύς : A C D W Θ f^{13} 892.1006.1506 M latt sy; while those who retain the text without any omission are: ℵ B L f^1 33. 205. 579. 1342. 2427 pc co; Or. Considering the witnesses, the latter are weightier. But on the internal examination, it is due to parallel influence from Luke 4:33. It is «a desire to rid the text of the awkward combination of εὐθύς and ἦν, "he was". The adverb normally goes with a verb of action; elsewhere in Mark it always does»[11]. On the grounds of «more difficult reading», Taylor suggests that it should be read with the latter witnesses[12].

Yet another minor problem is the insertion of ἔα in v.24. The variant readings are:

1)   ℵ² A C L $f^{1.13}$ 33.892.1006.1342.1506 M sy[h]; Or Cyr
2)   ℵ* B D W Θ 565.2427.2542 pc latt sy[s.p] co

Qualitatively number 2 has greater weight and geographical spread. Moreover, on the internal level, we are once more confronted with the problem of parallel with Luke 4:34. There is a tendency to harmonisation and clarification on the part of no. 1 witnesses. Thus, the insertion or omission does not change the meaning or sense of the text. Based on that we retain the text as it is.

The last textual problem we would like to examine is in v.27. This is the only textual problem in our pericope according to the GNT (4th revised edition). The variant readings are as follows:

1) τί ἐστι τοῦτο; τίς ἡ διδαχὴ ἡ καινὴ αὕτη; ὅτι κατ'ἐξουσίαν
   (A) C (f^{13}) 892.1006.   (1342, 1506) M lat sy[p.h]
2) τίς ἡ διδαχὴ ἐκείνη ἡ καινὴ αὕτη ἡ ἐξουσία ὅτι D (W it sy[s])
3) τί ἐστιν τοῦτο; διδαχὴ καινὴ αὕτη, ὅτι κατ'ἐξουσίαν Θ (579.
   1582*, 700)

---

[10] R.H. GUNDRY, Mark, 80. One can see this preference as follows: 2:1; 3:27; 5:39; 6:25; 7:24, 25; 11:15; 15:43 and 16:5.

[11] R.H. GUNDRY, Mark, 82.

[12] Cf. V. TAYLOR, Mark, 173.

4) τί ἐστιν τοῦτο; διδαχὴ καινὴ κατ'ἐξουσίαν· καί ℵ B L 33 (f¹ 205.565*, 2427: καινὴ αὕτη)

In the above variant readings we notice that the supporters of 2 and 3 are mainly Western witnesses or Caesarean, who often have the tendency of harmonisation and conflation. Likewise the supporters of 1, not only lack geographical distribution, but also are weak and cannot measure up to that of 4. Gundry remarks: «It is easier and therefore unoriginal, not to mention the weightier external evidence of ℵ B L 33 (f¹ 28* 565*) on the side of "What is this? A new teaching..."»[13]. This latter variant reading «seems to account best for the rise of the others. Its abruptness invited modifications, and more than one copist accommodated the phraseology in one way or another to the parallel in Lk 4:36»[14]. Another important problem confronting this verse is that of punctuation. The clause κατ'ἐξουσίαν may be joined either to διδαχὴ καινή or to ἐπιτάσσει. But in view of v.22 it seems preferable to take κατ'ἐξουσίαν with διδαχὴ καινή[15]. This assertion has the support of most modern editions of the Greek text and translations[16].

With this exercise of scrutinizing the textual problems in our pericope done, we can now be rest assured with the authenticity of our text to begin our exegetical work. But before then we must also examine the internal structure of our text.

1.4 *The Structure of the Text*

The Structure of this pericope can be seen from different ways depending on what one wants to achieve. Looking at the overall structure, one can see the story has the Narrative parts (21-24a, 25a, 26-27a, 28) and also three Direct Discourses (24b, 25b, 27b) which were made by the three main actors in the story: the Demoniac, Jesus and the People. However, we can examine the literary structure of this text through its main verbs, the characters in the story and the pericope's main themes.

---

[13] R.H. GUNDRY, *Mark*, 85.

[14] B.M. METZGER, *Textual Commentary*, 75.

[15] Cf. B.M. METZGER, *Textual Commentary*, 75; V. TAYLOR, *Mark*, 176; C.E.B. CRANFIELD, *Mark*, 80-81.

[16] R.G. BRATCHER – E.A. NIDA, *Translator's Handbook*, 53, confirms that, «the first is preferred by Tischendorf, Nestle, Vogels, Soden, Turner, Lagrange, Moffatt, Berkeley, Weymouth , Zürich, Gould, Taylor; the second is favored by AV, ASV, RSV, ... Knox, Synodale, Brazilian, Swete».

Based on the verbal elements of the pericope, we observe that Jesus' entry into Capernaum with his disciples gives a *general introduction* or title to the story; while the spreading of his fame throughout Galilee gives the story its *general conclusion*. The main body of the pericope can be divided into two unequal parts: Jesus' entry into the synagogue, his teaching, and the reaction of the People will form the first part; while the presence of a man with unclean spirit, his encounter with, and self-defence against Jesus, Jesus' reaction and command, the effect of Jesus' command on the unclean spirit (exorcism), and the reaction of the People form the second part. Now let us outline it thus:

21a General Introduction: Jesus and His Disciples *went* into Capernaum
21b A.   Jesus' *entry* into the Synagogue and His Teaching
22   The People's *reaction*: astonishment
23a B.   A man with Unclean Spirit *was* in the Synagogue
23b-24   The Unclean Spirit *cried out*: encounter and self-defence
25   Jesus' *reaction* and command
26   The Unclean Spirit *departs* (exorcism)
27   The People's *reaction*: amazement
28   General Conclusion: Jesus' Fame *spreads* throughout Galilee

Likewise when we consider the *dramatis personae* (the subject of the main verb) with their actions, we can see clearly the central position of Jesus, the chief protagonist of the story of our pericope.

A *Jesus*, entering the synagogue, *was teaching* (v.21)
  B *People are astonished* at his teaching (v.22)
    C *A man with unclean spirit cries out and confronts* Jesus (vv.23-24)
      D *Jesus rebukes and commands* the unclean spirit (v.25)
    C' *The unclean spirit comes out* of the man (v.26)
  B' *People are amazed* at his teaching and exorcism (v.27)
A' *Jesus' fame spreads* (v.28)[17]

This simple concentric chiasm above can show that all the actions are turning around Jesus. Moreover, «the day, as Mark narrates it, is eventful and full of action and the account of it is rich in depictive color and detail»[18]. As a working structure, we could also divide the pericope into three thematic parts: (a) Jesus' teaching with its peculiar vocabularies

---

[17] Cf. S. KUTHIRAKKATTEL, *The Beginning*, 126. I tried to adapt this structure to how I conceived the pericope.
[18] W.E. BUNDY, *Jesus and the First Three Gospels*, 74.

(vv.21-22); (b) Jesus' expulsion of an unclean spirit (vv.23-26); and (c) the Reactions to Jesus' Activity (vv.27-28)[19]. With this, we come to the end of our examination of the structure of our text.

Since we have tried to situate our pericope in its context, to establish it as a complex unit, confirm its textual authenticity, and examine its internal structure, we shall now compare it with other synoptic writers, Matthew and Luke.

1.5 *The Synoptic Comparison*

In this synoptic comparison, we want to examine the significance of the position of our pericope, and its function for the Gospel. Since our text falls within the first section of the beginning of Jesus' Galilean ministry, we shall therefore verify in the first three pericopes, the common elements among the synoptic evangelists, their differences, and the peculiarity of Mark. Thus, we shall find out in this Jesus' initial appearance, whether this pericope has a special function for Mark's Gospel.

1.5.1 Jesus begins his Ministry in Galilee

The beginning of Jesus' public ministry starts in Galilee, and is similar in the three synoptic writers. In fact, the three evangelists state that after Jesus' temptation in the wilderness (Mt 4:1-11; Mk 1:12-13; Lk 4:1-13), he came to Galilee and began his public ministry by preaching/teaching (Mt 4:12-17; Mk 1:14-15; Lk 4:14-15). In spite of these similarities, each evangelist emphasized one thing or the other, for example: while Mark emphasizes a temporal sequence between John's arrest and Jesus' arrival to Galilee; and Matthew stresses Jesus' withdrawal from hostile situation and gives geographical details (cf. Is. 9:1-2); Luke rather highlights Jesus' ministry under the power of the Spirit[20]. After this common beginning of Jesus' ministry for the three evangelists, in what follows begins the differences in the order of the individual synoptic writer.

1.5.2 Jesus' Initial Actions

a) The Call of the First Disciples (Mk 1:16-20; Mt 4:17-22)

The call of the first disciples (Simon and Andrew, James and John) in Mark and Matthew are the same, except for their individual favourite

---

[19] Cf. J. HARGREAVES, *A Guide*, 23.
[20] Cf. S. KUTHIRAKKATTEL, *The Beginning*, 84-85.

vocabularies and styles. But for Luke this call of the first disciples came later after a rather long ministry (cf. 5:1-11). Here Jesus' encounter with his disciples took place within a miraculous event of catching of fish, in which Simon Peter experienced the divine in Jesus. However, Luke in this second pericope has another theme.

b) Jesus' Visit at Nazareth (Lk 4:16-30)

Luke placed Jesus' visit at Nazareth (4:16-30) immediately after Jesus' arrival to Galilee under the power of the Spirit. This pericope is seen much later in Matthew and Mark (Mt 13:53-58; Mk 6:1-6). Indeed, many scholars affirm that Luke's placement of this pericope here is to serve a *programmatic purpose*, because «it presents in capsule form the theme of fulfilment and symbolizes the rejection that will mark the ministry as a whole»[21]. In fact, «its placement at this point in Luke's account makes it crucial in the overall development of the story»[22]. Hence for Luke this pericope, placed immediately at the beginning of Jesus' public ministry is programmatic for his Gospel.

1.5.3 Jesus' Other Initial Actions

a) Jesus' Appearance at Capernaum (Mk 1:21-28; Lk 4:31-37)

Both Mark and Luke have the story of Jesus' first appearance in the synagogue of Capernaum, where Jesus taught the people and cast out an unclean spirit from a man. The content of the story is the same but their favourite vocabularies and styles also prevail here. However, «Jesus' teaching and exorcism are treated almost independently in Lk 4,31-37 whereas in Mk 1,21-28 these two activities of Jesus are more integrated as emphasized in 1,27 where the people are deeply amazed at his teaching as well as his exorcism»[23]. On the other hand, this pericope is absent in Matthew, in its place he also has another theme.

b) The Sermon on the Mount (Mt 5-7)

After the summary statement of Jesus' ministry in Galilee (4:23-25), comes the theme of the «Sermon on the Mount», which is the first of the

---

[21] J.A. FITZMYER, *Luke I-IX*, 71, 529; Cf. D.L. BOCK, *Luke 1:1-9:50*, 394; I.H. MARSHALL, *Luke*, 177; J. NOLLAND, *Luke 1-9:20*, 191.

[22] J.H. HAYES - C.R. HOLLADAY, *Biblical Exegesis*, 78. Cf. J.B. GREEN, *Luke*, 207.

[23] S. KUTHIRAKKATTEL, *The Beginning*, 118, 119.

five great discourses[24] in Matthew. «The evangelist's placement of this first discourse toward the beginning of the Gospel indicates he attached importance to this material»[25]. This gives a programmatic to Jesus' ministry, especially in his teaching activity, because Mt places «teaching» ahead of «preaching» and «healing» (cf. 4:23). He also characterizes the Sermon on the Mount as «teaching» (cf. 5:2; 7:28). Hence, «the Sermon is the example par excellence of this facet of Jesus' activity»[26].

1.5.4 The Function of our Pericope for Mark's Gospel

Just as Matthew's and Luke's placement of their important materials (cf. Lk 4:16-30; Mt 5-7) at the beginning of Jesus' Galilean public ministry had an important significance for them, so also we think Mk 1:21-28 has for Mark. In fact, «the placement of this pericope at the beginning of Jesus' ministry is not fortuitous but intentional: 1,21-28 has a specific function in Mark»[27]. This «specific function» is discovered in Mark's positioning of this pericope here, at Jesus' first public appearance and activity, and most probably because it has a *programmatic purpose* of introducing Jesus' ministry in Mark's Gospel[28].

1.6 *Summary*

We have so far established our pericope in its larger context, textual unity, authenticity, and structure. From the synoptic comparison we affirmed, that the placement of our pericope at the beginning of Jesus' Galilean public ministry, gives it a specific function of introducing Jesus' ministry in Mark's Gospel. Now we shall look into the Linguistic-Syntactic Analysis of our text.

---

[24] The five discourses in Matthew are: the Sermon on the Mount (5:1-7:29); the discourse on Mission (9:36-11:1); the discourse of the Parables (13:1-53); the discourse for the Disciples (18:1-19:1); and the final discourse (23:1-26:1).

[25] D.A. HAGNER, *Matthew 1-13*, 82-83; Cf. A. STOCK, *Method and Message*, 67; W.D. DAVIES – D.C. ALLISON, *Matthew*, I, 413.

[26] A. STOCK, *Method and Message*, 68; R.H. GUNDRY, *Matthew*, 137, confirms that «because Mt is interested in Jesus' teaching and authority, he takes over Mark's statement about those topics with only one change».

[27] S. KUTHIRAKKATTEL, *The Beginning*, 141.

[28] Cf. K. STOCK, *Boten*, 25, 27.

2. Linguistic-Syntactic Analysis

In this section we shall examine the vocabulary, the grammar with its categories and forms, the syntax and the style of the author. We shall try to discover the programmatic character of our pericope, which its position in the Gospel has signalled. This will be done through the examination of Markan key-words or favourite terms in our pericope, and then establish Markan peculiarity in his arrangement of these key-words.

2.1 *The Vocabulary*

In this pericope of eight verses there are about 124 words. Among these words are repetitions of words, expressions or phrases. Repeated are words like: διδάσκειν (vv.21,22); διδαχή (vv.22,27); ἐξουσία (vv.22,27); συναγωγή (vv.21,23); πνεῦμα (vv.23,26,27); ἀκάθαρτον (vv.23,26,27); ἐξέρχεσθαι (vv.25,26,28); Ἰησοῦς (vv.24,25); λέγειν (vv.24,25,27); εὐθύς (vv.21,23,28)[29].

---

[29] The verb διδάσκειν occurs for the first time in Mk, and 2x in this introductory part, but it appears 17x in the whole of Mk: 1:21,22; 2:13; 4:1,2; 6:2,6,30,34; 7:7; 8:31; 9:31; 10:1; 11:17; 12:14,35; 14:49.

The importance of the word διδαχή is seen in its 2x appearance in this pericope, but 5x in the whole Gospel of Mk: 1:22,27; 4:2; 11:18; 12:38.

The word ἐξουσία appears 2x here and 10x in Mk's Gospel: 1:22,27; 2:10; 3:15; 6:7; 11:28(bis),29,33; 13:34.

The noun συναγωγή occurs 2x in this text but 8x in Mk: 1:21,23,29,39; 3:1; 6:2; 12:39; 13:9.

The substantive πνεῦμα appears 23x in the Gospel of Mark. This is the first appearance of «unclean spirit» and 3x in this pericope, but 11x times in Mk's Gospel: 1:23,26,27; 3:11,30; 5:2,8,13; 6:7; 7:25; 9:25.

The adjective ἀκάθαρτον qualifying the «spirit» occurs also 3x in this pericope but 11x in Mk.

The compound verb ἐξ-έρχεσθαι appears here for the first time and 3x (2x for unclean spirit) in our text. In the Gospel of Mk it occurs 39x, but for casting out unclean spirits or demons 9x: 1:25,26; 5:8,13; 7:29,30; 9:25,26,29.

The name, Ἰησοῦς, «Jesus» appears 81x in Mk's Gospel: it occurs only 6x in chapter 1 and 24x in the first half of the Gospel, but 2x in our pericope: 1:1,9,14,17, 24,25; 2:5,8,15,17,19; 3:7; 5:6,7,15,20,21,27,30,36; 6:4,30; 8:17,27; 9:2,4,5,8,23, 25,27,39; 10:5,14,18,21,23,24,etc.

The verb λέγειν often introduces a direct discourse as it is found 3x in our text, especially in present participle.

This is a very important adverb, εὐθύς, in the Gospel of Mk occurring 42x: 11x in chapter 1, 32x in the first half of the Gospel (chap.1-8), but 3x in our pericope. Here they are: 1:10,12,18,20,21,23,28,29, 30,42,43; 2:8,12; 3:6; 4:5,15,16,17,29;

We have other important words, though they were not repeated in the text. But these words appear for the first time in our text and have an important role in the Gospel of Mark. The prominent verbs among these are: ἀπολλύναι, εἰσπορεύεσθαι, ἐκπλήσσεσθαι, ἐπιτιμᾶν, ἐπιτάσσειν, συζητεῖν, θαμβεῖν, ὑπακούειν, σπαράσσειν, φωνεῖν[30]; and other words are: Καφαρναούμ, σάββατον, γραμματεύς, ἀκοή, Ναζαρηνός, καινός, πανταχοῦ, ὅλος, Γαλιλαία[31].

5:2,29,30,42(bis); 6:25,27,45,50,54; 7:25,35; 8:10; 9:15,20,24; 10:52; 11:2,3; 14:43,45,72; 15:1.

[30] The verb ἀπολλύναι appears first in our text but 10x in Mk: 1:24; 2:22; 3:6; 4:38; 8:35(bis); 9:22,41; 11:18; 12:9.

The verb εἰσπορεύεσθαι also appears for the first time in our text, but 8x in Mk: 1:21; 4:19; 5:40; 6:56; 7:15,18; 11:2.

The verb ἐκπλήσσεσθαι is an important one for Mk and it appears first in this pericope, but 5x in Mk's Gospel: 1:22; 6:2; 7:37; 10:26; 11:18.

Another important verb is ἐπιτιμᾶν, that appears first in our text but occurs 9x in Mk: 1:25; 3:12; 4:39; 8:30,32,33; 9:25; 10:13,48.

The verb ἐπιτάσσειν also appears for the first time in this pericope but 4x in Mk's Gospel: 1:27; 6:27,39; 9:25.

Συζητεῖν is a favourite verb of Mark. It occurs 6x in Mk's Gospel but appears first in our text: 1:27; 8:11; 9:10,14,16; 12:28.

The verb θαμβεῖν is also a favourite one for Mk, and it appears 3x in his Gospel but its first appearance begins here in our text: 1:27; 10:24,32.

The verb ὑπακούειν occurs only 2x in Mk's Gospel but its first occurrence is in our pericope: 1:27; 4:41.

The verb σπαράσσειν appears 2x in Mk's Gospel but for the first time occurs in this text: 1:26; 9:26.

Φωνεῖν occurs 9x in Mk but starts in our pericope: 1:26; 9:35; 10:49(thrice); 14:30,68,72(bis); 15:35.

[31] Καφαρναούμ is an important city in the public ministry of Jesus. It appears 3x in Mk's Gospel but the first appearance is in our text: 1:21; 2:1; 9:33.

The «sabbath day», σάββατον, is an important occasion for Jesus' public ministry. The word occurs 12x in the Gospel of Mk but its first appearance is in our pericope: 1:21; 2:23,24,27(bis),28; 3:2,4; 6:2; 16:1,2,9.

Among the chief opponents of Jesus in his public ministry were the «scribes», from the word γραμματεύς. They appear 21x in Mk's Gospel but their appearance as a word begins with our pericope: 1:22; 2:6,16; 3:22; 7:1,5; 8:31; 9:11,14; 10:33; 11:18,27; 12:28,32,35,38; 14:1,43,53; 15:1,31.

The word ἀκοή, is unique in its meaning here with regard to its other appearances in Mk's Gospel, however, it appears 3x in Mk but its first occurrence is in our text: 1:21; 7:35; 13:7.

The name Ναζαρηνός is important to Mk, it appears 4x in the Gospel but it begins its appearance in our text: 1:24; 10:47; 14:67; 16:6.

Also some expressions or phrases are repeated: καὶ εὐθύς (vv.21,23); ἐξέρχεσθαι ἐξ αὐτοῦ (vv.25,26); πνεῦμα ἀκάθαρτον (vv.23,26,27). Or some that are not necessarily repeated but can form a parallel, such as: εἰς τὴν συναγωγήν (v.21)// ἐν τῇ συναγωγῇ (v.23); τί ἡμῖν καὶ σοί; (v.24)// τί ἐστιν τοῦτο; (v.27).

One can see from the review of the words the importance and the privileged position of our pericope. Since most of the words appear for the first time in Mark's Gospel, and in a pericope that is placed at the beginning of Jesus' public ministry, these facts strengthen our thesis that our pericope has a programmatic in Mark's Gospel. Now we look at the categories and forms in which the grammatical organization of this pericope is arranged.

2.2 The Grammatical Categories and Forms

After considering the vocabulary of this text, it is also wise to see how the pericope is composed. We have already stated how many words therein, the breakdown of these words are: 28 verbs, 22 substantives[32], 18 pronouns, 16 conjunctions, 15 articles[33], 10 prepositions, 7 adjectives, 4 adverbs, 3 particles and 1 negative.

The primary position of the verb in the text is incontestable, having the highest number. The 28 verbs include: 14 finite verbs, 10 verbs infinite and 4 of εἰμί, which can be further divided into voice, mood, tense, number, person (and for participles - gender and case). We have only two voices in our text: active, 25 and passive, 3. For the moods: indicative, 16; imperative, 2; participle, 8; and infinitive, 2. The tenses of the

---

The adjective καινός appears 6x in Mk's Gospel but occurs first in this pericope: 1:27; 2:21,22; 14:24,25; 16:17.

This local indication in the public ministry of Jesus, signals something, however, πανταχοῦ appears only 2x in Mk beginning from our text: 1:28; 16:20.

The adjective ὅλος, appears 18x in the Gospel of Mk but its first appearance is our pericope: 1:28,33,39; 6:55; 8:36; 12:30(4x),33(3x),44; 14:9,55; 15:1,16,33.

The region Γαλιλαία has an important role in the public ministry of Jesus. It appears 12x in Mk's Gospel, and our pericope enjoys its appearance also: 1:9,14,16,-28,39; 3:7; 6:21; 7:31; 9:30; 14:28; 15:41; 16:7.

[32] The adjective ὁ ἅγιος, because it has an article is also regarded as a substantive in the text. Cf. BDF, 138, #263a.

[33] In the number for the articles, two articles qualified the adjectives also, thereby giving more emphasis to the substantive.

indicative verbs have historical present (3), aorist (5)[34], imperfect (4)[35], perfect (1)[36]; for the participles: present (5), aorist (3); infinitive has present (1) and aorist (1); while imperative has aorist (2)[37]. With regard to the number of the verbs: the singular has 23, while the plural 5. For the persons of the 18 finite verbs, we have: first singular, 1; second singular, 4; third singular, 9; third plural, 4. The participles, however, have for the gender: masculine, 6; neuter, 2; and for case: nominative, 7; and accusative, 1. That is how the verbs stand in the text.

The substantives reveal a noteworthy variety in its composition, in number[38], gender[39] and case[40]. The pronouns[41] highlight diversity in the composition of the text, both in number[42], gender and case[43]. Among the 15 articles, 2 govern adjectives qualifying the substantives. Apart from γάρ all the other 15 conjunctions are καί. The prepositions, the adjectives, the adverbs and particles are full of repetitions which we have in one way or the other seen.

---

[34] This includes one passive indicative aorist.

[35] These also include one passive indicative imperfect and a *periphrastic construction* of a participle with the verb εἶναι which is here ἦν (impf), thereby rendering the construction as an imperfect verb. Cf. *BDF*, 179, #353; M. ZERWICK, *Biblical Greek*, 125, #360.

[36] Here the verb οἶδα has indicative perfect but present in meaning. Cf. J. SWETNAM, *An Introduction* I, 306.

[37] This has one active aorist and one passive aorist.

[38] The striking thing is that the number of the singular is 19, while the plural is 3.

[39] The feminine has 11, masculine, 7, while neuter, 4. In the feminine, συναγωγή, διδαχή, ἐξουσία appeared 2x each thereby inflating the number to 11 instead of 8. The masculine has 7 instead of 6 because Ἰησοῦς occurred 2x. Likewise for the neuter πνεῦμα appeared 3x thereby increasing the number to 4 instead of 2.

[40] This has nominative: 7; vocative: 2; accusative: 5; genitive: 2; dative: 6. It must be noticed that accusative is 5 because Καφαρναούμ, which is feminine, is in the text not declined, if it were, it would have been in accusative because of the preposition εἰς.

[41] The 18 pronouns are divided thus: personal pronouns, 13; interrogative pronouns, 3; reflexive and demonstrative pronouns have 1 each respectively. Apart from 3 that are neuter all others are masculine.

[42] On the number of the personal pronouns, we have: second singular, 2; third singular, 7; first plural, 2; third plural, 2. The reflexive pronoun has 3rd plural, 1; while the interrogative pronoun, singular, 3; and demonstrative, 1.

[43] The nominative has 4; accusative, 5; dative, 4; while genitive, 5. Among the 5 of the genitive, 3 acted as possessive pronoun, 2 others are influenced by the preposition, ἐκ. Likewise πρός influenced one of the 5 in accusative.

The above classifications and forms of the grammar, based on the words of our text, reveal how the pericope is full of actions, especially when we observe the number of finite verbs that are dominant in active voice, in indicative mood and in the singular. Likewise in the substantives, the composition of the number, gender and case reflect action and individuality. Our next attention will turn to the syntax of the pericope.

2.3 *The Syntax and the Text*

The syntax helps us to know how the text or the sentence is arranged. Since we have already highlighted the importance of the verbs, substantives, adverbs, adjectives, and pronouns in the text, we shall now find out how they are arranged with the conjunctions, prepositions, and particles, to form a sentence or phrase. We shall also examine the relationship between the subject and object, the subject and predicate.

In our text, apart from the γάρ (v.22), almost all the conjunctions in our text is καί. Those other conjunctions are absent, except some particles like ὡς (v.22) or ὥστε (v.27). This shows the paratactical nature of our text. Thus the principal linking elements are: καί, γάρ, ὡς, ὥστε. However, the verb λέγειν also acts as a link between the narrative and the direct discourses, as we observed earlier.

It is common to introduce each sentence with καί, yet one can also notice a certain interest to do the same with the expression, καὶ εὐθύς (vv.10,12,18,20,21,23,29,30,42). The latter can serve as a literary device to increase tension, and a sense of urgency; and to fulfil the function of the storyteller's connecting link as part of the folk-narrator's art[44].

With regard to the relationship between the subject and object, one observes that there are very few explicit subjects or objects in our text. Rather, we see the use of implicit subjects (vv.21[bis],22[bis], indefinite pronouns or subjects (vv.23,27), or personal pronoun for the object (vv.22,26). One cannot forget the role of transitive and intransitive verbs in considering the subjects and objects of a verb. In fact, we have more intransitive verbs[45] than the transitive, which means less objects to the

---

[44] Cf. E.J. PRYKE, *Redactional Style*, 87-88.

[45] Apart from the 4 copulative verbs («verb to be»: εἰμί) and the 3 λέγειν introducing direct discourse, we have about 11 intransitive verbs and 10 transitive verbs. We should call to mind that verbs of movement or feeling could fall into the group of intransitive verbs. Cf. E.G. JAY, *New Testament Greek*, 40, 221, 259.

verbs, but more complements[46]. In the transitive verbs, some as a rule take dative (indirect object)[47] instead of direct objects. Even ἐδίδασκεν has no object except implicitly (cf. v.22). Since there are implicit subjects and objects, this reality gives more strength to the pronouns both to indicate the executor or sufferer of the actions, and to represent them in the sentences. There are also cases of change of positions of the subject and the object for the sake of stress or emphasis (vv.22b,26a,27c).

Having seen the relationship between subject and object, now let us look at subject and predicate in the sentences. Following Greek syntax, we have not much problems with the subject and predicate in our text. However, as the predicate must always be a finite verb, then we can refer to nominal sentence or clause (v.24) or clauses/sentences with verbs infinite (non-finite verbs) like participles (vv.21b,22bβ,26ab) and infinitive (v.27aβ). If indefinite subjects or pronouns are attested as being implicitly in the verb (predicate), then the problem of subject and predicate would not be a serious one, though for one to understand the sentence the subject must be sought from the predicate.

The use of the tenses is also striking. The preceding v.20 ended with aorist, but our pericope begins with historical present (v.21a), then changes to imperfect (v.21b), continues in the same tense until it changes to aorist (v.23b). The same aorist continues (vv.23-27) until v.27b when it changes once more to historical present, and finally again with aorist, v.28.

Now let us examine the types of sentences in our text. We notice that our pericope is made up of complex or compound sentences but few simple sentences. In v.21 we see a complex sentence made up of a co-ordinate clause (21a) – an intransitive verb with complement; this is connected to a main clause (21bβ) with a sub-ordinate clause (21bα) by καί. In v.22 there is also a complex sentence of a main or principal clause (22a), connected with a causal co-ordinative conjunction γάρ to a co-ordinate clause (periphrastic construction) [22bα], and a sub-ordinate clause (22bβ) linked together by a sub-ordinate conjunctive and comparative particle ὡς. While v.23 has a compound sentence of two co-ordinate clauses connected by a co-ordinative conjunction καί. In v.24 λέγειν — introductory verb to direct discourse — introduces simple sentences or

---

[46] The complements are many in our text, for example: vv. 21a,b; 22a; 23a; 25bβ; 26b,c; 27aβ; 28.

[47] These are in vv.25a; 27d,e.

clauses that are paratactically together. The first sentence or clause is elliptical[48], thus a nominal sentence. The second is a clause with «infinitive of purpose»[49] construction. And the third is a simple sentence with an enlargement of its object[50] (apposition of noun). While v.25 contains compound sentence of three co-ordinate clauses[51]. But v.26 as a complex sentence has two sub-ordinate clauses (participial) linked together by co-ordinative conjunction καί, and a main clause (an intransitive verb with complement) in an asyndetic connection. In v.27 we meet a very complex sentence which has in the narrative section — a main clause linked together with a sub-ordinate clause (infinitive of result)[52] by a sub-ordinate conjunctive particle ὥστε; then in the direct discourse that has a co-ordinate noun clause with a noun phrase in apposition, linked to two co-ordinate clauses by an ascensive καί. While v.28 is a simple sentence with an enlargement of the complement (an intransitive verb with complement).

One can see the syntactical nature of our text with its variety, especially the complex sentences dominated by implicit subjects and objections, intransitive verbs, and paratactical connections, all help to confirm actions and movements in our pericope. Now we shall still examine the writer's style to conclude this analysis.

2.4 *The Style*

In this section, we shall investigate whether Mark's style can be revealed in our pericope, in order to confirm what we have said so far. We shall therefore examine the different aspects, be it lexical, grammatical, syntactical, or even thematical elements of our text in the light of his style. We shall also compare his style with the other Gospel writers, in order to bring out Mark's peculiarity.

In the vocabularies, we saw that Mark has some interest for certain words or expressions. It becomes very conspicuous when placed side by side with other evangelists. Some of these words are εἰσπορευεσθαι,

---

[48] This is a case of an elliptical usage with dative, cf. *BDF*, 157, # 299,3.

[49] Here we see infinitive of purpose with verb of movement, cf. *BDF*, 197, #390,1.

[50] Cf. C.E.B. CRANFIELD, *Mark*, 76.

[51] We regarded the direct discourse as two co-ordinate clauses connected by καί.

[52] Cf. *BDF*, 197, # 391,2.

εὐθύς, διδαχή, etc[53]. These favourite words of Mark can illustrate the importance attached to our text.

Grammatically, he is also used to certain ways of expressing his ideas, for instance: historical present (vv.21,27)[54], indefinite/implicit plural (vv.21,22)[55], dual use of related verbs (v.21)[56], the γάρ-explanatory (v.22)[57], periphrastic construction (v.22)[58], and ὥστε + Infinitive construction[59].

[53]

	Mt	Mk	Lk	Jn	Acts	Paul	Rest	Total
Γαλιλαία	16	12	13	17	3	0	0	61
γραμματεύς	22	21	14	0	4	1	0	62
διδάσκειν	14	17	17	9	16	15	7	95
διδαχή	3	5	1	3	4	6	8	30
εἰσπορεύεσθαι	1	8	5	0	4	0	0	18
ἐκπλήσσειν	4	5	3	0	1	0	0	13
ἐξέρχεσθαι	43	39	44	29	29	8	24	216
ἐξουσία	10	10	16	8	7	27	24	102
ἐπιτάσσειν	0	4	4	0	1	1	0	10
εὐθύς	7	42	1	3	1	0	0	54
θαμβεῖν	0	3	0	0	0	0	0	3
καινός	4	5	5	2	2	7	17	42
ὅλος	22	18	16	6	19	14	13	108
πανταχοῦ	0	2	1	0	3	1	1	7
πνεῦμα ἀκάθ.	2	11	5	0	2	0	2	22
συζητεῖν	0	6	2	0	2	0	0	10
ὑπακούειν	1	2	2	0	2	11	14	21

[54] Cf. J.H. MOULTON – N. TURNER, Grammar, IV, 20; W. EGGER, Frohbotschaft und Lehre,147; R.H. STEIN, «Markan Seam», 84; M. ZERWICK, Markus-Stil, 49-57; J.C. HAWKINS, Horae Synopticae, 113-8.

[55] Cf. R.A. GUELICH, Mark, 55; V. TAYLOR, Mark, 47; W. EGGER, Frohbotschaft und Lehre, 147; R.H. STEIN, «Markan Seam», 84; C.H. TURNER, «Marcan Usage», (1923-24) 378-386.

[56] R.A. GUELICH, Mark. 55.

[57] R.A. GUELICH, Mark, 55; E.J. PRYKE, Redactional Style, 126-135; W. EGGER, Frohbotschaft und Lehre, 147; R.H. STEIN, «Markan Seam», 84.

[58] Cf. E.J. PRYKE, Redactional Style, 126-135; J.H. MOULTON – N. TURNER, Grammar IV, 20,26; C.H. TURNER, «Marcan Usage», (1926-27) 349-351; R.H. STEIN, «Markan Seam», 84; R. PESCH, «Eine neue Lehre», 249.

[59] Of the thirteen examples used by the evangelist, eleven are followed by the Acc + Infinitive construction (1:27,45; 2:2,12; 3:10,20; 4:1,32,37; 9:26; 15:5), and the other two by the indicative (2:28; 10:10). Cf. E.J. PRYKE, Redactional Style, 115-119, esp. 115; R. PESCH, «Eine neue Lehre», 254.

Some authors have observed the duality in Mark's Gospel. We observe that some compound verbs are followed by the same preposition[60], for instance, vv.21(bis),25, 26: εἰσπορεύονται εἰς ... εἰσελθὼν εἰς; ἔξελθε ἐξ; ἐξῆλθεν ἐξ[61]. Some verbs go with cognate accusative or dative (v.26)[62]; and multiplication of cognate verbs (vv.21, 21/22, 22/23, 28/29)[63]; we have also double participles (v.26)[64]; and double imperatives (v.25)[65] which are also characteristic of Mark. In some cases, there is a repetition of the antecedent, which occurred 2x in our text: v.22: ἐπὶ τῇ διδαχῇ αὐτοῦ (cf. v.21: ἐδίδασκεν); and v.23: ἐν τῇ συναγωγῇ) cf.v.21: εἰς τὴν συναγωγήν)[66].

As we continue to discuss on Mark's style, it has been observed other duplicate expressions and double statements, that are expressed in different ways in the text. Some of these are: a) Double Statement: temporal or local, in our text we observe two of it, though local: v.21: εἰσπορεύονται εἰς Καφαρναούμ / εἰσελθὼν εἰς τὴν συναγωγήν; v.28: πανταχοῦ / εἰς ὅλην τὴν περίχωρον τῆς Γαλιλαίας[67]; b) Double Statement: general and special, this is noticed also in v.21: εἰπορεύονται εἰς Καφαρναούμ· καὶ ... εἰσελθὼν εἰς τὴν συναγωγήν[68]; c) Synonymous Expressions, like in v.24: Ἰησοῦ Ναζαρηνέ ... ὁ ἅγιος τοῦ θεοῦ[69].

The correspondence within the pericope is part of Markan characteristic: i) Correspondence in Narrative, which can be seen in vv.23,26: ἄνθρωπος ἐν πνεύματι ἀκαθάρτῳ / καὶ σπαράξαν αὐτὸν τὸ πνεῦμα τὸ ἀκάθαρτον[70]; ii) Exposition and Discourse, like in vv.22,27: ἦν γὰρ διδάσκων αὐτοὺς ὡς ἐξουσίαν ἔχων, καὶ οὐχ ὡς οἱ γραμματεῖς

---

[60] F. Neirynck, *Duality in Mark*, 75; it was first published by the same author as «Duality in Mark», 394-463.

[61] F. Neirynck, *Duality in Mark*, 75, noted 63 occurrences, among which occur 24x (εἰσέρχεσθαι εἰς); 10x (ἐξέρχεσθαι ἐκ); and 6x (εἰσπορεύεσθαι εἰς).

[62] Cf. F. Neirynck, *Duality in Mark*, 76. These occur 27x in Mark, but in our text the verb is with the dative case.

[63] F. Neirynck, *Duality in Mark*, 77-81.

[64] F. Neirynck, *Duality in Mark*, 82-83.

[65] F. Neirynck, *Duality in Mark*, 84.

[66] F. Neirynck, *Duality in Mark*, 85-87.

[67] F. Neirynck, *Duality in Mark*, 94-96; Cf. V. Taylor, *Mark*, 51.

[68] F. Neirynck, *Duality in Mark*, 96-97.

[69] F. Neirynck, *Duality in Mark*, 101-106.

[70] F. Neirynck, *Duality in Mark*, 112-113.

/διδαχὴ καινὴ κατ᾽ ἐξουσίαν[71]; iii) Narrative and Discourse, vv.23,25: καὶ ἀνέκραξεν λέγων· ... / φιμώθητι; vv.25-26,27: ἐπετίμησεν αὐτῷ ὁ Ἰησοῦς ... καὶ ... τὸ πνεῦμα τὸ ἀκάθαρτον ... ἐξῆλθεν ἐξ αὐτοῦ / τοῖς πνεύμασι τοῖς ἀκαθάρτοις ἐπιτάσσει, καὶ ὑπακούουσιν αὐτῷ[72]; iv) Command and Fulfilment, vv.25,26: ἔξελθε ἐξ αὐτοῦ / καὶ ... ἐξῆλθεν ἐξ αὐτοῦ[73]; v) Direct Discourse preceded by Qualifying Verb, see of such in our text: vv.23,24; v.25; v.27[74]; vi) Double Question, like v.24ab[75]; vii) and also Inclusion, as can be observed in vv. 21,29: εἰσελθὼν εἰς τὴν συναγωγήν / ἐκ τῆς συναγωγῆς ἐξελθόντες[76].

One observes a constant change of characters in the story, which reflects how dynamic the text is, especially with actions[77]. The temporal and spatial setting remain the same. We have seen that Mark's style in his Gospel is very much alive in our pericope. This is evident in his favourite words, grammatical expressions, syntactical arrangements, all concentrated in our pericope.

2.5 *Summary*

We have seen so far the stylistic characteristics of the Gospel of Mark, be it in the choice of words, grammatic arrangement, syntactical organization or the manner of expressing oneself, all this add to the peculiarity of Mark.

The choice of words reflects very clearly the two activities (deeds) of Jesus in the synagogue: Teaching: σάββατον, συναγωγή, διδάσκειν, διδαχή, ἐκπλήσσειν, ἐξουσία, γραμματεύς, etc; Exorcism: πνεῦμα ἀκάθαρτον, ἀνακράζειν, φωνεῖν, ἀπολλύναι, ἐπιτιμᾶν, ἐπιτάσσειν, ἐξέρχεσθαι, σπαράσσειν, θαμβεῖν, etc. And these two activities

---

[71] F. NEIRYNCK, *Duality in Mark*, 114-115.

[72] F. NEIRYNCK, *Duality in Mark*, 115-119.

[73] F. NEIRYNCK, *Duality in Mark*, 119-121.

[74] F. NEIRYNCK, *Duality in Mark*, 122-124.

[75] F. NEIRYNCK, *Duality in Mark*, 125-126.

[76] F. NEIRYNCK, *Duality in Mark*, 131-133.

[77] The scene opened with Jesus and his disciples, then Jesus alone (v.21a,b). In v.22a,b, the people came in (though implicit) and the narrator. A man with unclean spirit appears (v.23-24), Jesus responds (v.25), the unclean spirit reacts to Jesus' command (v.26); then the people react again to the event (v.27), lastly, the narrator concludes (v.28).

are concluded in v.27b. In the grammar, we notice that «teaching» was described with imperfect (vv.21b-22a,b), while «exorcism» was with aorist (vv.23b-27a). Likewise two grammatic constructions accompanied them each: the γάρ- and peripharistic constructions (v.22a,b) for the former, while the infinitives of purpose and result (vv.24,27) for the latter. Also the explicit subjects are more in the latter, while the former have implicit subjects. In fact, this pericope highlights two important themes in Mark's Gospel (teaching and exorcism), nevertheless, it also raises other important motifs: the role of the scribes in Jesus' ministry; Jesus' authority, identity, and mission; the reaction of the people (crowd); Galilee in Jesus' public ministry.

In the syntax and style of the author, one observes that the act of teaching have narrative, while the act of expulsion has that of alternation of narrative and direct discourse. Our text enjoys the richness, variety, important and privileged position revealed in the «duality in Mark»: general and special (vv.21,28); correspondence in narrative (vv.23,26); exposition and discourse (vv.22,27); command and fulfilment (vv.25,26); double question (v.24), etc. This encourages us to dig deeper because a better understanding of this pericope is likely a key to understanding the section and even the whole Gospel.

3. Conclusion

At the end of this chapter, we would like to mention some important findings of our investigation. We can summarize them thus:

1. Our pericope (1:21-28) falls within the section of the beginning of Jesus' public ministry, where Jesus' authority was unique and extraordinary (cf. 1:14-3:6).

2. We have a text whose unity can easily be established through its double location, time, theme, persons and stylistic expressions.

3. We don't have any serious textual problems to doubt the authenticity of the pericope.

4. Structurally, Jesus is at the centre of all the actions in the story. Among possible structures, we observed that the two main themes are well delineated, and then linked together by the people's reaction to them: teaching (vv.21-22); exorcism (vv.23-26); and reactions to these Jesus' actions (vv.27-28).

5. The placement of our pericope at the beginning of Jesus' Galilean public ministry, when compared with Matthew and Luke, signals an important function of our text.

6. We discovered that most key-words in our pericope appeared for the first time, both in our text and in Mark's Gospel. This gives us another good sign of the importance of our pericope.

7. Grammatically, we noted that our pericope is full of actions and movements. The words are dominated by verbs, especially finite, intransitive, in active voice, indicative mood, and in singular.

8. In the syntax and style of the text, Mark's peculiarity was most evident, especially when we noticed that most of the key-words in our pericope were also Mark's favourite terms. Hence, the concentration of these Markan key-words and favourite terms in a pericope that is situated at the beginning of Jesus' public ministry must be another good signal of its significance for Mark's Gospel.

CHAPTER II

Semantic Analysis

After our detailed Linguistic-Syntactic analysis of the text, it is logical that we should embark on the Semantic analysis. In this chapter we shall try to find out the meaning of our text, through verse by verse analysis of the key-words, phrases and expressions in our pericope. We shall also discover the themes/motives latent in 1:21-28, especially highlighting important aspects therein. Our pericope will be divided into three structurally thematic parts: (a) 1:21-22 dealing with Jesus' teaching; (b) 1:23-26, on Jesus' exorcism; and (c) 1:27-28, the reactions to Jesus' activity.

1. Mk 1:21-22: Jesus' Teaching

In this first section of 1:21-28, we shall examine the introductory part of our pericope in order to discover what Jesus did at his first public appearance in the synagogue of Caperanaum on the sabbath day. Apart from his teaching which will be dominant, we shall also put in relief other important aspects of the text.

1.1 *Mk 1:21a: Jesus and his Disciples entered into Capernaum*

After the call of the first fishermen, the pericope (1:16-20) closed with the ἀπῆλθον ὀπίσω αὐτοῦ (they left ... followed him), of which its verb is in aorist. But the next pericope begins with εἰσπορεύονται («to go» or «to enter»), which is in historical present, thereby giving a completely new significant situation, in which, not only the location, time, audience is changed, but also the theme[1]. This verb is also observed to be in indefinite plural[2]. This entry into Capernaum is significant because it

---

[1] Cf. W. EGGER, *Frohbotschaft und Lehre*, 147; M. ZERWICK, *Markus-Stil*, 57.
[2] C.H. TURNER, «Marcan Usage», (1924-25) 225f,228-231. Here the indefinite plural is implicit because it relates to Jesus and his disciples.

officially opens Jesus' public ministry in Galilee. The v.21a acts as a general introduction[3] to Jesus' activity in this region. It could also be a *title* (like «in Capernaum»), both for this pericope and for the following pericopes (1:21-39)[4]. It must be emphatically remarked that this v.21a belongs to this pericope (21-28) and not to the preceding one (16-20)[5].

1.1.1 They entered

In Markan usage of this verb, εἰσπορεύεσθαι, we notice that among the 18x this verb appears in the NT, Mk has 8x (Mt 1x, Lk 5x, Acts 4x). This is indeed among his favourite words[6], as we saw earlier. In fact, this entry of Jesus with his first four disciples into Capernaum, is their first *common* action as indicated by Mark (1:2a). And since the next two verbs, εἰσελθὼν ... ἐδίδασκεν, single Jesus out as entering the synagogue and teaching (1:21b), one could say that the third person plural of εἰσπορεύομαι, is a way of indicating the presence of Jesus' disciples in the scene, and their company with him (cf. 1:29)[7]. As a verb of

---

[3] This verse could serve as introduction to the pericope and to the complex. Cf. R.H. STEIN, «Markan Seam», 84.

[4] Some have called some part of this section «a day in Capernaum», but there are divisions in the opinions as to which pericopes belong to this day of Jesus' effective and authoritative activity in Galilee. Some scholars limit it to Mk 1:21-31, Cf. W. GRUNDMANN, *Markus*, 41; E. LOHMEYER, *Markus*, 34; while some like R. PESCH extends it to 1:21-34, Cf. *Markusevangelium*, I, 116-117; ID., «Ein Tag», 114-115; ID., «Eine neue Lehre», 241; R.A. GUELICH, *Mark*, 55; P. GUILLEMETTE, «Un enseignement nouveau», 239; D.E. NINEHAM,*Mark*,74; still most extend it to 1:21-39, for example, Cf. E.K. BROADHEAD, *Teaching with Authority*, 56; V. TAYLOR, *Mark*, 90f, 170-171; J. ERNST,*Markus*, 61; R.BULTMANN, *History,* 209; P. CARRINGTON, *According to Mark*, 53; J. SCHNIEWIND, *Markus*, 18; E. KLOSTERMANN, *Markusevangelium*,11; B. WEISS, *Markus und Lukas*, 21; J. WELLHAUSEN, *Marci*, 8f. I think the emphasis is not so much on the «day» but the «authority» or «power» of Jesus' activities in this city and its effect on the people. This is because the argument of the change of time or place in vv.32/35, in order to deny 21-39, is the same for 21-34. I would agree with R. GUNDRY, *Mark*, 78, that «Chronology and topography are incidental to the power that Jesus displays in his activities. Mark's interest lies in the power».

[5] Cf. R. GUNDRY, *Mark*, 73; V. TAYLOR, *Mark*, 172; R.H. STEIN, «Markan Seam», 83-84; R. PESCH, «Eine neue Lehre», 245; «Ein Tag», 117; E. KLOSTERMANN, *Markusevangelium*, 13.

[6] Cf. Ch.I, sec. 2.4, n.53.

[7] This style of indicating the presence of the disciples with Jesus in plural, and then singling Jesus out for an action/s, can also be seen elsewhere, cf. 1:38-39; 5:1-2, 38-

movement, this verb also indicates that Jesus moves about with them. Henceforth, as we shall see later, Jesus' disciples will always accompany him in his movements and ministry. And the being-together of Jesus with his disciples, is an important motif in Mark's Gospel[8].

When Jesus called his first disciples (fishermen), he said to them: δεῦτε ὀπίσω μου, καὶ ποιήσω ὑμᾶς γενέσθαι ἁλιεῖς ἀνθρώπων («Follow me and I will make you become fishers of men»), 1:17. However, he later made his intention very clearly in Mk 3:14-15: ἵνα ὦσιν μετ'αὐτοῦ καὶ ἵνα ἀποστέλλῃ αὐτοὺς κηρύσσειν καὶ ... ἐκβάλλειν τὰ δαιμόνια («to be with him, and to be sent out to preach and ... to cast out demons»). Jesus' first intention (ἵνα ὦσιν μετ'αὐτοῦ)[9] is indeed being fulfilled in this implicit plural subject. In fact, his call is not only to form a community of inner attitude but he wants them to accompany him or to be his companions[10]. «Jesus demands from them in the first place, that they are near or close by, that they are present during his word and deed. It is not said what he intends with this their presence»[11]. Later on we shall see how the other two intentions of Jesus for his disciples were manifested even in our pericope. Meanwhile, even though the disciples are not playing any role now, they have to observe and learn until their formation is completed before they will be «sent out to preach and ... to cast out demons». However, one can observe that our first motif has just emerged, in which Jesus is in the company of his disciples in his movement and his ministry.

39; 8:22-23; 9:9, 30-31, 33; 10:33-34, 46; 11:1; 14:32.

[8] Cf. C.H. TURNER, «Marcan Usage», (1924-25) 225-231.

[9] The phrase εἶναι μετά finds itself in Mk in 1:13; 2:19; 3:14; 4:36; 5:18; 14:67 (cf. Lk 15:31; 23:43). It is used when Jesus is together with others (1:13; 2:19), or when others are together with him (3:14; 4:36; 5:18; 14:67). It is remarkably striking that this phrase in Mk is exclusively in connection with Jesus, which shows how much concentration and interest the Gospel has for the person of Jesus. The phrase speaks about physical presence or to be actually present, and does not only mean the inner attitude, that one declares oneself for another person (cf. Lk 11:23). Cf. K. STOCK, *Boten*, 17-18

[10] Cf. K. STOCK, *Boten*, 18; C.M. MURPHY, «Discipleship in Mark», 306, also rightly remarks, «Jesus for Mark is always "on the move", and the disciple of Jesus is precisely the one who is on the move with him». In fact, this so called movement with Jesus begins with εἰσπορεύονται.

[11] K. STOCK, *Boten*, 18, (the translation is *mine*); S. FREYNE, *The Twelve*, 120 (cf. 120-128, 137), referring to the Instruction or Teaching said: «They are with Jesus to learn from him, to learn about him».

1.1.2 Into Capernaum

Capernaum is one of the few or rare places identified by Mark as associated with Jesus' ministry. This name like Nazareth was not mentioned in the OT. Most modern scholars identify it with Tell Hûm on the north west shore of the lake[12] about two miles from the entrance of the Jordan. It was a boundary city between Herod Antipas and Philip[13], with a Toll station and Military Garrison. The name Καφαρναούμ from the Hebrew נחום כפר means «village of Nahum» or «village of consolation»[14] has two forms, being spellt either Καφαρναούμ or Καπερναούμ, while Josephus offers a third possibility with Καφερνώμη[15].

This city's name appears only in the Gospels[16] and no other place in both the OT and NT. That it appears in the four Gospels shows the importance it has in Jesus' public ministry. The usage in Mark has no parallels in the other Gospels except one (Mk 1:21//Lk 4:31). Capernaum was recorded as a dwelling place for Jesus in his ministry (Mt 4:13 cf. Jn 2:12); it was referred to in the «Woe» passages (Mt 11:23; Lk 10:15). Most importantly, it was recorded by all the Evangelists as a place of healing[17] and teaching[18].

---

[12] The Lake, can be the «Sea of Galilee» (Mt 4:18; Mk 1:16; 7:31), or «lake of Gennesaret» (Lk 5:1).

[13] Cf. D. LÜHRMANN, *Markusevangelium*, 49; W. GRUNDMANN, *Markus*, 42; R. PESCH, *Markusevangelium*, I, 120; E. KLOSTERMANN, *Markusevangelium*, 13.

[14] Cf. S.E. JOHNSON, *Mark*, 46;   J.S. KENNARD Jr., «Capernaum»,137; H.B. SWETE, *Mark*,17.

[15] Cf. E.F.F. BISHOP, «Jesus and Capernaum», 428. F.C. BURKITT,*Syriac Forms*, 27ff, suggests that the form «Capernaum» is a Syrian corruption. «Capharnaum» according to him, is the old and true text preserved by the Four Gospels and attested by MSS, including the Latin, Egyptian, Origen, Eusebius and Epiphanius. In order words, « Καπερναούμ, belongs to the Byzantine text and to that alone: there is no sign of its existence before the fourth century». Cf. ID., «Capernaum, Capharnaum», 386. The origin of Capernaum «is to be sought for not in Palestine but in Northern Syria, in the region of Theodoret and of Antioch». *Ibid.*, 388. Although, it is clear that Capharnaum is the old and original, yet in the later tradition Capernaum has predominated.

[16] Mt: 4x, Mk: 3x, Lk: 4x, Jn: 5x.

[17] Here we have Mt 8:5-13, 14-17; Mk 1:23-28, 29-34; 2:1-12; (cf. 3:1-6); Lk 4:33-37, 38-41; 7:1-10; Jn 4:46-54, etc. Cf. V.C. CORBO, «Capernaum»,866.

[18] This is well reflected at the beginning of Jesus' public ministry in Galilee: Mt 4:17; 4:23; 9:35; Mk 1:21-22, cf. v.27; 2:1-2; 9:33-50; Lk 4:31-32; Jn 6:59, etc.

The only three appearances of Mark (1:21; 2:1; 9:33) deal with, firstly, «teaching and healing», secondly, «healing», and lastly, «teaching». This can reveal to us the core of Jesus' mission and ministry. We can very well understand, why after having called his first disciples he came into Capernaum with them to begin his missionary programme.

1.2 *Mk 1:21b: Jesus enters and teaches in the Synagogue*

Jesus went to Capernaum with his disciples, and now in order to focus on the protagonist and his action, the evangelist specifies the time, place, and person. This first appearance of Jesus in the Synagogue and on the Sabbath-day is symbolic, because it begins and actualizes his mission. It is our task to find out what importance his activity here means to his missionary enterprise.

1.2.1 Immediately on the Sabbath

This adverbial phrase, καὶ εὐθὺς τοῖς σάββασιν, has an important link with the preceding sentence or clause. One is attracted to the word εὐθύς[19] which is also Mark's favourite word[20]. It could mean an adjective or adverb, but here it is an adverb[21]. Generally, εὐθύς means «immediately», «at once». But in our text it could mean a «connective conjunction»[22] or «transitional connective»[23] or an «inferential conjunction»[24]

---

[19] This is read in almost all the occurrences in Mark, as against the more common one in the Hellenistic form and even in the Koine, εὐθέως. Cf. J.H. MOULTON – G. MILLIGAN, *Vocabulary*, 262, 245; H.G. LIDDELL – R. SCOTT – H.S. JONES, *Greek-English Lexicon*, 716.

[20] Cf. Ch.I, sec. 2.4, n.53.

[21] The adverb arises from the nominative masculine singular of εὐθύς, there is also another normal form, εὐθέως, which does not exist in Mark's Gospel.

[22] According to J.H. MOULTON – N.A. TURNER, *Grammar*, III, 229, «Mark uses εὐθύς only 5x near the verb, that is, as an adverb; elsewhere it is probably merely a connective conjunction, occurring at the beginning of its clause (viz, 1:10,12,18,20,21,23,2,30,31, etc). Some thirty of these instances are καὶ εὐθύς: and so (consecutive, like the Heb)...»

[23] Cf R.A. GUELICH, *Mark*, 54, states that it functions here as transitional connective without its more literal meaning of immediacy.

[24] It sometimes acts as an inferential conjunction (e.g. Mk 1:21,23,29,30 «so then»). Cf. J.H. MOULTON – W.F. HOWARD, *Grammar*, II, 446; This inferential use could weaken the adverb to *then, so then, and so, now*. Cf. V. TAYLOR, *Mark*, 172; BURKITT in J. WEISS, «ΕΥΘΥΣ bei Markus», 125.

without having strictly that sense of immediacy. On the temporal level, one could use *immediately*, though mitigated, as it is qualifying another temporal element, *on the Sabbath*. Thus, inferring from the preceding clause, one can render it as «as soon as it was...» or «scarcely was it the sabbath when...»[25] Hence, it has that inferential or connective element which is conspicuous, without loosing completely that element of immediacy. The reality of the number of the verbs of motion in our text confirms the latter.

In Mark's usage of καὶ εὐθύς, in as much as it links the preceding action with the present, it also sets the action in motion. Here, it acts as a set phrase which appeared twice (vv.21b,23a) in a textual unit or pericope, and at the same time announces two «acts» or «actions»[26]. In other words, this phrase not only can delineate actions within a pericope, but can also connect and speed them up.

In the NT, the word, τὸ σάββατον («sabbath»), appears 67x (Synoptics 43x, John 13x; the remaining in Acts and a few letters)[27]; especially in the Gospels, it appears in the teachings of Jesus or in his conflicts with religious leaders. «The four Gospels record among eight sabbath incidents six controversies in which Jesus "rejected the rabbinic sabbath *halakah*"»[28]. The sabbath activities of Jesus are neither hurtful provocations nor mere protests against rabbinic legal restrictions, but are part of Jesus' essential proclamation of the inbreaking of the kingdom of God in which man is taught the original meaning of the sabbath, through which God manifests his healing and saving rulership over man. Thus, Jesus'

---

[25] Cf. R.G. BRATCHER–E.A. NIDA, *Translator's Handbook*, 45. «So, "immediately" tells us how soon Jesus enters the synagogue on the sabbath or more likely since it suits Mk's emphasis on Jesus'teaching, how soon Jesus starts teaching once he enters the synagogue on the sabbath». Cf. R.H. GUNDRY, *Mark*, 80; W. EGGER, *Frohbotschaft und Lehre*, 146.

[26] Cf. R. PESCH, «Eine neue Lehre», 245; «Ein Tag», 117, observes that this fact is attested in many Markan texts especially in chapter one: 1:10, 12; 29, 30, etc.

[27] Cf. G.F. HASEL, «Sabbath», 850.

[28] J. JEREMIAS, *Neutestamentliche Theologie* I, 201. These incidents: two are recorded in the three synoptics (Mt 12:1-8 = Mk 2:23-28 = Lk 6:1-5; Mt 12:9-14 = Mk 3:1-6 = Lk 6:6-11), one is recorded by two synoptics (Mk 1:21-28 = Lk 4:31-37) and the remainder are found in Mark (1:29-31), Luke (13:10-17; 14:1-6) and John (5:1-18; 9:1-41) only. In fact, only Jesus' inaugural sabbath sermon in Nazareth (Lk 4:16-30) and the healing of Peter's mother-in-law on the sabath (Mk 1:29-31) are outside of explicit controversies contexts. Cf. G.F. HASEL, «Sabbath», 854; L. GOPPELT, *Theology of NT* I, 92-94; E. LOHSE, «σάββατον», 21-25.

miraculous sabbath healings indicate once more that Jesus restores the sabbath to be benefit for humankind against any distortions of human religious and/or cultic traditions[29]. Hence, Jesus' ministry of healing suspended the sabbath while fulfilling through infringement its own intention of preserving human life[30].

In Mark's Gospel, σάββατον appears 11x, and also reflects the reality found in the other Gospels: teaching/healing and controversy[31]. The sabbath was therefore an opportunity for Jesus to «teach» and to «heal» (Mk 1:21-28, 3:2,4; 6:2) even though it brought him into conflict with the religious leaders, this did not deter him from fulfilling his salvific mission. In our pericope, these double activities are clearly well defined. Our text is not free from conflict, the unclean spirit who interrupted Jesus' teaching, in fact, began the conflict, on behalf of its world of spiritual beings, before the religious leaders entered the scene. Thus, the seed of conflict has already been sown. However, Jesus is equal to the task, and he did demonstrate it in word and deed.

1.2.2 He entered into the Synagogue

Jesus enters into the synagogue and began to teach. One notices that in the introductory clause of v.21a, there is a general statement made about entry into Capernaum, now it is more specific «entry into the synagogue». Comparing the verbs εἰσπορεύομαι and εἰσέρχομαι, one can see that they can be used interchangeably both in their use and meaning[32].

The verb, εἰσέρχομαι, which appears 30x in Mk (Mt 36x; Lk 50x; Jn 15x), can mean «come (in, into)», «go (in, into)», «enter»[33]. This could literally refer to entry into a *place*[34]; or the entry of the *unclean spirit/*

---

[29] G.F. HASEL, «Sabbath», 855.

[30] L. GOPPELT, *Theology of the NT*, 94.

[31] Among the 11x, it appears 7x in the controversy pericopes (Mk 2:23-28 = 5x; 3:1-6 = 2x - in healing); 2x in teaching (1:21-22; 6:2), then the last two in 16:1,2 (one sabbath, another week). It is striking that 9 out of 11x appeared in the first six chapters of Mark.

[32] One can refer to Mk 5:39, 40; 7:15, 17 to see the alternative use of these two verbs. for the meaning.

[33] Cf. *BADG*, 232-233.

[34] This *place* could have a city name, like «into Jerusalem» (Mt 21:10; Mk 11:11); Caesarea (Acts 10:24; 23:33), Capernaum (Mt 8:5; Mk 2:1; Lk 7:1). It could mean other places like: *into the sanctuary*, Heb 9:12, 24f; *temple*: Lk 1:9; Mk 2:26 (house of God); Rev 15:8; *house*: Mt 10:12; 12:29; Mk 7:17, 24; 9:28; Lk 1:40; 8:41; Acts

demon[35] into someone. Figuratively, it refers to the entry into the *kingdom of God*[36], or things like food into the mouth (Mt 15:11; Acts 11:8), or of thoughts (Lk 9:46). This verb often takes the preposition εἰς to qualify the person, place or thing entered.

In the usage of Mark, we notice that Jesus entering these synagogues, villages, cities or houses, have often the scope of teaching or healing. In fact, the texts where Jesus was the subject of this verb confirm this reality[37]. The figurative use was often used for the entry into the kingdom of God. So like εἰσπορεύομαι it has almost the same meaning and usage, thereby making room for variety.

This prepositional clause has εἰς with accusative of place; and the synagogue, although it appears here for the first time, has a definite article. Could this synagogue be a well known one to the readers? Or is it a special one in Capernaum? But what is a synagogue, συναγωγή? The meaning in our context can be reduced to two: an *assembly of Jews* formally gathered together to offer prayer and listen to the reading and exposition of the Holy Scriptures; the *building* where those solemn Jewish assemblies are held[38]. It is a well established fact that all the four Evangelists refer to teaching and preaching in the synagogue; it is

---

11:12; 16:15; 21:8; *synagogue*: Mk 1:21; 3:1; Lk 4:16; 6:6; Acts 14:1; 18:19; *city*: Mt 10:11; 27:53; Mk 1:45; Lk 10:8; 22:10; Acts 9:6; 14:20; *village*: Mk 8:26; Lk 9:52; 17:12; *tomb*: Mk 16:5; Jn 20:6; or other forms of houses or rooms like praetorium, sheepfold, ark, room, etc.

[35] Like demons or unclean spirits possessing or dwelling within someone, Mk 9:25; Lk 8:50; of demons entering a swine, Mk 5: 12, 13; Lk 8:32, 33; of Satan entering into Judas, Lk 22:3; Jn 13:27.

[36] It seems this is a technical term for expressing the *entry into the kingdom of God* (εἰσελθεῖν εἰς τὴν βασιλείαν τοῦ θεοῦ) Mt 5:20; 7:21; 19:24; Mk 9:47; 10:15, 23, 24, 25; Lk 18:17, 25; Jn 3:5; or *enter into eternal life* (which in structural parallelism is the same as «the kingdom of God» compare Mk 9:47 with 9:43, 45), Mt 18:8f; 19:17; Mk 9:43, 45.

[37] The texts where Jesus is the subject of this verb almost always, in the Gospel of Mark, relate to «teaching» or «healing». Mk 1:21, 45; 2:1; 3:1; 5:39; 7:17, 24; 9:28; 11:11, 15. Cf. Mt 8:5; 9:25; 21:10, 12; Lk 4:16, 38; 6:6; 7:1, 6, 44, 45; 8:41, 51; 17:12; 19:1, 45. Often in Lk it is related to an invitation to a meal, in some cases, there is a «teaching» or «healing» element also: Lk 7:36; 10:38; 11:37; 19:7; 24:29.

[38] People came to the synagogue to worship God: Mt 4:23; 6:2, 5; 9:35; 12:9; 13:54; Mk 1:39; 3:1; 6:2; Lk 4:15; 6:6; Jn 18:20. In the same buildings court was also held and punishment was inflicted: Mt 10:17; 23:34; Mk 13:9; Lk 12:11; 21:12; Acts 22:19; 26:11.

likewise evident that healings took place there too. According to the unanimous accounts of the Gospels Jesus often chose a synagogue for teaching and preaching[39]. In fact, συναγωγή, which appears 8x in Mk (Mt 9x; Lk 15x; Jn 2x), refers to Jesus' διδάσκειν 3x in Mk, Mt, Lk, and 2x in Jn, and to His κηρύσσειν 1x each in Mk and Lk, and 2x in Mt[40]. Truly speaking, the healing ministry of Jesus is less closely connected with the synagogue than His preaching or teaching ministry, yet according to Mk and Lk the first miracle of healing takes place in a synagogue, as does also the only Sabbath healing (Mt 12:9-14; Mk 3:1-6; Lk 6:6-11). «The synagogue is the site of the first battle between demonic powers and the ἅγιος τοῦ θεοῦ - this confession occurs only here in the synagogue sphere according to the Synoptists, Mk 1:24; Lk 4:34. It is also the site of Jesus' victory over these powers»[41]. Our topic naturally introduces us to the next important theme, which Jesus exercized in the synagogues: διδάσκειν.

1.2.3 And He taught

In Mark's Gospel, «teaching» is an important theme as we have seen in different ways. Compared with other synoptic writers, Mk seemed to have emphasized it so much, especially in his use of the verb διδάσκειν, the noun διδαχή, or even the title of a teacher διδάσκαλος or ῥαββί[42]. This act of teaching was the first act of Jesus in his first appearance in the synagogue of Capernaum. Teaching forms part of the sabbath service in the synagogue which consists of prayer, followed by readings from the Law and the Prophets, and exposition or sermon[43]. The concentration of

---

[39] W. SCHRAGE, «συναγωγή», 830-832.

[40] Cf. W. SCHRAGE, «συναγωγή», 833. The references to Jesus' teaching in the synagogue: Mk 1:21, 22; 6:2; Mt 4:23; 9:35; 13:54; Lk 4:15, 31 cf. 33; 13:10; Jn 6:59; 18:20; and his preaching: Mt 4:23; 9:35; Mk 1:39; Lk 4:44. One can also notice that typically Mt combines διδάσκω and κηρύσσω (4:23; 9:35; 11:1).

[41] W. SCHRAGE, «συναγωγή», 833.

[42] When we consider the shortness of Mark's Gospel in comparison with Matthew's or Luke's, we can appreciate the amount of occurrences of these words in his Gospel: διδάσκειν: Mk 17x; Mt 14x; Lk 17x; διδαχή: Mk 5x; Mt 3x; Lk 1x; διδάσκαλος: Mk 12x; Mt 12x; Lk 16x; ῥαββί: Mk 4x; Mt 4x; Lk 0x. On the use of these didactic terms for Jesus alone in comparison with other synoptic writers, cf. R.T. FRANCE, «Teaching of Jesus», 103-104.

[43] Cf. E. SCHÜRER, *History of the Jewish People*, II, 448; S.E. JOHNSON, *Mark,* 46; A.E.J. RAWLINSON, *Mark,* 16; E.P. GOULD, *Mark,* 21. This exposition or teaching can

this teaching vocabularies in our pericope, especially in vv.21,22 (3x), and a heightened emphasis in v.27 make this activity very important for our text. It is also a characteristic activity of Jesus: of the 17x in Mk, he was mentioned 15x as the subject of the verb (unlike Mt and Lk)[44]. The object of this teaching was chiefly the crowd or the disciples[45]. The place of teaching begins in the synagogue, and other places, but ended in the temple[46].

«Teaching» could be used *absolutely*, as in our text, in the sense that what is taught is not indicated. It is not peculiar to Mk (Mt 9x; Mk 8x; Lk 13x) to use this verb absolutely, but what disturbs scholars is that in spite of the undue emphasis on teaching, the content of that teaching is lacking[47]. But in other occasions the content of the teaching was also seen, like «many things in parable» (4:2), «many things» = πολλά (6:34); his passion foretold = παθεῖν (8:31; 9:31); the way of God (12:14), etc.[48]. Here διδάσκειν is in Imperfect Indicative Active, which is generally regarded as being in an *inceptive* sense[49]. «The Imperfect tense of ἐδίδασκεν (usually taken as inceptive, "he began to teach") is due to the

---

be done by a rabbi or other person present and competent to teach. This appointment is made by the ἀρχισυνάγωγος, *the ruler of the synagogue*.

[44] In Mt, of the 14x: Jesus 9x; disciples 1x; others 4x; in Lk of the 17x: Jesus 15x; disciples 0x; others 2x; and in Mk of the 17x: Jesus 15x; disciples 1x; others 1x.

[45] The crowd/people, ὄχλος: Mk 1:22; 2:13; 4:2; 6:2,34; 10:1; 11:17; 12:35; 14:49 (Mt 6x; Lk 8x); the disciples: 8:31; 9:31 (Mt 2x; Lk 2x); the nations (Mt 20:28) benefitted from Jesus' teaching.

[46] The places of teaching were: *synagogue* (Mt 4:23; 9:35; 13:54; Mk 1:21,22; 6:2; Lk 4:15; 6:6; 13:10); *temple* (Mt 26:55; Mk 11:17; 12:35; 14:49; Lk 19:47; 20:1; 21:37); along/beside the *sea* (Mk 2:13; 4:1,2; Lk 5:3) around the *villages/region* (Mt 11:1; Mk 6:6; 8:31; 10:1; Lk 13:22; 23:5); a *lonely place* (Mk 6:34); *house* (Mk 9:31).

[47] If one compares with Mt and Lk, it will be noticed that for Mt, the teaching material begins in *the Sermon on the Mount* (5-7) and in Lk *Jesus at Nazareth* (4:16-30). However, one has to look back, to infer from Mk 1:15, that he must have taught about the coming of the kingdom of God.

[48] On the subject-matter of the teaching material consult, R.T. FRANCE, «Teaching of Jesus», 118-123; Cf. J. DELORME, «Aspects doctrinaux», 84.

[49] This has the support of many scholars: Cf. R.H. GUNDRY, *Mark*, 73; E.K. BROADHEAD, *Teaching with Authority*, 58; R.G. BRATCHER – E.A. NIDA, *Translator's Handbook*, 44; C.E.B. CRANFIELD, *Mark*, 72; W.L. LANE, *Mark*, 71; C.S. EMDEN, «The Imperfect Tense», 147; C.H. TURNER, «Marcan Usage», (1926-27) 351. But for the tenses of Mark's 15 uses of διδάσκειν of the teaching of Jesus, see R.T. FRANCE, «Teaching of Jesus», 130, n.8.

linear nature of teaching and is common in other verbs of speaking, too»[50]. This is well justified, as this is the first appearance of this verb, and its use by Jesus in Mk, so Jesus begins to teach. The «beginning» and the «continuing» natures of this verb are represented here, as we shall see soon with the people's reaction.

In this verse, «like all the righteous in Israel Jesus and His disciples go to the synagogue on the Sabbath to take part in worship and to avail themselves of the right of every male Israelite to append a sermon or instruction to the reading of Scripture»[51]. Here Jesus did not only «append» but was also the protagonist of the day's worship, teaching and proclaiming the «nearness of the kingdom of God» (1:15)[52].

1.3 *Mk 1:22: People's Astonishment at Jesus' authoritative Teaching*

This is one of the most important verses in this pericope. One can observe this reality by the concentration of themes, motifs, grammatical constructions, particles and other unique elements revealed in this verse. The wonder motif, the insistence on the teaching theme, the γάρ-clause, the periphrastic construction, the first grammatic object of teaching, the authority motif, the double ὡς, the only negative particle, and the contrast of Jesus' teaching with the scribes, illustrate clearly the importance of this verse. On the other hand, the relevance of this verse is well attested by the synoptic evangelists (Mt 7:28b-29; Mk 1:22; Lk 4:32), though with few modifications but substantially the same.

The preceding verse (v.21b) highlighted Jesus' activity of teaching in the synagogue of Capernaum on the sabbath. And now this verse continues this narration by showing how this activity touched the people. The people reacted to it. The narrator also was not left out in giving us the reason for this reaction. So we shall now examine *how* the people reacted, *what* impact merited the reaction, and *why* such a reaction.

1.3.1 They were astonished at his Teaching

This is the main clause in the complex sentence of our verse. As the verb ἐκπλήσσομαι is an intransitive verb, it has no object but complement. This verb, has both the active and passive senses respectively. For

---

[50] R.H. GUNDRY, *Mark*, 73.

[51] E. LOHSE, «σάββατον», 21; Cf. J. ERNST, *Markus*, 63.

[52] Cf. P. GUILLEMETTE, «Un enseignement nouveau», 239; W. GRUNDMANN, *Markus*, 42; W.L. LANE, *Mark*, 71.

the active sense, it could mean «to amaze, astound, overwhelm (lit. strike out of one's senses)»; or «to drive out or away, expel». But in the passive sense, it could also mean «to be amazed, overwhelmed», or «to be struck with astonishment, astonished»[53]. In the NT only the passive form (ἐκπλήσσομαι) is found[54].

This verb introduces us to the motif of wonder, which Theissen describes as comprising,

all the narrative elements which express astonishment, fear, terror and amazement. Wonder may be described either by a verb: θαυμάζειν (Mt 8.27 etc.), ἐξίστασθαι (Mk 2.12 etc.), φόβεῖσθαι (Mk 4.41 etc.), θαμβεῖσθαι (Mk 1.27), ἐκπλήττεσθαι (7.37), or by a noun: ἔκστασις (Mk 5.42), φόβος (Mk 4.41; Lk 7.16), θάμβος (Lk 4.36)[55].

In fact, the verb ἐκπλήσσομαι) appears only 13x in NT, and mostly in the synoptic Gospels, except once in Acts.[56]. It is associated with the usual effect of Jesus' words and deeds[57], or a typical response to divine revelation in word or deed[58], or a characteristic reaction of the people (multitude) or/and the disciples[59] to Jesus' teaching or healing[60]. This strong verb of feeling expresses a profound amazement or astonishment.

In Mk, and even in Mt, we see clearly how this verb expresses this profound meaning for the people listening to this revelatory teaching of Jesus. Among the 5x (Mk) and 4x (Mt), each used this particular word 4x for teaching. Apart from ἐκπλήσσομαι Mk has other terms[61] to express the astonishment of the people or the disciples at the word and deed of

---

[53] Cf. *BAGD*, 244.

[54] Cf. *BAGD*, 244; J.H. MOULTON – G. MILLIGAN, *Vocabulary*, 197-198.

[55] G. THEISSEN,*Miracle Stories*, 69; Cf. T. DWYER, *Motif of Wonder*, 11; ID., «Motif of Wonder», 49; R. PESCH,*Markusevangelium*, II, 150.

[56] It occurs in Mt 4x, Mk 5x, Lk 3x and none in Jn, but 1x in Acts.

[57] Cf. V. TAYLOR, *Mark*, 172; E. KLOSTERMANN, *Markusevangelium*, 14.

[58] E. LOHMEYER, *Markus*, 35.

[59] Cf. W. LANE, *Mark*, 72; C.E.B. CRANFIELD, *Mark*, 73.

[60] Cf. R. PESCH, «Eine neue Lehre», 249; ID., «Ein Tag», 117-118. This is the effect of Jesus' *teaching* on the crowd (Mt 7:28; 13:54; 22:33; Mk 1:22; 6:2; 11:18; Lk 4:32), on the disciples (Mt 19:25; Mk 10:26) and the reaction to Jesus' *healing* (Mk 7:37; Lk 9:43).

[61] The variety of terms employed by Mk are as follows: θαυμάζω (5:20; 15:5, 44); ἐκθαυμάζω (12:17); θαμβοῦμαι (1:27; 10:24, 32); ἐκθαμβοῦμαι (9:15); ἐξίστημι (2:12; 5:42; 6:51); cf. φοβοῦμαι (4:41; 5:15, 33, 36; 6:50; 9:32; 10:32; 11:18) and ἔκφοβος (9:6). Cf. CRANFIELD, *Mark*, 73; LANE, *Mark*, 72, no. 110.

Jesus. This shows that amazement occasioned by Jesus are a striking feature of the gospel. To confirm this reality Dwyer remarks:

Mark is worthy of an examination of wonder more so than Matthew or Luke because its use of wonder is more frequent and intense (32x in Mark, 27x in Matthew, which is a full third longer, 34x in Luke, which is 8370 words longer). Wonder is also more varied in Mark (six of Mark's terms for wonder are not used by Matthew, and five are not used by Luke). Further, it can be said that language of wonder in Mark has a mystery which surpasses that of the other Synoptics (cf. Mk 3.21; 10.32; 14.33; 16.8). Wonder in Mark serves as more than a mere element of the miracle tradition[62].

We must also remark straightaway, that this verb in our context is an Imperfect tense and also an implicit or indefinite plural[63]. The tense of this verb is well fitted because it «makes the audience's astonishment match Jesus' activity of teaching: as long as he taught, astonishment overwhelmed them»[64]. So the people were «knocked out of their senses», dumbfounded, while they were in the synagogue. But what made this impact is explained by the use of ἐπί with *dative* which means «at». This is generally used to indicate the basis or ground for an action[65]. This preposition gives the ground for the astonishment, which is attached to the reality of the activity of teaching: διδαχή. Here in Mk and as many places «the amazement is always a specific reaction, as indicated by a reference to the object (ἐπί with dative) (1.22; 10.24; 11.18; 12.17) or by explicit questions (10.26; 6.2, cf. 1:27)»[66]. Carrington affirms that «this reaction of wonder and amazement is the primary reaction in Mark to the gospel teaching of Jesus»[67].

---

[62] T. DWYER, «Motif of Wonder», 50. Matthew does not use ἐκθαμβέομαι, θαμβέομαι, ἐκθαύμαζω, τρόμος, ἔκστασις or ἔκφοβος; while Luke also does not use ἐκθαμβέομαι, θαμβέομαι, ἐκθαύμαζω, ἔκφοβος, τρόμος.

[63] Cf. C.H. TURNER, «Marcan Usage», (1923-4) 378 (here simply means «people were astonished»); V. TAYLOR, *Mark*, 172; C.E.B. CRANFIELD, *Mark*, 73; R.G. BRATCHER – E.A. NIDA, *Translator's Handbook*, 45.

[64] Cf. R.H. GUNDRY, *Mark*, 73; Cf. C.S. EMDEN, «The Imperfect Tense», 147.
According to the latter, this imperfect is for giving the effect of continuity in narration. Moreover, the feeling of amazement, or wonder is given depth by being described in imperfect tense.

[65] Cf. M. ZERWICK, *Biblical Greek*, # 126; V. TAYLOR, *Mark*; R.G. BRATCHER – E.A. NIDA, *Translator's Handbook*, 46.

[66] G. THEISSEN, *Miracle Stories*, 71.

[67] P. CARRINGTON, *According to Mark*, 50.

This substantive, διδαχή generally means «teaching», «instruction»[68]. In the NT, when the Synoptists speak of the διδαχή of Jesus (Mt 7:28; 22:33; Mk 1:22 and par., etc), «they do not mean a particular dogmatics or ethics, but His whole διδάσκειν, His proclamation of the will of God as regards both form and content»[69]. In Mk, διδαχή, appears 5x, but all referring to Jesus' teaching[70]. It is this Jesus' teaching which causes astonishment to the people, though its content is not indicated. «The non-specification of the content and the emphasis instead on authoritative manner favor a dynamic meaning for τῇ διδαχῇ αὐτοῦ, "his activity of teaching", over a static meaning, "what he taught"»[71]. Ambrozic sees in Jesus' teaching «the revelatory and active character» which is further brought out «by the amazement, astonishment and fear which it evokes». He then concluded, «however imperfect the response of amazement may be in Mark's eyes, it is considered by him to be a sign of the recognition that God is at work in Jesus' teaching»[72].

1.3.2 He was teaching Them

In the above section we tried to show the «how» and the «what» of the reaction of the people in the synagogue, which reveals itself in the «amazement» and «teaching» motifs. Here we want to show also the *why* of this reaction. And to this, we have the γάρ-particle to do this work. We must remark also that the narrator intervenes here to give us this reason with this γάρ-construction.

Our text concerns the aspect of γάρ that deals with the «reason and cause of a foregoing statement», which takes up «the causal or argumentative force of the particle, *for*»[73]. The γάρ-clause usage is important for Mk as well as for the other Evangelists (Mt 124x; Mk 64x; Lk 97x; Jn 64x).

The periphrastic construction ἦν ... διδάσκων (imperfect of εἰμι + present participle) in our pericope offers us the Imperfect tense of διδάσκειν. This construction helps to give a «progressive and continu-

---

[68] K.H. RENGSTORF, «διδαχή»,163-164.

[69] K.H. RENGSTORF, «διδαχή», 164.

[70] Cf. Mk 1:22, 27; 4:2; 11:18; 12:38; in Mt among the 3x only 2x refers to Jesus (7:28; 22:33); while in Lk only 1x and to Jesus (4:32).

[71] R.H. GUNDRY, *Mark*, 73.

[72] A.M. AMBROZIC, «New Teaching», 137-138.

[73] Cf. *BAGD*, 151, 1; Cf. R. PESCH, «Eine neue Lehre», 249. Here it is absolute, it can also combine with other particles and conjunctions.

ous» treatment of the theme of teaching in our text[74]. We have earlier shown that this construction is a favourite one for Mark[75]. For the first time we see αὐτούς, the grammatical object of this verb διδάσκειν, referring to the people (the implicit and indefinite subject, v.22a, cf. v.23: αὐτῶν).

The insistence on the teaching activity of Jesus has been so much emphasized in this early part of the pericope, that we think we could still develop an aspect we have not yet touched. In fact, this is the relationship between διδάσκειν and κηρύσσειν («teaching» and «preaching»). When we compare with other synoptic writers like Matthew, the difference in the use of Mark becomes clear. We notice that Mt combines the two often (cf. Mt 4:23; 9:35; 11:1), and it is typical of him. This, on the other hand, is not so with Mark.

The verb, κηρύσσειν has the basic meaning of «to cry out loud», «to proclaim», «to declare», «to announce», or «to make known»[76]. Mk described with κηρύσσειν (preaching) the activity of the Baptist 2x; Jesus 3x; the disciples (the Twelve) 2x; and the universal Church 2x[77]. The object of this verb, strictly speaking revolves around two elements: μετάνοια and εὐαγγέλιον («repentance» and «gospel»)[78]. But if we follow it as it occurs in Mk, we can see that it includes: baptism of repentance (βάπτισμα μετανοίας) (1:4); the Gospel (τὸ εὐαγγέλιον) (1:14; 13:10; 14:9; 16:15); about Jesus' coming (1:7); the experience of Healing (1:45; 5:20 cf. 7:36). This word also is used absolutely (without an object): 2x of Jesus (1:38,39) and 2x of the disciples (3:14; 6:12; cf. 16:20)[79].

---

[74] Cf. G. BJÖRCK, *Die Periphrastischen Konstruktionen*, 41ff, 61; Cf. J. GNILKA, *Markus* I, 78.

[75] Cf. V. TAYLOR, *Mark*, 45, 62; R. PESCH, «Eine neue Lehre», 249, n.30. Cf. Mk 1:6,13,22,33,39; 2:6,18; 3:1; 4:38; 5:5,11,40; 6:31,44,52; 8:9; 9:4; 10:22,32; 14:4,40,54; 15:7,26,40,43,46.

[76] G. FRIEDRICH, «κηρύσσω», 697; Cf. *BAGD*, 431.

[77] Cf. E. SCHWEIZER, «Theologische Leistung», 340; ID., «Anmerkungen zur Theologie», 93f; H. FLENDER, «Lehren und Verkündigung», 702. These four protagonists of κηρύσσειν: the Baptist, Jesus, the Twelve, the universal Church, are what K. STOCK, *Boten*, 20, calls «a chain of preachers» («Kette der Verkündigungsträger»).

[78] E. SCHWEIZER, «Theologische Leistung», 340; ID., «Anmerkungen zur Theologie», 94.

[79] Cf. K. STOCK, *Boten*, 20.

On the relationship between κηρύσσειν and διδάσκειν in Mark's Gospel, Stock, among other things, said:

> According to Mark's word usage, «to proclaim» seems to mean: the first, proclaiming announcement to those, who have not yet had any experience. It brings something completely new and sets the beginning. It is more likely a unique event and can hardly be repeated before the same hearers. It corresponds well, that the word was used only in the first chapter of Mark for Jesus, even for his initial activity. «Teaching» means, on the other hand, the continuing, explaining clarification. It does not amount to a unique event, but it can be repeated to the same hearers (audience). So also it is with Mark throughout the whole Gospel and stands for Jesus' mission through word[80].

For Mk, κηρύσσειν is rather the first announcement and is placed at the beginning of a process; while διδάσκειν constitutes the successive development[81]. The fact of the comparison between «teaching» and «preaching», puts in relief the importance of teaching in our pericope, and also emphasizes its exclusiveness to Jesus in the whole Gospel, as in our text. Now we shall examine what makes Jesus teaching different, and contrasts him with his contemporaries.

1.3.3 As One Having Authority

This sub-ordinate clause is the kernel of this verse because it gives the reason for the astonishment of the people. In view of its central importance both to the verse, the pericope and even the Gospel, we shall give a closer attention to its meaning, before relating it to other aspects of the text. In fact, this clause begins with the particle ὡς, which is a relative adverb of the relative pronoun ὅς. This particle, ὡς[82]. could be used as «a comparative particle, indicating the manner in which something proceeds», or «a conjunction denoting comparison», or other uses, like «a temporal conjunction». But in our text, it falls on the third, among the four different uses[83]. Here, ὡς «introduces the characteristic quality of a

---

[80] K. STOCK, *Boten*, 20-21. The translation is *mine*.

[81] Cf. M. GRILLI, *Comunità e Missione*, 86; R.T. FRANCE, «Teaching of Jesus», 104; K. STOCK, *Boten*, 101.

[82] The particle, ὡς occurs in Mk 21x; Mt 40x; Lk 29x; Jn 13x. It seems Mt is in the habit of doubling or tripling it: 3x (Mt 10:16); 2x (Mt 7:29; 10:25; 17:2; 28:3; Mk 1:22; Lk 22:26). One can notice that only in our verse that Mk has ὡς doubled in a verse.

[83] Cf. *BAGD*, 897-899.

person, thing, or action»: Firstly, it introduces the «actual quality» (ἐξουσία); and secondly,«ὡς with the participle (ἔχων) gives the reason for an action *as one who, because*»[84].

The construction in our text combines three different uses of ὡς: a comparative particle indicating the manner in which something (teaching) proceeds[85]; the characteristic quality (ὡς ἐξουσία) of Jesus is highlighted; and the reason for the superiority of Jesus' activity of teaching is implied by the use of «ὡς with the participle ἔχων»[86] — just as if he had or as one who has ἐξουσία. Thus, this prepares the setting on which we are going to engage our attention from now on.

a) Ἐξουσία in General

Ἐξουσία has been mentioned so much that it is now necessary to begin to discuss it. It is derived from ἔξεστιν, meaning «it is free», «it is possible», «it is permitted» which denotes ability to perform an action to the extent that it denies the presence of any hindrance or obstacle to do so[87]. It is mostly used in connection with legal transactions, whereby the possibility or freedom to act, decide and dispose (something) is derived from a higher norm or authority[88].

It is not always easy to distinguish the relationship between ἐξουσία and δύναμις («authority» and «power»). Their meanings are not the same, even though their boundaries are not often very distinct. The distinction between them, says Dillon, «is the distinction between *right* and *ability*, between the warrant to do something and the intrinsic capacity to do it»[89]. Both freedom/right and ability/power to act are necessary for authority to be effective. Authority without power has no meaning. This can be seen

---

[84] *BAGD*, 898, III, 1a & b.

[85] Cf. V. TAYLOR, *Mark*, 173. He states that ὡς ... ἔχων indicates the manner of the teaching.

[86] This construction (ὡς + participle) occurs 5x in Mark: 1:10,22; 6:34; 8:24; 13:34. R. PESCH, «Eine neue Lehre», 249, n.32, recorded 4x (without Mk 13:34).

Likewise, it is observed that the construction of ἐξουσίαν ἔχειν occurs again in Mk 2:10, still referring to Jesus. Cf. *ibid.*, 250. We must also remark that the same combination with a change in position (ἔχειν ἐξουσίαν) appears in Mk 3:15, but here referring to the disciples.

[87] W. FOERSTER, «ἐξουσία», 560, 562.

[88] Cf. M. YOUNG-HEON LEE, *Autorität*, 94; W. FOERSTER, «ἐξουσία», 562.

[89] R.J. DILLON, «As One Having Authority», 97; Cf. K. SCHOLTISSEK, *Vollmacht Jesu*, 50; W. FOERSTER, «ἐξουσία», 563; J. MARSH, «Authority», 319.

clearly in the delegated or commissioned «authority».

In the OT there is no technical term or direct equivalent for ἐξουσία both in Hebrew or Biblical Aramaic[90]. However, the LXX uses ἐξουσία to translate a number of Hebrew words, ממשלה and the root שלט[91]. The usage of ἐξουσία in LXX first means right, authority, power, permission or freedom in the legal or political sense, and it is then used for the right or permission given by God, or for the permission granted or withheld by the Jewish law[92]. In the NT, the word ἐξουσία occurs 102x, and its usage is also closest to that of the LXX, and it denotes the absolute or creative power of God[93] and the spiritual world[94], the power which Satan exercises and imparts[95], and especially the power or freedom which Jesus exercises[96], and given by Him to His disciples[97]. This usage is also extended

---

[90] Cf. K. SCHOLTISSEK, *Vollmacht Jesu*, 47, 55; J. MARSH,«Authority», 319.

[91] E. HATCH – H.A. REDPATH,*Concordance to the Septuagint*, 500-501; Cf. K. SCHOLTISSEK, *Vollmacht Jesu*, 31; W. FOERSTER, «ἐξουσία», 565; J. MARSH, «Authority», 319.

[92] W. FOERSTER, «ἐξουσία», 564; Cf. K. SCHOLTISSEK, *Vollmacht Jesu*, 55; M. Y.-H. LEE, *Autorität*, 95.

[93] Lk 12:5; Acts 1:7; Rev 16:9; Jude 25; Rom 9:21. Cf. W. FOERSTER, «ἐξουσία», 566-567; K. SCHOLTISSEK, *Vollmacht Jesu*, 67; M.Y.-H. LEE, *Autorität*, 96; A.M. AMBROZIC, «New Teaching», 121-122; W. GRUNDMANN, *Begriff der Kraft*, 18-21.

[94] The ἐξουσία and the power of God are variously displayed in the sphere of nature. It is used to describe the power of Angels (Rev 14:18; 18:1), the forces of destruction in nature (Rev 6:8; 9:3,10,19). Cf. W. FOERSTER, «ἐξουσία», 567; M.Y.-H. LEE, *Autorität*, 96.

[95] ἐξουσία describes Satan' sphere of dominion (Eph 6:12) or his power (Lk 4:6; Acts 26:18; Col 1:13; Eph 2:2). Thus it is described as Satan's power (cf. Mk 3:27 and par.). Cf. M.Y.-H. LEE, *Autorität*; W. FOERSTER, «ἐξουσία», 567-568; W. GRUNDMANN, *Begriff der Kraft*, 49-53.

[96] Here ἐξουσία denotes Jesus' divinely given power and authority to act (Mt 28:18; Mk 1:22 and par., 27; 2:10 and par.; 3:15; Lk 4:36; Jn 5:27; 10:18; 17:2). This authority unfolds especially in Jesus' Word and Deed. Jesus exercises his Authority with free will and in agreement with his Father, God. Hence, being the Son, this authority is not a restricted commission. Cf. M. Y.-H. LEE, *Autorität*, 96-97; K. SCHOLTISSEK, *Vollmacht Jesu*, 121-128; K. STOCK, «Die Machttaten Jesu», 200-201; W. FOERSTER, «ἐξουσία», 568-569.

[97] Likewise here ἐξουσία denotes the Authority which Jesus gives to his disciples to exercise. (Mt 10:1; Mk 6:7; Lk 9:1; 10:19; cf. 2 Cor 10:8; 13:10). The disciples are authorized or empowered through Jesus, and their authority is exercized in the continuing or carrying on of Jesus' already begun Work. Cf. M.Y.-H. LEE, *Autorität*, 97; R.J. DILLON, «As One having Authority», 99, and n.25; K. STOCK, *Boten*, 21, 87-

to the political relationships[98].

b) Ἐξουσία in Mark's Gospel

The word ἐξουσία appeared 10x in Mk (Mt 10x; Lk 16x; Jn 8x): 7x referring to Jesus (1:22,27; 2:10; 11:28bis,29,33), while 3x refer to Jesus' gift to the disciples (3:15; 6:7; 13:34)[99]. In its grammatical construction, we have the verbs ἔχειν (1:22; 2:10; 3:15) and διδόναι (6:7; 11:28; 13:34), with prepositions κατα (1:27) and ἐν (11:28,29,33). This statement form gives the content and range of ἐξουσία. It describes here authority, right of disposal, entitlement or power, which only refers to Jesus and his disciples[100]. From the general idea of «power to act» ἐξουσία in the LXX and NT expresses the thought of «authority» rather than «power»[101]. And Jesus possesses this ἐξουσία (authority) which manifests itself in his teaching (1:22,27), healing (23-27) and forgiveness of sins (2:10). He does these because he is the Son of God, and «as herald and instrument of God's reign, exerted the "authority" of God in the proper sense of God's right to rule the universe»[102]. Jesus himself gives directly to his disciples the ἐξουσία (authority) to cast out demons (3:15), and unclean spirits (6:7), and suggestively indicates the continuous responsible service (13:34)[103]. Jesus is also questioned as to the nature and source of his authority for doing «these things» (11:27-28,29,33).

91; W. FOERSTER, «ἐξουσία», 569.

[98] This has to do with authority or power to govern (Lk 19:17), of the Sanhedrin (Acts 9:14; 26:10,12), of Pilate (Lk 20:20; Jn 19:10), of the power of kings (Rev 17:12,13), and of freedom of self-determination (Acts 5:4; 1 Cor 7:37). It is used sometimes in plural for the «authorities» (Lk 12:11; Rom 13:1; Tt 3:1), but in singular for «government»(Rom 13:2f; Mt 8:9 and par). Cf. W. FOERSTER, «ἐξουσία», 565; K. SCHOLTISSEK, Vollmacht Jesu, 69.

[99] Mark's use of the term differs somewhat from the other Synoptics: while others speak of the ἐξουσία of God (Lk 12:5), of men (Mt 8:9; Lk 7:8), and of Satan (Lk 4:6), or to govern (Lk 19:17; 20:20), besides that of Jesus, Mark predicates it only of Jesus or depicts it as his gift to the disciples. Cf. A.M. AMBROZIC, «New Teaching», 122; K. SCHOLTISSEK, «Nachfolge und Autorität», 74; K. STOCK, Boten, 21, 87-91; J. COUTTS, «Authority of Jesus», 111-118, esp. 111.

[100] Cf. M. Y.-H. LEE, Autorität, 99.

[101] V. TAYLOR, Mark, 173.

[102] R.J. DILLON, «As One having Authority», 98; Cf. D.J. DOUGHTY, «Authority», 178; W. HARRINGTON, Mark, 16; K. KERTELGE, Die Wunder Jesu, 57-58.

[103] Cf. M.Y.-H. LEE, Autorität, 99.

This «authority» of Jesus is not the Rabbinic רשׁוּת or prophetic authority[104] or the Hellenist «wonder-worke's»[105] or like a King's[106] or like an Emperor's[107], but the authority of the Son of God, the Messiah[108]. Thus, «the authority of Mark's Jesus, then, is ultimately dependent on his status as God's beloved son and heir»[109]. This is the authority which Jesus demonstrated both in his word and deed in this pericope.

c) Ἐξουσία and Jesus' Teaching

What astonished the people in the synagogue was Jesus' teaching «as one having authority». We have so far tried to establish what this «authority» is, but now we shall see how it relates to teaching. This link between both motifs of teaching and authority has a programmatic character: on the one hand, for the reader of Mark's Gospel from now on always wherever there is the talk of the teaching of Jesus, it is associated with the connotation «powerful teaching»; on the other hand, it is even this authority character of Jesus' teaching which opens an immense conflict potential[110]. If we observe the insistence or occurrence of the terms of «teaching» (διδάσκειν/διδαχή: 3x) in vv.21-22, and yet the

---

[104] Cf. D. DAUBE, «ἐξουσία in Mark», 45-59; criticized by A.W. ARGYLE, «The Meaning of ἐξουσία», 343; Cf. W. EGGER, Frohbotschaft und Lehre, 148; R.H. STEIN, «Markan Seam», 88.

[105] This is especially when «an extraordinary and superhuman or divinely delegated power» is linked with Exorcism. Cf. J. STARR, «The Meaning of "Authority"»,302-5, esp. 304; R. GUNDRY, Mark, 81; L. BIELER, ΘΕΙΟΣ ΑΝΗΡ, 80ff; Pesch recommends against interpreting ἐξουσία exclusively in terms of the pneumatic power of the wonder-worker. Cf. R. PESCH, «Eine neue Lehre», 271-72.

[106] Cf. H.J. FLOWERS, «ὡς ἐξουσία ἔχων», 254.

[107] Cf. D.F. HUDSON, «ὡς ἐξουσία ἔχων», 17.

[108] As R.H. GUNDRY, Mark, 81, suggests, «we should not distinguish sharply between ἐξουσία as inherent divine authority, like that of a Hellenistic divine man, and ἐξουσία as delegated divine authority like that of a Hebrew prophet; for Jesus is not only God's agent, "Christ", but also God's Son, who does not need to say, "Thus saith the Lord,"...»

[109] T.-S.B. LIEW, «Tyranny, Boundary, and Might», 16. Hence, «Jesus, as God's son and heir, has absolute authority in interpreting and arbitrating God's will». Ibid., 27, cf. 20,21.

[110] Cf. K. SCHOLTISSEK, Vollmacht Jesu, 121-122; καὶ οὐχ ὡς οἱ γραμματεῖς - «and not as the scribes». So «it is not that he, in contrast to them, has the "right" to teach, but that his teaching was in and of itself authoritative, i.e. power-full». Cf. T.L. BUDESHEIM, «Jesus and the Disciples», 193.

teaching material was lacking, it shows that it is «authority» that is been emphasized: the «manner» of teaching which is being characterized by «authority»[111]. Coincidentally, in Mark's Gospel *teaching* and *authority* are uniquely reserved only for Jesus. We shall now see the effect of Jesus' authority on the scribes.

1.3.4 And not like the Scribes

This noun phrase, καὶ οὐχ ὡς οἱ γραμματεῖς, concludes v.22. The reason for the astonishment of the crowd or people have been furnished by the γάρ-clause: that Jesus was teaching them «as one having authority». Our attention will now go to the comparative aspect which the second ὡς in the verse introduces. The only negative particle οὐχ in our pericope refers to «characters» who never functioned in the scene. This makes their appearance here very curious. We shall try to find out what type of relationship, which the narrator wants to highlight among the characters in the text. However, we shall go straight to the discovery of the main subject of this phrase: «and not as the scribes».

In the Gospel of Mark, the «scribes» have an important role to play compared with other religious authorities or leaders. The scribes appear 21x[112] as against the Pharisees, 12x[113]; the chief priests, 14x[114]; the elders, 5x[115]; and others. In Mark the «scribes» always appear at counterpoint to Jesus - alone (1:22; 2:6; 3:22; 9:11,14; 12:28,38), linked with the Pharisees (2:16; 7:1,5), with the chief priests (10:33; 11:18; 14:1; 15:31)

---

[111] As a hallmark of Jesus' teaching, ἐξουσία is «a more comprehensive characteristic of his activity, causing offence to others» (cf Mk 2:1-12; 11:28-33). Cf. R. PESCH, «Eine neue Lehre», 271; R.J. DILLON, «As One having Authority», 98, n.21; P. GUILLEMETTE, «Un enseignement nouveau», 239-240.

[112] When we compare the length of Matthew and Luke, we can see that Mark has more emphasis on the «scribes» than them: Mk 21x; Mt 22x; Lk 14x; Jn 0x. Apart from 4x in Acts, and 1x in Pauline Letter, there was no other appearance in the NT of the 62x occurrences. Thus the Synoptics supplied the necessary information about this «class of professionals». These 21x in Mk are: 1:22; 2:6,16; 3:22; 7:1,5; 8:31; 9:11,14; 10:33; 11:18,27; 12:28,32,35,38; 14:1,43,53; 15:1,31.

[113] The Pharisees appear 12x in Mark (Mt 29x; Lk 27x; Jn 19x) as follows: 2:16,18,24; 3:6; 7:1,3,5; 8:11,15; 9:11; 10:2; 12:13.

[114] The chief priests' appearance in Mk are about 14x (Mt 18x; Lk 12x; Jn 10x): 8:31; 10:33; 11:18,27; 14:1,10,43,53,55; 15:1,3,10,11,31.

[115] The elders appear 5x in Mk (Mt 11x; Lk 4x; Jn 0x): 8:31; 11:27; 14:43,53; 15:1.

and with the elders and chief priests (8:31; 11:27; 14:43,53; 15:1)[116].

On the location of Jesus' opponents, Saldarini says, «The Pharisees along with the scribes are the chief opponents of Jesus in Galilee; the chief priests, scribes and elders are his opponents in Jerusalem at the time of his death; the Sadducees appear only once»[117]. Malbon sees the two halves of Marcan narrative, in terms of spatial setting depicting a general movement from Galilee to Jerusalem and from synagogue to temple[118]. There is some consensus that in Mark's mind there is a direct continuity between Jesus' opponents in his Galilean ministry and his enemies in Jerusalem[119]. On the base of the hostility towards Jesus, Shae says, «The source of this resistance and the headquarters of the enemy forces was Jerusalem»[120].

a) The Scribes and Jesus

The «scribe», (γραμματεύς) generally denotes, «a secretary, clerk, recorder, or copyist»; but in the NT means «a learned theologian, rabbi, or scribe». However, what type of «scribes» contrast with Jesus especially

---

[116] Cf. R.A. GUELICH, *Mark*, 56; J.D. KINGSBURY, «The Religious Authorities», 44-45; A.J.SALDARINI, *Pharisees, Scribes and Sadducees*, 147; E.S. MALBON, «The Jewish Leaders», 265; J. GNILKA, *Markus*, 79; J.C. WEBER, «Jesus' Opponents», 214. It must also be noted that the scribes were part of the Sanhedrin, and also play an important role in it. Cf. E. SCHÜRER, *History of the Jewish people*, II, 210-214; 330-335.

[117] A.J. SALDARINI, *Pharisees, Scribes and Sadducees*, 146; Cf. J.D. KINGSBURY, «The Religious Authorities», 44-45.

[118] Cf. E.S. MALBON, «The Jewish Leaders», 272-274; For further discussion also see, ID., *Narrative Space*; and «Galilee and Jerusalem», 242-255.

[119] The scribes who challenge Jesus' authority actually begins in Capernaum (2:6-7) and feature as chief enemies (2:16; 3:22; 7:1) in his Galilean ministry. They were also acting in continuity with the members of Sanhedrin, the protagonists of his crucifixion (8:31; 10:33; 11:18; 14:1,43,53; 15:1;31) in Jerusalem. Mark specified twice that they were «scribes who had come down from Jerusalem» (3:22; 7:1). Cf. R.J. DILLON, «As One having Authority», 102; J.D. KINGSBURY, «The Religious Authorities», 44-46; W. WEISS, *Eine neue Lehre*, 80, 172, 342; D. LÜHRMANN, «Die Pharisäer und die Schriftgelehrten», 172.

[120] G.S. SHAE, «Authority of Jesus», 26. Furthermore he said: «It was from Jerusalem that the scribes went to Jesus in Galilee to do battle with his power (Mk iii 22). In Mk. xi 1f Jesus carried his warfare to the enemy headquarters itself. Just as he had subdued the master of the house and had repatriated the victims of Satan's dominion by his ἐξουσία, so did he by the same ἐξουσία destroy the kingdom of his enemies and reclaim it for all nations». [*ibid.*]

in Mark's Gospel? To this D. Daube added the third meaning of γραμματεύς: «"elementary", "inferior", or "Bible" teacher»[121]. Thus he affirmed that Jesus taught with Rabbinic authority (רשׁוּת) like an ordained scribe (Rabbi), and not like the scribes (elementary teachers) who were unordained[122]. Many Scholars did not agree with him because they held that the scribes of Jesus' time were really «the learned Jewish theologians», privileged and known teachers of the people, and not «the inferior or elementary teachers»[123].

From the foregoing, one can observe that the *common denominator* between Jesus and the scribes is *teaching*. In fact, «the Scribes are the authoritative teachers of the Law in Mark»[124]. This confirms that teaching can likewise be said to constitute the principal activity Mark attributes to the religious authorities[125], Saldarini says, «their teachings are referred to in an offhand way, which suggests that they were recognized as authoritative teachers of Jewish law and custom (Mk 1:22; 9:11)»[126].

On the other hand, of all that Jesus does during his public ministry, Mark uses teaching more to characterize him; and teaching is habitual or «customary» to him (10:1: ὡς εἰώθει)[127]. Thus the focus of v.22 is not only the *manner* of Jesus' teaching (as against its matter) but also the *uniqueness* of Jesus.

From the above established points, we can affirm that the node of the *tertium comparationis* is teaching, not authority. Both Jesus and the

---

[121] D. DAUBE, «ἐξουσία in Mark», 50-52 esp. n.5: He concludes «it seems that all three significations, "scholar", "elementary teacher", and "copyist", are to be explained by the fact that the art of writing was not too common in ancient times».

[122] Cf. D. DAUBE, «ἐξουσία in Mark», 45-49; ID., *The New Testament*, 205-233.

[123] Cf. G.R. OSBORNE, «Structure and Christology», 150, n.11; R. GUNDRY, *Mark*, 81-82; R.A. GUELICH, *Mark*, 56; J. GNILKA, *Markus* I, 79-80; C.E.B. CRANFIELD, *Mark*, 73-74; W.L. LANE, *Mark*, 72 and n.111; R.H. STEIN, «Markan Seam», 82, 88. A.W. ARGYLE, «Meaning of ἐξουσία», 343, also argued whether such levels of authority existed within Judaism in Jesus' day, since not one of the fifty occurrences of ἐξουσία in the LXX renders רשׁות, the suggested Hebrew term behind ἐξουσία in 1:22. Cf. R.A. GUELICH, *ibid.*; G.R. OSBORNE, *ibid.*

[124] E. RIVKIN, «Scribes, Pharisees, Lawyers, Hypocrites», 137.

[125] Cf. J.D. KINGSBURY, «The Religious Authorities», 53.

[126] A.J. SALDARINI, «Scribes»,1015.

[127] And this teaching characterization emphasizes more on who teaches than on the content of his teaching. Cf. B.D. CHILTON, «Exorcism and History», 255-256; A.M. AMBROZIC, *Hidden Kingdom*, 84, 85. For a fuller discussion on the phenomenon cf. R.T. FRANCE, «The Teaching of Jesus», 101-136.

scribes are teachers, but only he teaches with authority; the hallmark of his teaching is not something he shares with them or anybody[128]. Gundry adds that «teachers enjoy high respect in Mark's environment. But with the phrase "not as the scribes" he has Jesus vault far higher than other teachers. We might think that in their teaching they *appeal* to authority whereas in his teaching he *assumes* authority»[129].

Considering the *nature* and *source* between the teaching of Jesus («from heaven») and that of the scribes («You abandon the commandment of God and hold fast to mere human tradition», 7:8), we observe the comparison of content between the διδαχή of Jesus and that of the scribes[130]. So, Jesus' teaching coming «from heaven» and being the Son of God, «thinks the things of God», that is, he perceives reality from a divine point of view (8:33c)[131]. While Mark characterizes the Religious Authorities (without authority) as those who «think the things of men», that is, to view reality from a purely human perspective (8:33c). This is, in fact, to be on the side of Satan (8:33)[132]. Thus the teaching of the scribes is not only destructive of God's word and command[133]; it is also part and parcel of their consistent hostility, in word and deed, to Jesus, and thus participates in Satan's and the demons' opposition to him[134].

---

[128] Cf. R.J. DILLON, «As One Having Authority», 103; K. SCHOLTISSEK, *Vollmacht Jesu*, 124-125. Scholtissek here rightly remarks that ἐξουσία is a distinguishing mark of Jesus' ministry *alone*. Mark never concedes authority to the scribes. Moreover with Mark there is no direct description of ἐξουσία with regard to men (cf. Mt 8:9), to God (cf. Lk 12:5) or to Satan (cf. Lk 4:6), but exclusively to Jesus.

[129] R.H. GUNDRY, *Mark*, 74. He concludes that Mark tells what feature of the scribes' teaching betrays a lack of authority no more than he tells what feature of Jesus' teaching exhibits authority. Such contrast interests him and helps him to exalt the figure of Jesus.

[130] Cf. R.J. DILLON, «As One having Authority», 103, 108 and n.60; K. SCHOLTISSEK, *Vollmacht Jesu*, 125; A.M. AMBROZIC, «New Teaching», 121. Scholtissek points out that only in this passage, with its quotation of Isa 29:13 (LXX), does Mark allow anyone other than Jesus to become the subject of the verb διδάσκω, (the exception being the apostles, cf. Mk 6:30).

[131] Cf. J.D. KINGSBURY, «The Religious Authorities», 51; on «divine point of view» in Mark, cf. ID., *Christology of Mark*, 47-50.

[132] Cf. J.D. KINGSBURY, «The Religious Authorities», 52; Cf. A.M. AMBROZIC, «New Teaching», 120-121.

[133] Cf. R. SCHNACKENBURG, *Markus I*, 48.

[134] Cf. A.M. AMBROZIC, «New Teaching», 120-121; ID., *Hidden Kingdom*, 56-62.

b) The Role of Ἐξουσία in the Comparison

Since we have noted that «teaching» is the medium of comparison, and authority was exclusively reserved for Jesus, what does Mark want to achieve by emphasizing Jesus' manner of teaching, as against that of the scribes? To this, Kingsbury sees this verse as the «key to his entire presentation of Jesus' conflict with the authorities»[135]. Furthermore he affirms that fundamentally «the issue of authority, underlies every controversy Jesus has with the religious authorities and is, in fact, at the root of his entire conflict with them»[136]. Thus, the theme of conflict or controversy had already been introduced by this verse, even without the personnel involved playing any role in the pericope. This contrast or conflict is most evident by the only negative particle, οὐχ, in our text. Since there is also a comparative particle ὡς in our text, then we have both a *comparing* and *contrasting* element in our pericope. Therefore this points to a strong contrast between Jesus and the scribes, which his authority occasions.

1.4 *Summary*

At this first part of our chapter, we want to highlight most of the terms and themes/motives, which we discovered in our pericope. These are as follows:

1. Jesus entry into Capernaum with his disciples after calling them (1:16-20), was discovered in the verb, εἰσπορεύονται (1:21), to be a theme for their being together both in Jesus' movements and ministry.

2. The most important activity of Jesus in his public ministry, the exclusive use of διδάσκειν, διδαχή and other didactic terms for Jesus, demonstrate and highlight the principal theme of Teaching in the pericope.

3. The motif of Wonder (ἐξεπλήσσοντο) as a response of the people to Jesus' word and deed, is also an important theme.

4. The theme of authority (ἐξουσία) is an important one for Mark. It is not only exclusive to Jesus, but it was also identified as the root issue

---

[135] J.D. KINGSBURY, «The Religious Authorities», 51.

[136] J.D. KINGSBURY, «The Religious Authorities», 47, 52-53, 54, 56, 59, 60-61; ID., *Conflict in Mark*, 66-67, 86; R.J. DILLON, «As One having Authority», 102, and n.38; P. GUILLEMETTE, «Un enseignement nouveau», 239-240. That the central issue in all controversy stories mediated by the Synoptic traditions had to do with the authority of Jesus, was also confirmed by other scholars. Cf. D.J. DOUGHTY, «Authority», 178; H. TÖDT, *The Son of Man*, 113-125, 138.

that underlies every controversy or conflict Jesus had with the Religious Leaders, which even led to his death.

5. If Jesus was the protagonist, the scribes (οἱ γραμματεῖς) were the antagonists in Jesus' public ministry. The contrast between Jesus and the scribes was sharpened by the authority issue. So this contrast with Jesus reveals another important theme for Mark.

6. We also met other key-words in our pericope, for instance, Καφαρναούμ, σάββατον, συναγωγή, and εἰσέρχεσθαι.

We shall now go to the second thematic part dealing with Exorcism.

2. Mk 1:23-26: The Expulsion of an Unclean Spirit

As we have treated the first thematic part dealing with teaching, now we turn to the next part concerning exorcism. In the first part, we noticed a lot of indefinite and implicit subjects, but here we meet characters or subjects of the story; there, there was more of narration, but here there are both narration and discourse. If one accuses the former, of lack of content, here is manifested in concreteness both in words and actions: here actions give rise to reactions or even counter-actions.

Mark, in fact, reported in his Gospel many miracles, exorcisms and healings[137]. But the first miracle recorded in his Gospel is *exorcism*[138]. Here there is an encounter between Jesus and the «agent» of Satan. The importance the evangelist attaches to this struggle can be shown by the number or frequency of such an encounter in his Gospel, and at what points he situates these scenes[139]. Now, let us look at Jesus' first expulsion of an unclean spirit at the beginning of his public ministry, and discover other programmatic aspects of our periocpe.

---

[137] Cf. R.H. GUNDRY, *Mark*, 74.

For exorcism stories we have these passages: 1:21-28; 5:1-20; 7:24-30; 9:14-29; for miraculous healings: 1:29-31, 40-45; 2:1-12; 3:1-6; 5:21-43 (two intertwined stories); 7:31-37; 8:22-26; 10:46-52; and for nature-miracles: 4:35-41; 6:35-44, 47-52; 8:1-9; 11:12-14, 20-25.

[138] In spite of the above recorded reports, Mark recognizes a clear distinction between exorcism and healings. It is also clear from the above, that there are *four* exorcism stories and *nine* healing stories. However, one observes that exorcism has the most dominant and largest single category of healing story in the Gospel of Mark. Cf. G.H. TWELFTREE, «ΕΚΒΑΛΛΩ», 362, 364; Cf. J.M. ROBINSON, *The Problem of History*, 83, n.2; P.W. HOLLENBACH, «Jesus, Demoniacs», 568; A.E.J. RAWLINSON, *Mark*, 18.

[139] Cf. J. BRIÈRE, «Le cri et le secret», 40.

2.1 *Mk 1:23a: A Man with Unclean Spirit in the Synagogue*

This verse which begins a new scene has two clauses, of which we shall begin with the first (23a). Although a new scene, yet it demonstrates some affinity with the preceding one. In fact, this preceding textual unit (vv. 21-22) on Jesus' teaching sets the stage and locale for the exorcism (vv.23-28). The exorcism itself follows a «classical exorcism form» which according to Guelich[140] are: encounter (v.23), defence (vv.23b-24), command to depart (v.25), exorcism (v.26), and the bystanders' reaction (v.27). Bultmann called it the «typical characteristics» of a miracle story, especially of an exorcism[141]. However, both of them are the same contentwise.

Comparing this verse with Lk 4:33a (which is the only parallel pericope), one notices that Luke omitted εὐθύς and αὐτῶν, substituted ἔχων for ἐν connected with πνεῦμα ἀκάθαρτον; but added δαιμονίου ἀκαθάρτου to πνεῦμα. On the hand, Luke changed the position of φωνῇ

---

[140] R.A. GUELICH, *Mark*, 55; Cf. G.R. OSBORNE, «Structure and Christology», 150; Cf. J. GNILKA, *Markus*, 76. R. PESCH has also the same form but more divided as follows:
a) Die *Begegnung* (in Synagoge): vv.21b.23a.
b) Die *Abwehrformel* (des Dämons): vv.23b.24.
c) Die *Drohung* (des Exorzisten): v.25a.
d) Die *Schweigegebot* (des Exorzisten): v.25b.
e) Die *Ausfahrbefehl*, die *Apopomp* (des Exorzisten): v.25b.
f) Die *Ausfahrt* (des Dämons unter letztem *Aufbegehren*): v.26.
g) Das *Staunen* (der Zeugen): v.27a.
h) Der *Chorschluß* (der Zeugen): v.27b,c,e.
i) Der *Erfolgsbericht* (vom Wundertäter): v.28
R. PESCH, «Ein Tag», 119; ID., *Markusevangelium* I, 119; ID., «Eine neue Lehre», 256-261; Cf. K. THRAEDE, «Exorzismus», 44-117, esp. 59-60; Cf. K. KERTELGE, *Wunder Jesu*, 32; ID., *Markusevangelium*, 24-25; D.-A. KOCH, *Die Bedeutung*, 55-56; Cf. P. GUILLEMETTE, «Un enseignement nouveau», 235, n.60; Cf. A. SUHL, «Überlegungen zur Hermeneutik», 31. One can observe that in Pesch, the «command to depart», has c,d,e and the «bystanders' reaction» has g,h (as he stated in «Ein Tag», 119-120, that they are variable); while the last (i): v.28, is not a part of exorcism story, but a commentary on it. Koch has, on the other hand, only *a-f*.

[141] These are: 1) the demon recognizes the exorcist and puts up a struggle; 2) a threat and a command by the exorcist; 3) the demon comes out, making a demonstration; 4) an impression is made on the spectators. Cf. R. BULTMANN, *History*, 209-210; Cf. O. BAUERNFEIND, *Die Worte der Dämonen*, 33; J. BRIÈRE, «Le cri et le secret», 36; R. YATES, «Jesus and the Demonic», 46; P. GUILLEMETTE, «Un enseignement nouveau», 234-237 (He added the description of the sickness); Cf. E. BIANCHI, «Esci da costui», 115.

μεγάλη («in or with a loud voice»), which is found at the departure of the unclean spirit in Mk 1:26, and places it earlier at the «crying out» (Lk 4:33b). He also added what it cried out: ἔα (which is not in Mk). Nevertheless, they have both common elements, content and meaning.

In our text there is another connecting phrase καὶ εὐθύς (cf. v.21b), the same location, συναγωγή (synagogue, cf. v.21b), and there is a reference to the same audience, αὐτῶν (cf. v.22b: αὐτούς). The new element is the introduction of a new actor or character into the scene, ἄνθρωπος ἐν πνεύματι ἀκαθάρτῳ (a man with unclean spirit). Our text also betrays some Semitic textual features[142] which we shall treat as they appear.

2.1.1 And immediately there was in their Synagogue

Jesus is still in the synagogue of Capernaum. While he was still teaching, there was an unusual encounter that took place. In short, there was an interruption in Jesus' teaching activity in the synagogue. To introduce this unusual scene, Mk used again his favourite phrase καὶ εὐθύς, which can function as the (temporal) connection of the narrative units in a section or pericope[143]. Here also it acts as a link or connection between the former scene of teaching (words) and the present one of exorcism (deeds). So καὶ εὐθύς that normally means «and immediately» plays a double role here as in v.21b: as a connector, and as a sign of surprise or «shows the rapid sequence of events»[144].

The presence of εὐθύς creates both a textual and syntactical problem for both ἦν and ἀνέκραξεν. This was observed in the *textual criticism*. To solve this problem, some hold that εὐθύς («immediately», «at once») is to be taken with ἀνέκραξεν («cried out»): «who at once shrieked out»[145]. There is also some difficulty in connecting the adverb with ἦν, of which «neither "immediately" nor "so then" is a satisfactory translation»[146]. To get rid of this awkward combination, some witnesses

---

[142] Cf. M. REISER, *Syntax und Stil*; E.C. MALONEY, *Semitic Interference*; Cf. R.H. GUNDRY, *Mark*, 75, 82; J. GNILKA, *Markus I*, 77-78; H.C. KEE, «Terminology of Mark, 232-246; E. LOYMEYER, *Markus*, 36.

[143] Cf. W. PÖHLMANN, «εὐθύς»,78.

[144] E.P. GOULD, *Mark*, 22.

[145] Cf. R.G. BRATCHER– E.A. NIDA, *Translator's Handbook*, 48; V. TAYLOR, *Mark*, 173.

[146] Cf. V. TAYLOR, *Mark*, 173

suggested its omission. Bratcher and Nida offer two alternatives: «(1) *euthus* may be understood in a general sense "now", "then"; (2) *ēn* "was" may be taken as equivalent to *egeneto* "came", "appeared". The second is probably to be preferred»[147]. Thus, it would probably read: «and no sooner in the synagogue than this demoniac appeared»[148]. However, it is reasonable to observe that the adverb (εὐθύς) probably modifies the whole of the following story rather than ἦν[149]. But this story is happening in the synagogue, as we indicated earlier, which here should mean a synagogue building[150]. This synagogue is not only with a definite article but has also a personal pronoun, αὐτῶν -«their», acting as a possessive pronoun[151]. Therefore this refers us to the «astonished people» (ἐξεπλήσσοντο) of v.22a, and the direct object (in v.22b: αὐτούς) of the teaching activity of Jesus.

2.1.2 A Man with Unclean Spirit

Now we come to the subject of the verse, who is not a simple character but a complex one: a double personality. Instead of using a word to describe this new actor in the scene, Mk employed a circumlocutive construction. In fact, the above phrase betrays Semitic textual features. Ἄνθρωπος can have indefinite meaning, «someone, anyone», which in Greek is τις and thus «a man»[152]. Likewise the phrase ἐν πνεύματι ἀκαθάρτῳ reflects this Semitic interference. While Mark used the preposition ἐν, which represents the Hebrew ב = «with»[153] (cf. Mk 5:2,

---

[147] R.G. BRATCHER – E.A. NIDA, *Translator's Handbook*, 48.

[148] E.P. GOULD, *Mark*, 22; cf. R.G. BRATCHER – E.A. NIDA, *Translator's Handbook*, 48.

[149] R.H. GUNDRY, *Mark*, 74.

[150] In fact, Markan usage has strongly affected the tradition and also determined the meaning: without exception συναγωγή refers to the *synagogue building/synagogue*. Cf. H. FRANKEMÖLLE, «συναγωγή», 293.

[151] To show possession there is a tendency to use the genitive case of the personal pronoun (αὐτός) in a reflexive sense instead of the possessive pronoun, though the latter is legitimate. Cf. J. SWETNAM, *An Introduction* I, 53.

[152] Cf. E.C. MALONEY, *Semitic Interference*, 131-134, esp. 134; R. PESCH, «Eine neue Lehre», 251; M. BLACK, *An Aramaic Approach*, 250. This indefinite usage of ἄνθρωπος is not only here in v.23, but could be found elsewhere in the Gospel: 3:1; 4:26; 5:2; 12:1; 13:34, etc.

[153] Cf. R.H. GUNDRY, *Mark*, 75; R.G. BRATCHER – E.A. NIDA, *Translator's Handbook*, 48; E. KLOSTERMANN, *Markusevangelium*, 14.

25); Luke used ἔχων, «having» (4:33 cf. Mk 3:30; 7:25; 9:17). And ἐν standing in relation to πνεύματι ἀκαθάρτῳ, «unclean spirit» carries the merely Greek sense «under the special influence of a demonic spirit»[154]. The use of *unclean spirit* instead of *demon* reveals also this Semitic origin[155]. Mark is most faithful to the specifically Jewish usage (πνεῦμα ἀκάθαρτον = רוח הטמאה, cf. Zech 13:2)[156].

The verbal noun πνεῦμα[157], which has variety of meaning, is derived from the verb, πνέω designating the elementary power of nature and life: wind, breeze; breath, as both matter and process together. This is often translated by the Heb. רוח, which fundamentally means also «wind» and «breath». «In the OT *rûah* often refers expressly to the "Spirit" of God that acts as life power and beyond that bestows special gifts or inspires a person»[158]. In the NT, on the other hand, is essentially characterized by the Heb. equivalent *rûah* and its use in Judaism. However, in both Greek and NT concepts, πνεῦμα is seen as a power that fills, generates, catches away, inspires and discloses. But the contrast lies in the difference of origin and content. Thus, concludes Kleinknecht, «the secular Greek concept of πνεῦμα, whether understood physiologico-cosmologically, mantico-enthusiastically or in the last resort spiritually, is distinguished from the NT concept by the fact that the God who stands behind it is quite different»[159].

In Markan usage of the πνεῦμα sayings, one observes that of the 23x (Mt 19x; Lk 36x; Jn 24x), he applied 11x (+3x) to πνεῦμα ἀκάθαρτον («unclean spirit»)[160]; 6x to πνεῦμα ἅγιον (Holy Spirit)[161]; 2x to πνεῦμα

It is not likely that ἐν is instrumental or indicative of manner since this employs the semitic construction we mentioned above, cf. V. TAYLOR, *Mark*, 173.

[154] *BAGD*, 260, I.5.d; Cf. R.H. GUNDRY, *Mark*, 82; H. VAN DER LOOS, *The Miracles of Jesus*, 379; R.G. BRATCHER – E.A. NIDA *Translator's Handbook*, 48.

[155] Cf. G.H. TWELFTREE, *Jesus the Exorcist*, 60; P. PIMENTEL, «Unclean Spirits», 173-5; P. GUILLEMETTE, «Un enseignement nouveau», 227; W. FOERSTER, «δαιμόνιον», 16.

[156] W. FOERSTER, «δαιμόνιον», 16.

[157] J. KREMER, «πνεῦμα», 117-122; *BAGD*, 674-678; H. KLEINKNECHT, «πνεῦμα», 334-339.

[158] J. KREMER, «πνεῦμα», 118.

[159] H. KLEINKNECHT, «πνεῦμα», 359.

[160] Mark uses «unclean spirit» 11x (Mt 2x; Lk 5x; Jn 0x: cf. Mt 10:1; 12:43; Lk 4:33,36; 8:29; 9:42; 11:24) which are: 1:23,26,27; 3:11,30; 5:2,8,13; 6:7; 7:25; 9:25. Although 9:17,20,25b refer to either the dumb, or deaf and dumb spirit, yet there they

αὐτοῦ (his [Jesus'] spirit)[162]; and finally 1x to πνεῦμα πρόθυμον («willing spirit»)[163]. From the statistics of the classification of the appearances of πνεῦμα in Mark's Gospel, it is clear that πνεῦμα ἀκάθαρτον «unclean spirit» dominated. On the other hand, Mark also uses another term δαιμόνιον «demon» alternatively or synonymously to «unclean spirit»: 11x[164] (Mt 11x; Lk 23x; Jn 6x)[165]; or its verbal adjective δαιμονίζομαι «demonize»: 4x[166] (Mt 7x; Lk 1x; Jn 1x). Looking at the terms to describe «demons» in Mark one can observe the importance of this theme. In our text, which is the very first mention of «unclean spirit» in the Gospel, we notice that of the 11x usages of πνεῦμα ἀκάθαρτον, it occurs 3x (vv.23,26,27). In fact, 8x of these occurrences were in the four exorcism stories[167]; while the remaining 3x were in the context of: a) the Beelzebul controversy (3:20-30); b) Jesus' healing and exorcizing activity (3:7-12); c) the mission of the Twelve (6:6-12). The frequency of these synonymous words of exorcism highlights the place this activity has in Jesus' mission.

The adjective, ἀκάθαρτον «unclean», qualifies and predicates the noun or substantive, πνεῦμα «spirit», thus *unclean spirit*. Unclean or evil

---

all refer to «unclean spirit» in v.25a, thus bringing the usage to 14x. Cf. E. SCHWEIZER, «πνεῦμα», 396; R.A. GUELICH, *Mark*, 56.

[161] Whereas Mk has only six places in which he mentioned the Holy Spirit (cf. 1:8,10,12; 3:29; 12:36; 13:11), Mt has 12x; Lk 17x; and Jn 15x. Cf. J.A. FITZMYER, *Luke I-IX*, 227.

[162] πνεῦμα is used purely anthropologically in Mk 2:8; 8:12, where it is the source and seat of insight, feeling, and will, generally representing the part of the inner life of man. Cf. *BAGD*, 675, 3b; E. SCHWEIZER, «πνεῦμα», 396.

[163] Here there is that antithesis set between πνεῦμα πρόθυμον («willing spirit») and σὰρξ ἀσθενής («weak flesh»), cf. Mk 14:38. Cf. E. SCHWEIZER, «πνεῦμα», 396-397.

[164] These are: Mk 1:34[bis],39; 3:15,22; 6:13; 7:26,29,30; 9:38. Of the 11x, 8x refer to Jesus, while 2x refer to his disciples (3:15; 6:13), but 1x refers to the «unknown disciple» (9:38).

[165] This usage of «unclean spirits» and «demons» as interchangeable or synonymous expressions is very much established in Mark, for instance: Mk 3:30 cf. 3:22; 6:7 cf. 6:13; 7:25 cf. 7:26,29,30 (cf. Mt 10:1,8; Lk 4:33-36; 8:29 cf. vv.29,30,33). Cf. R.A. GUELICH, *Mark*, 56; K. KERTELGE, *Markusevangelium*, 25; E. BIANCHI, «Esci da costui», 113, 136, n.4; M.L. GRUENTHANER, «The Demonology», 6.

[166] These are: Mk 1:32; 5:15,16,18. It is interesting to note that these words appear not in verbs but only in verbal nouns (participles).

[167] Of these 8x, occur 3x in Mk 1:21-28; 3x in 5:1-20; 1x in 7:24-30 and 1x in 9:14-29. Cf. P. PIMENTEL, «Unclean Spirits», 174-75; R.A. GUELICH, *Mark*, 56.

spirits are generally opposed or hostile to God, and to possess or be in a person, means separating the person both from God and the society. Thus, Kampling sees the possession of a man by an «unclean spirit» or «demon» to mean the full destruction of the personality which that person has, that the person does not act any more rather the demon acts in his place. So the person speaks no more but rather the demon, who has him under his power (cf. Mk 1:23,26) and forces him to do things, which are absolutely opposite or against his own interest (cf. Mk 9:20,22)[168].

So in our text, we meet a person destroyed in his personality and under the power of the unclean spirit, who encounters Jesus in the synagogue in the course of a community worship. This demoniac is ritually and morally unfit for any public worship. But how did he enter the synagogue: as a seemly normal person or as a demoniac? However he attracted attention by his action. Since this is Jesus' first appearance in his public ministry to the people, it was an initial challenging battle or encounter that could not be ignored, because it will surely have its consequences. In other words, this meeting fulfils the *encounter* of the demon with Jesus. What did the demoniac do during this encounter? That is what will occupy us next.

2.2 Mk 1:23b,24: The Words of the Unclean Spirit

The unclean spirit cries out its resistance to Jesus' presence through the man in the synagogue. We shall now examine the meaning and implication of these demonic utterances.

2.2.1 And He cried out

This is the first discourse in the pericope, and it was made by the man with unclean spirit. To introduce this discourse, one observes the presence of two verbs ἀνακράζειν (aorist) and λέγειν (participle), which is the clause of the narrative part. The καί links the two clauses of the verse together (v23a,23b), which is governed by one subject (ἄνθρωπος...). ἀνακράζειν is a compound verb (ἀνα+κράζειν) with a perfective preposition[169], and it means «to cry out» or «shout out». It is not a very

---

[168] Cf. R. KAMPLING, «Dämonismus und Exorzismus», 308; L. SABOURIN, «The Miracles of Jesus (II)»,157, n.72; W. FOERSTER, «δαιμόνιον»,18-19; S.V. MCCASLAND, «Demonic Confessions», 33.

[169] Cf. R.H. GUNDRY, *Mark*, 75.

common verb, in fact, it appears only in Mark and Luke in the NT[170], The simple verb κράζειν is more often used, while the former shows the intensity of the action, which is well demonstrated in our text.

In the use outside the NT, one discovers that κράζειν and ἀνακάζειν have religious significance in the sphere of the demonic in the Greek world. Likewise it has a sense of proclamation. But in the NT, these terms have an important significance with regard to demons in Jesus' public ministry. Other uses of the terms especially, κράζειν, include: the cry out of fear; the cry for help to save; the cries of jubilation; the cry of a woman in childbirth; the cries of hate; or even last cry of death[171].

Mark uses ἀνακράζειν in our text (v.23 cf. Lk 4:33; 8:28) and elsewhere only at 6:49[172], but he often uses the simple form κράζειν at least 10x (3:11; 5:5,7; 9:24,26; 10:47,48; 11:9; 15:13,14)[173]. Among the usages, he has 4x for the cry of the demons (3:11; 5:5,7; 9:26; cf. Mt 8:29; Lk 4:41; 9:39); 3x for the cry for help to save (9:24; 10:47,48; cf. Mt 9:27; 20:30,31; 15:22,23; Lk 18:39); the cries of jubilation (11:9; cf. Mt 21:9,15); the cries of hate (15:13,14; cf. Mt 27:23). Thus, in this first appearance, Mark uses ἀνακράζειν to describe the intensity of the crying out of the demon or unclean spirit, while elsewhere he uses the simple form.

One would be tempted to ask: who is speaking, the demoniac or the unclean spirit? Surely this man is forced by the evil spirit to violate both the sacred time and place, for he yells out his objection to Jesus.

2.2.2 What is between us and you, Jesus of Nazareth?

The first part of the speech sets the tone of the encounter between the demoniac and Jesus. It is an aggressive question: τί ἡμῖν καὶ σοί[174]. This

---

[170] Cf. Mk 1:23; 6:49; Lk 4:33; 8:28; 23:18.

[171] Cf. W. GRUNDMANN, «κράζω, ἀνακράζω», 900-903; H. FENDRICH, «κράζω», 313-314; cf. «ἀνακράζω», 83; BAGD, 56, 447-448.

[172] Mk 6:49 describes the cry of the Disciples, who, when they saw Jesus walking on the sea, thought he was a Ghost, so that they cried out with fear cf. Mt 14:26 with κράζειν.

[173] While Mk used κράζειν 10 (11)x, Mt has 12x, Lk 4x, Jn 4x.

[174] This could also be, or often is, τί ἐμοί καὶ σοί (in Heb. מה לי ולך). Cf. BAGD, «ἐγώ», 217; G.H. TWELFTREE, Jesus the Exorcist, 61, n 25; ID., «ΕΚΒΑΛΛΩ» 373-378.

phrase has a semitic background[175]. In fact, this initial expression seen here in v.24 (par.Lk 4:34; cf. 5:7 // Mt 8:29; Lk 8:28 and Jn 2:4) is a very common formula within the context of combat or judgment in the OT[176]. In the classical Greek it means, «What have we in common?»[177], while in the Hebrew usage (מה לנו ולך, literally, «What to us and to you») it means, «Why are you interferring with us»[178] or even «Mind your business!» To clarify the above, Brown suggests that in OT this Hebrew expression has two shades of meaning: (a) When one party is unjustly bothering or disturbing another (Judg.11:12; 2 Chron 35:21; 1 Kgs 17:18); and (b) when someone is asked to get involved in a matter which he feels is no business of his (2 Kgs 3:13; Hos 14:8). Thus, there is always some refusal of an inopportune involvement, and a divergence between the views of the two persons concerned, yet (a) implies hostility while (b) implies simple disengagement[179]. Thus, «the question has the defensive function of placing the one questioned in the position of responsibility for what follows and thereby creates an irreconcilable distance between the two parties»[180].

Many scholars see this expression in Mk 1:24 as leaning on the parallel text of 1 Kgs 17:18, the story of the encounter between the widow of Sarepta with Elijah (1 Kgs 17:17-24)[181]. Bauernfeind synoptically

---

[175] Cf. G.H. TWELFTREE, Jesus the Exorcist, 64; M. REISER, Syntax und Stil, 20-21; E.C. MALONEY, Semitic Interference, 183-185; P. GUILLEMETTE, «Mc 1,24», 88; R.E. BROWN, John I-XII, 99; E. KLOSTERMANN, Markusevangelium, 17.

[176] Cf. Josh 22: 24; Judg.11:12; 2 Sam 16:10; 19:23; 1 Kgs 17:18; 2 Kgs 3:13; 2 Chron 35:21. Cf. O. BÄCHLI, «Was habe ich», 69-80; R.A. GUELICH, Mark, 56-57; A.M. MAYNARD, «τί ἐμοὶ καὶ σοί», 582; O. BAUERNFEIND, Die Worte der Dämonen, 3-10, 14f., 28-31, 68f.

[177] Cf. G.H. TWELFTREE, Jesus the Exorcist, 63; ID., «ΕΚΒΑΛΛΩ», 373; A.M. MAYNARD, «τί ἐμοὶ καὶ σοί», 582; V. TAYLOR, Mark, 174; R.G. BRATCHER – E.A. NIDA, Translator's Handbook, 49; C.E.B. CRANFIELD, Mark, 75; H.B. SWETE, Mark, 19.

[178] Cf. G.H. TWELFTREE, Jesus the Exorcist, 63; «ΕΚΒΑΛΛΩ», 373; C.S. MANN, Mark, 212; A.M. MAYNARD, «τί ἐμοὶ καὶ σοί», 582; H. ANDERSON, Mark, 91; W.L. LANE, Mark, 73; J. BRIÈRE, «Le cri et le secret», 35; E.P. GOULD, Mark, 23.

[179] R.E. BROWN, John I-XII, 99; Cf. P. GUILLEMETTE, «Mc 1,24», 88.

[180] R.A. GUELICH, Mark, 57; cf. O. BÄCHLI, «Was habe ich», 80.

[181] Cf. G.H. TWELFTREE, Jesus the Exorcist, 63-64; ID., «ΕΚΒΑΛΛΩ», 374; S. BECKER-WIRTH, «Jesus treibt Dämonen aus», 182; A. SUHL, «Überlegungen zur Hermeneutik», 32; J. ERNST, Markus, 63; P. GUILLEMETTE, «Un enseignement nouveau», 229-230, 240-241; ID., «Mc 1,24», 86-89; E. ARENS, The ΗΛΘΟΝ-sayings,

compared Mk 1:24 with 1 Kgs 17:18 and Philo's *Quod Deus sit immutabilis*, # 138 and came to the conclusion that this text is a «defensive saying or formula» (*Abwehrspruch/Abwehrformel*)[182]. In fact, Bauernfeind used Philo's book, *Quod Deus sit immutabilis*, #138, the Greek Magical Papyri and the motif of resistance of the demons in the ancient world to prove that Mk 1:24 -the demon's saying- was a *magic defensive mechanism* to counter-attack their enemy, Jesus.

In Markan usage, this phrase appeared only twice (1:24; 5:7)[183] and they were all (including their parallels) in the context of the encounter between Jesus and the demons. The dialogue was not between admiring friends but deadly enemies. If we compare on a general level Mk 1:24 with 1 Kgs 17:18 within their contexts, one notices that Jesus plays the role of Elijah, while the unclean spirit that of the widow[184]. One can then observe the rebuff, the hostility, the warding off, the refusal to enter into relation on the part of the unclean spirit with Jesus[185]. This is because it

---

210-211; W. GRUNDMANN, *Markus*, 42.

[182] O. BAUERNFEIND, *Die Worte der Dämonen*, 3-10; Cf. K. KERTELGE, *Markusevangelium*, 26; G.H. TWELFTREE, *Jesus the Exorcist*, 64, n.43; D. LÜHRMANN, *Markusevangelium*, 51; A. SUHL, «Überlegungen zur Hermeneutik», 32; P. GUILLEMETTE, «Mc 1,24», 83-86; W.L. LANE, *Mark*, 73; J. GNILKA, *Markus*, 80; E. KLOSTERMANN, *Markusevangelium*, 17; A. FRIDRICHSEN, «Conflict of Jesus», 124.

[183] In the NT, as we have pointed out above, this expression occurs only 6x: Mk 1:24, par. Lk 4:34; Mk 5:7, par. Mt 8:29; Lk 8:28; and in another context (the wedding of Cana) in Jn 2:4. Cf. A.M. MAYNARD, «τί ἐμοὶ καὶ σοί», 583.

[184] There is a marked difference between Jesus and Elijah: while Elijah invokes Yahweh, who grants his request by restoring to life the widow's son; Jesus as the Holy One, and Son of God, acts through his word. The truth of Elijah's word depends on its fulfilment by God, while Jesus acts on behalf of God, and His word is the same as God's word. On the function attributed to Elijah by the widow, and that to Jesus by the unclean spirit, there is still a striking difference. Elijah proved the widow wrong (that he came to recall his sins or faults and to kill his son) by raising his dead son to life; Jesus proved that the unclean spirit was right (that he came to destroy them) through his exorcism. However, both 1 Kgs 17:18 and Mk 1:24 have distinct roles to play. Indeed, Mk 1:24 makes us discover Jesus of Nazareth as the Holy one of God, who came to destroy the unclean spirits: it is both an affirmation and a revelation on the person of Jesus; while 1 Kgs 17:18 presents to us Elijah as a man of God, who was responsible for the death of the widow's son, but it is not a revelation on the person of Elijah. Cf. P. GUILLEMETTE, «Un enseignement nouveau», 240-241.

[185] Cf. R.A. GUELICH, *Mark*, 57; J.M. ROBINSON, *The Problem of History*, 84-85; P. GUILLEMETTE, «Mc 1,24», 88; J. GNILKA, *Markus*, 80; O. BÄCHLI, «Was habe ich», 80; E. ARENS, *The* ΗΛΘΟΝ-*sayings*, 211,n.7, 220; J. BRIÈRE, «Le cri et le secret», 35;

realizes the intention or mission of Jesus and sees him as a deadly enemy.

The «us» in the demonic question could mean the man along with the spirit, or the people in the synagogue along with the spirit[186]. But in view of the plural «unclean spirit» in v.27, Mark most probably means that this unclean spirit speaks on behalf of all unclean spirits[187]. This really enjoys the consensus of most scholars, and I share the view that this unclean spirit speaks for the class of the whole unclean spirits[188].

The unclean spirit mentions Jesus' personal name with his home-town: Ἰησοῦ Ναζαρηνέ. This is in the vocative case. Ναζαρηνός occurs 4x in Mark (1:24; 10:47; 14:67; 16:6) and 2x in Lk, and only in these two can one see it in the NT; otherwise Ναζωραῖος is used (Mt 2x; Lk 1x; Jn 3x; Mk 0x; Acts 7x)[189]. One can see the preference and dominance of this word, Ναζαρηνός by Mark. The meaning and derivations of these two words have engaged the discussions of many scholars[190]. But when all is said, there is the conclusion that the two words (Ναζαρηνός, Ναζωραῖος) are different Greek forms of the Aram. nāsrāyā, derived from nāsrat, Ναζαρέθ, that is, the name of the city Nazareth[191]. Thus, the demon mentions the personal name and the

---

R.E. BROWN, *John I-XII*, 99.

[186] One cannot easily accept the interpretation of Keenan that «us» is «the entire synagogue structure and congregation». Cf. J.P. KEENAN, *Gospel of Mark*, 69.

[187] Cf. R.H. GUNDRY, *Mark*, 75-76.

BRUCE puts it thus: «The diseased man speaks for the demon in him, and the demon speaks for the fraternity as all having one interest». as seen in H. VAN DER LOOS, *The Miracles*, 380.

[188] Cf. K. KERTELGE, *Markusevangelium*, 26; R.A. GUELICH, *Mark*,56; A. STOCK, *Method and Message*, 74; D. LÜHRMANN, *Markusevangelium*, 51; V. TAYLOR, *Mark*, 174; B.D. CHILTON, «Exorcism and History», 258; W.L. LANE, *Mark*, 73; R. PESCH, *Markusevangelium* I, 122; D.E. NINEHAM, *Mark*, 75; T.A. BURKILL, *Mysterious Revelation*, 63, n.2.

[189] Cf. V. TAYLOR, *Mark*, 174; C.E.B. CRANFIELD, *Mark*, 76.

[190] The suggested derivations include: (1) from Ναζαρέτ (-θ), Ναζαρά; (2) from נצר «shoot», «branch»; (3) from נזיר «consecrated», «holy»; (4) from נוצרי, the Jewish name for the followers of *Jeshu ha nosri*. Nos 1 and 3 enjoy more consensus in the discussion. For Bibliography on this, see, V. TAYLOR, *Mark*, 177-178; E. SCHWEIZER, «Nazoräer», 90-93; H.H. SCHAEDER, «Ναζαρηνός, Ναζωραῖος»,874-879.

[191] Cf. H.H. SCHAEDER, «Ναζαρηνός», 875, 877, 879; C.E.B. CRANFIELD, *Mark*, 76.

hometown of Jesus (Jesus the Nazarene or Jesus of Nazareth)[192]. We must remark that apart from the mention of Nazareth earlier (1:9), we have here a name (Ναζαρηνός)[193]. Now we go to the next utterance of the unclean spirit.

2.2.3 Have you come to destroy us?

This is the second clause of the words of the unclean spirit. One can observe that it is the focal point in the demon's direct discourse. This clause, however, has two verbs with the construction of infinitive of purpose[194], thereby introducing the intention/mission of Jesus as the demon identified it. This statement has not obtained an agreed consensus on whether it is a question or a declaration. Some Greek editions of the text, commentators and translations understood it as a *question*[195]; while a good number of others have taken it as an *assertion* or a *declaration*[196]; and yet some see the same effect in either way[197]. Thus, one can agree with Bratcher & Nida when they said: «there is nothing in grammar or context definitely to decide which should be preferred»[198]. However, I would say, it is better taken as a question based on the crisis, fear or consternation the demon faces in the presence of Jesus - it could be a

---

[192] Cf. R.H. GUNDRY, *Mark*, 76; D. LÜHRMANN, *Markus*, 51; C.S. MANN, *Mark*, 212-213; G. ALLAN, «Nazirite», 81-82; D.B. TAYLOR, «Jesus of Nazareth», 336-337; R. PESCH, «Eine neue Lehre», 258.

[193] An article has been written that highlights the importance and position of Nazareth or «the Nazarene image» in the Gospel of Mark. Cf. E.K. BROADHEAD, «Jesus the Nazarene», 3-18.

[194] The infinitive of purpose here has a verb of motion, ἔρχεσθαι. Cf. *BDF*, # 390, 1.

[195] These are: Nestle, Westcott and Hort, Kilpatrick, Souter; AV ,ASV, RSV, etc; Cf. R.G. BRATCHER – E.A. NIDA, *Translation's Handbook*, 49-50; J. GNILKA, *Markus*, 80; E. KLOSTERMANN, *Markusevangelium*, 17; M.-J. LAGRANGE, *Saint Marc*, 23; H.B. SWETE, *Mark*, 19.

[196] Cf. M.D. HOOKER, *St Mark*, 64; R. PESCH, *Markusevangelium* I, 122; ID., «Eine neue Lehre», 258, n.73; E. ARENS, *The* ΗΛΘΟΝ-*sayings*, 211, n.5; W.L. LANE, *Mark*, 73; V. TAYLOR, *Mark*, 174; E. LOHMEYER, *Markus*, 36-37; R.H. LIGHTFOOT, *Mark*, 21.

[197] It could be read as a question or a statement. In either case it expresses a mixture of fear and defiance. Cf. C.E.B. CRANFIELD, *Mark*, 76; D.-A. KOCH, *Die Bedeutung*, 58, n.18.

[198] R.G. BRATCHER – E.A. NIDA, *Translator's Handbook*, 50.

rhetoric question; and also considering Markan style of double question which is characteristic of him[199].

Now we look at the text itself. ἦλθες is the main verb of this infinitive of purpose clause, and the subject of the «coming» here is Jesus. Among the «ἦλθον/ἦλθεν-sayings», Mk 1:24/Lk 4:34 (cf. Mt 8:29) is significant because «it is the only statement made by anyone, addressed to Jesus (not pronounced by him), about the latter's coming and its significance»[200]. And what is more, it was pronounced by the unclean spirit. This «Have you come...?» of Jesus is not «from Nazareth», nor his «entry into the synagogue» but his coming from God (heaven) *into the world*[201]. This verb can also carry the hint of divine commission since Jesus spoke and acted on behalf of God (*an Gottes Statt*)[202]. Hence, as the Son of God, Jesus' coming carries also a hint of divine origin. However, Jesus' coming has always a purpose[203], among many others, which in our text is expressed by the next verb, ἀπολέσαι.

The verb ἀπόλλυμι occurs 10x in Mark (Mt 20x; Lk 28x; Jn 10x). There are three ways in which Mark used it in his Gospel: (1) in active «to destroy», «to cause to perish», cf. 1:24; 3:6; 9:22; 11:18; 12:9; (2) «to lose», cf. 8:35 (bis); 9:41; (3) in the middle or passive «to be destroyed», «to perish», «to be lost» cf. 2:22; 4:38[204]. Among the 5x dealing with «to destroy», only in our text (1:24) is it dealing with unclean spirits (demons). The ἡμᾶς (like ἡμῖν in v.24a) refers to the whole class of the

---

[199] Cf. Mk 2:7; 2:8,9; 3:4; 4:21; 4:40; 6:2; 6:3; etc. cf. F. NEIRYNCK, *Duality in Mark*, 125-126.

[200] E. ARENS, *The ΗΛΘΟΝ-sayings*, 194.

[201] Cf. W. HENDRIKSEN, *Mark*, 65; R. PESCH, «Eine neue Lehre», 258; J.M. ROBINSON, *The Problem of History*, 85; BRATCHER– NIDA, *Translator's Handbook*, 50.

[202] Cf. R.H. GUNDRY, *Mark*, 76; R. PESCH, «Eine neue Lehre», 258; E. LOHMEYER, *Markus*, 37.

[203] Cf. Mk 2:17; 10:45; Mt 5:17; 9:13; 10:34,35; 18:11; 20:28; Lk 5:32; 9:56; 12:49; 19:10. Meye refers to Mk 1:38 as a statement of purpose, and at the same time mentions other statements of purpose in Mark's Gospel which state other purposes for Jesus' appearance. These are: a) the demons state that Jesus has *come to destroy* them (1:24); b) Jesus states that he has *come to call* sinners (2:17); and c) Jesus also states that he has «come to serve and to give his life a ransom for many» (10:45). Cf. R.P. MEYE, *Jesus and the Twelve*, 53-54; K. STOCK, «Die Machttaten Jesu», 198.

[204] R.G. BRATCHER – E.A. NIDA, *Translator's Handbook*, 50.

unclean spirits, which is also the object of this clause. Thus, Jesus has come to «destroy» the unclean spirits[205].

The consequence of Jesus' coming or his presence is very clear to the demons (unclean spirits) because it brings along the menace of destruction[206]. In fact, Mark sees in the liberation from the power of the demons an essential part of Jesus' mission, which is evident as he reports exorcism as Jesus' first miracle[207]. Hence the coming of Jesus from God into the world is to crush or destroy the power of Satan's emissaries or unclean spirits (demons) and all unclean and unholy powers against God[208]; and to establish the kingdom of God in the world.

2.2.4 I know who you are, the Holy One of God.

This is the third and the last part of the words of the unclean spirit. Here there are two clauses: the main and the subordinate: οἶδα σε + τίς εἶ, ὁ ἅγιος τοῦ θεοῦ. The object of the main clause is the personal pronoun, σε «you»; while τίς «who» which is in apposition to σε (in accusative case) becomes the subject of the subordinate clause, τίς εἶ, «who you are». Then ὁ ἅγιος τοῦ θεοῦ, «the Holy (One) of God» becomes the predicate of the sentence. When the clauses are combined the σε may be redundant[209]. The article with the adjective, ὁ ἅγιος, makes it a substantive, that is, «the holy one». But when considered with τοῦ θεοῦ, it is *Genitive of origin and relationship*[210]. Thus, the clause will literally mean «I know (you), who you are, the Holy One of God».

The phrase οἶδα σε τίς εἶ shows that the demonic powers possess a certain knowledge of Jesus' identity. This is illustrated clearly by the cry

---

[205] Twelftree observes that Jesus is portrayed in the Gospels as one who destroys the evil powers (cf Mt 12:28ff/Lk 11:20ff). Yet, neither in Mark, nor in the rest of the New Testament is ἀπόλλυμι used in relation to the ministry of Jesus. Cf. G.H. TWELFTREE, *Jesus the Exorcist*, 66; A. OEPKE, «ἀπόλλυμι», 394-396. I think one could say that that is what makes our text unique, that Jesus is the subject of the verb, and has the crushing of these powers as part of his mission.

[206] E. ARENS, *The HΛΘON-sayings*, 209, 220; W.L. LANE, *Mark*, 73; V. TAYLOR, *Mark*, 174.

[207] Cf. K. STOCK, «Die Machttaten Jesu», 198.

[208] Cf. G.H. TWELFTREE, *Jesus the Exorcist*, 66; D.E. GARLAND, «I am the Lord», 333, 339; L. SCHENKE, *Die Wundererzählungen*, 100; E. LOHMEYER, *Markus*, 37.

[209] Cf. V. TAYLOR, *Mark*, 174; H.B. SWETE, *Mark*, 20. It is redundant but it produces a very vivid effect on the narration.

[210] BDF #162, 1. Cf. R.G. BRATCHER – E.A. NIDA, *Translator's Handbook*, 50.

of recognition, «I know who you are, the Holy One of God». This formula of recognition is not limited to the demoniacs, even the ordinary sick people also expressed themselves in their own ways[211]. Some scholars see the parallels of this «I know-formula» as connected with the exorcism in the Hellenistic world in which it has much to do with magic[212]. In this case, this recognition-formula would not be a manifestation of knowledge by the unclean spirits but a defensive mechanism or manoeuvre[213] to gain control of Jesus in accordance with the common concept of that day, that the use of the precise name of an individual or spirit would secure mastery over him[214]. Thus, apart from the initial words of general defence, the demon has made known Jesus' origin (Nazareth) and his activity (the demon's destruction). Now the climax of the defence comes with the «I know» formula, that is, knowledge of Jesus' identity. It is also worth noting that the verb, οἶδα, which appears 23x in Mark (Mt 25x; Lk 26x; Jn 83x), makes its first appearance in our pericope.

Now let us turn to the title given to Jesus: ὁ ἅγιος τοῦ θεοῦ. The term «the Holy One of God» (v.24) has no recognizable tradition and does not occur in the ancient Jewish literature as a messianic title[215], and in the rest

---

[211] The sick individuals appeal to Jesus thus: «Lord» (7:28), «Teacher» (9:17), «Son of David» (10:47-48) or «Master» (10:51); while the demoniacs, on the other hand, address him as: «the Holy One of God» (1:24), «the Son of God» (3:11) or «the Son of the Most High God» (5:7), formulations which identify Jesus as the divine Son of God. Cf. W.L. LANE, *Mark*, 74; A. STOCK, *Method and Message*, 75-76; W.R. DOMERIS, «The Holy One», 11; H. VAN DER LOOS, *The Miracles*, 363.

[212] Cf. O. BAUERNFEIND, *Die Worte der Dämonen*, 11-18; P. GUILLEMETTE, «Mc 1,24», 89-93; G.H. TWELFTREE, *Jesus the Exorcist*, 66-67; ID., «ΕΚΒΑΛΛΩ», 374-375; R. BULTMANN, *History*, 209, n.1; A. FRIDRICHSEN, «Conflict of Jesus», 125.

[213] Cf. G.R. OSBORNE, «Structure and Christology», 151; G.H. TWELFTREE, *Jesus the Exorcist*, 62, 66-68; D. GARLAND, «I am the Lord», 333; P. GUILLEMETTE, «Un enseignement nouveau», 229-230; ID., «Mc 1,24», 85-86, 93-94; K. KERTELGE, *Die Wunder Jesu*, 53; H. VAN DER LOOS, *The Miracles*, 380; O. BAUERNFEIND, *Die Worte der Dämonen*, 10-18, 33-34. This position was not unchallenged especially by some: D.-A. KOCH, *Die Bedeutung*, 57-61; P. GUILLEMETTE, «Mc 1,24», 81-96, esp. 90-93, 94-96; R.A. GUELICH, *Mark*, 57-58.

[214] Cf. W.L. LANE, *Mark*, 74; B.D. CHILTON, «Exorcism and History», 261.
T.A. BURKILL, *Mysterious Revelation*, 76, was right in observing that «the demon knows the divine purpose of Jesus' coming and the divine character of his status; and by giving full expression to its knowledge it seeks to ward off the threatened offensive of its dangerous opponent».

[215] Many scholars agree that the term is not a messianic title: Cf. G.R. OSBORNE, «Structure and Christology», 152; G.H. TWELFTREE, *Jesus the Exorcist*, 67; D.E.

of the NT (outside the parallel Lk 4:34) it occurs only at John 6:69. We also see in the OT some close parallels, like referring to Aaron in Ps 106 (LXX 105):16 as «the Holy One of the Lord» (τὸν ἅγιον κυρίου)[216]; or Elisha in 2 Kgs 4:9 as «a holy man of God» (ἄνθρωπος τοῦ θεοῦ ἅγιος). Even holiness is also ascribed to Samson in Judges (LXX) 16:17B, «a holy one of God» (ἅγιος θεοῦ)[217], to the prophets and some people like Moses in the OT and NT. These texts, in fact, show that to call someone «holy» or «a Holy One of God» need mean nothing than that the individual had a special relationship with God[218]. This relationship with God was also expressed about Jesus in similar designations in other occasions by the unclean spirits, for example, «the Son of God» (3:11), «the Son of the Most High God» (5:7).

That Jesus is «the Holy One of God» contrasts with the character of the spirit as «unclean», in other words, «holy» by virtue of being possessed by the Holy Spirit. This contrast is because «there is a mortal antithesis between πνεῦμα ἅγιον and πνεῦμα ἀκάθαρτον which the demons recognise»[219]. Although many scholars see the «I know» formula of the demon as defensive mechanism, some still see it as a confession[220].

GARLAND, «I am the Lord», 333; D. LÜHRMANN, *Markusevangelium*, 51; C.S. MANN, *Mark*, 213; P. GUILLEMETTE, «Mc 1,24», 90; O. BAUERNFEIND, *Die Worte der Dämonen*, 16.

[216] Cf. G.H. TWELFTREE, *Jesus the Exorcist*, 67-68; ID., «ΕΚΒΑΛΛΩ», 376; M.D. HOOKER, *St. Mark*, 64; R.A. GUELICH, *Mark*, 57; J.H. NEYREY, «The Idea of Purity», 105-106; W.R. DOMERIS, «The Holy One», 9; J. GNILKA, *Markus*, 81. The holiness of the priesthood and especially that of Aaron is undisputed (cf. Num 16:3-5; Sir 45:6).

[217] Cf. R.A. GUELICH, *Mark*, 57; G.H. TWELFTREE, «ΕΚΒΑΛΛΩ», 376; G.R. OSBORNE, «Structure and Christology», 152.

[218] Cf. G.R. OSBORNE, «Structure and Christology», 152; G.H. TWELFTREE, «ΕΚΒΑΛΛΩ», 376; R.A. GUELICH, *Mark*, 57.

[219] O. PROCKSCH, «ἅγιος», 101-102; Cf. H. VAN DER LOOS, *The Miracles*, 363; W.L. LANE, *Mark*, 74; W.R. DOMERIS, «The Holy One», 11.

[220] Cf. W.R. DOMERIS, «The Holy One», 11; E. ARENS, *The ΗΛΘΟΝ-sayings*, 211; L. SCHENKE, *Die Wundererzählungen*, 100; E. KLOSTERMANN, *Markusevangelium*, 17; A. FRIDRICHSEN, «Conflict of Jesus», 125; M.F. SADLER, *Mark*, 15. R. PESCH, «Ein Tag», 120-121, 122 also refers to it as «constrained confession», (*Zwangs «Bekenntnis»*). However, S.V. MCCASLAND, «Demonic Confessions», 36, refuted this with two reasons: (1) that the conversations between Jesus and the demons reflect a desperate struggle between enemies who are bent on thwarting or destroying one another; they are not friendly confessions or recognitions; (2) that the «confessions» are really not confessions but identifications intended to strip the exorcist of his power.

Some scholars have also associated this term «the Holy One of God» with the designation «Jesus the Nazarene», from which association they see the demon's demonstration of knowing the true identity of Jesus. Thus naming him is an apotropaic or a typical exorcistic device for the demon to overpower the exorcist. But what is more difficult, is the association of these two designations for Jesus as stemming from a play on words (*Wortspiel*)[221]. This word play is seen from the LXX translation of the MT radicals behind Nazareth (נצר), and «holy or consecrated one» (נזיר). The LXX translated נזיר אלהים, in Judg. 13:7 and 16:17, in two ways (Codex A: ναζιραῖον/ναζιραῖος θεοῦ; and Codex B: ἅγιον/ἅγιος θεοῦ) with reference to Samson. The same is also found in LXX Codex B as ναζιρ θεοῦ. One can see that in both texts ναζιραῖος and ἅγιος θεοῦ are translation variants to «a holy or consecrated one of God». In other words, the «Nazarene» in v.24 is been associated in two steps, through the combination of «a Nazirite of God» and «a holy one of God» in the LXX texts, to obtain the true nature of Jesus of Nazareth. It makes sense and is also exciting in such a combination which confirmed the idea that Jesus is «the Holy One of God». However, this hypothesis is not without problems[222]. Hence, «the Holy One (ὁ ἅγιος) of God» would therefore be an interpretation of Jesus' place name (Ναζαρηνέ) as well as a revelation of his true nature or identity[223]. This designation («the Holy One of God») establishes the relation with God, but raises the question of Jesus' identity at this beginning of his public ministry.

The unclean spirit, through the words it cried out against Jesus, has demonstrated the supernatural knowledge about Jesus, by revealing his

---

[221] Cf. F. MUSSNER, «Ein Wortspiel», 285-286; R. PESCH, «Ein Tag», 124; ID., *Markusevangelium* I, 122, n.20; E. SCHWEIZER, «Nazoräer», 90-93; J. GNILKA, *Markus* I, 80-81; K. BERGER, «Nasoräer/Nasiräer», 330.

[222] R.H. GUNDRY, *Mark*, 82, has drawn our attention to about half a dozen of them. But I would like to mention the most important problems with the hypothesis: (1) the trail from Jesus as a «Nazarene» to «Nazirite» through 2 textual traditions of the LXX to «the Holy One of God»; (2) the differences between α and ι, -ηνος and -αιος in the Greek behind «Nazarene» and «Nazirite» respectively; (3) the uncertainty of the LXX textual tradition/s known to Mark; (4) that Jesus was not ascetic to be a «Nazirite»; (5) the double definite articles in Mark (in ἅγιος and θεός), which is completely lacking in Judges.

[223] Cf. C.S. MANN, *Mark*, 212-213; R.A. GUELICH, *Mark*, 57; A. SUHL, «Überlegungen zur Hermeneutik», 32; R. PESCH, *Markusevangelium* I, 122; F. MUSSNER, «Ein Wortspiel», 286.

name and origin, his mission and his true identity; but at the same time wanted to use it as a defensive mechanism against Jesus. The demoniac by his crying out has disturbed the worshipping community, we look at Jesus' reaction to this demonic encounter.

2.3 *Mk 1:25: Jesus' Word of Command*

This shortest verse of the pericope introduces us to the second direct discourse in our pericope. It is a turning point in the story, which has so far highlighted the words of the unclean spirit to Jesus. Here we shall examine Jesus' reaction to the unclean spirit's provocation, especially what he said.

2.3.1 But Jesus rebuked him

As this is the central moment of the story, it is wise that the principal actor should be mentioned, thus: ὁ ᾽Ιησοῦς[224]. Jesus' name being once more expressly mentioned here (after the unclean spirit's mentioning in v.24), the climax of the narration, is an effective feature or impulse in the story[225]. This is even more so after the unclean spirit has accused him, and revealed his person, identity and mission. Thus the highest tension is reached: can this Nazarener Jesus withstand such a power? It is therefore necessary that Jesus at this point should intervene to react or defend himself.

Jesus did really intervene and his reaction is described in the verb, ἐπιτιμᾶν. This verb could mean in classical Greek or literally, «to raise or lay a price or value upon», «to honour»; but in the NT could mean «to rebuke, reprove, censure»[226] or also «to speak seriously, warn in order to prevent an action or bring one to an end»; or even «to punish»[227]. The

---

[224] The name of Jesus (ὁ ᾽Ιησοῦς), as the explicit subject, almost always comes up at an important moment in the story (cf. 1:9, 14, 17, 25; 2:5, 8, 17, 19; etc). So far in this pericope we have been content with Jesus as the implicit subject from vv.21-24, until now and after (vv.26-28), but only here in v.25, he appears as the explicit subject.

[225] Cf. P. GUILLEMETTE, «Un enseignement nouveau», 236-237; R. PESCH, *Markusevangelium* I, 123; ID., «Eine neue Lehre», 258-259; ID., «Ein Tag», 121; E. LOHMEYER, *Markus*, 37.

[226] *BAGD*, 303, 1; Cf. C.S. MANN, *Mark*, 213; H.C. KEE, «Terminology of Mark», 235-240; V. TAYLOR, *Mark*, 175; E. STAUFFER, «ἐπιτιμάω», 623; R.G. BRATCHER – E.A. NIDA, *Translator's Handbook*, 51; G.A. BARTON, «ἐπιτιμᾶν in Mark», 233-234.

[227] *BAGD*, 303,1, 2; E. STAUFFER, «ἐπιτιμάω», 623; R.G. BRATCHER – E.A.

meaning cannot be exhausted but the context will help to clarify the specific understanding of the verb.

Kee in his article noted that ἐπιτιμᾶν[228] stems from the technical Semitic term גער, used in the Qumran and Jewish Apocalyptic literatures as the «commanding word, uttered by God or by his spokesman, by which evil powers are brought into submission, and the way is thereby prepared for the establishment of God's righteous rule in the world»[229]. Even there «rebuke» is not an adequate translation for such a concept in the Qumran documents[230], as also seen in the NT[231]. It is interesting to note that this term did not even occur in the Hellenistic exorcistic literature or miracle accounts[232]. However, Kee establishes in his article that «in the biblical and apocalyptic material, the subjugation of the demonic powers is understood as a necessary part in preparing for the establishment of God's rule over his creation»[233]. In other words, contrasting the creating Word of God (ברא) which brings about life, and the reproving Word of God (גער) which calls down destruction as seen in the OT thoughts in the LXX, one can say that «ἐπιτιμάω becomes a technical term for the powerful divine word of rebuke and threat»[234].

In the NT this verb, ἐπιτιμᾶν, appears mostly in the Gospels, especially in the Synoptics. It is in Mark 9x; Matthew 7x; and in Luke

---

NIDA, *Translator's Handbook,* 51; G.A. BARTON, «ἐπιτιμᾶν in Mark», 234.

[228] All the 11x occurrences of ἐπιτιμᾶν in the LXX are translated by the Hebrew verb גער. This verb גער, which occurs 14x in the Hebrew Bible, is usually translated «rebuke». Cf. J.M. KENNEDY, «The Root G`R »,47-64, esp. 47; A. CAQUOT, «גער», 49-53, esp. 49.

[229] H.C. KEE, «Terminology of Mark», 232-246, esp. 235; Cf. G.R. OSBORNE, «Structure and Christology», 151-152; S. KUTHIRAKKATTEL, *The Beginning*, 137; R.A. GUELICH, *Mark*, 57; W.L. LANE, *Mark*, 75-76, n.121; K. KERTELGE, *Die Wunder Jesu*, 54, n.86. However some are contrary, Cf. R.H. GUNDRY, *Mark*, 84; G.H. TWELFTREE, *Jesus the Exorcist*, 45-46, 68-69.

[230] Cf. 1 QapGen 20:28-29; 1 QM 14:9; 1 QH 9:11, etc.

[231] H.C. KEE, «Terminology of Mark», 235; Cf. C.S. MANN, *Mark*, 213; G.A. BARTON, «ἐπιτιμᾶν in Mark», 234.

[232] H.C. KEE, «Terminology of Mark», 241; Cf. R.H. GUNDRY, *Mark*, 84; C.S. MANN, *Mark*, 213.

[233] H.C. KEE, «Terminology of Mark», 235-240, esp. 239.

[234] E. STAUFFER, «ἐπιτιμάω», 634; Cf. J. GNILKA, *Markus*,I, 81; R. PESCH, *Markusevangelium*,I, 123; ID., «Eine neue Lehre», 258; ID., «Ein Tag», 121; C.E.B. CRANFIELD, *Mark*, 77.

12x. Generally speaking, one can say that the NT maintains the same tradition in the OT, especially the Wisdom literature, which established that, if men have any right of ἐπιτιμᾶν among themselves, it can only be in terms of judicial, paternal or fraternal correction. Therefore, it forbids rebuking except as brotherly correction, and treats effective threating and reproof as the prerogative of God and His Christ alone[235].

In Mark's Gospel, among the 9x occurrences, 6x has Jesus as the subject of the verb; the remaining 3x has, Peter, the disciples and the crowd, as the subjects. These three were: a) when Peter tried to rebuke Jesus as the suffering Messiah (8:32); b) when the Disciples were reproaching those bringing their children to Jesus (10:13); and c) when the people were rebuking Bartimaeus to be silent (10:48). In all these cases, Jesus did not fail to correct them, that they should not be obstacles to God's salvific action. Thus, that it is not their prerogative to rebuke.

The object of the verb with regard to Jesus' 6x use are as follows: the disciples (2x: 8:30, 33), the elemental or cosmic forces [wind and sea] (1x: 4:39), and the demons [unclean spirits] (3x: 1:25; 3:12; 9:25). The number of the use of the verb mainly by Jesus in Mark's Gospel, and the objects of the verb, establish that ἐπιτιμᾶν is a prerogative of Jesus in the Gospels, and rightfully declares his position as the Lord[236].

In our text what sense has this verb in the context? The Narrator used this verb to describe the action or reaction of Jesus before the provocative words of the unclean spirit. Although many see this verb as «to rebuke», while I would prefer to see it more as «to command» though with some element of rebuke. This is because: a) the word describes the action of Jesus which is reflected in the direct speech in two-fold command; b) the people also describe Jesus' action towards the unclean spirit as «to command» (ἐπιτάσσειν), v.27; c) the importance of Jesus' authority makes it clear that it is more of «command» than «rebuke»; because, «it is in the exorcisms that the authority of Jesus is supremely manifest»[237]; (d)

---

[235] Cf. E. STAUFFER, «ἐπιτιμάω», 625.

[236] Cf. E. STAUFFER, «ἐπιτιμάω», 625.
Likewise among the 14x of the verb נער's occurrence in the Hebrew Bible, Yahweh is the grammatical subject 11x; while the other three have human beings as subjects. Cf. J.M. KENNEDY, «The Root G`R», 47. Thus this confirms the Lordship of God and Christ through the use of this word.

[237] H.C. KEE, «Terminology of Mark», 242. Moreover «the word of command and the word of exorcism are combined in ἐπιτιμᾶν in Mk 1:25 (Lk 4:35)». Cf. E. STAUFFER, «ἐπιτιμάω», 626, n.18.

Taylor states, «Jesus *rebukes* the unclean spirit and *charges* it to be silent and come out of him»[238] (*italics* is mine); why did he use both verbs to translate ἐπιτιμᾶν? May be because the first did not do justice to it; (e) through the defensive mechanism of the unclean spirit, it wanted to frustrate Jesus' mission in his first public appearance, but Jesus demonstrated his lordship through his authoritative command: «the unconditional lordship of Jesus is powerfully revealed in this ἐπιτιμᾶν»[239]. Thus, «Jesus utters the commanding word by which the demon, as representative of the forces opposed to God and his purposes, is overcome»[240]. This commanding word is addressed to αὐτῷ, not to the «man with an unclean spirit» but the «unclean spirit»[241] itself. In fact, Jesus makes a separating operation in this text between the «man ...» in v.23 (ἐξ αὐτοῦ) and the «unclean spirit» identified with him also in v.23 (αὐτῷ).

2.3.2 «Be Silent!»

Jesus' first command is φιμώθητι. This commanding word comes from the verb φιμόω (φιμοῦν) which has a *literal* sense of «to muzzle», and a *figurative* one of «to silence»[242]. Some also see φιμοῦν as equivalent to καταδεῖν («to bind»), thus as a technical term used in magic or incantations for *binding* a person by a means of a spell so as to make him powerless or inoperative to harm[243]. However, in the NT this word appears only 8x, and it is generally used in the sense of «to muzzle, bind» (cf. 1 Cor 9:9; 1 Tim 5:18), and «to silence» (cf. Mk 1:25; 4:39; Mt 22:12, 34; Lk 4:35; 1 Pet 2:15).

---

[238] V. TAYLOR, *Mark*, 175.

[239] E. STAUFFER, «ἐπιτιμάω», 626.

[240] H.C. KEE, «Terminology of Mark», 242.

[241] Cf. W.L LANE, *Mark*, 74; V. TAYLOR, *Mark*, 175; R.G. BRATCHER – E.A. NIDA *Translator's Handbook*, 51; C.E.B. CRANFIELD, *Mark*, 77; H.B. SWETE, *Mark*, 20.

[242] Cf. B. KOLLMANN, «Jesu Schweigegebote», 268; J. BRIÈRE, «Le cri et le secret», 45, n.5; C.E.B. CRANFIELD, *Mark*, 78; MOULTON – MILLIGAN, *Vocabulary*, 672; H.B. SWETE, *Mark*, 20; E.P. GOULD, *Mark*, 24.

[243] Cf. E. ROHDE, *Psyche II*, 424; Cf. G.H. TWELFTREE, *Jesus the Exorcist*, 70, n.79; ID., «ΕΚΒΑΛΛΩ», 378; B. KOLLMANN, «Jesu Schweigegebote», 268-269, n.9; P. GUILLEMETTE, «Un enseignement nouveau», 231; R. PESCH, *Markusevangelium*, I, 123; K. KERTELGE, *Die Wunder Jesu*, 54, n.87; V. TAYLOR, *Mark*, 175; T.A. BURKILL, *Mysterious Revelation*, 74; R.G. BRATCHER – E.A. NIDA, *Translator's Handbook*, 51.

In Mark's Gospel, as we can see, it appeared only 2x. Apart from our text, the next has to do with the calming of the Sea-storm (4:39). In our text (1:25) it is aorist imperative passive, which could mean «be muzzled, be bound»[244] or «be silenced, be silent!»[245] Looking at the context, our text has the most probable meaning of «be silent!» Thus, it is a command to silence or to end the speech of the unclean spirit that attempts to embarrass Jesus through its defensive mechanism. In other words, φιμώθητι is the real response or reaction to this defensive or «protective» words (*Abwehrformel*, cf. v.24) of the demon[246]. This is analogous to the injunction in 1:34 and 3:12 to the unclean spirits to keep silent[247]. In fact the silencing of the spirit starts the process of exorcism, and introduces us to the next immediate commanding word, «to come out of him».

Before we go to the next command, we must remind ourselves that it is also from here that Wrede developed his *Messianic Secret* theory[248].

Jesus' silencing of the demons could be interpreted in many ways but importantly, it is rather to stop the apotropaic use of his name and titles[249], and to prevent a premature revelation of his true nature through the «confessions» of the demons[250].

2.3.3 «Come out of him!»

Jesus' second command is ἔξελθε ἐξ αὐτοῦ[251]. This is the most

---

[244] Cf. G.H. TWELFTREE, *Jesus the Exorcist*, 69; ID., «ΕΚΒΑΛΛΩ», 378; E. ROHDE, *Psyche II*, 424; *BDF # 346*; F. PFISTER, «Beschwörung»,174.

[245] Cf. M.D. HOOKER, *St. Mark*, 65; W. HENDRIKSEN, *Mark*, 66, n.42; *BAGD*, 861; R.G. BRATCHER – E.A. NIDA, *Translator's Handbook*, 51.

[246] K. THRAEDE,«Exorzismus», 51, maintains that φιμώθητι in v.25 (which refers to the demon's *Abwehrspruch*) corresponds to a «rough command to silence» (*barsches Schweigegebot*) typical of Exorcism ritual. Cf. B. KOLLMANN, «Jesu Schweigegebote», 267, n.3; R. PESCH, *Markusevangelium I*, 123; «Ein Tag», 121; «Eine neue Lehre», 259.

[247] Cf. S. KUTHIRAKKATTEL, *The Beginning*, 137, n.97.

[248] Cf. W. WREDE, *Das Messiasgeheimnis*.

[249] Cf. R.H. GUNDRY, *Mark*, 84.

[250] Cf. B. KOLLMANN, «Jesu Schweigegebote», 273; T.A. BURKILL, *Mysterious Revelation*, 73. S. LÉGASSE, *L'Évangile de Marc*, I, 128-129, observes that this is the first example of Jesus' refusal to see his identity divulged by a demon (cf. 1:34c; 3:11-12), even when it says something in Jesus' favour by its supernatural knowledge.

[251] The Lukan form of this phrase (4:35) is with ἀπό in place of ἐκ. However, ἐξέρχεσθαι (in the sense of «come out, go out») is often used with ἀπό, especially

important element, in fact, a typical formula or technical term (*terminus technicus*) in Exorcism[252]. It corresponds to the *Ausfahrbefehl* (the command to come out), the ἀποπομπή (Apopompe) found in the ancient exorcism rituals and other stories of other exorcists of the period[253].

The verb ἐξέρχεσθαι, which appears 38x in Mk (Mt 43x; Lk 44x; Jn 29x), has a literally or figurative sense of «to go out», «to come out», «to go away», «to retire» or «to leave». In the Synoptics ἐξέρχεσθαι is the characteristic word for the «going forth» of demons (unclean spirit) from those possessed by them (Mk 1;26 and par.; cf. Act 8:7; 16:18)[254].

In Mark's Gospel, of the 38x, the local sense dominated with 27x; followed by 9x[255] referring to the going or coming out of demons or unclean spirits. Strikingly, we have ἐξέρχεσθαι 3x in our pericope: vv.25, 26, 28. Firstly, v.25 follows Jesus' command, which implies a *physical movement* of the unclean spirit out of its victim. Secondly v.26, still a physical movement, but here effects *exorcism* itself. Thirdly, v.28 has a figurative sense of Jesus' report or fame (going out) *spreading* beyond the vicinity of the synagogue and around the whole country.

In describing Jesus' activity of exorcism, Mk very often links the word δαιμόνιον with ἐκβάλλειν, Mk 7x (Mt 7x; Lk 7x), but with ἐξέρχεσθαι, Mk 2x (Mt 1x; Lk 6x)[256]. While he uses the phrase πνεῦμα

---

with Luke (13x in the gospel, and never with ἐκ, in contrast with Mark who has ἐξέρχεσθαι with ἀπό 1x only (11:12) but 10x with ἐκ)... This confusion of ἐκ and ἀπό is indeed common enough in Hellenistic Greek, but in the NT Hebrew influence is perhaps not entirely absent. Cf. M. ZERWICK, *Biblical Greek*, 29, #88.

[252] Cf. S. KUTHIRAKKATTEL, *The Beginning*, 137; R. PESCH, «Eine neue Lehre», 253.

G.H. TWELFTREE, «ΕΚΒΑΛΛΩ», 379, affirms that «the command to the demons to "come out" is the basic command found regardless of whether or not we would categorize them as "magical"».

[253] Cf. R.A. GUELICH, *Mark*, 58; K. THRAEDE, «Exorzismus», 52, 59-60; F. PFISTER, «Beschwörung», 174; J. SCHNEIDER, «ἐξέρχομαι», 678-680, esp. 679.

[254] Cf. J. SCHNEIDER, «ἐξέρχομαι», 679; *BAGD*, 274,1 a, δ.

[255] While Mark has 9x out of 38x for demons or unclean spirit, Mt has 4x out of 43x, and Lk has 11x out of 44x. These 9x are: 1:25,26; 5:8,13; 7:29,30; 9:25,26,29. It is also interesting that ἐξέρχεσθαι appears in all the four exorcism accounts.

[256] Mark's use of δαιμόνιον («demon») with ἐκβάλλειν («to cast out») are as follows: 1:34,39; 3:15,22; 6:13; 7:26; 9:38) and with ἐξέρχεσθαι («to go out») are: 7:29; 30. The verb ἐκβάλλειν in the NT has particularly the sense of «to expel» or «to repel» especially in the case of demons, who have settled in men as in a house. This is clearly illustrated in Mk 3:27, and par. Cf. F. HAUCK, «ἐκβάλλω», 527; K. STOCK,

ἀκάθαρτον almost always with ἐξέρχεσθαι 4x (1:26; 5:8,13; 9:25; cf. Mt 12:43; Lk 4:36; 8:29; 11:24); and never with ἐκβάλλειν[257]. We have earlier indicated that Mark used both «demon» and «unclean spirit» the same number of times: 11x. However, we want to emphasize here the *technical term* often used for each is: «cast out» for demons; «go or come out» for unclean spirits. The verb ἐξέρχεσθαι with the preposition ἐκ is employed in two ways in Mk: of place (1:29; 5:2; 6:54; 7:31) and of person (1:25,26; 5:8,30; 7:29; 9:25). In the latter group, except 5:30, all the occurrences are either Jesus' command (in the imperative) to the unclean spirits to come out of the person (1:25; 5:8; 9:25)[258] or the narration of the actual coming out of the unclean spirits from the person (1:26; 7:29)[259]. This confirms the technicalness of our term. We must point out that this verb, both in the local sense, and as a technical term for driving out unclean spirits, makes its first occurrence in our pericope.

It is here, at this point, the apex of the story, that the power or the ἐξουσία (authority) of the exorcist is tested. Here Jesus combats the demons with divine-peremptory authority, through his simple command which drives out the unclean spirit. This corresponds to the climax of our story, as well as its christological message: Jesus should absolutely be shown as the Holy One of God, the Son of God, who acts on God's behalf with divine authority[260]. Now we have seen Jesus' authoritative command to the unclean spirit, we shall then find out how it will react to this command.

2.4 *Mk 1:26: The Unclean Spirit departs*

This verse has a link with the foregoing one, in the sense that Jesus, the chief actor of the story has spoken, and his speech needs a reaction from

---

Boten, 22, n.43.

[257] The verb ἐκβάλλειν («to cast out») usually goes with δαιμόνιον («demon») and never with πνεῦμα ἀκάθαρτον («unclean spirit»), but rather the latter always with the verb ἐξέρχεσθαι («to go out»). Cf. R.H. GUNDRY, *Mark*, 91; K. STOCK, *Boten*, 22.

[258] The firmness and authoritative nature of Jesus' command is well revealed in the three parallel texts: Mk 1:25: φιμώθητι καὶ ἔξελθε ἐξ αὐτοῦ.

Mk 5:8 : ἔξελθε τὸ πνεῦμα τὸ ἀκάθαρτον ἐκ τοῦ ἀνθρώπου.

Mk 9:25: τὸ ἄλαλον καὶ κωφὸν πνεῦμα, ἐγὼ ἐπιτάσσω σοι, ἔξελθε ἐξ αὐτοῦ, καὶ μηκέτι εἰσέλθῃς εἰς αὐτόν.

[259] Cf. S. KUTHIRAKKATTEL, *The Beginning*, 137.

[260] Cf. R. PESCH, *Markusevangelium I*, 123; «Eine neue Lehre», 259; «Ein Tag», 121.

his opponent, the unclean spirit. The first two verbs are in aorist participle neuter sing., while the principal verb is in aorist indicative active. The object of the sentence remains the man (αὐτόν; ἐξ αὐτοῦ): this verse reminds us of v.23, where these two beings were also together. The explicit subject (πνεῦμα ἀκάθαρτον) is well stressed, with double articles, and by the change of position; likewise the object receives its emphasis by the change of position.[261] Hence in this verse we shall see, on the one hand, a battle between the «man» and the «unclean spirit»; and on the other hand, we shall also expect the fulfilment of Jesus' command that the unclean spirit should come out of the man.

2.4.1 The Unclean Spirit convulsed him

The first part of this verse deals with the last battle between the unclean spirit and the possessed man (its victim), which was sparked off by the powerful command of Jesus. To describe this action the narrator used the verb σπαράσσειν, which means «to tear» or «to rend», «to pull to and fro», or «to convulse»[262]. This verb occurs only 3x in the NT: Mk 1:26; 9:26; Lk 9:39[263]. And these 3x of σπαράσσειν and 2x of συνσπά-ρασσειν all occurred within the context of exorcisms.

In Mark's Gospel, as we have observed above, we have 2x (1:26; 9:26) of σπαράσσειν, and 1x (9:20) of συνσπάρασσειν. The violent action of the unclean spirit on the possessed man, is generally interpreted as «convulsing»[264]. However, some see the man as having a symptom of

---

[261] The normal word order in Greek in the simple sentence is «the *verb* or nominal predicate with its copula stands immediately after the conjunction; then follow in the order the *subject*, *object*, supplementary partciple, etc» (*italics* is mine). Cf. *BDF* #472. So the change of these positions call for attention or emphasis.

[262] *BAGD*, 760; V. TAYLOR, *Mark*, 175; C.E.B. CRANFIELD, *Mark*, 79; H.B. SWETE, *Mark*, 21.

[263] It has also a compound verb συνσπάρασσειν, cf. Mk 9:20; Lk 9:42. The σπαράσσειν can be referred to the LXX reading of the Heb. 2 Sam 22:8 (וַיִּגְעַשׁ), cf. H.B. SWETE, *Mark*, 21; or to Dan 8:7 LXX, cf. E. LOHMEYER, *Markus*, 37; E. KLOSTERMANN, *Markusevangelium*, 17.

[264] Cf. R.H. GUNDRY, *Mark*, 77; G.H. TWELFTREE, *Jesus the Exorcist*, 70; ID., «ΕΚΒΑΛΛΩ», 382-383; M.D. HOOKER, *St. Mark*, 65; R.A. GUELICH, *Mark*, 58; C.E.B. CRANFIELD, *Mark*, 79; H.B. SWETE, *Mark*, 21; E.P. GOULD, *St. Mark*, 24. Thus, C. BONNER, «Technique of Exorcism», 49, affirms that the last convulsions of the possessed man must be seen as the final combat with the demon although we can attribute them to the mental malady. Cf. P. GUILLEMETTE, «Un enseignement nouveau», 232, n.45 (the author mistakes the title of the article). However, some think

Epilepsy, or that the attack points to Epilepsy itself.[265]

The parallel text of our pericope, Lk 4:35, although replaces σπαράσσειν with ῥίπτειν, yet suggests convulsive movements, when it says that the demon threw him down without doing him any harm[266]. Likewise, the examination of the parallel text, 9:26 in Mark is also illuminating, as we shall notice now:

Mk 1:26	Mk 9:26
καὶ σπαράξαν αὐτὸν...	καὶ κράξας
καὶ φωνῆσαν φωνῇ μεγάλῃ	καὶ πολλὰ σπαράξας
ἐξῆλθεν ἐξ αὐτοῦ	ἐξῆλθεν

The three elements in both texts (the first and last exorcism stories in Mark) are observable: the *violent movements* between the unclean spirit and the man, the *shouting*, and the *departure* of the unclean spirit from the man. And both are described with two aorist participles and an aorist indicative (cf. Lk 4:35). However, in Mk 9:26 it is clear that the violent convulsions of the boy, which follow Jesus' command of expulsion (v.25), are linked to the sickness described in vv.18 and 20[267]. With this in mind, and added to it the ἀνέκραξεν of v.23, and the parallel text of Lk 4:35, one can conclude that the sickness must resemble that of Mk 9:20-26. Moreover, this violence is only accentuated by the presence of Jesus. His command of exorcism produces convulsions and shouting (1:26; 9:26)[268]. Therefore, we can more confidently establish that the man

---

of the unclean spirit as tearing (*zerren*) or pulling the man to and fro. Cf. J. ERNST, *Markus*, 64; R. PESCH, *Markusevangelium* I, 123-124; H. VAN DER LOOS, *The Miracles*, 381; W. GRUNDMANN, *Markus*, 43. I agree with the above positon, as it interpretes our text better.

[265] Cf. C.S. MANN, *Mark*, 213; J. ERNST, *Markus*, 64; W. HENDRIKSEN, *Mark*, 66; H. VAN DER LOOS, *The Miracles*, 382, n.1. In fact, J.H. WASZINK, «Besessenheit», 184, attests that in most cases it concerns Epilepsy to which indicates also that the possessed man is often being thrown on the ground by the demon. Cf. R. PESCH, *Markusevangeliuℵm I*, 123, n.28; «Eine neue Lehre», 253, n.55. For more discussion on Epilepsy, see E. LESKY – J.H. WASZINK, «Epilepsie»,819-831; J.H. WASZINK, «Besessenheit», 183-185.

[266] Cf. V. TAYLOR, *Mark*, 175; H.B. SWETE, *Mark*, 21.

[267] Cf. P. GUILLEMETTE, «Un enseignement nouveau», 232.

[268] Cf. J.M. ROBINSON, *The Problem of History*, 87. At the sight of Jesus the demon convulses the epileptic boy, who, falling on the ground, rolls about foaming (9:20).

was convulsed by the unclean spirit. And that was the most hectic and final battle it had with him before departing from him. Now we move to the next action of the unclean spirit.

2.4.2 And cried with a loud voice

The next action of the unclean spirit is described by this phrase, φωνῆσαν φωνῇ μεγάλη. It is in a cognate construction with dative (literally, «shouting with a loud shout or voice») which adds to emphasis. The unclean spirit is still the grammatical subject of the clause. The action is described by the verb, φωνεῖν which denotes the production of sound or noise by musical instruments, animals, or men[269]. In the NT φωνεῖν denotes the «loud speaking», «calling», or «crying» of men, angels, or demons[270]; and also the «crowing» of the cock[271]. Just as φωνεῖν can mean κράζειν («shout or cry out»), so also it can mean καλεῖν («to call or summon»). Thus it has many uses in the NT. Now we turn to its use in Mark's Gospel.

The verb, φωνεῖν, follows the uses or meanings as observed in the NT. This verb occurs 9x in Mk (Mt 5x; Lk 10x; Jn 13x), but only 1x, in our text (1:26), which refers to the crying or shouting of the unclean spirit. And to describe how this sound was produced the phrase, φωνῇ μεγάλη was used. Both in the OT and NT, φωνή means first of all, «noise», «sound» or «human voice». The substantive φωνή, occurs 7x in Mk (Mt 8x; Lk 14x; Jn 15x). However, this phrase φωνῇ μεγάλη appears 4x among the 7x in Mk (Mt 2x; Lk 6x; Jn 1x): 2x are linked with unclean spirits or demons (1:26; 5:7); while the other 2x are with Jesus' death cry or wail (15:34, 37).

So in Mk's Gospel, we observe that the unclean spirit uses for the last time the man's voice or vocal organs to make a loud, horrid cry[272]. This loud cry becomes a demonstration signal (cf. 5:13; 9:26) for the departure of the demon, a visible and audible sign of the effectiveness and success

---

[269] As a rule, the verb is used only of living creatures with a lung and throat. Man, however, is the chief subject of φωνεῖν. This can come in form of, «to lift up the voice», «to speak», «to call», «to cry», «to summon», etc. Cf. O. BETZ, «φωνέω», 301-302.

[270] Cf. O. BETZ, «Φωνέω», 303.

[271] Mk 14:30, 72 (bis); Mt 26:34, 74, 75; Lk 22:34, 60, 61; Jn 13:38; 18:27.

[272] Cf. W. HENDRIKSEN, *Mark*, 66; V. TAYLOR, *Mark*, 175; E. LOHMEYER, *Markus*, 37; W. GRUNDMANN, *Markus*, 43; E. KLOSTERMANN, *Markusevangelium*, 17; H.B. SWETE, *Markus*, 21.

of Jesus' exorcistic command[273]. These two actions (convulsions and shouting) of the unclean spirit, on the one hand, show that it obeys unwilling, that is, not without resistance. On the other hand, they prepare the stage for its final exit or depature from the man, its victim. So now we come to the exorcism proper in the next action of the unclean spirit.

2.4.3 It came out of him

The aim of Jesus' command is here fulfilled. Following Jesus' command verbatim, one can see that the fulfilment report corresponds to the punctual execution of that command. Bratcher & Nida state that «"convulsing... and shouting" are both aorist participles, whose action is simultaneous with that of the main verb "went out"»[274]. So after this seemingly resistance the unclean spirit left its victim, thereby giving up or leaving its dwelling place[275].

In fact, the «loud voice» or death wail (*Todesschrei*)[276] of the possessed, who gives up his unclean spirit (cf. 9:26; 15:37), really announces the final departure of the unclean spirit from the man. Thus the expulsion of demons by a single command exhibits Jesus' power in the highest degree. Thus «the lack of an adjuration, of an incantation, of an appeal to some deity or supernatural power, of a physical manipulation — all techniques normally used in exorcisms — lets all emphasis fall on the authority of

---

[273] Cf. J. ERNST, *Markus*, 64, 65; P. GUILLEMETTE, «Un enseignement nouveau», 237; R. PESCH, *Markusevangelium* I, 124; «Eine neue Lehre», 259; «Ein Tag», 122; L. SCHENKE, *Die Wundererzählungen*, 101; D.-A. KOCH, *Die Bedeutung*, 56, n.6, 57, n.11; G. THEISSEN, *Miracle Stories*, 66-67. E. SCHWEIZER, *Markus*, 28, affirms that the loud shouting of the outgoing demon demonstrates the force or impact of the battle and the greatness of the victory. On the other hand, R. GUNDRY, *Mark*, 77, observes that the distinction 9:20, 26 (cf. 1:23, 26) between convulsions and outcries prior to Jesus' command as proof of demonic possession, and after his command as proof of exorcism.

[274] R.G. BRATCHER – E.A. NIDA, *Translator's Handbook*, 52.

[275] Cf. J. GNILKA, *Markus*, 81-82; E. LOHMEYER, *Markus*, 37.

[276] Cf. R.A. GUELICH, *Mark*, 58; J. GNILKA, *Markus* I, 82; O. BÖCHER, *Dämonenfurcht*, 22-23; ID., *Christus Exorcista*, 45-46; K. THRAEDE, «Exorzismus», 52; F. PFISTER, «Beschwörung», 174. R. PESCH, *Markusevangelium* I, 121; ID., «Eine neue Lehre», 253, notes that the loud shout is the sign of the bearer of the spirit, positive: one who is filled with Holy Spirit (cf. 15:37); negative: one who is possessed by the unclean spirit. Cf. O. BÖCHER, *Dämonenfurcht*, 22-23; 103-104; *Christus Exorcista*, 44-46, 85-86.

Jesus' own simple but effective command»[277].

This naturally leads us to examine some of the similarities and differences between the exorcism of Jesus and his contemporaries. Twelftree notes about five areas of parallel between Jesus and his contemporaries: an initial dramatic confrontation; the words of the demons; the words of exorcism; the demon's plea (in Mk 5:10-12, but not here); the violent cure[278]. However, the uniqueness of Jesus is demonstrated in the differences: the absence of material or mechanical devices (e.g., burning incense, amulets, herbs, etc); the refusal to use «proofs» to demonstrate success; the absence of prayer in Jesus' exorcism; the refusal to invoke other authorities (like Solomon or the Spirit of God or angelic forces); and the absence of the binding formula[279]. Thus the uniqueness of Jesus lies «primarily in the authority he possessed in and of himself»[280]. Through the casting out of the unclean spirit (demon) the impression of Jesus' authority is still being strengthened. This is because Jesus' word of command on the unclean spirit is so valid and powerful that it obeys him[281]. We must remember that Jesus' exorcism is the second main theme of our pericope.

2.5 *Summary*

After this second thematic section, it is most evident that all the necessary elements to establish that exorcism is the second main theme in the pericope are present. These are: (a) the man possessed by unclean spirit (v.23a, 26), (b) the unclean spirit (vv.23b-24, 26), that has destroyed the man's personality and rendered him virtually and morally unfit for public worship, and (c) Jesus (v.25), who is the exorcist and main character of the story. However, we shall highlight other important aspects of the pericope in this section:

---

[277] R.H. GUNDRY, *Mark*, 77; Cf. G.R. OSBORNE, «Structure and Christology», 152-153; G.H. TWELFTREE, «EΚΒΑΛΛΩ», 383-386, esp. 386.

[278] G.H. TWELFTREE, «EΚΒΑΛΛΩ», 371-383; Cf. G.R. OSBORNE, «Structure and Christology», 152; C.E.B. CRANFIELD, *Mark*, 80; T.A. BURKILL, *Mysterious Revelation*, 72-73; C.K. BARRETT, *The Holy Spirit*, 55-57.

[279] G.H. TWELFTREE, «EΚΒΑΛΛΩ», 383-386; G.R. OSBORNE, «Structure and Christology», 152; R.H. GUNDRY, *Mark*, 77.

[280] G.R. OSBORNE, «Structure and Christology», 153.

[281] Cf. K. STOCK, «Die Machttaten Jesu», 201.

1. The concept of demonic possession is seen through the initial and repeated presence of πνεῦμα ἀκάθαρτον (vv.23,26,27) in our pericope.

2. The intensity of the demonic cry is described in our pericope with ἀνακράζω (only 2x in Mark), while in other places the simple form (κράζω) is used.

3. In the words of the unclean spirit, important motives were also raised: (a) the phrase, τί ἡμῖν καὶ σοί, which expresses hostility and warding off of deadly enemy (Jesus), introduces conflict between Jesus and the demonic world; (b) the name, Ναζαρηνός, reminds us of Jesus' hometown (1:9), or his natural identity (Nazarene), with which he will be identified from now on; (c) Jesus' mission includes breaking the powers of evil spirits on human beings, which is revealed in the only ἦλθον-saying uttered by anyone/unclean spirit (outside Jesus); (d) the revelation of Jesus, as «the Holy One of God», affirms his special relationship with God, which the unclean spirits will also express in other occasions with similar designations (3:11: «the Son of God»; 5:7: «the Son of the Most High God»).

4. Jesus' command/rebuke was described with ἐπιτιμάω, which reveals the unconditional lordship of Jesus, both in its meaning and use in the Gospel.

5. Jesus' command to silence, effected by φιμόω, with regard to the unclean spirit, was a reaction to its words, but also initiates this tendency throughout Mark's Gospel.

6. Jesus also commanded the unclean spirit to come out of the man, with a technical term for driving out unclean spirits, ἐξέρχομαι (vv.25, 26; cf. ἐκβάλλω for δαιμόνιον).

7. The unclean spirit staged the last and hectic battle with its victim before departing from its dwelling place, and this is described with σπαράσσω.

8. To give an audible sign of its departure from the man, the unclean spirit cried with a loud voice (φωνῆσαν φωνῇ μεγάλη), a death cry.

10. The actual exorcism took place, after the visible and audible signals described above, thus the unclean spirit obeyed Jesus by coming out of the man.

11. Besides these motives and their terms mentioned above, there are still some key-words that emerged in our pericope during our investigation, for example: ἀπόλλυμι, οἶδα, ἐπιτιμάω, ἐξέρχομαι (both in a local sense and technican term of exorcism), and φωνέω with its other meanings.

12. Here one observes the centrality of Jesus in the story. Both the demonic encounter with him in words, his double command to the unclean spirit, and his command being fulfilled in the departure of the unclean spirit, affirm this central position.

3. Mk 1:27-28: The Reactions to Jesus' Activity

In this third section, we shall examine the people's response to Jesus' activity. First of all, we shall find out how those in the synagogue are moved by this; and finally how those outside the synagogue heard it. What was the consequence of these reactions? We shall also try to discover other themes of our pericope.

3.1 *Mk 1:27: People react to Jesus' Teaching and Exorcism*

This very verse has an important role, in fact, a most important role to play in the whole pericope. It is a uniting factor between the preceding units. The exorcism of the foregoing verses set the stage for a heightened response of the people in the synagogue. Not only that the narrator had earlier indicated the reaction of the bystanders, but here the characters acted it out. Indeed, this is the third and last direct discourse in our pericope: we have heard from the unclean spirit (through the man) and Jesus himself, now we shall listen to the people who were present.

In our text the motif of wonder comes up again (cf. v.22), in other words «the pericope is thus framed by the language of wonder which emphasises the motif».[282] We shall now examine the type of feeling the people in the synagogue had, and how they expressed it.

3.1.1 The People were amazed

The narrator had earlier described the reaction of the people at Jesus' teaching with the verb ἐκπλήσσειν (v.22); but here after the experience of the exorcism, he still described their reaction with another verb θαμβεῖσθαι[283]. This is a very strong verb, in classical Greek it is chiefly

---

[282] T. DWYER, *Motif of Wonder*, 92.

[283] These are among the verbs often used to describe the crowd's or people's response to Jesus' teaching, and miracles (exorcisms and healings inclusive), which we observed in the analysis of v.22. Cf. J.R. EDWARDS, «Authority of Jesus, 222, n.22; R.T. FRANCE, «Teaching of Jesus», 106; R. PESCH, «Eine neue Lehre», 253, n.58; E. SCHWEIZER, «Die theologische Leistung», 340, n.8. J. GNILKA, *Markus* I, 82, observes

found in poetry, and occasionally in the LXX[284]. This verb is generally defined as «to be astounded», «to be astonished», «to be amazed»[285], or «to strike», «to be struck»[286], and occurs most commonly in the transitive or passive[287]. The verb, θαμβεῖσθαι has also a noun θάμβος, and a compound counterpart, ἐκθαμβεῖσθαι which is intensive; and all «refer to the absolute terror pressed upon a person in the context of divine revelation. It indicates a sudden bewilderment and total shock»[288]. In other words, «it denotes emotions between astonishment and fear as these are evoked by things seen»[289]. Some see in the people's reaction of amazement, astonishment or fear as «a stereotyped closing motif in the miracle stories»[290]. In other words, «amazement» is a technical term for describing the crowd's response in the miracle style[291].

It is observed that this verb and its group appear only in Mark and Luke in the NT: θαμβεῖσθαι occurs 3x only in Mk (1:27; 10:24, 32); ἐκθαμβεῖσθαι, 4x also only in Mk (9:15; 14:33; 16:5, 6); while θάμβος occurred 3x only in Lukan writings (Lk 4:36; 5:9; Acts 3:10). Thus, the usage in Mark has an important role in determining the meaning of this verb.

In Markan usage, θαμβεῖσθαι appears, apart from our text, in the context of the «rich man» who met Jesus, and asked for what it requires for one to inherit eternal life (cf. 10:17). The saddening departure of the

---

that this is the only place in the NT where it occurs in a miracle story. Cf. T. DWYER, *The Motif of Wonder*, 97, n.22.

[284] C.S. MANN, *Mark*, 214; V. TAYLOR, *Mark*, 175; H.B. SWETE, *Mark*, 21.

[285] Cf. T. DWYER, *The Motif of Wonder*, 95; *BAGD*, 350; V. TAYLOR, *Mark*, 175; G. BERTRAM, «θαμβέω», 4; R.G. BRATCHER – E.A. NIDA, *Translator's Handbook*, 53.

[286] W. GRIMM, «θαμβέω», 128; G. BERTRAM, «θαμβέω», 4.

[287] Cf. T. DWYER, *The Motif of Wonder*, 95; W. GRIMM, «θαμβέω», 128; *BAGD*, 350; V. TAYLOR, *Mark*, 175; G. BERTRAM, «θαμβέω», 4.

[288] W. GRIMM, «θαμβέω», 128.

[289] G. BERTRAM, «θαμβέω», 4.

[290] Cf. T. DWYER, *Motif of Wonder*, 96, n.18; G.H. TWELFTREE, *Jesus the Exorcist*, 59; G. THEISSEN, *The Miracle Stories*, 70; R. PESCH, *Markusevangelium* I, 124; C.K. BARRETT, *The Holy Spirit*, 57; E. KLOSTERMANN, *Markusevangelium*, 17 (sees v.27 as a stylistic expression of amazement of the people); G. BERTRAM, «θαμβέω», 6, notes that «the term also serves, as customarily in ancient miracle stories, to indicate the accreditation of the miracle by the spectators». Cf. R. PESCH, «Eine neue Lehre», 260; «Ein Tag», 122.

[291] Cf. H. VAN DER LOOS, *The Miracles*, 382.

man provoked Jesus' hard saying on the rich; and this caused the disciples' amazement (v.24). Jesus' repetition of this hard saying aroused once more «an exceedingly astonishment» (περισσῶς ἐξεπλήσσοντο, v.26) on the part of the disciples[292]. The next is Jesus on his way to Jerusalem (cf. 10:32); his person, destiny and the desire to fulfil the latter, caused amazement and fear on the disciples and those following him. The examination of the contexts of the occurrence of the intensive verb, ἐκθαμβεῖσθαι, reveals clearly the strong mixture of amazement and fear or terror in its meaning. After the Transfiguration (9:15), at the garden of Gethsemane (14:33), or at the women's visit to the empty tomb (16:5,6), all show that «the terror of man is rather a typical element in a revelation or epiphany. The use of θαμβεῖσθαι is thus a sign that for the author the account relates to a theophany»[293].

In our text, v.27, the elements of amazement and fear or terror are also not very much lacking, especially if those present in the synagogue have had the experience of Jesus' authoritative teaching (v.22) and were astonished, now with the expulsion of an unclean spirit from a man, this amazement is heightened[294]. Thus, some scholars see θαμβεῖσθαι as connoting here amazement and dread or alarm (Erschrecken und Staunen)[295], or even a frightening or shocking amazement (erschreckendes Staunen)[296]. But Grimm stated, «the reaction of the bystanders to an exorcism is described in Mk 1:27 par. Lk 4:36 with θαμβέω/θάμβος: Fear in the presence of a theophany is intended, as is indicated by the flashing and bewildered knowledge of the "holy God" (Mk 1:24) and of his unique authority (v.27)»[297]. On my own part, as indicated above, I

---

[292] Here we meet again these two wonder vocabularies (ἐκπλήσσειν, cf. 1:22; 10:26; and θαμβεῖσθαι, cf. 1:27; 10:24), though they interchanged their positions. R.H. GUNDRY, Mark, 77, sees both as synonyms. Cf. W. HENDRIKSEN, Mark, 67. Thus, Jesus' divine and authoritative teaching provokes amazement and even preoccupation.

[293] G. BERTRAM, «θαμβέω», 6; Cf. W. GRIMM,«θαμβέω», 129.

[294] Cf. K. STOCK, «Die Machttaten Jesu», 200.

[295] G.R. OSBORNE, «Structure and Christology», 153; Cf. J. GNILKA, Markus I, 80; R. PESCH, Markusevangelium I, 124; L. SCHENKE, Die Wundererzählungen, 101; W.L. LANE, Mark, 76; H.B. SWETE, Mark, 21.

[296] Cf. R. PESCH, Eine neue Lehre, 260; Ein Tag, 122; E. LOHMEYER, Markus, 38.

[297] W. GRIMM, «θαμβέω», 129. In the German original of this translation, we have: «... Damit ist ein Erschrecken vor einer Theophanie gemeint,...» (italics is mine).

would say that there is an element of fear in this amazement, or if you like a «frightening amazement».

But if one would ask, what is the object of this amazement? To this, it is not very easy to find a consensus among the scholars, especially in the subtle differences of their opinions. On the one hand, some say that the people's amazement refers to «the "authority" (*exousia*) that Jesus demonstrated»[298], Jesus' teaching[299], or Jesus' authoritative teaching[300]; while some say it refers to exorcism[301] or Jesus' authoritative healing/exorcism[302]. On the other hand, some hold that it refers to both Jesus' authoritative teaching and exorcism[303]; or Jesus' authority in word and deeds[304]. However, I would answer in two ways: (1) as καί which precedes ἐθαμβήθησαν is linking it to the exorcism in v.26, one would be tempted to say that v.27a («and they were all amazed») concerns exorcism alone; (2) but when one considers the result of the discussion that followed, which calls attention to two major themes in the pericope (teaching: v.27c, cf. vv.21-22; exorcism: v.27de, cf. vv.23-26), and the heightened emphasis on ἐξουσία (authority), then one would be able to make a balanced conclusion. And this is that the divinely authority which Jesus exercised in teaching and at same time concretized in exorcism provoked the people's deeped amazement. So it is neither teaching alone, nor exorcism alone, rather both are responsible for the people's reaction.

The explicit subject of θαμβεῖσθαι is ἅπαντες («all», «everyone»), even though it is not so specific, but it is presumed to be all those in the synagogue. Dwyer notes that «this is the only place in Mark where a form

---

[298] S.H.T. PAGE, *Powers of Evil*, 145.

[299] Cf. C.S. MANN, *Mark*, 214; A.M. AMBROZIC, «New Teaching», 130.

[300] Cf. T. DWYER, *The Motif of Wonder*, 95, 97; W. GRIMM, «θαμβέω», 129; R.T. FRANCE, «Teaching of Jesus», 106.

[301] Cf. R.H. GUNDRY, *Mark*, 77.

[302] Cf. M.D. HOOKER, *St. Mark*, 65; R.A. GUELICH, *Mark*, 58; D. LÜHRMANN, *Markusevangelium*, 51 (linked to the authority of Jesus' teaching); V. TAYLOR, *Mark*, 176 («it is occasioned also by the teaching of Jesus»).

[303] This refers to all that had taken place in the synagogue: the teaching and the demon-expulsion (exorcism). Cf. J.C. OKOYE, «Mark 1:21-28», 240-241; W. HENDRIKSEN, *Mark*, 67; K. TAGAWA, *Miracles et Évangile*, 89; G. BERTRAM, «θαμβέω», 6; E.P. GOULD, *Mark*, 24.

[304] Cf. W.L. LANE, *Mark*, 76; H. VAN DER LOOS, *The Miracles*, 382; E. KLOSTERMANN, *Markusevangelium*, 17.

of ἅπας is used with amazement»[305]. Gundry attests that «"all" emphasizes the universality of their amazement and thereby the impressiveness of the exorcism»[306]. In vv.21-22 we observed that it was characteristic of Mark to use indefinite third person plural, and he «usually attributes amazement to people who are not further specified (third person plural)»[307], but here it is different especially as it has ἅπαντες as the subject. So all the people in the synagogue, who observed all that happened were utterly amazed.

This amazement gave rise to questioning each other, and the narrator introduced it with this clause: ὥστε συζητεῖν πρὸς ἑαυτούς. Dwyer notes that this is the only place in Mark or the New Testament where a clause introduced by ὥστε follows a reaction of wonder[308]. Συζητεῖν occurs only 10x in the NT: 6x in Mk without any parallels (1:27; 8:11; 9:10,14,16; 12:28), and the rest 4x in the Lukan writings (Lk 22:23; 24:15; Acts 6:9; 9:29). The consecutive particle ὥστε plus the infinitive of the verb, συζητεῖν, expresses result here, and elsewhere in Mark's Gospel[309]. The meaning of this verb could be «to discuss», «to dispute» or «to debate»[310]. It can also mean «to reflect» or «to meditate»[311]. Here the verb is used absolutely.

---

[305] T. DWYER, *Motif of Wonder*, 95. Otherwise it is often πᾶς, cf. 2:12; 5:20; 6:50; 9:15; 11:18. In fact, ἅπας is not common with Mark, it occurs there only 3x (Mt 3x; Lk 17x; Jn 1x): 1:27; 8:25; 11:32; but is very common in Lk-Acts. Cf. V. TAYLOR, *Mark*, 176. In Attic, there is a distinction that ἅπας follows consonants, while πᾶς follows vowels, though this is not consistent in the NT. Cf. *BDF* #275; *BAGD*, 81.

[306] R.H. GUNDRY, *Mark*, 77; Cf. W. GRUNDMANN, *Markus*, 43 (*allgemeines* [ἅπαντες] *erregtes Staunen*).

[307] G. THEISSEN, *The Miracle Stories*, 69. But Matthew almost always gives a specific subject: men (8:27; cf. Mk 4:41), disciples (21:20), the crowds (9:8; cf. Mk 2:12; Mt 9:33; 12:23; 15:31; cf. Mk 7:37). While Luke nominalises «fear» and «trembling», makes them the grammatical subject, so that it appears as though numinous states were taking hold of people, thus Lk recasts the sentence in the form: καὶ ἐγένετο θάμβος ἐπὶ πάντας (4:36; cf. καὶ ἐθαμβήθησαν Mk 1:27). Cf. G. THEISSEN, *ibid.*, 69-70; K. TAGAWA, *Miracles et Évangile*, 96.

[308] T. DWYER, *Motif of Wonder*, 95.

[309] These can be seen thus: Mk 1:27,45; 2:2,12; 3:10,20; 4:1,32,37; 9:26; 15:5. Cf. S. KUTHIRAKKATTEL, *The Beginning*, 123, n.30; P. GUILLEMETTE, «Un enseignement nouveau», 232; R. PESCH, «Eine neue Lehre», 254; V. TAYLOR, *Mark*, 176; R.G. BRATCHER – E.A. NIDA, *Translator's Handbook*, 53.

[310] E. LARSSON, «συζητέω», 284; *BAGD*, 775; J. SCHNEIDER, «συζητέω», 747; V. TAYLOR, *Mark*, 176; R.G. BRATCHER – E.A. NIDA, *Translator's Handbook*, 53.

[311] Cf. E. LARSSON, «συζητέω», 284; *BAGD*, 775.

In Markan usage, the verb means: (i) «to discuss» or «to question» in v.27, and 9:10; (ii) while «to dispute» or «to debate» is seen in 8:11; 9:14,16; 12:28. «As Markan usage demonstrates, a group is always implied, so that the sense is that of an exchange (if not conflict) of opinions»[312]. This word is predominantly Markan, and as Guelich observes «the motif of argument or intense discussion (συζητεῖν) seems rather characteristic of Mark»[313]. In fact, there are also some examples were Jesus' action led to a discussion among those present, like, 2:12; 4:41; 6:2-3; 7:37. So, the «infinitive of result» construction will then read: «so as to question or discuss».

The subject of this verb or verbal construction which is supposed to be in accusative case, is under the prepositional influence, πρὸς ἑαυτούς[314]. Some textual witnesses would prefer the use of αὐτούς to ἑαυτούς[315], all the same, whichever use will not change the meaning in the text. Thus πρὸς ἑαυτούς would mean then «among themselves». So the people's aweful amazement caused them to discuss or question among themselves what this mysterious event before them meant. This narrative description of the reaction of the people resulted in direct discourse which x-rayed their minds.

3.1.2 A New Teaching with Authority

Once more λέγειν introduces us into the last direct discourse of our pericope. This direct discourse here with the preceding clause after the people's amazement, is what scholars call *Chorschluß* which also results to *Acclamation*. Here we may not meet the classical Acclamation, but following Theissen's statement, «we use the term "acclamation" for all linguistic comments on miracles, whatever particular nuance may be predominant,....»[316]. In our text, Pesch maintains that the *Chorschluß* is

---

[312] R.G. BRATCHER – E.A. NIDA, *Translator's Handbook*, 53.

[313] R.A. GUELICH, *Mark*, 58. In Lk 4:36, instead of συζητεῖν he used a normal verb of talking to each other: συλλαλέω, (cf. Mk 9:4).

[314] Luke used πρὸς ἀλλήλους instead of Mk's πρὸς ἑαυτούς. Mark's preference for this prepositional construction can be shown below: Cf. S. KUTHIRAKKATTEL, *The Beginning*, 123, n.32.

	Mt	Mk	Lk	Jn
πρὸς ἑαυτούς	0	7	2	2
πρὸς ἀλλήλους	0	4	8	4

[315] Cf. V. TAYLOR, *Mark*, 176.

[316] G. THEISSEN, *Miracle Stories*, 71. This particular nuance could be joy, praise,

not «acclamation» (cf. e.g. Mk 2:12; 7:37) but rather a «question» (cf. 4:41)[317], in other words the «acclamation» was changed[318].

This question opens the direct discourse thus: τί ἐστιν τοῦτο. This interrogative form of «What is this?» which Swete described as «incoherent and excited remarks of the crowd in their natural roughness»[319], demonstrates actually their amazement, that is, of what happened (both Jesus' teaching and exorcism)[320], especially the exorcism[321]. But some scholars feel it should rather read, τίς οὗτός ἐστιν (Who is this?)[322]. The basis of their argument rests strongly on the similarly constructed narrative in Mk 4:35-41[323]. Surely they have verbal similarities, as we have pointed out, but they cannot be directed to the same objective. So

thanksgiving, confession, etc. But pointing out the difference between acclamation and wonder, he maintains that «in acclamation there is always a verbal comment on the miracle or the miracle-worker, which may vary considerably».

[317] Cf. R. PESCH, *Markusevangelium* I, 124. T. KLAUSER states: «By acclamation are meant the cheers, often rhythmically phrased and uttered in chorus, with which a crowd expresses applause, praise and congratulation or rebuke, execration and demand». «Akklamation», 216-233, esp. 216; Cf. G. THEISSEN, *Miracle Stories*, 71. However, T. DWYER, observed in our text, as remarked by Pesch, that «Mark uses also a form of λέγω following amazement in 2:12 (a doxology), 4:41 (a question), 6:2 (a question), 7:37 (an acclamation) and 10:26 (a question). Thus there is a Markan pattern of amazement leading to a question or statement pointing to Jesus' identity». *Motif of Wonder*, 95.

[318] R. PESCH, «Eine neue Lehre», 260; ID., «Ein Tag», 122; D.-A. KOCH, *Die Bedeutung*, 45.

[319] H.B. SWETE, *Mark*, 21.

[320] Cf. W. HENDRIKSEN, *Mark*, 67.

[321] Cf. P. GUILLEMETTE, «Un enseignement nouveau», 242.

[322] Cf. R.H. GUNDRY, *Mark*, 85; R.A. GUELICH, *Mark*, 58; L. SCHENKE, *Die Wundererzählungen*, 98; K. KERTELGE, *Die Wunder Jesu*, 51; R. PESCH, *Markusevangelium* I, 118, 124; ID., «Ein Tag», 118, 123-124; ID., «Eine neue Lehre», 254, 272-274.

[323] We have already made many references to this passage, now let us see some striking verbal affinities or parallels between Mk 1:21-28 and 4:35-41, as follows: (i) ἀπολέσαι (1:24) // ἀπολλύμεθα (4:38); (ii) ἐπετίμησεν (1:25) // ἐπετίμησεν (4:39); (iii) φιμώθητι (1:25) // πεφίμωσο (4:39); (iv) τί ἐστιν τοῦτο (1:27) // τίς ἄρα οὗτός ἐστιν (4:41); (v) ὑπακούουσιν (1:27) // ὑπακούει (4:41). Cf. E. BIANCHI, «Esci da Costui», 118; P. GUILLEMETTE, «Un enseignement nouveau», 231, n.38; J. BRIÈRE, «Le cri et le secret», 38-39. J.M. ROBINSON, *The Problem of History*, 88, traces the language of exorcism in this Markan pericope (4:35-41).

«there it will be a question of Jesus' identity; here it is a question of teaching»[324].

To the question of whether reactions of wonder in Mark, especially here, imply negative connotations or insufficient understanding on the part of those involved, scholars give diverse opinions. Lohmeyer says that the effect of the *Chorschluß* «is not confessing and belief, but rather dull frightening amazement and questioning»[325]. While Chilton sees the reaction in 1:27 as «no guarantee that one has understood correctly. It is a necessary, but in itself insufficient, response»[326]. Also Ambrozic opines that amazement at Jesus' words and works is an imperfect response, though positive to a degree, allies with lack of understanding[327]. Dwyer agrees that the amazement in 1:27 «*may* be the first step towards either faith or stumbling»[328].

I would respond to this question by comparing v.27c with v.24c: τί ἐστιν τοῦτο; («What is this?») // οἶδα σε τίς εἶ... («I know who you are,...»). What Pesch[329] was looking for in Mk 4:41 is here in 1:24c, that is, between «Who» and «What» or between the question about Jesus' identity and the happenings in the synagogue. From the above parallels, one can see that «on being confronted by Jesus, the demons at once acknowledge his Messiahship, whereas the human beings who witness his words and works are moved only to amazement or to surprised questionings among themselves»[330]. And «this contrast between the knowledge of the demons and the ignorance of human beings is maintained until the occasion of Peter's confession at Caesarea Philippi (8:29)»[331]. So I would suggest that here it is a matter of ignorance or lack of understanding[332].

---

[324] R.H. GUNDRY, *Mark*, 77. For the criticism on Pesch for insisting on the change of the question from «What is this?» to «Who is this?» thereby changing the object of the people's amazement from Jesus' authoritative teaching and exorcism to Jesus' identity, see R.H. GUNDRY, *Mark*, 85.

[325] E. LOHMEYER, *Markus*, 38.

[326] B.D. CHILTON, «Exorcism and History», 267, n.18.

[327] Cf. A.M. AMBROZIC, «New Teaching», 130-131.

[328] T. DWYER, *Motif of Wonder*, 98; Cf. C.E.B. CRANFIELD, *Mark*, 73.

[329] R. PESCH, *Markusevangelium*, 118; 124; ID. «Ein Tag», 118; 123-124; ID., «Eine neue Lehre», 254; 272-274.

[330] T.A. BURKILL, *Mysterious Revelation*, 66.

[331] T.A. BURKILL, *Mysterious Revelation*, 67.

[332] With regard to the identity of Jesus, those in the synagogue do not have the information of 1:1, 9-11 about him.

However, the people's question among themselves is an initial and spontaneous reaction to God's marvels, which they have never experienced before. This questioning of the people is, indeed, the first time human characters question about Jesus' activity or identity (cf. the unclean spirit, v.24).

Now comes up the first reason for the people's amazement: διδαχὴ καινὴ κατ' ἐξουσίαν. The punctuation of this verse is really a bit problematic. The phrase κατ' ἐξουσίαν («according to or with authority») may be joined either to διδαχὴ καινή («new teaching») or to ἐπιτάσσει («he commands»). I have dealt with this problem in the textual criticism, however, I only wanted to highlight it here before going on. Most scholars favour the first construction, that is, as it stands in our text (διδαχὴ καινὴ + κατ' ἐξουσίαν)[333], especially as it recalls διδαχή and ἐξουσία in v.22[334]. The next task is, what does «a new teaching with authority» mean in our context. Since we had earlier discussed «teaching» and «authority», we shall now ask ourselves what καινός means.

The two words generally used for «new» in the NT are νέος and καινός. In classical Greek, the basic meaning of καινός is «new, fresh, newly-made, newly-invented, novel»[335]. But in the NT, it means something «unused», or «not yet used»[336], or «something not previously present, unknown, strange»[337], or «what is old and become obsolete and should be replaced by what is new»[338]. While νέος signifies «what was not there before», «what has only just arisen or appeared» or «young»[339]. The

---

[333] The mention of some of those who favour this construction here is not exhaustive: Cf. R.J. DILLON, «As One Having Authority», 93, n.3; R.H. GUNDRY, Mark, 77, 85; M.D. HOOKER, St Mark, 65; D. DAUBE, New Testament, 212-216; E. GOULD, Mark, 24.

[334] R.H. GUNDRY, Mark, 77, observes that «the repetition of "teaching" and "authority" (cf. vv.21-22) completes the framing of the exorcism so as to make it support Jesus' authority as a teacher». Likewise the διδαχη here (as in v.22) is a teaching activity. Cf. L. WILLIAMSON, Mark, 51.

[335] Cf. LIDDELL – SCOTT – JONES, A Greek-English Lexicon, 858; R.A. HARRISVILLE, «The Concept of Newness», 69; BAGD, 394; J. BEHM, «καινός», 447.

[336] Cf. J. BAUMGARTEN, «καινός», 229; BAGD, 394; J. BEHM, «καινός», 448.

[337] Cf. S. KUTHIRAKKATTEL, The Beginning, 139; BAGD, 394; LIDDELL - SCOTT - JONES, A Greek-English Lexicon, 858.; R.A. HARRISVILLE, «The Concept of Newness», 69.

[338] BAGD, 394; cf. S. KUTHIRAKKATTEL, The Beginning, 139.

[339] G. SCHNEIDER, «νέος», 462; BAGD, 536; J. BEHM, «καινός», 447; R.A.

adjective νέος is new in time or origin, while καινός is new in nature, different from the usual, impressive, better than the old, superior in value or attraction[340]. So, καινός is new in quality, while νέος is new in time[341]. However, Harrisville notes that this distinction is not always observed in the NT, and concludes that both terms are synonymous: both have qualitative and temporal newness[342]. This not withstanding, theologically καινός is «the epitome of the wholly different and miraculous thing which is brought by the time of salvation», and especially «the reality of salvation which we know already in Christ»[343].

In Mark's Gospel καινός appears 5x (4x), while in Mt 5x; Lk 5x; Jn 2x. Apart from our text (1:27), it occurs again in 2:21,22; 14:(24),25. From the above data, there are only two other contexts in which this adjective occurs. In Mk 2:21f, in the context of «new» garment, it is in the sense of *unused* or *not yet used*[344]; while in Mk 14:25 and par., it appears in the context of the new wine of the eschatological banquet. But in our pericope, καινός made its first appearance in Mark's Gospel, in the context of the amazement of the people, which was aroused by Jesus' teaching and the exorcizing of the unclean spirit. The «new teaching» of Jesus does not refer to the presentation of his personal views in contrast to rabbinic tradition, or to mean strange doctrine[345]. But the element of

---

HARRISVILLE, «The Concept of Newness», 70.

[340] Cf. J. BEHM, «καινός», 447; *BAGD*, 394.

[341] Cf. R.H. GUNDRY, *Mark*, 77-78; S. KUTHIRAKKATTEL, *The Beginning*, 139, n.104; V. TAYLOR, *Mark*, 176; R.A. HARRISVILLE, «The Concept of Newness», 70, 71, 72. P. LAMARCHE, *Evangile de Marc*, 79, confirms that καινός refers not to a temporal, recent newness (cf. νέος), but a qualitative newness.

[342] R.A. HARRISVILLE, «The Concept of Newness», 69-79, esp 72; BRATCHER-NIDA, *Translator's Handbook*, 53. Harrisville also added that in the NT there are four distinctive features of the concept of newness: the element of contrast, continuity, dynamic and finality. Cf. *ibid.*,73-77, esp. 77.

[343] J. BEHM, «καινός», 449; Cf. S. KUTHIRAKKATTEL, *The Beginning*, 139; R.H. STEIN, «Marcan Seam», 91, n.73.

[344] Cf. J. BAUMGARTEN, «καινός», 229; *BAGD*, 394; J. BEHM, «καινός», 448. The other NT texts with the same sense, cf. Mt 9:17; Lk 5:36,38; also Mt 27:60; Jn 19:41.

[345] Cf. R.A. HARRISVILLE, «The Concept of Newness», 77. Some scholars see the newness of Jesus' teaching as reflecting the Jewish belief that the messianic age will bring new eschatological teaching of the Law. Cf. R.H. STEIN, *The Proper Methodology*, 137-138; E. LOHMEYER, *Markus*, 38; W. GRUNDMANN, *Markus*, 43. But R.H. GUNDRY, *Mark*, 85, to this replied, «Mark's accent rests solely on authority as such; and he can hardly expect his Gentile audience to fill in Jewish legal content».

newness in Jesus' teaching lies in his ἐξουσία (his divine authority)[346]. So the «new teaching» could then be interpreted as Jesus' authority in word and deed (teaching and exorcism)[347] or that Jesus' authoritative teaching is demonstrated by act or exorcism[348]. Thus, «the ἐξουσία gives to his work an essential newness in contrast to rabbinic teaching»[349], which is «that something wholly new at work in the person and ministry of Jesus»[350].

The importance of authority in Jesus' words and works makes this element of «newness», strange, remarkable and impressive, and places Jesus in a different and special position in contrast with his contemporaries. Thus the cause of the people's wonder or amazement is not only the freshness and vigour of the teaching, or the extraordinary way of effecting exorcism, but also the note of divine authority inherent in Jesus, who teaches, heals, and exorcizes and acts on behalf of God. Hence, in the final analysis, Jesus' ἐξουσία in teaching and exorcism causes the wonder, amazement, fear and the discussion on the newness of his teaching[351].

---

[346] Cf. S. LÉGASSE, L'Évangile de Marc, 131; R.H. GUNDRY, Mark, 77, 85; K. SCHOLTISSEK, Vollmacht Jesu, 122, 123-124; R.T. FRANCE, «Teaching of Jesus», 106; L. SCHENKE, Wundererzählungen, 105; R.A. HARRISVILLE, «The Concept of Newness», 77.

[347] Cf. G.R. OSBORNE, «Structure and Christology», 153; J.R. EDWARDS, «The Authority of Jesus», 222; R.A. GUELICH, Mark, 59; K. KERTELGE, Die Wunder Jesu, 56; K. TAGAWA, Miracles et Évangile, 89; E.P. GOULD, Mark, 24.

[348] Cf. R.A. GUELICH, Mark, 59; D. LÜHRMANN, Markusevangelium, 51; K. KERTELGE, Die Wunder Jesu, 57, 59; H.B. SWETE, Mark, 21. P.J. ACHTEMEIER, «He taught them», 478, states that «the power inherent in Jesus' teaching is precisely the power that enable him to overcome demonic forces». Cf. A.M. AMBROZIC, «New Teaching», 141; R.H. STEIN, «Marcan Seam», 90-91.

[349] R.A. HARRISVILLE, «The Concept of Newness», 77. The relation between 1:22, διδαχῇ ... ὡς ἐξουσίαν ἔχων and 1:27, διδαχὴ καινὴ κατ'ἐξουσίαν, demonstrates that the «newness» lies in this authority which distinguishes Jesus from the scribes.

[350] C.S. MANN, Mark, 214.

[351] R. PESCH, «Eine neue Lehre», 275, summarized the «newness» of Jesus' authoritative teaching thus: «The teaching is therefore new because it is effected in authority (power), because Jesus works in the Spirit, because he teaches not like the Scribes, but above all, because he is the "Son of God" (1:11; 3:11; 5:7; 9:7: hear him). Jesus' teaching is therefore new also, because it touches (moves) people again, frees them from the demons, sins, false burdens (7:1-16). His teaching is therefore new, because it is being constantly put into action» (translation is mine). Cf. M.Y.-H. LEE, Autorität, 100, n.8.

3.1.3 The Unclean Spirits obey Him

We meet the second reason for the amazement of the people: «he commands even the unclean spirits, and they obey him». Here an ascensive καί («even»)[352] introduces these two co-ordinate clauses, thereby marking the climax of the astonishment of the people (not only teaching but also exorcism). The object of the first clause, τοῖς πνεύμασι τοῖς ἀκαθάρτοις...(unclean spirits) is placed forward for the sake of emphasis (both the substantive and the adjective). These two paired clauses (v.27de) refer us to the event of vv.25 and 26: where Jesus with a simple but authoritative command effected an exorcism in the synagogue. Now let us examine more closely the rest of this verse.

The important actions in these two clauses are ἐπιτάσσειν and ὑπακούειν, and it is our task to find out the meaning in the text. The verb ἐπιτάσσειν, which means «to command» or «to order»[353], occurs only 10x in the NT, 4x each in Mk and Lk, and 1x each in Acts and Philemon. In the NT, this verb appears in the contexts of (a) one having authority over a people - Jesus on his disciples (Mk 6:39), king Herod (Mk 6:27), high priest Ananias (Acts 23:2), or a master (Lk 14:22); (b) Jesus' forcible and powerful command to demons (Mk 1:27 par. Lk 4:36; Mk 9:25; Lk 8:31) or to demonic cosmic powers (wind and sea: Lk 8:25)[354]; (c) and Paul's encouraging command to a believer. In the Gospels, except in Mk 6:27 (king Herod) and Lk 14:22 (a master), the main subject of this verb ἐπιτάσσειν is always Jesus (6x out of the 8x in Mk and Lk).

In Mark's Gospel, it is clear that among the 4x occurrences, 2x (1:27; 9:25) refer to the unclean spirits. The other 2x refer to king Herod's order to the soldier to behead John the Baptist in prison; and Jesus' command to his disciples to bid the people (5,000) to sit down for their miraculous feeding. It is observable that the command to the unclean spirits dominated in Mk's Gospel (as seen also in Lk). One can also notice that both in 1:27 and 9:25, ἐπιτάσσειν appeared in direct discourses: the people's discussion among themselves, on the one hand; and Jesus' emphatic direct command to the «dumb and deaf spirit»[355], on the other

---

[352] Cf. R.H. GUNDRY, *Mark*, 78; V. TAYLOR, *Mark*, 176; R.G. BRATCHER – E.A. NIDA, *Translator's Handbook*, 53; H.B. SWETE, *Mark*, 22.

[353] Cf. W. GRIMM, «ἐπιτάσσω», 41; *BAGD*, 302.

[354] Cf. W. GRIMM, «ἐπιτάσσω», 41.

[355] Ἐπιτάσσω indicates the authority of his words (cf. esp. 1:27); and «ἐγώ, "I",

hand. Likewise these two occurrences are in the Present Indicative, unlike the two others (6:27, 39: in Aorist Indicative), thereby making vivid this Jesus act of command. Thus, the discussion in v.27 is based on the episode of v.25, the forceful, powerful and double authoritative command of φιμώθητι καὶ ἔξελθε ἐξ αὐτοῦ («be silent, and come out of him!»), described with a powerful word ἐπιτιμᾶν[356].

This command is not a simple directive as seen in 6:39, but an order given to an unclean spirit that must leave its abode unwillingly: it is an aggressive command that leaves absolutely no freedom of action for the unclean spirit. In fact, it is an exorcistic command. We have seen earlier that for anyone to command, one must be a superior, master, king or high priest, in other words, one must possess authority. So here Jesus' relation with the unclean spirit must be like a master before his servant, or a king before his slave (cf. Mk 6:27; Lk 14:22; Acts 23:2)[357]. Jesus possesses the authority above all these we have mentioned: he acts with a divine authority as the «Holy One of God», and on behalf of God. And as Kee rightly puts it, the authority of Jesus is supremely manifest in the exorcisms[358].

The object of Jesus' command refer to the unclean spirits (τοῖς πνεύμασι τοῖς ἀκαθάρτοις). We meet once more πνεῦμα ἀκάθαρτον, which is the third time in our pericope (cf. vv.23, 26), but here it is in plural. The plural «spirits» generalizes from the one case; if Jesus can expel one he can expel any number[359]. However, the plural in «unclean spirits» refer to v.24 which speaks of the class of the unclean spirits[360]. Thus, it is a characteristic feature in the Gospels, especially in Mk, that Jesus commands unclean spirits, here is the beginning and it did not end

---

highlights the authority of his person in giving a command to come out and sets him in contrast with the failed disciples». R.H. GUNDRY, *Mark*, 491.

[356] W. GRIMM, «ἐπιτάσσω», 41, confirms our stand that ἐπιτιμᾶν is a divine powerful command, by saying with regard to ἐπιτάσσειν «a synonymous verb is ἐπιτιμάω ("reprimand, rebuke", Heb g`r) seen in Mk 1:25, 27; 9:25; Lk 8:24, 25)».

[357] Cf. P. GUILLEMETTE, «Un enseignement nouveau», 238.

[358] H.C. KEE, «Terminology of Mark», 242, states, «it is in the exorcisms that the authority of Jesus is supremely manifest, and it is through the exorcisms that the kingdom can be seen as having drawn near (i. 15). In the exorcisms, the authority of Jesus' word and the authority of his action are united».

[359] Cf. W. HENDRIKSEN, *Mark*, 67.

[360] Cf. P. GUILLEMETTE, «Un enseignement nouveau», 233; R. PESCH, «Eine neue Lehre», 254.

here, but continued until the most extraordinary command to a «dumb and deaf spirit» in 9:25.

What follows in the next clause is the attestation of the people, that the unclean spirits obey him (Jesus). And this refers to the action of the unclean spirit in v.26, where it fulfils the command of Jesus, by departing from the possessed man. The verb ὑπακούειν, which is a compound derived from ἀκούω («to hear»), occurs 21x in the NT particularly in the Epistles, but 5x in the Gospels, especially in the Synoptic Gospels. This verb can mean «to obey»[361], «to follow, be subject to»[362], or literally «to open or answer (the door)»[363]. This word is adequately rendered as «obey», and especially in the Epistles, it relates to persons such as «children, slaves or wives who stand in a divinely willed relation of subordination (Eph 6:1,5; Col 3:20,22; 1 Pt 3:6)»[364]. But in the Synoptic Gospels, it describes the relation of the demons or unclean spirits (Mk 1:27) or natural elements (Mk 4:41 par. Mt 8:27; Lk 8:25) to Jesus' authoritative command. Only in Lk 17:6 does it refer to the faith of the disciples.

It is remarkable that, apart from the obedience of the natural elements (wind and sea) in 4:41, ὑπακούειν occurs only here with regard to the unclean spirits, both in Mk's and other Gospels. The parallel text in Lk 4:36 has ἐξέρχονται («they come out»), thereby referring directly to Lk 4:35 (cf. Mk 1:26). But here Mk used ὑπακούειν («they obey»), instead of ἐξέρχεσθαι, thereby using a corresponding word of «to command» and «to obey»[365]. Mark has no doubt that the unclean spirits must obey Jesus especially, as he has demonstrated his unchallenged authority in the text (cf. vv.25, 26), thus Jesus' divine authoritative command subjects, and forces the unclean spirits to obey. And the unclean spirits know this because their spokeman had already attested Jesus' superiority and his mission towards them (1:24b). They have no choice but to bow to the divine rule, which Jesus has come to inaugurate.

---

[361] Cf. G. SCHNEIDER, «ὑπακούω», 394; *BAGD*, 837; G. KITTEL, «ὑπακούω», 223.

[362] *BAGD*, 837.

[363] Cf. G. SCHNEIDER, «ὑπακούω», 394; *BAGD*, 837; G. KITTEL, «ὑπακούω», 223. The only case about this literal sense is in Acts 12:13, where Rhoda came «to answer» or open the door for Peter who was delivered from prison by an angel of the Lord.

[364] G. KITTEL, «ὑπακούω», 223.

[365] Here in Mk 1:27de is the only place in Mk's Gospel where «to command» and «to obey», are paired together; we also observe such in Lk 8:25 (with regard to wind and sea), all this stress the personal authority of Jesus. Cf. R.H. GUNDRY, *Mark*, 78.

Among the 5x occurrences of ὑπακούειν in the Gospels (only Synoptics), except in Lk 17:6 where the object of the verb is ὑμῖν (the apostles), all the 4 others (Mk 1:27; 4:41; Mt 8:27; Lk 8:25) are αὐτῷ, and all refer to Jesus alone. So in Mk, it is clear that the 2x refer to Jesus alone, thereby confirming that Jesus is the only one to be obeyed. And he receives this obedience because he is the Son of God.

The emphasis made on our text on the relation of Jesus to the unclean spirits, in the realm of «commanding» and «obeying», places Jesus in a superior level. That Jesus commands, and they obey, establishes the fact that Jesus needs only to utter a word, and helplessly these demons yield. Thus the pericope attracts attention to the power of the word of Jesus. Jesus is therefore in a position of authority with regard to the unclean spirit, because he can give it orders (cf. 6:27; Lk 14:22; Acts 23:2). Jesus is, in fact, the master of the unclean spirit through his word of command. Moreover, it is a clear fact, that it is Jesus who is the central figure or character in the text, and not the unclean spirit, nor the possessed man himself[366].

3.1.4 The Relationship between Teaching and Exorcism

Since we mentioned at the beginning of the analysis of this verse, that this verse (v.27) has a uniting character with regard to the pericope, now we want to examine, both from the pericope, and the verse, how this unity is realized. We shall then investigate the relationship between teaching and exorcism in our pericope. It is clear in this pericope (1:21-28) that there exists some connection between teaching and exorcism. As Ambrozic observes «while Matthew sees teaching and miracles as existing side by side, in the hands of Mark they blend into one in such a way that miracles reveal the God-willed significance of Jesus' mission»[367]. This combination of teaching and exorcism in 1:21-28 have been seen by some scholars as *programmatic* with regard to Mark's Gospel (cf. 1:39)[368]. The problem is not the reality of the connection or combination that exists but *how* it is done.

---

[366] Cf. P. GUILLEMETTE, «Un enseignement nouveau», 237-238.

[367] A.M. AMBROZIC, «New Teaching», 139; Cf. K. KERTELGE, *Die Wunder Jesu*, 56; R.H. STEIN, «Marcan Seam», 90.

[368] Cf. J.C. OKOYE, «Mark 1:21-28», 241; K. SCHOLTISSEK, *Vollmacht Jesu*, 122; P. GUILLEMETTE, «Un enseignement nouveau», 243; K. STOCK, *Boten*, 25, 27.

Some NT scholars have the opinion that Mark focused primarily on Jesus as teacher[369] (most of them were writing about Jesus as teacher) and that the miracles are subordinate to Jesus' teaching[370]. They substantiated their view on the basis of Mk 1:21-28 (cf. also Mk 2:1-12) that exorcism was subordinated to teaching[371], by deducing from it that Mark intended to illustrate or demonstrate Jesus' authoritative teaching by means of an exorcism[372]. This verse highlights what is evident in the pericope for some scholars, that teaching and exorcism have both intimate relationship (illumining each other), as well as an equal, distinctive and independent value and function in the mission of Jesus[373]. However, this close combination between these two activities, seen as belonging together, emphasizes the unity of Jesus' words and works[374]. In fact, this uniting force is fundamentally based on his (ἐξουσία) divine authority[375], which is evident both in Jesus' powerful word and deed[376].

---

[369] Cf. P.J. ACHTEMEIER, «He Taught Them», 465-481; W. EGGER, *Frohbotschaft und Lehre*, 159-160, 166; R.P. MEYE, *Jesus and the Twelve*, 46-47.

[370] M.M. JACOBS, «Mark's Jesus», 64.

[371] Cf. R.J. DILLON, «As One Having Authority», 93, n.5; L. WILLIAMSON, *Mark*, 49; P.J. ACHTEMEIER, «He Taught Them», 480; J. BRIÈRE, «Le cri et le secret», 42, 43-44, 46, n.18.

[372] Cf. M.M. JACOBS, «Mark's Jesus», 64; W. WEISS, *Eine neue Lehre*, 125; J. ERNST, *Markus*, 62, 64; L. SCHENKE, *Die Wundererzählungen*, 104-106, 397-398; D.-A. KOCH, *Die Bedeutung*, 52-55; A.M. AMBROZIC, «New Teaching», 139, n.49, 141; R.P. MEYE, *Jesus and the Twelve*, 46; R. PESCH, «Eine neue Lehre», 270, 272; E. SCHWEIZER, «Anmerkung zur Theologie», 97, n.17.

[373] Cf. J.C. OKOYE, «Mark 1:21-28», 240; R.J. DILLON, «As One Having Authority», 93, n.5; K. SCHOLTISSEK, *Vollmacht Jesu*, 122-123; R.A. GUELICH, *Mark*, 59; R.T. FRANCE, «Teaching of Jesus», 110-111; A.M. AMBROZIC, «New Teaching», 140-141; K. KERTELGE, *Die Wunder Jesu*, 56; K. TAGAWA, *Miracles et Évangile*, 87, 88.

[374] Cf. S.H.T. PAGE, *Powers of Evil*, 145; K. SCHOLTISSEK, *Vollmacht Jesu*, 122; ID., «Nachfolge und Autorität», 66; M.D. HOOKER, *St. Mark*, 66; R. KAMPLING, «Dämonismus und Exorzismus», 309; K. STOCK, «Die Machttaten Jesu», 200; J. KALLAS, *Synoptic Miracles*, 77-78.

[375] Cf. K. SCHOLTISSEK, *Vollmacht Jesu*, 123; L. WILLIAMSON, *Mark*, 49. J. DELORME, «Aspects Dotrinaux», 85, states that «one could say that for him the word which teaches and that which casts out the demons are one and the same word, expression of one and the same divine power» (translation is *mine*).

[376] Cf. J.C. OKOYE, «Mark 1:21-28», 240; K. STOCK, «Die Machttaten Jesu», 200; L. WILLIAMSON, *Mark*, 49; W. EGGER, *Frohbotschaft und Lehre*, 149.

I would agree with those who negate the idea of subordination of exorcism to teaching. Scholtissek states: «Teaching and mighty deeds of Jesus were neither in isolation placed side by side nor super-or subordinated to each other. ... Both dimensions of Jesus' deeds are integrated to each other»[377]. Gundry adds «the result of this combination is not subordination of exorcism to teaching, but a coordination in which the two support each other (cf. 2:10-11; 6:2; etc)... Verse 27 simply coordinates the two, and follows the order of vv.21-22 and 23-26 in doing so»[378].

On the other hand, one gains one thing and loses the other: Teaching has the support of (i) receiving much *emphasis* through frequency of didactic terms (vv.21,22 [bis], 27); (ii) it has an *inclusion* of «teaching» (διδάσκειν/διδαχή) and «authority» (ἐξουσία) in vv.22 and 27; and (iii) the *reaction* of the people - ἐκπλήσσειν (astonishment), cf. v.22. While Exorcism on its part gains (a) the visible and *concreteness* of Jesus' action (vv.23-26); (b) it has also an *inclusion* of ἐπιτιμᾶν and ἐπιτάσσειν in vv.25 and 27d; and also (c) the *reaction* of the people - θαμβεῖν (amazement), cf. v.27a. In this way, we can establish once more that these activities of Jesus are combined to serve different functions and to support and illumine each other.

At this juncture, we ask ourselves: did this double synagogue event definitely end in this synagogue, or did it go beyond it; and how did it happen? The answer to this question will be taken up in the next verse.

3.2 *Mk 1:28: Jesus' Fame spreads throughout Galilee*

The last verse (v.27) seemed to be the concluding verse of the pericope, especially with its uniting factor, which we have already indicated. But

---

[377] K. SCHOLTISSEK, *Vollmacht Jesu*, 122 (translation is *mine*). I am not so convinced with the conclusion of Ambrozic, when he says: «The relationship between it (teaching) and the miracles would thus seem to be primarily that of *cause and effect*. While the miracles seem to be the most visible and striking result of the teaching and thus serve the *purpose of illustrating* its comprehensive effectiveness, they are by no means its only or its most important consequence» (*italics* is mine). A.M. AMBROZIC, «New Teaching», 142-143.

[378] R.H. GUNDRY, *Mark*, 74. He went further to show that «the last statements in the story proper — "even the unclean spirits he commands, and they obey him" — form an independent sentence, not a subordinate clause introduced by a characteristically Marcan γάρ, "for" (as we would expect for a subordination of exorcism to teaching)». Moreover Jesus teaches in vv.21-22 before he casts out an unclean spirit in vv.23-26. *Ibid*.

the evangelist went on to introduce this verse (v.28), to highlight the effect of Jesus authoritative word and deed, which news could not be confined to the synagogue or to Capernaum alone, but must go beyond. So this verse also adds to the emphasis on Jesus' authority[379].

This is a simple sentence with an enlargement of the complement, which has merited more attention in this verse. On this detailed ending, Turner describes it as «a redundant expression quite in Mark's style»[380], while Pesch calls it the «hyperbolic conclusion» (der hyperbolische Abschluß)[381]. All this shows and emphasizes how Jesus' reputation or fame spreads throughout Galilee. Now we take up the analysis of the text.

3.2.1 Jesus' Fame spreads

Once more καί connects us to the foregoing event of Jesus' powerful teaching and exorcism in the synagogue. The only verb of the verse ἐξέρχεσθαι[382] (the third time in the pericope) appears, to introduce the strong effect of Jesus' action, and to be connected with ἀκοή is unique[383]. It does not constitute a «second exorcism» but a strong way of describing the «sensational effect»[384] of Jesus' activity, including exorcism that had just taken place. The subject of this verb is ἡ ἀκοὴ αὐτοῦ, and ἀκοή which occurs 24x in the NT, has Mk 3x (Mt 4x; Lk 1x; Jn 1x). The substantive ἀκοή[385] could have (1) an active meaning of the «faculty of hearing», «act of hearing» or «organ of hearing», the «ear»; or (2) of the passive sense, of what is heard: i) «fame», «report», «rumour»[386]; ii)

---

[379] Cf. R.H. GUNDRY, Mark, 78.

[380] C.H. TURNER, «Text of Mark I», 155; cf. V. TAYLOR, Mark, 177; R.G. BRATCHER – E.A. NIDA, Translator's Handbook, 54.

[381] R. PESCH, Markusevangelium I, 125; «Eine neue Lehre», 261.

[382] I.H. MARSHALL, The Gospel of Luke, 194, observes that having used ἐξέρχομαι in Lk 4:36, Luke here uses ἐκπορεύομαι, no doubt for the sake of variety.

[383] Cf. R. PESCH, «Eine neue Lehre», 255. This verb is very frequent in Mk, as we have seen earlier, but only here with ἀκοή.

[384] Cf. G.R. OSBORNE, «Structure and Christology», 153.

[385] Cf. I.H. MARSHALL, The Gospel of Luke, 194, Luke uses ἀκοή, «report», to mean «ear» (7:1), but here he uses ἦχος, which may be either «report» (masc. Heb 12:19) or «sound, noise» (neuter 21:25).

[386] G. SCHNEIDER, «ἀκοή», 53; BAGD, 30-31; V. TAYLOR, Mark, 177; G. KITTEL, «ἀκοή», 221; R.G. BRATCHER – E.A. NIDA, Translator's Handbook, 54; C.E.B. CRANFIELD, Mark, 81; H.B. SWETE, Mark, 22.

«account», «report», «preaching»[387].

In Mk's Gospel, ἀκοή appears only 3x (1:28; 7:35; 13:7). Beside our text, in 7:35 it refers to «ears» in the context of the man whose ears were opened; while in 13:7, it refers to the «rumours» of war, in the context of the last days (eschatology). But in our text, it has to do with «report», «news» or «fame» of Jesus. Thus, this ἀκοή concerning Jesus, which has to do with Jesus' activity in the synagogue (teaching and exorcism)[388], is the subject of «going out» or «spreading». It was not indicated by the narrator *how* and *who* spreads it, but his concern was *when* and *where* it went out. So he used two adverbs εὐθύς (temporal) and πανταχοῦ (local) to modify the verb ἐξέρχεσθαι. This is the third time we meet εὐθύς («immediately») in this short pericope[389]. This shows the immediacy (immediateness), fastness or the speed with which such a demonstration of Jesus' authority spreads[390]. There is no time to spare in disseminating this «good news» beyond its vicinity. The element of speed characterized by εὐθύς which is peculiar to Mk, especially in the first chapter and first half of the Gospel, is also testified here as the report or news about Jesus' actions go round and far.

The spreading of Jesus' fame, as we pointed out above with the temporal and local adverbs (εὐθύς, πανταχοῦ), therefore affects both *time and space*. Thus πανταχοῦ («adverb of place») which appears only 6x (7x) in the NT, and occurs only in 1:28 (cf. Lk 9:6) means «everywhere» or «in all directions»[391]. This therefore introduces us to the local dimension of the spread of Jesus' fame. Here we want to mention it as it modifies the verb, indicating that this report went in all directions («everywhere»), however we shall take it up again as it affects the region where this divine activity is taking place.

---

[387] G. SCHNEIDER, «ἀκοή,», 53; *BAGD*, 31.

[388] I disagree with M. MEISER, *Die Reaktion des Volkes*, 132-133, who holds that the ἀκοή Mk 1,28 does not relate to the miracle (exorcism), but rather to Mk 1,22.27c as divinely authorized preaching person of Jesus (ἀκοή αὐτοῦ). In this case, he negates one of Jesus' double action, by favouring only teaching, instead of teaching and exorcism (cf. vv.22, 23-26, 27c, de).

[389] E.P. GOULD, *Mark*, 24, observes that Luke, in spite of his general verbal resemblance to Mark, omits it in every case.

[390] Cf. G. THEISSEN, *Miracle Stories*, 72; W. HENDRIKSEN, *Mark*, 67; V. TAYLOR, *Mark*, 177; E.P. GOULD, *Mark*, 24.

[391] *BAGD*, 608.

3.2.2 The Region of Galilee

Jesus' actions took place in the synagogue of Capernaum, a city of Galilee. Galilee as a region was very important in Jesus' public ministry. It is the highest and northernmost of the mountain regions of Israel. The region is divided into northern Upper Galilee and southern Lower Galilee. «Since Galilee was geographically distant from Jerusalem, the seat of the Judean palace, temple, archives, and scribes, events occurring there are rarely mentioned in the Hebrew bible...»[392] Thus, since it is relatively isolated from the main arteries of commerce and centres of government, «its role as a kind of *hinterland* was much more important than would appear from the historical sources»[393]. However, because «Galilee was the location for much of the ministry of Jesus, for the military activity of the Jewish historian Josephus, and for the post-70 C.E. Palestinian Judaism, it is mentioned prominently in the NT (especially the Gospels), in the writings of Josephus, and in early rabbinic writings»[394].

Jesus' association with this region was the most significant period in its history. «Almost the entire career of Jesus of Nazareth lay within the borders of this tiny region»[395]. Many of the evangelists focus on different aspects of Jesus' association with this region. For Mark, «Galilee stands in opposition to Jerusalem as the place in which Jesus conducts a successful ministry of healings and exorcisms and where he is to be reunited with his chosen disciples (16:7)»[396]. When one views the relation between Galilee and Jerusalem from the Markan context, this opposition is real. Although the destiny of Jesus (that is, the decision to destroy him) is mentioned as early as 3:6 in the Gospel, as planned or led by the Pharisees (with the Herodians, 3:6, cf. 8:15; 12:13); yet the actual enemies of Jesus, and the executors of this plan in Mark's Gospel, were the Scribes, who accused him of blasphemy that led to his condemnation and death (2:6-7, cf. 14:64). This fact will be demonstrated later, because the initial contrast of the Scribes with Jesus here later on developed into total hostility. And moreover, the evangelist indicated twice that the Scribes came from Jerusalem to oppose Jesus in Galilee (cf. 3:22; 7:1). However, «a certain opposition between Jerusalem and Galilee is already

---

[392] R. FRANKEL, «Galilee, 879.

[393] Y. AHARONI, *The Land of the Bible*, 27.

[394] R. FRANKEL, «Galilee», 879.

[395] K.W. CLARK, «Galilee», 347.

[396] S. FREYNE, «Galilee», 899.

given with the geographical references themselves»[397]. I would not conclude this brief introduction on the region of Galilee without mentioning the importance of the Sea of Galilee[398] in Jesus' Galilean ministry.

Now we take up our text again with the adverb πανταχοῦ, which when it is joined with the following phrase εἰς ὅλην τὴν περίχωρον τῆς Γαλιλαίας, forms a «double statement»[399]. Both statements are describing the spreading of the news within the region. It can also refer to a «double statement: general and special»[400] since πανταχοῦ generalizes it, while the next phrase, εἰς ὅλην...τ. Γαλιλαίας specifies it. When one compares with the parallel text in Lk 4:37, *where* this report went out εἰς πάντα τόπον τῆς περιχώρου («into every place in the surrounding region»), then we can feel the conglomeration of words used to emphasize this spread, the redundancy characteristic of Mark's style. Jesus' fame went out «immediately», and «in all directions». It spreads (εἰς ὅλην...) «into the whole... region», and it is in τὴν περίχωρον which means «the surrounding region» or «region around» or «neighbourhood»[401]. The word περίχωρος appears 9x in NT but only once in Mk (Mt 2x; Lk 5x; Acts 1x), and here (therefore *hapax legomenon*). And this is happening in the region (τῆς Γαλιλαίας), «of Galilee». So the spread of this report did not leave any part missing[402].

But the true interpretation of this phrase εἰς ὅλην τὴν περίχωρον τῆς Γαλιλαίας has not received the consensus of the scholars. This phrase may be understood in three senses: (1) «the region which surrounds

---

[397] B. VAN IERSEL, *Reading Mark*, 22, went further to say that, «the inherent contrasts between Galilee and Jerusalem are considerably reinforced by what the story locates in each».

[398] E.S. MALBON, «Sea of Galilee», 363; states: «The Sea of Galilee is the geographical focal point for the first half of the Gospel of Mark, the center of the Markan Jesus' movement in the space (7:31). By the sea Jesus calls disciples (1:16,19,20) and teaches and heals the crowds (2:13; 3:7; 4:1). Jesus crosses the sea freely (4:35; 5:1,18,21; 6:53,54; 8:10,13) and at one point commands his disciples to cross the sea before him (6:45). Three voyages are dramatically marked by events or conversations of consequence: stilling the storm (4:37ff.), walking on the sea (6:47ff.), conversation about bread (8:14ff.)».

[399] Cf. F. NEIRYNCK, *Duality in Mark*, 94; this refers to «Double Statement: Temporal or Local», but in our own case it is *local*.

[400] Cf. F. NEIRYNCK, *Duality in Mark*, 96; (although he did not include it in this category, but I think that like 1:21, it also belongs here).

[401] *BAGD*, 653.

[402] Cf. R.H. GUNDRY, *Mark*, 78.

Galilee» which indicates a wider area than Galilee; apparently Mt 4:24 understood it thus by writing ὅλην τὴν Συρίαν «all Syria»[403];(2) «all the region of Galilee *around Capernaum*», which designates an area less than the whole of Galilee; some see this corresponding to the parallel text of Lk 4:37[404]; and (3) «the whole surrounding region, that is, Galilee», this is thus taken as an epexegetic genitive[405] or genitive of apposition[406]. The majority of scholars, translations and commentators favour the third interpretation[407].

I share the opinion of those who hold that Jesus' fame spread throughout the whole region of Galilee (the third interpretation), because: firstly, this is the initial stage of Jesus' actions in his public ministry; secondly, Jesus' fame spreading throughout Galilee precedes him, thereby anticipating his going soon throughout Galilee (1:39)[408]; thirdly, Jesus' ministry from the beginning (1:14) up to 3:6 is exclusively restricted to the region of Galilee (contrast this with 3:7-8)[409]; and fourthly, the news could not be held back but swept throughout the «whole region of Galilee» (cf. 1:33-34, 39, 45)[410].

The word, ἡ Γαλιλαια appears 61x in the NT, and among these occurrences Mk has 12x (Mt 16x; Lk 13x; Jn 17x; Acts 3x). Apart from

---

[403] Cf. M.D. HOOKER, *St. Mark*, 66; E. KLOSTERMANN, *Markusevangelium*, 18.

[404] Cf. R.G. BRATCHER – E.A. NIDA, *Translator's Handbook*, 55; C.S. MANN, *Mark*, 214; V. TAYLOR, *Mark*, 177; E.P. GOULD, *Mark*, 24.

[405] Cf. *BAGD*, 653; J. GNILKA, *Markus*, 82; W. LANE, *Mark*, 76, n.123; E. LOHMEYER, *Markus*, 38, n.4; V. TAYLOR, *Mark*, 177; BRATCHER – NIDA, *Translator's Handbook*, 55; C.E.B. CRANFIELD, *Mark*, 81; H.B. SWETE, *Mark*, 22.

[406] R.H. GUNDRY, *Mark*, 85.

[407] Cf. G.R. OSBORNE, «Structure and Christology», 153; K. KERTELGE, *Markusevangelium*, 27; R.H. GUNDRY, *Mark*, 85; S. KUTHIRAKKATTEL, *The Beginning*, 140; D. LÜHRMANN, *Markusevangelium*, 51; P. GUILLEMETTE, «Un enseignement nouveau», 244; W. HENDRIKSEN, *Mark*, 67; L. SCHENKE, *Die Wundererzählungen*, 98; R.G. BRATCHER – E.A. NIDA, *Translator's Handbook*, 55; W. GRUNDMANN, *Markus*, 44; H.B. SWETE, *Mark*, 22.

[408] Cf. E.S. MALBON, «Galilee and Jerusalem», 248-249; R.H. GUNDRY, *Mark*, 85.

[409] Cf. S. KUTHIRAKKATTEL, *The Beginning*, 140. In Mk 3:7-8, the evangelist makes a clear distinction between those from Galilee and those from other countries or regions: the multitude from Galilee *followed* (ἠκολούθησεν) him while the multitude from other regions *came* (ἦλθον) to him. And those from other regions coming to him anticipates Jesus' reciprocal visits to them. Cf. E.S. MALBON, «Galilee and Jerusalem», 249, n.33.

[410] Cf. G.R. OSBORNE, «Structure and Christology», 153.

3x in Acts, the rest were all in the Gospels, none was in the Pauline writings and the rest of the NT. This can be justified because it has almost always been associated with Jesus. And it shows also the importance Galilee has in the public ministry of Jesus. In Mk's Gospel Jesus' ministry began in Galilee (1:9,14,16,28,39) and also ended in it (14:28; 16:7); it also linked him with the «Sea of Galilee» (1:16; 7:31) and his movements often took place there, as we have mentioned earlier. The only reference to Galilee that has no association with Jesus was in 6:21, where it referred to «... the officers and the leading men of Galilee» invited for Herod's birthday party.

The deliberate emphasis on Galilee together with the absence of any detailed information about it, when contrasted with Josephus' detailed account of the physical features, the boundaries, the characteristics of its inhabitants, and governorship, arouses our curiosity[411]. Some scholars have highlighted the mediating function of Galilee, as Freyne observes in Mk 3:7-8, that «the listing of Jewish and non-Jewish territories without any concern for their differences shows that as far as the author is concerned such distinctions are unimportant»[412]. While Malbon sees this as a conscious juxtaposition which has deeper significance in terms of overcoming the tension between the familiar and the strange[413]. Thus Galilee provided a condusive atmosphere and a fertile ground for Jesus' ministry, where he moved freely and easily from the *familiar* to the *strange* regions, thereby inaugurating a new order of no differences between «the Jews and the Gentiles».

In relation to our text, there is a strong emphasis on the spreading of Jesus' fame (a result of his word and deed) in the entire region, whose effect attracted many people to Jesus, and also increased his popularity (1:33-34,37,45; 2:2-4,13; 3:7-8) in the vicinity and beyond[414]. Freyne observed that the diverse social and economic world of Galilee helped for the appearance of crowds and the spreading of the news about the main character (Jesus) and his activity throughout the region[415]. Since the

---

[411] Cf. S. FREYNE, *Galilee, Jesus and the Gospels*, 35; JOSEPHUS, *The Wars of the Jews*, 3:35-40.

[412] S. FREYNE, *Galilee, Jesus and the Gospels*, 36.

[413] Cf. E.S. MALBON, «Galilee and Jesusalem», 249-251, 252; S. FREYNE, *Galilee, Jesus and the Gospel*, 36.

[414] Cf. K. STOCK, «Die Machttaten Jesu», 201.

[415] S. FREYNE, *Galilee, Jesus and the Gospels*, 39-41, esp. 40; «Because of the links

diverse social structures helped to spread the news throughout the whole region, no one should be surprised that only a day of Jesus' authoritative activity in Capernaum could attract so many people, and initiate the increase of his popularity immediately. Like all human reactions, his popularity will please some people, and also displease some others. However, Jesus continues his ministry of salvation unabated.

Thus this verse stresses the magnitude of the wonder performed by Jesus in his word and deed, and also emphasizes its success[416]. And its effect is already holding on the people through the spread of the news throughout the surrounding region of Galilee, the gathering of the people, the bringing to him «all who were sick or possessed of demons», every one searching for him, and the crowd following him.

3.3 *Summary*

In this last section of our chapter, we have tried to examine the reactions to Jesus' activity, both within and outside the synagogue of Capernaum; and at the same time highlighted some important aspects of our pericope. They are as follows:

1. The heightened reaction of the people's frightened amazement raised, (a) the discussion among themselves which indirectly questions about Jesus' identity, (b) the «newness» of Jesus' teaching which emphasizes his divine authority, (c) Jesus' authoritative command on the unclean spirits and their submissive obedience to him.

2. The news about Jesus' fame (activity of teaching and exorcism) spread immediately throughout the whole region of Galilee.

3. We also observed some key-words in our section, like, θαμβέω, συζητέω, καινός, ἐπιτάσσω, ὑπακούω, and ἀκοή.

---

that existed between villages and other rural settlements with the cities, and particularly because of the markets, important information could be disseminated quickly, it is assumed, and the healer and his travelling retinue, for their part, made a point of visiting those places where people gathered for secular as well as religious activity». The same easy assess to the crowds and quick dissemination of news was also experienced by Josephus. Cf. *The Life of Flavius Josephus*, 99f., 102f., 205f.; *The Wars of the Jews*, 2:602; Cf. S. FREYNE, *ibid.*, 40, n.13.

[416] Cf. R. PESCH, «Eine neue Lehre», 260; L. SCHENKE, *Die Wundererzählungen*, 98.

4. Conclusion

At the end of our semantic analysis, we shall like to give a synthetic conclusion to this chapter, since we have already given a summary conclusion to each of the three sections. We were able to discover the themes/motives, and confirm the key-words in our pericope. These themes/motives are: Jesus' company with his disciples, Jesus' teaching, the people's motif of wonder at Jesus' word and deed, Jesus' authority, and Jesus' contrast with the scribes. Likewise other themes were evident, like: demonic possession, Jesus' identity, and his mission, Jesus' command to silence, and his exorcism of the unclean spirit. Jesus' fame spreads throughout the vicinity, and its echo attracted the crowd motif. Galilee has also an important place in Jesus' public ministry. The important significance of Mark's key-words/favourite terms observed in the linguistic-syntactic analysis were also confirmed in this chapter.

The discovery of the concentration of these dominant themes/motives and their key-words in our pericope, gives us an important signal of the function of our pericope in the Gospel. However, we shall demonstrate this fact in Part II. But meanwhile, we shall examine our pericope in the narrative analysis, to see how the author (evangelist/ narrator) communicates his message to his reader/hearer.

CHAPTER III

Narrative Analysis

After our investigation into the vocabulary, organization and meaning of our text in the previous analyses (linguistic-syntactic and semantic), we want now to continue with the narrative analysis. In this chapter, therefore, we shall examine how the author/narrator communicated his message to his readers/hearers, and how he characterized the persons in the story of our pericope. We shall also find out whether this analysis can help to identify some important aspects of our pericope.

1. Introduction

Narrative Analysis is a text-centred one, and investigates the «formal features» of the narrative, «which include aspects of the story-world of the narrative and the rhetorical techniques employed to tell the story»[1]. Thus a narrative has two aspects: story and discourse, which is the «what» and the «how» of narrative.[2] *Story* refers to the content of the narrative, and includes the events, the characters and the settings of the narrative. While *Discourse* refers to how the story is told, including: the plot, the narrator, point of view, style and rhetorical devices. However, «the "what" and the "how", story and discourse, content and form, are obviously inseparable

---

[1] D. RHOADS, «Narrative Criticism», 411-412. This will include what M.H. ABRAMS categorized as the «objective criticism» which is text-centred and regards the literary work in isolation, and analyzes it as «a self-sufficient entity constituted by its parts in their internal relations, and sets out to judge it solely by criteria intrinsic to its own mode of being». Cf. *The Mirror and the Lamp*, 26-29; M.A. POWELL, *Narrative Criticism*, 11.

[2] S. CHATMAN, *Story and Discourse*, 9, 15-42; R.M. FOWLER, *Let the Reader Understand*, 16, 23.

in narrative, and their interrelation is integral to the impact of a narrative»[3].

Although the narrative elements we mentioned above are interrelated, yet the analysis of the text makes scholars emphasize one more than the other. Egger maintains that the narrative analysis limits itself methodically to actions and actors[4]. For Aristotle actions are primary and agents are their necessary corollary[5]. According to Broadhead, synchronic analysis must first investigate the actions by which the plot of the narrative is constructed[6]. He further clarifies that actions and agents are interdependent, correlative elements of a narrative. Thus, «overemphasis on one or the other tends to blur the dynamics of the coexistence of agents and actions within a narrative»[7]. On the other hand, Ska states that «the two chief elements» of a narrative are the narrator (voice) and the plot»[8]. However, this depends on where one begins the analysis, but we must continue to emphasize the interrelationship existing between these narrative elements. For example, the plot, actions and characters are interdependent; the sequence of events or incidents is not enough, but it is the plot that renders and organizes them (actions and characters) so as to achieve their particular effects[9]. This goes to confirm the integral nature of the narrative.

Every narrative or text has a message sent by someone to somebody or an audience. So there is a communicative structure (sender, message, receiver) associated with the narrative. This communicative structure of a narrative can be enlarged to seven elements. There is a «Real author» and «Implied author»; an «Implied reader» and «Real reader»; a «Narrator» and a «Narratee»; and the «Narration»[10]. Thus one can observe the

---

[3] D. RHOADS, «Narrative Criticism», 414.

[4] Cf. W. EGGER, *Methodenlehre*, 126, cf. 120.

[5] I. BYWATER, «Poetics, Chap. II», 2317; S. CHATMAN, *Story and Discourse*, 108-109.

[6] E.K. BROADHEAD, *Teaching with Authority*, 36.

[7] E.K. BROADHEAD, *Teaching with Authority*, 40.

[8] J.L. SKA, *Our Fathers*, 2, 39; ID., «L'analisi narrativa», 147. The narrator is the storyteller and the «mediator» between the world of the narrative and the world of the audience; while the plot is the ordered arrangement of the actions, incidents or events.

[9] Cf. M.H. ABRAMS, *Glossary*, 137.

[10] The «Real author» is the ancient writer of the text; while the «Implied author» is the author as perceived in the text; the «Implied reader» is the one presupposed by the narrative itself; while the «Real reader» is the one reading the text now. The sender of the message is the «Narrator», the receiver is the «Narratee», while the message itself

communicative structure in the order below:

Narrative text

Real author = Implied author = Narrator = Narration = Narratee = Implied reader = Real reader[11].

We cannot exhaust the content of this Narrative analysis here, lest it becomes a lecture. It will be better to go into our text, there we can highlight other nuances of the analysis. As we go on, these will appear and we shall give a concise explanation of them. Now we turn to our text.

2. Narrative Analysis and Mk 1:21-28

We shall now try to apply the narrative analysis to our pericope, and see what this analysis will highlight for us about our text.

2.1 *Jesus prepares for his Ministry*

Mark's Gospel opens with a prophetic message of preparing the «way of God». This divine initiative took place in two stages: the first was the «forerunner» John the Baptist who prepares the mind of the people for the Son of God (Jesus Christ). He was a true forerunner both in his *mission* and *destiny*: he proclaimed (1:4, 7: κηρύσσειν) in the wilderness the Baptism of repentance (1:4-6); about Jesus' coming and mission (1:7-8); he was handed over to death (παραδίδοναι: 1:14, cf. 6:14-29; 9:11-13). Thus John the Baptist presented Jesus not only in his mission but also in his destiny, in the process of preparing the way of the Lord.

The second stage introduces Jesus into the scene, first with Baptism which gave him a triple presentation (the baptism of John, v.9; the descending power of the Spirit, v.10; and the heavenly voice, v.11: «this is my Son, the beloved one,...» Then the temptation in the wilderness (1:12-13), which foreshadows the conflict with Satan and his agents in his ministry. His divine power was tested here, and he was assured of divine assistance and victory before his actual mission began.

Jesus' ministry began in Galilee (1:14-15) from where he left (v.9: Nazareth of Galilee) for Jordan to receive his mandate through Baptism[12]

---

is the «Narration».

[11] Cf. M.A. POWELL, *Narrative Criticism*, 19-20, 25-27; R.M. FOWLER, *Let the Reader Understand*, 31; J.L. SKA, *Our Fathers*, 39-43; S. CHATMAN, *Story and Discourse*, 151.

[12] R.C. TANNEHILL sees the Gospel of Mark as «the story of the commission which

(vv.9-11). He actually began his ministry by proclaiming (κηρύσσειν, v.14) the gospel of God (v.14, cf 1:1). The content of Jesus' preaching is based on «the fulfilment of time» and «the nearness of the kingdom of God» (v.15); he then called for repentance and the belief in the gospel (v.15). With this central message, he began his Galilean ministry, and along the Sea of Galilee he called the first four fishermen, whom he promised to become «fishers of men» (his disciples). The authority and power of his message made them follow (ἀκολουθεῖν, v.18, cf. v.20; 2:14) him immediately (εὐθύς, vv.18,20). The speedy response of these fishermen to Jesus' call, will characterize or echo the response of the people to Jesus' message throughout his Galilean ministry.

2.2 Jesus' First Sabbath at Capernaum

The delimitation of this pericope (vv.21-28) is easy to decipher. Jesus left the Sea of Galilee (local setting) with the four fishermen who followed him (ἀπῆλθεν ὀπίσω αὐτοῦ, v.20). Then they went into (εἰσπορεύονται, v.21) Capernaum (local setting); and immediately on the sabbath (temporal setting) Jesus entered the synagogue (another local setting) and began to teach. At the end of the sabbath worship, they left the synagogue (ἐξελθόντες ἦλθον, v.29) and went into the house of Simon and Andrew. The change of place, time and characters initiates a new pericope. The v.29 closes and at the same time opens another pericope (vv.29-31).

Looking at the plot (arrangement) of this narrative, one observes that there are two important motifs or themes within the pericope. The narrator chose two ways of narrating the story: the first is a «summary», while the second is a «scene».[13] The plot[14] here is episodic, and there is an

---

Jesus received from God and of what Jesus has done (and will do) to fulfill his commission». Thus the baptism scene could be understood «as the communication of this commission». Cf. «Narrative Christology», 61.

[13] To consider the duration of a story, one must call to mind the difference between the narrative (story) time and the narration (plotted) time. The narrative time is the duration of the actions or events in the story-world (eg. years, months, days, etc); while the narration time is the duration it takes to read the narrative as written (eg. chapters, paragraphs, sentences, verses, etc). Thus in «summary» the narration time will be shorter than the narrative time; while in «scene» the duration of both times will almost be equal. Cf. M.A. POWELL, Narrative Criticism, 38; J.L. SKA, Our Fathers, 12-13; ID., «L'analisi narrativa», 151-152; G. GENETTE, Narrative Discourse, 86-112; S. CHATMAN, Story and Discourse, 67-70, 72.

[14] There are two types of plot: the unified and the episodic plot. Cf. J.L. SKA, Our

element of conflict within the narrative plot. In fact, there are two conflicts shown by the narrator, one is foreshadowed, while the other is actualized in the story. The omniscient narrator intrudes and furnishes necessary information that helps in the development of the conflict. The protagonist of this plot is Jesus, while the antagonist is the unclean spirit (speaking through a man). The people in the synagogue (and the disciples in the background) form a character-group that reacts to this eventful episode in the synagogue. The language of the narrative is violent. However, this is also a plot of resolution[15] because the conflict eventually ended, thereby changing the situation and lessening the tension already created by this conflict in the synagogue. And this episode caused amazement among the people, and soon spread out in the vicinity. This is just a brief summary of what we shall see in the narrative before us for analysis.

2.3 *Jesus teaches in the Synagogue*

The plot begins with the initial action of Jesus who *comes into* (εἰσπορεύονται, v.21) Capernaum accompanied by his disciples. And immediately on the sabbath he *entered* the synagogue and *taught*. Here in a summary form the implied author/narrator[16] has presented the protagonist or the main character of the story, Jesus (though implicitly), and his actions, which will give rise to subsequent actions. The settings are also clearly indicated both local (Capernaum, synagogue) and temporal (sabbath). This could be called an introduction or an exposition[17] of a plot.

Fathers, 17.

[15] There is also the distinction between the «plot of resolution» and the «plot of revelation». Cf. J.L. SKA, *Our Fathers*, 18; S. CHATMAN, *Story and Discourse*, 48.

[16] I will be using these two designations (implied author, narrator) interchangably which in another way will be called «Mark», because as D. RHOADS says, «in a narrative like the Gospel of Mark, with a wholly reliable narrator, there is little or no difference (or distance) between the norms and choices of the implied author and the point of view of the (reliable) narrator». *Narrative Criticism*, 422; Cf. J.G. COOK, *Structure and Persuasive Power*, 144. R.M. FOWLER, *Let the Reader Understand*, 78, went further to say, «The absence of distance between the implied author and the narrator of Mark's Gospel, along with the narrator's unlimited third-person stance, is a rhetorical strategy calculated from the start to win over the reader to becoming not only the implied reader but also the credulous narratee of the omniscient narrator».

[17] Exposition provides the necessary information as the background to the story, that is, a) the setting of the narrative (time, place); b) the main characters and the relations among them (e.g. Who? Where? When?); and c) a key to the understanding of the

The narrator did not tell us what Jesus taught and how long he taught in the synagogue, however he succeeded in characterizing Jesus as a teacher. In short, as the one who directs the story (story-teller), after the general introduction of Jesus and his disciples, he focused on Jesus alone, thereby placing the disciples in the background (we did not hear about them until v.29, when they left the synagogue). So here Jesus is characterized as the one who «comes» and «teaches». But his teaching is in Imperfect (it could be seen both as inceptive and iterative - with regard to its frequency in the narrative).

Although the actions of Jesus are summarized in the verse, the narrator goes further to present the immediate effect of Jesus' activity of teaching. The people *were astonished* (ἐξεπλήσσοντο, v.22a) at Jesus' teaching. He introduces the reaction of the character-group (the people in the synagogue, and most likely the disciples inclusive). As a summary, he did not tell us how they reacted. However, the response of the people (crowd) initiates their characterization in the story[18]. Then at this juncture, the omniscient narrator[19] intrudes to explain to the reader or his audience the reason for the astonishment: «for he was teaching them as one having authority, and not as the scribes» (v.22b). He distinguishes Jesus' teaching

---

narrative. Cf. J.L. SKA, *Our Fathers*, 21; M. STERNBERG, *Expositional Modes*, 1-2. One can say a) and b) are almost here, but the picture will be completed in v.23; on the other hand, c) will come in v.22. But we have here already the greater part of the exposition.

[18] E.K. BROADHEAD, *Teaching with Authority*, 58.

[19] Here our attention is drawn to the «point of view» of the narrator. Mark's narrative, explains N.R. PETERSEN, belongs to that type of third-person point of view known as the omniscient point of view of an intrusive narrator. Cf. «Point of View», 105-106. And M.H. ABRAMS explained that in the *omniscient point of view* «the narrator knows everything that needs to be known about the agent and events; that he is free to move as he will in time and space, and to shift from character to character, reporting (or concealing) what he chooses of their speech and actions; and also that he has priviledged access to a character's thoughts and feelings and motives, as well as to his overt speech and actions». Thus within this mode «the *intrusive narrator* is one who not only reports but freely comments on his characters, evaluating their actions and motives and expressing his views about human life in general; ordinarily, all omniscient narrator's reports and judgments are to be taken as authoritative». Cf. *Glossary*, 143. This is clearly reflected in our text. For further treatment of the role of the narrator in Mark's Gospel, Cf. R.M. FOWLER, *Let the Reader Understand*, 61-80; M. STERNBERG, *The Poetics*, 84-87; D. RHOADS – D. MICHIE, *Mark as Story*, 35-43.

from that of the scribes, and characterized that of Jesus with authority, thereby developing further the characterization of Jesus as teacher. Thus «this qualification takes on a sense of linear duration through the use of the periphrastic construction (ἦν ... διδάσκων); authority is a durative narrative trait which serves to characterize Jesus»[20]. On the other hand, he has characterized the scribes (although not present) as «without authority»[21]. In fact, this is the first thing that the reader learns about them and it is the only trait considered so important that the implied author has the narrator tell the reader this outright[22]. Likewise in judging the duration of the narrative, one observes that there is a *pause* here[23]. The authority, as a character trait, foreshadows and anticipates the conflict that will later arise between Jesus and the religious Leaders, especially the scribes (cf. 2:1-12).

In presenting the story to the reader, the implied author uses some styles and narrative patterns which help the reader to articulate the narrative easily. It has been noted that «Mark's style is terse, words being suggestive rather than exhaustive, concrete rather than abstract»[24]. This is not all, but so far this is verifiable in our narrative. We also notice some *narrative patterns*[25] or *rhetorical devices*,[26] the narrator uses to tell the

---

[20] E.K. BROADHEAD, *Teaching with Authority*, 59.

[21] In Mark's Gospel, one observes that the root character traits of the religious leaders is that they are «without authority» (1:22). Cf. M.A. POWELL, *Narrative Criticism*, 62; For further treatment of the character traits (of religious authorities) in Mark, cf. J.D. KINGSBURY, *Conflict in Mark*, 14-21.

[22] Cf. J.D. KINGSBURY, *Conflict in Mark*, 15. In fact, R.M. FOWLER, *Let the Reader Understand*, 61, confirms that «one of the chief ways the reliable narrator of the Gospel directs the reading experience is by providing "reliable commentary"». Cf. *Ibid.*, 81-126; ID., *Loaves and Fishes*, 149-179. And this calls to mind what M. STERNBERG, *Expositional Modes*, 102-104, observes about the literary importance of the «primary effect», by which information conveyed early in the narrative shapes the reader's perception most critically, especially by the omniscient narrator. Cf. M.A. POWELL, *Narrative Criticism*, 118, n.21. This also satisfies the c) part of the Exposition, already mentioned above.

[23] «Pause» refers to instances when the narrative (story) time stops while narration (discourse) time continues. Thus the narrator takes «time out» to describe or explain something to the reader and then picks up the story again where he or she left off. Cf. M.A. POWELL, *Narrative Criticism*, 38-39; J.L. SKA, *Our Fathers*, 12.

[24] D. RHOADS, «Narrative Criticism», 424; D. RHOADS – D. MICHIE, *Mark as Story*, 44.

[25] There are 15 categories of «compositional relationships» found in the biblical

story: (i) In the local setting (Capernaum, synagogue), we notice what one can call *duality* (Neirynck), *two-step progression* (Rhoads & Michie), or *particularization* and *generalization* (Powell);[27] and this is the most pervasive stylistic feature in Mark's Gospel[28]. (ii) Sometimes *repetition* occurs within the episode, as we see with teaching words (vv.21b, 22a,b) in the narrative text. To this, Rhoads & Michie remark, «this repetition alerts the reader to major themes in an episode, and its recurrence keeps the motif before the reader»[29]. (iii) In v.22b one notices also *contrast* that places Jesus and the scribes in opposite positions. (iv) There is also *preparation* in v.22b, which makes the reader anticipate (*prolepsis*) the controversy or conflict between Jesus and the scribes (religious leaders). (v) And above all, we have *summarization* which we have already mentioned as characterizing this two verses. Thus the narrative patterns so far met, can help the reader to be attentive to the narration being guided by the narrator. It is very clear that all this emphasis is based on the theme or motif of *teaching*, and helps to develop this characterization of the main character in the narrative.

So far the narrator has made known to his reader or audience that Jesus' characteristic activity is teaching, and also underlined his character trait, authority. This divine authority is already known to the reader, when in Baptism Jesus was vested with divine power (1:10), and by the fact of being the Son of God (1:1, 11). And this personal trait of authority will accompany his actions, as the reader is already aware of Jesus' desert

---

narrative. Cf. M.A. POWELL, *Narrative Criticism*, 32-34; D. BAUER, *The Structure*, 13-20; see also, D. RHOADS – D. MICHIE, *Mark as Story*, 45-55.

[26] D. RHOADS, «Narrative Criticism», 424.

[27] Cf. M.A. POWELL, *Narrative Criticism*, 33-34.

[28] Cf. D. RHOADS – D. MICHIE, *Mark as Story*, 47-49; F. NEIRYNCK, *Duality in Mark*, 75-136, esp. 96-97. «This is no mere repetition, for the second part adds precision and clarifies the first part», say RHOADS - MICHIE, 47.

[29] D. RHOADS – D. MICHIE, *Mark as Story*, 46; R.M. FOWLER, *Let the Reader Understand*, 140, adds, «The most obvious rhetorical use of repetition is to drive home a point by a succession of hammer blows... Things that are repeated demand attention, and so the narrator may stress the importance of something by repeating what he wants to highlight». R. ALTER also remarks that in the frequent repetitions in storytelling «the authors of the biblical narratives astutely discovered how the slightest strategic variations in the pattern of repetitions could serve the purposes of commentary, analysis, foreshadowing, thematic assertion, with a wonderful combination of subtle understatement and dramatic force». Cf. *Biblical Narrative*, 91. For the Techniques of Repetition, see 88-113.

experience with Satan, and his calling of his first disciples. It is important that this information is being revealed to the reader by the omniscient narrator, on Jesus' first public appearance, and at the beginning of his ministry. The reader has also been informed of the character trait of the people (crowd), and that of the scribes (in anticipation).

2.4 *Jesus encounters an Unclean Spirit in the Synagogue*

As we mentioned above, the narrator told the foregoing story in a «summary» form. Now the story will be presented in a scenic form. Here the narrator will let the characters speak, beginning with the unclean spirit (through the man), then Jesus, and finally the people in the synagogue. And the narrator will close the scene and the story with his comment. In this case, one can observe how the narration time is almost equal or very close to the narrative time.

Now the implied author in vv.23-24 introduces a new character[30] into the scene. He repeats the local setting (synagogue), indicating that the other characters have not changed their location. And the new character in question is a «man with an unclean spirit», the antagonist of the narrative. As the narrator informs us, this demoniac *was* (ἦν) in the synagogue. He did not tell us when he came in or whether he was there from the beginning of the sabbath worship. However, as stative verb states, he was there may be unnoticed. Then according to the story-teller he *cried out* (ἀνέκραξεν). This action attracted the attention of all in the synagogue (including Jesus) to him, and interrupted the worship, at least, for a while. The narrator introduced the unclean spirit's speech with *speaking* (λέγων). This introduces into the scene, what one can call crisis or confrontation, thereby initiating into the narrative an important moment of the plot[31]. This is the *inciting moment*[32] of the plot. The antagonist

---

[30] The entrance of a new character into the scene completes the picture of the Exposition, which we have already indicated. Thus the characters are: Jesus - the main character and protagonist, the unclean spirit (the antagonist), and the people in the synagogue (including the disciples).

[31] The different «moments of the plot» which was proposed by G. FREYTAG, as cited by J.L. SKA; in the original German terms are: Einleitung (Exposition), das erregende Moment, Steigerung, Höhepunkt, das tragische Moment, Fall oder Umkehr, das Moment der letzten Spannung, Katastrophe. In English: exposition, inciting (exciting) moment, complication, climax, turning point, falling action, resolution, last delay, denouement (conclusion). These «moments of the plot» do not correspond exactly to well delimited sections of the narrative. Cf. *Our Fathers*, 20-30; ID., «L'analisi

(unclean spirit) appeared unnoticed, but its cry has registered the beginning of a conflict or an encounter with the protagonist, Jesus. Thus, this «provides the initial portrait of those who oppose Jesus, and it initiates the plot action»[33].

Since the narrator has let the character (the antagonist) speak, the reader will now in v.24 hear his addressing words to the protagonist. In the first place, he addresses the protagonist by name, «Jesus the Nazarene», wanting to ward him off from his presence. The unclean spirit acknowledges the destructive threat[34] his presence will create for his group. He firmly reveals Jesus' true identity, by calling him «the Holy One of God». This encounter is really a conflict, like most conflicts in Mark's Gospel, which «evoke dramatically intense, emotional, and often violent words and actions»[35]. Broadhead to this address remarks, «Jesus' opponent serves here as a mirror in which the character image of Jesus is intensified and reflected to the implied reader. The demonic speech further specifies the character qualities of Jesus ("the holy one of God"), and it is a demon who first names Jesus in the story (1.24)»[36]. One also observes that both the functions of plot action and of characterization are linked together here. This is because, though the plot development is focused on the antagonist and his actions, in the final analysis the result is the characterization of Jesus[37].

This speech can be seen as a self defence mechanism of the unclean spirit against Jesus. In this case it wants to solve the problem of this conflict by getting rid of the presence of the protagonist. Here one can find the moment of «complication»[38] in the plot development of the

---

narrativa», 155-156. I have plotted our narrative thus: exposition (vv.21-23a), inciting moment (v.23b), complication (v.24), climax, turning point (v.25), resolution (v.26), last delay (v.27), denouement (conclusion) v.28.

[32] J.L. SKA maintains that the inciting moment is the moment in which the conflict or the problem appears for the first time and arouses the interest of the reader. Cf. *Our Fathers*, 25; ID., «L'analisi narrativa», 156.

[33] E.K. BROADHEAD, *Teaching with Authority*, 59.

[34] R.C. TANNEHILL maintains that «in order to be the one who brings salvation to people, Jesus must be the destroyer of the powers that oppress them». Cf. «Narrative Christology», 65.

[35] D. RHOADS – D. MICHIE, *Mark as Story*, 73.

[36] E.K. BROADHEAD, *Teaching with Authority*, 59.

[37] E.K. BROADHEAD, *Teaching with Authority*, 59.

[38] Here in the «complication» one usually finds the different attempts to solve the

narrative. The other characters in the scene may have heard the crying out of the unclean spirit (through the man), but what was uttered did not come to their hearing: it was on the supernatural plane. However, the reader heard it all, because he was privileged to have the «reader-elevating»[39] position. But it created in the reader enormous tension and suspense. Indeed, this is what helps for the development of the plot and gives it a conflict character.

Now the narrator continues the narrative by introducing Jesus (v.25), thereby showing his reaction towards his antagonist. This is the first time the narrator is presenting Jesus with his proper name explicitly. The reader had anxiously been expecting (though with tension and suspense) the outcome of this encounter, and what Jesus' reaction towards his opponent would be. The story-teller informs us that Jesus *rebuked/ commanded* (ἐπετίμησεν) the unclean spirit. All the same, he presents him to speak directly by his usual *saying* (λέγων). Jesus' commanding speech was short, harsh and terse: the only two imperatives in the narrative. Thus he strongly calls the unclean spirit to *be silent* (θιμώθητι - to stop revealing his identity), and to *come out* (ἔξελθε) from its victim (the man held in bondage by him). This heightens the tension and suspense of the reader, who sees now power matching against power. But he knows that with Jesus' divine authority and assistance he will surely subdue the unclean spirit, since he has done so before (1:12-13). In fact, this is the apex, the climax or the turning point[40] of the narrative plot. Broadhead confirms this thus, «here the plot action and the authority

---

problem or conflict. Thus the unfolding of the narrative normally creates suspense and the reader keeps asking «what will happen?» or «what does this mean?» Cf. J.L. SKA, *Our Fathers*, 25-26; «L'analisi narrativa», 156.

[39] Scholars have discovered three main reading positions: reader-elevating, character-elevating, evenhanded. The reader-elevating position is therefore when a reader knows more than the character(s) in the narrative. Cf. M. STERNBERG, *The Poetics*, 163-172, esp. 164-165; J.L. SKA, *Our Fathers*, 54-56.

[40] The «climax» can be the moment of highest tension, the appearance of a decisive element or character, the final stage of a narrative progression. While the «turning point» normally inaugurates the falling action. Thus at this point an element appears that will lead the movement of the narrative to its conclusion. Cf. J.L. SKA, *Our Fathers*, 27. The introduction of the protagonist with his character traits already highlighted by the narrator, satisfies these requirements that will bring the development of the plot to its conclusive end.

image of Jesus reach a common apex»[41]. Furthermore he adds, «here the exorcism is accomplished by command alone. This simplicity serves to intensify the thematic characterization of Jesus as "one having authority"»[42]. However, the effect of Jesus' action on the reader is really great, because Abrams states, «as a plot progresses it arouses expectations in the audience or reader about the future course of events, and how characters will respond to events»[43]. And that is why one can talk about «suspense»[44] here.

The narrator takes up the story again in v.26, telling his reader what type of effect the commanding speech of Jesus had on the unclean spirit. The narrator was very graphic in showing how unwilling the unclean spirit's response was, in leaving its victim. The sequence of actions that preceded its exit was described by two participles, thereby giving impression of some duration of struggle between the man and his oppressor. However, the unclean spirit, *convulsing* (σπαράξαν) the man and *crying* (φωνῆσαν) with a loud voice, *came out* (ἐξῆλθεν) of him. In fact, it is here that the exorcism is effected: the problem is resolved, the conflict ends, and the plot action is completed. And Jesus is the victor. Broadhead observes that «the description is brief and violent: convulsing, screaming, departing... The story intensifies the evil characterization of Jesus' opponents»[45]. This also demonstrates Jesus' divine power over the unclean spirit, and thus heightens his authority further. This is also the moment of «resolution»[46] in the plot line of the narrative, which initiates

---

[41] E.K. BROADHEAD, *Teaching with Authority*, 59.

[42] E.K. BROADHEAD, *Teaching with Authority*, 60.

[43] M.H. ABRAMS, *Glossary*, 138.

[44] *Suspense* according to M.H. ABRAMS is an anxious uncertainty about what is going to happen, especially to those characters whose qualities are such that we have established a bond of sympathy with them. While if what in fact happens violates our expectations, it is known as *surprise*. Cf. *Glossary*, 138. Surely the narrator has created sympathy with Jesus (main character) in the mind of the reader, whom he guides with his point of view.

[45] E.K. BROADHEAD, *Teaching with Authority*, 60. Commenting on the language of the story in his article, E.K. BROADHEAD, «Jesus the Nazarene», 8, says, «the language of the story is violent, crying out (ἀνέκραξεν), destroying (ἀπολέσαι), warning (ἐπιτίμησεν), muzzling (φιμώθητι), tearing (σπαράξαν), making a loud noise (φωνῆσαν φωνῇ μεγάλη)».

[46] In a plot of action (resolution), this resolution is called *peripeteia* or *perpety*. It is the change of action from one state of affairs to its exact opposite. Cf. J.L. SKA, *Our Fathers*, 27; ID., «L'analisi narrativa», 154; S. CHATMAN, *Story and Discourse*, 85.

a change of situation. The suspense of the reader with regard to the narrative ends with the resolution.

In the encounter between Jesus and the unclean spirit (vv.23-26), the narrator used some narrative patterns to communicate to his reader the story. In the first place, the protagonist and the antagonist are able to speak out their thoughts. He also used *repetition* of words or phrases, to keep the reader alert, like «and immediately» (vv.21, 23, cf. v.28); «synagogue» (vv.21, 23); «unclean spirit» (vv.23, 26, cf. v.27); «Jesus» (vv.24, 25: by the character, and the narrator); «speaking» (vv.24, 25, cf. v.27); «crying out» (vv.23, 26); and the phrase, «come out of him» (ἐξέρχεσθαι ἐξ αὐτοῦ, vv.25, 26)[47]. There is also the presence of *two-step progression* (duality)[48] in the narrative. Likewise the narrative patterns came as *questions*[49] within the story. Hence these narrative patterns keep the reader attentive and involved in perusing the narrative.

The narrator has tried in this scene, which is not yet completed (since we have not heard the people in the synagogue), to show the characters (the unclean spirit, Jesus) especially involved in the conflict. He presents the characters both in what they do and say, which helps to characterize them. The unclean spirit in its speech characterizes itself as evil, since it abhors Jesus' presence, and sees it as destructive. While in Jesus' case,

---

[47] Among the repetitions which occur within episodes, D. Rhoads – D. Michie include «the words in commands or requests are repeated in the descriptions of their fulfillment». Cf. *Mark as Story*, 46.

[48] Here it appears «where direct discourse is preceded by a qualifying verb, the first step being a verb or verbal phrase which characterizes generally the statement of the speaker while the second step specifies precisely the actual statement». D. RHOADS – D. MICHIE, *Mark as Story*, 48. The examples of these are obviously in vv.24, 25, 27.

[49] With regard to questions in Mark's story, D. RHOADS – D. MICHIE observe that «questions heighten the drama by creating suspense and tension for the reader. Because the interrogative mood intensifies conflicts between the characters, the reader becomes absorbed in the narrative, awaiting answers to the questions and resolutions to the conflict. The questions also reveal character». Cf. *Mark as Story*, 49. These observations are so evident in the narrative, especially in «What have you to do with us, Jesus of Nazareth? Have you come to destroy us?» (1:24); «What is this? A new teaching with authority?» (1:27). On these, R.M. FOWLER, *Let the Reader Understand*, 132-133, observes, on the one hand that each of these questions remains unanswered in the story, cf. ID., *Loaves and Fishes*, 167-168; and on the other hand that, «Each of these questions is in fact a double question, a common stylistic trait in Mark... Double questions contribute to training the reader to follow the lead of the narrator as he takes incremental steps in his discourse». Cf. *Let the Reader Understand*, 133.

both the actions and words of the unclean spirit, and that of Jesus himself, help to intensify the characterization of Jesus, and also heighten his authority image.

2.5 *The People's Reaction to Jesus' Actions*

After the scene of the conflict between Jesus and the unclean spirit, the narrator now focuses on the people, by showing the reader how they reacted to the events in the synagogue. The people's response in v.22a was in summary form, but here (v.27) it is in scenic. However, the story-teller shows the reader that the people *were awfully amazed* (ἐθαμ-βήθησαν) at Jesus' authoritative teaching and exorcism. In fact, these raised *discussion* or *question* (συζητεῖν) among the people. Here, the narrator let them speak out for themselves by the verb of *saying* (λέγοντας). In their speech, they were amazed at Jesus' new teaching with authority, and how Jesus commands the unclean spirits and they obey him. On the one hand, the people themselves (the characters in the story) confirm what the narrator had told the reader about the character traits of Jesus in v.22b: that Jesus teaches with authority. For them it is a «new teaching». On the other hand, they expressed their judgement on the simple command of Jesus, which just effected exorcism (vv.25-26). For them, this single episode of exorcism is a foreshadow of Jesus' victory over the unclean spirits. On the people's speech, Broadhead comments, «dual themes are focused anew: teaching and authority. This provides summarization of the character portrait of Jesus. The display of authority is expressed in dramatic and durative terms through the use of the present tense - he is commanding (ἐπιτάσσει) and they are obeying (ὑπακού-ουσιν). Thus, the display of authority becomes a durative trait which characterizes the entire ministry of Jesus»[50]. I would take this verse to be the «last delay»[51] in the plot of the narrative.

To bring the story of Jesus' first appearance for his public ministry to a conclusion, the narrator informs the reader, even before Jesus left the synagogue with his disciples, what was the effect of Jesus' word and deed. In a graphic and densed manner, the story-teller tells the reader that immediately Jesus' actions were made manifest, Jesus' fame (report)

---

[50] E.K. BROADHEAD, *Teaching with Authority*, 60.

[51] The «last delay» is the moment of delay or retardation (final suspense) between the resolution and the final conclusion. Cf. J.L. SKA, *Our Fathers*, 28.

spread (ἐξῆλθεν, v.28) everywhere throughout all the surrounding region of Galilee. So the report about Jesus goes out immediately and everywhere, «not only within the narrative but also to the implied reader of the narrative»[52]. This spread of Jesus' fame foreshadows the response that will accompany Jesus' galilean ministry, and the crowd that will follow him, whether far or near. Here, I will say is the *denouement* (French for «unknotting») or the conclusion[53] of the narrative.

At this juncture, one can see clearly the narrative as a whole and make some observations. Apart from the fact, that the omniscient narrator authoritatively intrudes to offer the reader key information to understand the story, he does other things in the narrative. He is not bound by time or space; so he «knows what happens in every place, unlike a character-narrator who would have to be present or hear about an event indirectly in order to be able to recount it realistically»[54]. Likewise, among other functions, «the narrator establishes a relationship with the reader which is different from the relationship the narrator engenders between the reader and the characters, thereby guiding the reader to be distant from or to identify with the different characters»[55].

In addition to what we said earlier about Mark's style, one observes that «the brevity of style and rapidity of motion give the narrative a tone of urgency. Thus, through the style of the narrative, the reader experiences the urgency which the protagonist conveys by his central message: The right time is fulfilled, and the rule of God has come near»[56]. Some narrative patterns also attract our attention: the *repetition* of words or

---

[52] E.K. BROADHEAD, *Teaching with Authority*, 60.

[53] This is the «conclusion» because it contains the result and the sequels of the resolution, the final outcome of the events. Cf. J.L. SKA, *Our Fathers*, 28. It is the «denouement» because «the action or intrigue ends in success or failure for the protagonist, the mystery is solved, or the misunderstanding cleared away». Cf. M.H. ABRAMS, *Glossary*, 139; J.L. SKA, *Our Fathers*, 28. In our own case, the plot (conflict) ends in success for the protagonist, Jesus; that is why his fame spread throughout the vicinity, and will soon attract people to him.

[54] D. RHOADS – D. MICHIE, *Mark as Story*, 37.

[55] D. RHOADS – D. MICHIE, *Mark as Story*, 41. For the interrelation between narrator, reader and characters, cf. N.R. PETERSEN, «Point of View», 100-102.

[56] D. RHOADS – D. MICHIE, *Mark as Story*, 45. This is confirmed by the presence of many participles, frequent occurrence of καὶ («and») and εὐθύς («immediately»), which reinforce the rapid movement of action and characters. And this is evident in the narrative.

phrases also bridges episodes. For example, διδαχή («teaching») and ἐξουσία («authority») in vv.22, 27, which form an *inclusio*[57] in the narrative, also «weave their way through the story, giving the fabric of the story an intricate design and unity it would not otherwise have»[58]. Likewise the *two-step progression* (duality), which we noted earlier (v.21) in «particularization» and «generalization» of the local setting repeated itself in (v.28). Here the narrator tells the reader, that Jesus' fame spread πανταχοῦ («everywhere» or «in all directions»), which is generic. Then he specifies it: «throughout all the surrounding region of Galilee». Even the double occurrence of the peoples' response (vv.22, 27) should also move the reader to ask himself, what his response would have been, if placed in the same situation. This double occurrence of the people's reaction could make one think of *Chiasm*[59] in the narrative.

These two last verses (vv.27 and 28) reflect the effect of Jesus' authoritative teaching and exorcism on the people. It seems like one is a summary of Jesus' actions, while the other is the conclusion of this story. The narrator lets the people (characters) speak out their impression and reaction to Jesus' activities in the synagogue. Finally, the narrator in his conclusive remark informs the reader how Jesus' fame, in no time, went out or spead throughout the region of Galilee. And this foreshadows the response Jesus will receive in his ministry: both from the crowd who will follow him from everywhere; and from the religious leaders who will be envious about his success and will intend to kill or destroy him. And that will be the paradox of popularity: love and hatred.

---

[57] «Inclusio» refers to a repetition of features at the beginning and end of a unit. Cf. M.A. POWELL, *Narrative Criticism*, 33.

[58] D. RHOADS – D. MICHIE, *Mark as Story*, 46.

[59] «Chiasm» has to do with a repetition of elements in an inverted order: «a, b, b, a». Cf. M.A. POWELL, *Narrative Criticism*, 33.

We can demonstrate it according to the narrative thus:

A *Jesus* enters and teaches in the synagogue (v.21)
  B *People* were astonished at his teaching (v.22)
    C A man with *unclean spirit* cries out, confronts Jesus (v.23-24)
      D *Jesus* commands the unclean spirit (v.25)
    C' The *unclean spirit* cries out, came out of the man (v.26)
  B' *People* were amazed at his teaching and exorcism (v.27)
A' *Jesus 'fame* spreads throughout Galilee

It is very clear from the above structure that Jesus is the central figure in the narrative, and the narrator tries with narrative devices to communicate to the reader this fact.

2.6 *The Characterization of Jesus*

As we have examined the narrative, we can now look more closely on the role of the protagonist in the development of the plot of the story. It is observed that in Mark «the development of plot predominates over the development of character»[60]. We also noticed that there is a link between the development of plot action with the characterization of the main character. After the general introduction of Jesus and his first four disciples (fishermen) into the scene (Capernaum, v.21a), the narrator immediately focused on Jesus (v.21b), the main character and protagonist of the story. From here onwards, as the plot develops so also the characterization of Jesus, be it by the characters' reactions or actions, the narrator's evaluative point of view or comments, or even what Jesus said or did. I intend, therefore, to examine here the characterization of Jesus in the narrative.

In order to appreciate the central position of Jesus, it will be helpful to look briefly at the narrative features, and see how much attention was given to them. In the first place, let us consider the characters in the narrative. Nothing was said about the *disciples*, except, by implication, they came into Capernaum with Jesus (εἰσπορεύονται). The *people* are not introduced into the narrative but assumed, and they are focused upon through their reactions, and later on through their speech. The *possessed man* (demoniac) had no name, nothing was known about him, except what the unclean spirit (through him) said about Jesus, and its response to Jesus' command. Even what happened to him after the exorcism (healing) is not known (cf. 1:45; 2:12; 5:20; 8:26; 10:52). Secondly, no further information about the Setting, both local and temporal (Capernaum, synagogue; sabbath), was given. Thirdly, the Event, which here is a conflict, was not given a background preparation. Suddenly at the middle of the story, it began without prior information. This brings to relief that the concern of the narrator is to focus and characterize Jesus in the narrative. That is why the development of plot actions in the narrative are all geared towards the characterization of Jesus, the protagonist.

2.6.1 Jesus' Characterization in the Narrative

To define «characterization», Rhoads says that it «refers to authors' bringing characters to life in a narrative by telling about them and/or by

---

[60] D. RHOADS, «Narrative Criticism», 417.

showing them through (a) what they say, (b) what they do, and (c) how other characters perceive them or react to them»[61]. And this is not difficult to verify in our narrative. In Mark's Gospel, however, «the narrator creates a very complex characterization of Jesus. What Jesus *says* discloses his understanding of himself and his purposes. What Jesus *does* reveals primarily the extent and nature of his authority from God. Both what Jesus does and says determine his values and the dynamics of his relations with other characters... what others say and how they react reveal the unusual, enigmatic, and controversial aspects of this character»[62].

The main actions of Jesus or «what he does» in the narrative are teaching[63] (cf. vv.21b, 22a,b) and exorcism (v.25a), and they really revealed his divine authority. His word (the simple command) or «what he says» - «Be silent, and come out of him!» (v.25b) is what actually effected the exorcism, which is both the event and conflict in the plot of the narrative. With regard to how the other characters perceive or react to Jesus, (i) the people are astonished at his authoritative teaching (v.22a); and are awfully amazed at both his powerful and authoritative teaching and exorcism (v.27); (ii) while the unclean spirit, on the one hand, reacts with hostility, and fear of imminent destruction; and on the other hand, perceives Jesus as the «Holy One of God» (v.24a,b,c). The narrator's point of view, shall be treated later.

2.6.2 Aspects of Characterization

There are two aspects of characterization that are especially important: evaluative point of view and character traits[64]. We shall examine how these reflect in the narrative.

---

[61] D. RHOADS, «Narrative Criticism», 417. On characterization, R. ALTER, *Biblical Narrative*, 116-117, says that «character can be revealed through the report of actions; through appearance, gesture, posture, costume; through one character's comments on another; through direct speech by the character; through inward speech, either summarized or quoted as interior monologue; or through statements by the narrator about the attitudes and intentions of the personages, which may come either as flat assertions or motivated explanations».

[62] D. RHOADS – D. MICHIE, *Mark as Story*, 103.

[63] This «teaching» though is in the action of Jesus, because of the summary. It is likewise a part of «what he says», because it is based on v.15, which continues the proclamation he set as his purpose, or if one may say, his *statement of purpose*.

[64] Cf. M.A. POWELL, *Narrative Criticism*, 53.

a) Evaluative Point of View

Evaluative point of view refers to the norms, values, and general world-view or perspective that the implied author establishes to guide the story. It can be defined as «the standard of judgment by which readers are led to evaluate the events, characters, and settings that comprise the story»[65]. In fact, it is the narrator's point of view that guides the reader, and represents the standard of judgment in the story. Thus the narrative reveals the point of view of the narrator, and the narrator in turn shows us the points of view of the characters, in the course of telling the story[66]. One can therefore distinguish between the narrator's point of view (narrator's voice) and a character's point of view. Uspensky[67] gave a comprehensive analysis of point of view in narrative in four planes: *ideological* plane, referring to belief and values; *phraseological* - speech; *spatial-temporal* - actions; *pyschological* - thoughts. These distinctions have been used in the Gospel of Mark, with insightful results[68].

The way the narrator introduces a character into the narrative shows how much regard he has for him. In Mark's Gospel, the narrator presents Jesus to the reader as a reliable character[69]. Jesus, as the Son and Holy One of God, represents the normative evaluative point of view in the Gospel, which also corresponds to God's evaluative point of view[70]. The narrator presents the people as astonished at Jesus authoritative actions, in other words, associate with the reliable character; while the scribes (though not present) and the unclean spirit, are the antagonists. The reader naturally adopts the narrator's view of the characters and evaluates them as the narrator does. Jesus and the narrator share the same ideological

---

[65] M.A. POWELL, *Narrative Criticism*, 24.

[66] Cf. D. RHOADS, «Narrative Criticism», 421; D. RHOADS - D. MICHIE, *Mark as Story*, 43.

[67] B. USPENSKY, *Poetics of Composition*, 8-100; Cf. N.R. PETERSEN, «Point of View», 106-118; D. RHOADS, «Narrative Criticism», 421-422; M.A. POWELL, *Narrative Criticism*, 52.

[68] Cf. N.R. PETERSEN, «Point of View», 106-118.

[69] The narrator introduced Jesus as the Son of God (1:1), confirmed by John's prophecy (vv.7-8), the spirit's descent (v.10), the voice from heaven (v.11), and Jesus' successful encounter with Satan in the desert (v.13). Thus, «by the time Jesus first speaks, the reader accepts him as a reliable character and is ready to hear and trust what he says». Cf. D. RHOADS - D. MICHIE, *Mark as Story*, 40, 44.

[70] Cf. M.A. POWELL, *Narrative Criticism*, 24; J.D. KINGSBURY, «The Figure of Jesus», 3-36, esp. 5-7.

point of view («thinking the things of God»)[71], while Jesus' antagonists (the scribes and the unclean spirit) follow another point of view («thinking the things of men», cf. 8:33)[72]. Powell confirms this assertion, thus: «In Mark's Gospel, Jesus is seen to espouse a true evaluative point of view because he always acts, speaks, thinks, and believes in ways that accord with God's point of view»[73].

Even here in this narrative, the character's (unclean spirit) *phraseological* point of view recognizes that Jesus is the Holy One of God (v.24c), but does not share Jesus' *ideological* point of view, because they are antithetically opposed to each other. Hence the narrator guides the story with the standard of judgment, which corresponds to that of Jesus (God), that of «thinking the things of God». Those outside this point of view may not enjoy the empathy of the reader. The narrator did not reveal to the reader Jesus' thought[74] (*psychological* point of view) in the narrative, but he gave his *spatial-temporal* point of view, by letting the reader know that Jesus teaches and exorcizes with authority. Thus, both the narrator (vv.22b,28), the unclean spirit (vv.24b,26), the people (vv.22,27) and even Jesus himself (vv.21b,25) through their evaluative points of view characterized Jesus in the narrative, as one who with divine authority and relationship with God, teaches and exorcizes unclean spirits.

b) Character Traits

As an aspect of characterization, characters may also be distinguished by traits that are attributed to them in the narrative. A «trait» is therefore defined as «a personal quality of a character which persists over whole or part of a story»[75]. Narrative critics sometimes distinguish different kinds

---

[71] J.G. COOK, *Structure and Persuasive Power*, 144, confirms this when he says, «Mark blends the perspective of the narrator and Jesus and gives the text one single dominant point of view, with the result that the story has no moral or ideological ambiguity». And R.M. FOWLER, *Let the Reader Understand*, 73, adds that, «the narrator establishes his authority by establishing the authority of his main character, Jesus. The two become indistinguishable; we could say that they share the same voice or that they share the same conceptual point of view».

[72] Cf. N.R. PETERSEN, «Point of View», 107-108.

[73] M.A. POWELL, *Narrative Criticism*, 54.

[74] As R.C. TANNEHILL, «Narrative Christology», 58, remarks, «in the Gospel of Mark there is little description of the inner states of the story characters. Instead, characterization takes place through the narration of action».

[75] D. RHOADS, «Narrative Criticism», 417; D. RHOADS – D. MICHIE, *Mark as Story*,

of characters on the basis of their traits. Forster made such distinctions: *round* characters as those, whose traits are many and conflicting, complex and unpredictable; while *flat* characters are those, whose traits are fewer, consistent and predictable[76]. Likewise Abrams proposed *stock* characters as those who are completely flat, having only one trait[77].

Looking at Jesus' personal traits as they appear in Mark's Gospel, Rhoads says, «atlthough Jesus is not a round character in the sense of having conflicting or changing traits, he certainly has a rich complex of many traits, the full extent of which only gradually unfolds in the course of the narrative»[78]. And this gives a rich characterization of Jesus. In the narrative before us, the omniscient narrator has revealed to the reader, as «primary effect» Jesus' personal trait, authority (v.22b). And this authority becomes a durative trait which will unfold gradually, and will characterize the entire ministry of Jesus. Hence authority, as a personal trait, becomes an important element that helps in the characterization of Jesus in the narrative.

3. Conclusion

In the Narrative Analysis we have tried to apply the formal features of the narrative to our pericope. We highlighted the story-world of the narrative, that is, the characters (Jesus, unclean spirit, the people), the settings, and the events (actions) - which reveal a conflict in our context. The expressive features of the narrative were also put in relief: the roles of the plot, narrator, point of view, style and narrative patterns.

Although there are many characters in the narrative, the narrator chose to focus on Jesus, the main character. The result of this shows that the development of the plot, the narrator's point of view, the reactions and words of the other characters to Jesus, Jesus' actions (teaching, exorcism, authoritative command), the narrative patterns (like repetition, contrast, inclusio, chiasm, foreshadowing, etc), all help to characterize Jesus in the

---

102; M.A. POWELL, *Narrative Criticism*, 54.

[76] Cf. E.M. FORSTER, *Aspects of the Novel*, 65-82; S. CHATMAN, *Story and Discourse*, 131-133; D. RHOADS, «Narrative Criticism», 417; D. RHOADS – D. MICHIE, *Mark as Story*, 102-103; J.L. SKA, *Our Fathers*, 84; M.A. POWELL, *Narrative Criticism*, 55.

[77] Cf. M.H. ABRAMS, *Glossary*, 185; D. RHOADS, «Narrative Criticism», 417; D. RHOADS – D. MICHIE, *Mark as Story*, 103.

[78] D. RHOADS, «Narrative Criticism», 418; RHOADS - MICHIE, *Mark as Story*, 104.

public ministry, should be given such prominence, and therefore it foreshadows the *programmatic* significance of our pericope in Mark's Gospel.

Jesus, having received his commission, begins to act, speak, think on behalf of God, and becomes the point of reference in knowing and «thinking the things of God». This scene of teaching and public encounter with the unclean spirit becomes a paradigmatic one with regard to the exercise of Jesus' divine authority in his ministry.

As we have highlighted the role of the author/narrator in the text through our narrative analysis, we shall now find out what is the role of the reader in the interpretation of the text, through the pragmatic analysis or reader-response criticism.

CHAPTER IV

Pragmatic Analysis

Earlier we have, through linguistic-syntactic, semantic and narrative analyses, investigated into our pericope by examining the vocabulary, organization, meaning of the text, and the role of the author/narrator in the art of communication. We shall now, in this chapter try to find out, through the pragmatic analysis (reader-response) the function and effect of our text on the reader/hearer. At the same time, we shall verify the role of the reader in the process of reading and interpretation. Since we began our investigation from the *text* to the *author*, it is therefore, natural to conclude it with the *reader*.

1. Introduction

The pragmatic analysis is primarily concerned with the reader: in fact it is «reader-centred». Most recent scholars call it «Reader-Response Criticism»[1]. Powell calls the *Reader-Response Criticism*, «a pragmatic approach to literature that emphasizes the role of the reader in determining meaning»[2]. This criticism or analysis studies «the dynamics of the reading process in order to discover how readers perceive literature and on what bases they produce or create a meaning for any given work»[3]. For Heil, in the reader-response approach, «we are concerned with what the

---

[1] In our analysis, we shall be using these two terms («pragmatic analysis» or «reader-response criticism») interchangeably in the course of the treatment. For more on Reader-Response Criticism, cf. R. DETWEILER, ed., *Reader-Response Approaches*.

[2] M.A. POWELL, *Narrative Criticism*, 16.

[3] M.A. POWELL, *Narrative Criticism*, 16; J.L. SKA, *Our Fathers*, 54; J.L. RESSEGUIE, «Reader-Response Criticism», 307.

text *does* to and how it *affects* its reader,...» [4] On the other hand, Egger sees the pragmatic analysis of written scripts as trying «to respond to the question: why and for what scope was a text written». Thus, according to him, the author utilizes a written expression, as an instrument, «to establish a linguistic communication, for influencing the reader according to the situation and to induce the reader to a determinate behaviour (comportment)»[5]. One can observe that in spite of different angles of handling this «reader-centred» analysis, all is directed towards the reader. To express the diversity of this method, Tompkins in her introduction says, «reader-response criticism is not a conceptually unified critical position, but a term that has come to be associated with the work of critics who use the words *reader, the reading process*, and *response* to mark out an area for investigation»[6]. And I think that area for investigation is the role of the reader in determining meaning in a text.

As the reader-response criticism focuses on the reader's actions in responding to a text, the diversity of the scholars' interpretation of this reality is based primarily on the relation of text to reader. Some critics focus on the reader's dominance *over the text* (e.g. Holland); here meaning is largely subjective since it is «a creation by and in the individual reader»[7]. Among those in this category, some scholars fear that such extreme attention to the role of the reader in determining meaning will lead to interpretive anarchy. So S. Fish suggested in his theory of «interpretive communities», that «readings may be recognized as being in or out of accord with the accepted strategy»[8]. Some others focus on the

---

[4] To specify this assertion, he says further, «what actions the text calls forth, what mental moves, emotional feelings, anticipations, attitudes, persuasions, realizations, convictions, etc. the text causes its reader to experience in order to produce the meaning latent in the text and thus to bring its act of communication to completion». J.P. HEIL, *The Gospel of Mark*, 2; J.L. RESSEGUIE, «Reader-Response Criticism», 307.

[5] W. EGGER, *Methodenlehre*, 135 (translation is *mine*).

[6] J.P. TOMPKINS, «An Introduction to Reader-Response Criticism», ix.

[7] Cf. J.L. RESSEGUIE, «Reader-Response Criticism», 307; M.A. POWELL, *Narrative Criticism*, 17. N. Holland in his *transactive criticism*, as cited by POWELL, understands interpretation as being largely determined by the defenses, expectations, and wish-fulfilling fantasies of the reader. Thus, he stresses the effect of personality on perception: a reader makes sense out of a text by transforming the content in accord with his or her own identity. cf. *Ibid*.

[8] Cf. S. FISH, «Interpreting the *Variorum*», 182-184 (dealing with «interpretive communities»); ID., *Is There a Text*, 171-173; M.A. POWELL, *Narrative Criticism*, 17. Thus, «readers may control texts, but anarchy does not result because interpretive

reader *in the text*. Here the reader is inscribed or encoded in the text, is a property of the text, and is part of the text's meaning. Thus the critic's function is to interpret the signals transmitted to the inscribed reader of the text[9]. Powell sees this category in «structuralism» and «narrative criticism», and not in reader-response criticism[10]. Still other scholars see the act of reading as a dialectical process, in which the reader interacts *with the text*. So meaning is not seen as something a reader creates out of a text but as the dynamic product of the reader's interaction *with* the text[11]. This interacting process between the reader and the text is explained by Fish (in his *affective stylistics*)[12] and Iser (in his *phenomenological criticism*). I would prefer to elaborate on this last category, as a help in the analysis of our text; because here meaning is not subjected to the reader alone, and moreover, neither the reader's nor the text's role in obtaining meaning is overemphasized, rather it is a product of interaction of both. In fact, «during the reading of a text both reader and text are present and in direct contact with each other»[13].

These two scholars (Fish, Iser) see this interaction of reader and text in this reading process, which is a temporal experience. For Fish, through interaction with the text, the reader is encouraged to continually check his or her responses and review them according to ongoing developments within the text[14]. On the other hand, Iser sees the reading process as an

---

communities control readers». Cf. R.M. FOWLER, *Let the Reader Understand*, 35-36; ID., «Reader Response Criticism», 14.

[9] Cf. J.L. RESSEGUIE, «Reader-Response Criticism», 307.

[10] M.A. POWELL, *Narrative Criticism*, 18. He says, «despite similarities, structuralism and narrative criticism differ from the reader-response approaches in that the former focus on ways in which the *text* determines the reader's response rather than on ways in which the *reader* determines meaning» (*italics* mine).

[11] Cf. M.A. POWELL, *Narrative Criticism*, 17-18; J.L. RESSEGUIE, «Reader-Response Criticism», 307.

[12] According to S. FISH, *Is There a Text*, 26-27, «the concept is simply the rigorous and disinterested asking of the question, what does this word, phrase, sentence, paragraph, chapter, novel, play, poem, *do*? And the execution involves an analysis of the developing responses of the reader in relation to the words as they succeed one another in time». Cf. ID., «Literature in the Reader», R.M. FOWLER, *Let the Reader Understand*, 42.

[13] B.M.F. VAN IERSEL, *Reader-Response Commentary*, 20.

[14] Cf. S. FISH, *Is There a Text*, 156-157, 158-159; ID., «Interpreting the *Variorum*», 172; M.A. POWELL, *Narrative Criticism*, 18; J.L. RESSEGUIE, «Reader Response Criticism», 316. Accordingly «the reader thus engages in a process of forming

evolving process of anticipation and retrospection, of consistency-building and illusion, and of reconstruction[15]. The reading process also recreates the author's original act of creating the work[16]. He also emphasized the creative role of the reader in filling up the «gaps» and indeterminate elements in the text[17]. On the text's influence on the reader, Iser maintains that the author of a text takes the conventions or familiar territory (what he calls *repertoire*), and places it in a new or different context so that the familiar appears unfamiliar to the reader, a process known as *defamiliarization*[18]. Whereas Fish focused on the sequential line by line reading, Iser is more interested in the unfolding of the work as a whole[19]. With this brief explanation we shall conclude this introduction to the Reader-Response Criticism (Pragmatic Analysis), in order to take up our text.

---

expectations and then experiences the shattering of those expectations. The wide range of reading activities include "the making and revising of assumptions, the rendering and regretting of judgments, the coming to and abandoning of conclusions, the giving and withdrawing of approval, the specifying of causes, the asking of questions, the supplying of answers, the solving of puzzles"». Cf. J.L. RESSEGUIE, *ibid.*; S. FISH, *Is There a Text*, 158.

[15] Cf. W. ISER, *The Implied Reader*, 278-290; M.A. POWELL, *Narrative Criticism*, 18; R.M. FOWLER, «Reader Response Criticism», 20; J.L. RESSEGUIE, «Reader-Response Criticism», 317.

[16] This recreation is a part of that anticipation and retrospection in the reading process. To this W. ISER says: «We look forward, we look back, we decide, we change our decisions, we form expectations, we are shocked by their nonfulfillment, we question, we muse, we accept, we reject; this is the dynamic process of recreation». *The Implied Reader*, 288; Cf. R.M. FOWLER, *Let the Reader Understand*, 43; ID., «Reader Response Criticism», 20; J.L. RESSEGUIE, «Reader-Response Criticism», 317.

[17] W. ISER, *The Implied Reader*, 38-40, 279-280, 283; Cf. B.M.F. VAN IERSEL, *Reader-Response*, 18; M.A. POWELL, *Narrative Criticism*, 18; R.M. FOWLER, *Let the Reader Understand*, 34, 46; J.L. RESSEGUIE, «Reader-Response Criticism», 317. «The technique mobilizes the reader's imagination, not only in order to bring the narrative to life, but also - and even more essentially - to sharpen his sense of discernment». ISER, *ibid.*, 39.

[18] In other words, there are two main structural components within the text that influence the reader's response or reaction: «first, a repertoire of familiar literary patterns and recurrent literary themes, together with allusions to familiar social and historical contexts; second, techniques or strategies used to set the familiar against the unfamiliar». W. ISER, *The Implied Reader*, 288; J.L. RESSEGUIE, «Reader-Response Criticism», 309.

[19] Cf. M.A. POWELL, *Narrative Criticism*, 18; J.L. RESSEGUIE, «Reader-Response Criticism», 316-317.

Other details about this analysis will follow according to the exigencies of this interaction between the reader and the text, as seen in our pericope.

2. The Pragmatic Meaning of Mk 1:21-28

Before entering into the pericope, we are aware that the reader[20] knows up to this time all that it takes to prepare for Jesus' ministry: beginning from the prophetic preparation of the «way»; John's prophecy about Jesus (as the stronger one coming after him, and baptizing with the Holy Spirit); Jesus' baptism, filled with power of the spirit, and acknowledged as the beloved Son of God; and he defeated victoriously Satan's temptation in the wilderness. To the reader, «Mark then uses this wilderness episode to give a preliminary picture of who Jesus is»[21]. After the arrest of John, he proclaimed at the fulness of time that the kingdom of God is at hand, and encouraged people to repentance and belief in the gospel. He also called four fishermen, with whom he came into Capernaum.

Jesus' initiates his ministry, after calling his four disciples, with entering and teaching in the synagogue. This attracted reaction from the people, because of the authoritative manner of his teaching. He also drove out the unclean spirit who imprisoned a man. This also heightened both his authority, and the people's amazement. At crucial points, the narrator guides the reader by his comments or information. It is therefore our task, to read this text closely, and discover what in the text evokes the reader's response, and how it affects the reader.

2.1 *Jesus' authoritative Teaching and the People's Reaction*

Jesus' appearance in the synagogue of Capernaum on the sabbath opens officially the chapter of his ministry (cf. 1:14). In the first two verses

---

[20] I would not like to go into the question of whether the «reader» is the «ideal», «informed», «real» or «implied» reader, but here our position is that he is the implied reader. I would share Resseguie's description, that «the implied reader is an individual who comes to a text with certain social and cultural norms as well as a degree of literary competence, is able to take the clues or guidelines transmitted in a text, and can concretize the meaning». J.L. RESSEGUIE, «Reader-Response Criticism», 308. In other words, «the implied reader is the reader/hearer/audience that every text presupposes in order to be actualized as an act of communication; it is "the reader" anticipated and created by the text in the process of reading or listening to it». Cf. J.P. HEIL, *The Gospel of Mark*, 2; for different types of readers, see R.M. FOWLER, *Let the Reader Understand*, 26-40; ID., «Reader Response Criticism», 5-18.

[21] J.G. COOK, *Structure and Persuasive Power*, 161.

(vv.21-22), Jesus' teaching is emphasized; the reaction of the people; the narrator's intervention which stressed the authority trait to this teaching theme, and above all the contrast with the scribes' teaching. We shall concentrate on the role of the reader in the reading process of this text. Thus the implied reader of this text must assume or take some information for granted, must look backward in retrospection, fill up some gaps, and above all must look forward or anticipate certain things.

To describe Jesus' entry into Capernaum, the implied author says, «and they went into Capernaum;...» (v.21a). Since the subject of the action is indefinite and implicit, the implied reader must look back to discover that «Jesus and the four fishermen» (1:16-20) went together into Capernaum, and also form the subject of the verb. Not only that Jesus' first public appearance carries its expectations (his main purpose for coming), one also needs both the anticipation and retrospection to make a meaning of the text[22]. And going further the implied author adds, «and immediately on the sabbath Jesus entered the synagogue and taught» (v.21b). The connection between these two phrases calls for some reflection, which tends to call for some gap to be filled in[23]. One could ask: Did they enter the synagogue the same day they came into Capernaum from the Sea of Galilee? Was that day a sabbath? Or was the sabbath the next immediate one on their arrival to Capernaum? «It is the set of answers given that

---

[22] According to W. ISER, «while these expectations arouse interest in what is to come, the subsequent modification of them will also have a retrospective effect on what has already been read. ... Thus, the reader, in establishing these interrelations between past, present and future, actually causes the text to reveal its potential multiplicity of connections». *The Implied Reader*, 278.

[23] On filling in the gaps in the literary work, M. STERNBERG maintains that «the literary work consists of bits and fragments to be linked and pieced together in the process of reading: it establishes a system of gaps that must be filled in». *The Poetics*, 186; for gaps, ambiguity, and the reading process, cf. 186-229, esp. 186-190. For W. ISER, «it is only through inevitable omissions that a story gains its dynamism. Thus whenever the flow is interrupted and we are led off in unexpected directions, the opportunity is given to us to bring into play our own faculty for establishing connections - for filling in the gaps left by the text itself». *The Implied Reader*, 280, 282-283. R.M. FOWLER, *Let the Reader Understand*, 46, suggests that, «the gap metaphor helpfully reminds us that the job of reading requires us to make sense of what the text does not give us, as much as of what it does give us; we must wrestle with what the text does not say as much as with what it does say». But I would add that the reader's creativity in the reading process must begin first with the understanding of the text, and then with his/her imagination fill in the gaps or bring the narrative to life.

enables the reader to reconstruct the field of reality devised by the text, to make sense of the represented world»[24]. However, to worship on a sabbath is familiar, but for a «non-scribe» or a non-ordained scribe (Jesus) to teach on a sabbath, is new, and as such defamiliarization of the familiar (which we shall see soon), and this calls for the reader's response. In other words, it is through our imagination or picturing of these indeterminate elements or gaps, which are the unwritten parts of the text, that the reader can contribute to the meaning of the text.

Another important gap in our text is the content of Jesus' teaching. This also activates the reader's imagination, to find out why so much emphasis was given to teaching but no content. Here the process of anticipation and retrospection in reading comes up once more. When one looks back in retrospection to Jesus' initial words (vv.14-15), or the relation between «preaching» and «teaching», κηρύσσειν, διδάσκειν - that teaching prolongs or continues what preaching began or is synonymous with it -, then one can imagine what Jesus must have delivered in detail to this synagogue worshippers. And that would be this gospel message: «The time is fulfilled, and the kingdom of God is at hand; repent, and believe in the gospel» (v.15). The unwritten content also arouses our anticipation of the full content, which will gradually unfold itself in the subsequent parts of the Gospel.

The next verse (v.22a) says, «They were astonished at his teaching,...» Here again the reader is given the opportunity to imagine that «they» - which is both indefinite and implicit - must be those in the synagogue for the sabbath worship. Now the question is: how did the people express this astonishment? The content of the teaching which aroused the people's reaction is still an open question. These unanswered questions will then provide the reader the chance to bring to life this text, through his imagination and filling in the gap of the unwritten text.

The narrator's intrusion and explanation (through the γάρ-clause) is directed to no other but the reader, when he says, «for he taught them as one who had authority, and not as the scribes» (22b)[25]. The authority of

---

[24] M. STERNBERG, *The Poetics*, 186.

[25] This is the second γάρ in the Gospel (cf. 1:16). To this, B.M.F. VAN IERSEL, *Reader-Response Commentary*, 21, says, «after reading only a few pages, the reader is aware that the narrator is fond of the explanatory "for" (γάρ), which characterizes his voice as that of someone taking great pains to be understood correctly». And R.M. FOWLER, *Let the Reader Understand*, 94, adds, «one of the chief rhetorical effects of the *gar* clause is reinforcing the reader's dependence upon the narrator... The *gar*

Jesus which is emphasized here refers us to his direct authority from God as the «beloved Son» (v.11), and this enables him to proclaim the «gospel» of the kingdom of God authoritatively, and to give authoritative command to repentance and belief in this gospel of God. To this Heil states:

> That Jesus teaches with such authority and «not like the scribes» not only establishes the superiority of Jesus' teaching to that of the Jewish scribes, who lack this direct divine authority..., but also arouses suspense with the implication of a contrast and conflict between the teaching of Jesus and that of the «scribes» as the professional and official teachers of the Jews[26].

Here the narrator uses the text to present the familiar (repertoire) against the unfamiliar (defamiliarization)[27]. Through the textual strategy, the narrator uses the technique of defamiliarizing the familiar (teaching) by placing Jesus and the scribes in analogy and contrast, in order to highlight Jesus' divine authority. This arouses in the reader the attraction to Jesus, which leads to «identification» with him[28]. This is because the omniscient narrator presents Jesus to the reader (his point of view) as a reliable character[29], who teaches with divine authority. The narrator gives the reason for the people's reaction as authoritative teaching of Jesus, but also induces the reader to make his own response, and that is what the text does to the reader. Likewise through the narrative patterns or rhetorical devices, as we noted earlier in the Narrative Analysis, the implied author/narrator keeps the reader alert.

2.2 *A Man with Unclean Spirit encounters Jesus*

While the reader is expecting more to be said about the scribes, or to hear more about Jesus' teaching, the implied author introduces another

---

clause simultaneously reveals and fills a gap in the reader's knowledge, but probably more important it teaches the reader to follow the narrator, even in momentary retreat». On his discuss on Markan γάρ clauses, see, ID., *Loaves and Fishes*, 77-78, 162-164, 207.

[26] J.P. HEIL, *The Gospel of Mark*, 46. B.M.F. VAN IERSEL, *Reader-Response Commentary*, 135, confirms that the scribes «are the professional, though unpaid, teachers of the Torah who, since they are also authorities on the oral traditions, interpret the written law for present-day situations».

[27] Cf. W. ISER, *The Implied Reader*, 288-289; J.L. RESSEGUIE, «Reader-Response Criticism», 309-311.

[28] Cf. W. ISER, *The Implied Reader*, 291-292; J.L. RESSEGUIE, «Reader-Response Criticism», 321.

[29] Cf. RHOADS – MICHIE, *Mark as Story*, 40, 44.

character into the scene. And there was the enigmatic presence of the unclean spirit (demoniac) in the synagogue, while Jesus was still teaching (v.23). This change creates a gap or jump between the preceding and the following verses. This sets the reader to imagine and question: when and how did he come into the synagogue; and what is his mission there? Then he cried out, thereby creating both fear and tension to both the people in the synagogue and the reader himself. Now, the reader develops sympathy for the man who is a victim of demonic possession, and he begins to expect what Jesus could do to rescue the man from his oppressor. However, the words which the unclean spirit addresses to Jesus (through the man) are both ironical and rhetorical questions. Moreover, «a rhetorical question seeks not only a response from the opponents in the text but also from the reader of the gospel ... is an effective means of creating reader participation ... refocalizes issues, thereby allowing the reader to see an accepted norm in a new context»[30]. The first rhetorical question is: «What have you to do with us, Jesus of Nazareth?» (v.24a). But is it true that Jesus has nothing to do with the demonic world? To this Heil maintains, that «this question functions as an ironic understatement for the reader, who knows that Jesus, as God's Son (1:11) who has already overcome the testing of Satan through divine protection (1:12-13), is indeed very much involved with combatting the demonic powers of evil»[31].

Here as it were, the unclean spirit hit the nail at the head, by saying, «have you come to destroy us?» (v.24b). This also «functions as another ironic understatement, since Jesus has powerfully proclaimed the advent of God's kingship (1:15), which stands in diametrical opposition to the demonic kingship of Satan»[32]. Indeed, Jesus has come to destroy the demonic stronghold and usher in the kingdom of God. The desert experience of Jesus with Satan (vv.12-13), assures the reader that Jesus will surely accomplish his mission.

The unclean spirit trying to play its last card, wanted to ward off Jesus' threatening power and escape being destroyed, as this was imminent, by using his superior and spiritual knowledge to make a bold assertion about Jesus: «I know who you are, the Holy One of God» (v.24c). Thus, «the unclean spirit reveals to the reader its knowledge of the more profound

---

[30] J.L. RESSEGUIE, «Reader-Response Criticism», 310.

[31] J.P. HEIL, *The Gospel of Mark*, 47.

[32] J.P. HEIL, *The Gospel of Mark*, 47.

identity of Jesus of Nazareth as God's "Holy One"»[33]. In other words, the unclean spirit «knows Jesus' name, knows that Jesus has come to destroy them, and even knows who he is, "the Holy One of God". Through this identification the unclean spirit puts Jesus on the side of the Holy Spirit»[34]. Hence, Jesus is antithetically opposed to this unholy and unclean spirit.

It is now the duty of the reader to evaluate the different points of view (perspectives) about Jesus' identity that come out of the textual strategy, especially the four of them: the narrator's, the characters', the plot's and the implied author's. This can apply not only to Iser's process of anticipation and retrospection, but also to what he called «consistency-building». This is «the process of grouping together all different aspects of a text to form the consistency that the reader will always be in search of. While expectations may be continually modified, and images continually expanded, the reader will still strive, even if unconsciously, to fit everything together in a consistent pattern»[35]. And this is consistent with the «picturing» which the reader's imagination does in order to form the *gestalt*[36] of a literary text, which is often coloured by his own characteristic selection process.

Now, the *narrator* had informed the reader at the beginning that Jesus is the Christ (Messiah), the Son of God (1:1). So «we may assume that the narrator does view the title Son of God as an appropriate one for Jesus»[37]. Among the *characters*, the disciples and Jesus have not said anything yet about who Jesus is. But God and the unclean spirit have said something: (a) the reader assumes that the voice from heaven is the voice of God, who refers to Jesus as «my Son, the Beloved» (1:11, cf. 9:7). Thus, this pronouncement establishes the narrator as a reliable one and also the title, Son of God, as the one that best captures Jesus' identity[38]. (b) The unclean spirit knows Jesus as «the Holy One of God» (1:24, cf. 3:11; 5:7), but

---

[33] J.P. HEIL, *The Gospel of Mark*, 47.

[34] B.M.F. VAN IERSEL, *Reader-Response Commentary*, 136.

[35] W. ISER, *The Implied Reader*, 283-284; J.L. RESSEGUIE, «Reader-Response Criticism», 319.

[36] In this case, according to Iser, the «consistent interpretation» or gestalt «is a product of the interaction between text and reader, and so cannot be exclusively traced back either to the written text or the disposition of the reader». W. ISER, *The Act of Reading*, 119; Cf. J.L. RESSEGUIE, «Reader-Response Criticism», 319.

[37] W.R. TATE, *Reading Mark*, 102.

[38] Cf. W.R. TATE, *Reading Mark*, 103; J.D. KINGSBURY, *Christology of Mark*, 48-50.

Jesus forbids it. Is it because it lacks something essential or because it is premature for publicity? Why did Jesus not say anything here? The *plot's* point of view establishes that Jesus is a teacher (1:21,22, cf. v.27). And the narrator saturates the narrative with references to Jesus' teaching; and the crowds also refer to Jesus as a teacher or to his teaching (1:22,27)[39]. The reader must therefore find out the relationship between Jesus' identity as the Messiah, Son of God, teacher and fill it up.

2.3 *Jesus drives out the Unclean Spirit*

Jesus really reacted with a terse and rebuking command: «be silent, and come out of him!» (v.25) The divine authority of Jesus is once more in evidence. Here «Jesus silences not only the unclean spirit's vain struggle to avoid the exorcising power of Jesus but also the inappropriate revelation by the unclean spirit of Jesus' more profound identity as the Holy One of God. Jesus vigorously compels the unclean spirit to free the man from the grisly grip of demonic power by "coming out" of him»[40]. Here the process of defamiliarization would apply. The familiar convention of exorcism with conjuration rituals, cantations and other exorcistic techniques, will be replaced with the unfamiliar, Jesus' simple command, which has divine authority behind it. So the implied reader, with his cultural and social background, would then ask whether Jesus' simple command, would effect anything at all on the unclean spirit. Jesus' authoritative command surely heightened the reader's tension, suspense and even expectations, because there is a fatal conflict going on between those possessing spiritual powers (Jesus and the unclean spirit). But most importantly, would the unclean spirit submit to Jesus' double command or not? At this high point of the story, the reader must be moved in a profound way in his imagination, what the result of this event would be, since any change makes a great impact in the narrative.

The implied author informs the reader that «the unclean spirit, convulsing him and crying with a loud voice, came out of him» (v.26). To confirm the authoritative command of Jesus, the unclean spirit with audible and visible signs came out of the possessed man. Thus, «freed from demonic possession the man personally experiences the salvation

---

[39] Cf. W.R. TATE, *Reading Mark*, 111, 112; V.K. ROBBINS, *Jesus the Teacher*, 108, argues that 1:21-28 establishes Jesus' basic social identity as a teacher.

[40] J.P. HEIL, *The Gospel of Mark*, 48.

Jesus has come to actualize as part of the kingdom of God»[41]. Surely the reader must have imagined what could have happened to the «possessed» man after the departure of the unclean spirit. This is indeed a big gap or unwritten information, that calls the attention of the reader. With regard to the healed demoniac, was he «sitting there, clothed and in his right mind» (5:15)? Or was he «like a corpse; so that most of them said, "He is dead"» (9:26)? Was he crying or talking; conscious or unconscious; rejoicing or sad? Did he go home with other worshippers (alone or accompanied); or he remained behind? In any case, he has become the first person to experience in his life Jesus' salvific ministry: the nearness of the kingdom of God has been brought home to him. Jesus' successful expulsion of the unclean spirit, heightens the admiration for him, which will assure the reader's identification with him. On the other hand, the reader will also experience the fulfilment of his expectation of what Jesus could do for this man, a victim of demonic possession. Thus, «by vicariously identifying with this man (possessed)…, we realize that Jesus as the "Holy One of God" possesses the divine power to liberate our personal lives also from the inextricable grasp of the evil powers that can totally control and overwhelm us»[42]. The reader would now, not only rely on the narrator's point of view, but also on what he has personally experienced from Jesus' authoritative word and deed.

2.4 *The People are amazed and Jesus' Fame spreads out*

At this point, the narrator introduces the people's reaction once more, when he says: «And they were all amazed, so that they questioned among themselves, saying, "What is this? a new teaching with authority, even he commands the unclean spirits, and they obey him"» (v.27)[43]. The reader must again assume that the indefinite «they» are those worshipping in the synagogue (not excluding the disciples). This is strengthened by the

---

[41] J.P. HEIL, *The Gospel of Mark*, 48.

[42] J.P. HEIL, *The Gospel of Mark*, 49.

[43] R.M. FOWLER, *Let the Reader Understand*, 104, observes that the ὥστε clause offers us here twofold of inside view: the amazement of the audience in the synagogue, and their private questioning about Jesus' evident authority. It also echoes another inside view that was offered to the reader earlier in same episode in 1:22, which was then followed by a *gar* clause in which the narrator explained that people were amazed because Jesus taught with authority, a discreet way of raising the authority issue for the reader for the first time in the Gospel.

indefinite or implicit «all» - all without exception were amazed. Thus, «this impressive exorcism of Jesus reinforces and increases the previous astonishment of the people at his authoritative teaching (1:22), so that now "all" are "amazed" and question the meaning of this extraordinary event»[44]. This verse is dedicated to the reactions or responses of the people and the unclean spirits (generalizing the episode). If the people react to Jesus' authoritative word and deed with amazement and question, and the unclean spirits with obedience; what is the reader's response? What is the effect of this extraordinary event on the reader: identification or empathy with Jesus, or filial or trusting obedience to him? But what should be the right response to Jesus' authoritative actions? Or could such an enormous divine power possessed by Jesus frighten or scare the reader? The rhetorical question («What is this?»), as we noted earlier, calls for the participation of the reader too, in supplying the answer. And a most important gap or unwritten text, which the reader must fill in, is that the reactions are all based on Jesus' actions, but nothing is said about the author of these actions. It will be, I think, the task of the reader to call to mind, that the source of all these actions (word and deed) should be referred or directed to Jesus' origin, person, identity and mission.

The defamiliarizing process of the familiar, which we have seen both in teaching and exorcism, functions as a textual strategy to highlight the *newness* element in Jesus' actions, which is seen in his divine authority. It is well combined in this verse, which expresses the people's profound and awful amazement. Thus it impresses upon the reader to imagine how authoritative Jesus is, both in his word and in his deed. Likewise the consistency-building which results to the gestalt of a text, is evidenced here as the reader actively selects and organizes perspectives[45] in the text.

---

[44] J.P. HEIL, *The Gospel of Mark*, 48.

[45] The perspectives are constantly changing and the reader in the flow of the reading must select and organize them. In fact, «there are four perspectives through which the pattern of the repertoire first emerges: that of the narrator, that of the characters, that of the plot, and that marked out for the reader». W. ISER, *The Act of Reading*, 96. In the face of the interacting and changing perspectives the reader cannot embrace all perspectives at a time, so that the one he is involved at a particular moment is the «theme»; and this is read against the «horizon» of the other perspective segments in which he had previously been situated. Thus, «the structure of theme and horizon constitutes the vital link between text and reader, because it actively involves the reader in the process of synthetizing an assembly of constantly shifting viewpoints, which not only modify one another but also influence past and future syntheses». W. ISER, *The*

And «the reader's task is not simply to accept, but to assemble for himself that which is to be accepted»[46]. Since the reader is at present concerned with Jesus' «new teaching with authority» (the theme), the reader's attitude must be conditioned by the horizon of the past attitudes towards Jesus from the narrator's point of view, the other characters, the plot, and Jesus himself. When the theme changes, the horizon is also modified. He also fills in the «blanks» between the theme and horizon, and this helps to give consistent interpretation to the text.

The narrator in his concluding remark says, «And at once his fame spread everywhere throughout all the surrounding region of Galilee» (v.28). Jesus' authoritative word and deed in the synagogue on the sabbath, and on his first public appearance, was so great and exciting that it could no longer be limited to the architectural structure of the synagogue, but must be spread out beyond it, for the nearness of God's kingdom to be actualized in others too. But the question the reader must ask the text is; who did the spreading of Jesus' fame: the amazed people, the healed demoniac, or the accompanying disciples? Could Jesus' fame go out of the synagogue (v.28), before Jesus actually leaves the synagogue with his disciples (v.29)? Or is that a summary or a conclusive statement of the narrator, to describe for the reader the effect of Jesus' actions outside the synagogue experience? Most likely the people in the synagogue spread this «good news» to the whole region. As the reader identifies with their excited astonishment and amazement at this dramatic evidence of God's power over evil, he is likewise motivated by his evaluative response «to extend this good news to others, realizing that the deliverance from demonic power that Jesus offers is not limited to selected individuals or groups but applies to all human beings»[47].

2.5 *The Reader and Effect of the Text*

This dialectical relationship between the reader and the text in the process of reading is most evident in our pericope. There are conventional norms (repertoire) which are shared by both the reader and the text, and also textual strategies; while the reader on its part have expectations, anticipations and retrospection as he meets the text.

Act of Reading, 97; J.L. RESSEGUIE, «Reader-Response Criticism», 319.

[46] W. ISER, *The Act of Reading*, 97; J.L. RESSEGUIE, «Reader-Response Criticism», 319.

[47] J.P. HEIL, *The Gospel of Mark*, 49.

To be in the synagogue of Capernaum on a sabbath is familiar, but to meet an «unknown leader» who teaches with authority, begins the process of defamiliarizing the familiar, and thereby creating an element of surprise and expectation on the reader. The analogy and contrast introduced by the narrator between Jesus and the scribes, increases the reader's possibility of identifying himself with Jesus, because «positive descriptions or evaluations of characters are likely to create involvement and sympathy for a character, whereas negative comments or evaluations promote alienation and distance from a character»[48]. And that is the case with the narrator's point of view with regard to Jesus' and the scribes' teaching.

In spite of the unfamiliar presence of the unclean spirit in the synagogue during sabbath worship, the reader must confront the surprise, defamiliarization, and also evaluate the different perspectives (points of view) about Jesus' identity (narrator, character, plot, and implied reader), and synthesize the changing themes (teaching, mission, identity, exorcism) from the horizon, and then fill the gaps, for a meaningful understanding. However, Jesus' command of exorcism to the unclean spirit heightens the reader's expectations, which could be fulfilling or disappointing/ frustrating. It is fulfilling for the reader, both on the part of the possessed man healed, and also gives a more positive image of Jesus' authority. Thus, the reader's identification with Jesus increases. And the familiar method of exorcism is defamiliarized by Jesus' simple command.

The people's heightened amazement at Jesus' teaching and exorcism and their discussion about them increases the identification with Jesus, whose teaching is referred to as «new»[49]. The reader must therefore evaluate again the narrator's point of view that Jesus teaches with authority (1:22), which the people are now confirming, with an added experience of his exorcism of the unclean spirit. The narrator's last comment of the spread of Jesus' fame everywhere around Galilee must also involve the anticipation and retrospection of the reader, who must assess, evaluate and synthesize the different perspectives, in order to give

---

[48] J.L. RESSEGUIE, «Reader-Response Criticism», 312.

[49] J.G. COOK, *Structure and Persuasive Power*, 288, observes that, «Mark's text encourages a complete allegiance to Jesus, faith in him, and a disciple/teacher relationship with Jesus. It pictures Jesus as a teacher sent by God and as the Son of God and Son of Man who dies on the cross, rises from the dead, and who will judge human beings after his return».

an adequate response to this text, and the identification with dominant character of the story.

3. Conclusion

Both in the theoretical and practical part of the reader-response method, it is evident that the reader is not passive but also active, especially in the reading process of the text. However, «the text as a written act exerts a strong pull on readers and hearers»[50]. The text indicates familiar conventions, which through defamiliarization introduces new ideas; through narrative techniques suggests different perspectives and filling up of the gaps. On the other hand, the reader with his deliberative acts forms expectations or experiences shattered or frustrated expectations, forms anticipations and retrospections, themes and horizons, gives evaluation of the different points of view, and also makes identification with the impressive character. All these we saw in our pericope.

The reader, in his reading process, identified himself with Jesus, when the people were astonished at his teaching, and the narrator gives a positive perspective of him (teaching with authority), to the detriment of the scribes. Thus, the analogy and contrast of the narrator puts Jesus' quality of teaching in relief. He identified himself with Jesus, when with a simple command he casts out the unclean spirit. Likewise when the people confirmed Jesus' authority in teaching and exorcism. And lastly, when the narrator concludes that Jesus' fame spread everywhere.

It is the duty of the reader to fill up the gap, where there is unwritten text, like between Jesus' arrival in Capernaum and the synagogue; what Jesus exactly taught on the sabbath that astonished the people; how, when and why the demoniac was in the synagogue; and who spreads Jesus' fame while he is still in the synagogue.

The reader must go back and forth with the changing themes and points of view in the text, in order to evaluate, reexamine, assess, and synthesize for the product of meaning. Our minds go to the identity of Jesus in the text, what the narrator, characters, plot or implied reader say/s: whether the Son of God, Holy One of God, teacher, etc. is the appropriate title for Jesus. However, the anticipation and retrospection helps the reader, to decide that «what one is» is more important than «what one does». And the quality of perspectives assure us that Jesus' relationship with God

---

[50] J.G. COOK, *Structure and Persuasive Power*, 289.

(1:1,11,24) authorizes him to perform any mission, and that is why he is endeared to the reader.

Just as in the narrative analysis, Jesus remains central in the story, so also here, in the pragmatic (reader-response) analysis. Therefore, the reader cannot but identify himself with Jesus, who is the centre of anticipation and expectation, of surprise, of admiration, of fulfilment, of positive perspectives, of themes (teaching, authority, mission, identity, exorcism, etc) and horizon, of discussion, and of spreading of his words and actions everywhere.

PART TWO

SYNTHETIC-THEOLOGICAL ANALYSIS

INTRODUCTION

In the first part of this work, we concentrated on the exegetical analysis of this pericope (1:21-28); while in this second part, we shall prove how the elements dominant in this pericope anticipate and combine many important themes in Mark's Gospel. With the help of that analysis, we were able to identify and highlight some of the themes and motives latent in the pericope. These themes/motives could be listed as follows: the disciples being with Jesus (being in Jesus' company); Jesus' teaching activity; the motif of wonder (astonishment/amazement) among the people with regard to Jesus' activities; the authority in Jesus' words and deeds; the role of the scribes (religious authorities) in Jesus' public ministry (controversy/conflict); Jesus' identity (the Nazarene, the Holy One of God); and his mission (especially with demonic powers); Jesus' command to silence, and his Exorcism; Jesus' fame (echo of his activities) and the role of the crowd in his public ministry; the place of Galilee in Jesus' entire ministry. We have moreorless given a summary of the content of our pericope under consideration.

On the basis of the above attestation, it would be our task to show or demonstrate in this part, that most of these themes run through (develop throughout) the Gospel of Mark. In fact, some authors have already demonstrated this affirmation with some of these themes, to mention but a few: Jesus' authority[51]; the motif of wonder[52]; Jesus' identity (Jesus, the Son of God)[53]; the Nazarene image (Jesus of Nazareth)[54]. In spite of this, we shall try to demonstrate that these themes are dominant in Mark's Gospel, and that their concentration in our pericope reveals clearly the function of this pericope in the Gospel of Mark: it has a *programmatic character*.

---

[51] K. SCHOLTISSEK, *Die Vollmacht Jesu*.
[52] T. DWYER, «The Motif of Wonder», 49-59; ID., *The Motif of Wonder*.
[53] C.R. KAZMIERSKI, *Jesus, the Son of God*.
[54] E.K. BROADHEAD, «Jesus the Nazarene.

In this second part, we shall concentrate on the themes/motives that concern or relate to Jesus, as the central figure of our story. But in order to prove our affirmation in Mark's Gospel, the most ideal thing would have been to follow the order of these themes as they appeared in the pericope, as seen above. However, one would also observe that some of these themes repeated themselves within the pericope. Therefore, if followed systematically one would duplicate or repeat them, for example: Jesus' teaching (vv.21,22,27); the people's wonder (vv.22,27); Jesus' authority (vv.22,27); Jesus' identity (v.24a,c); and Jesus' exorcism (vv.25-26,27). In view of this, I thought it wise to organize it, in such a way, that these repetitions could be avoided. To this, I have divided the themes in three chapters: (a) the themes dealing with Jesus personally: the Identity of Jesus, the Authority of Jesus, and the Mission of Jesus; (b) the themes dealing with Jesus' activity in the pericope: the Teaching of Jesus, and the Exorcism of Jesus; (c) and the themes on Jesus' relationship with the characters in the story: Jesus and the Disciples (being with him), Jesus and the Crowd (motif of Wonder), and Jesus and the Scribes (contrast/conflict).

CHAPTER V

The Person of Jesus

In our analysis in Part One, we noticed the importance of the presence of Jesus in the pericope, as the dominant character (protagonist) of the story. His natural and supernatural (true) identity was mentioned by the unclean spirit (v.24a,c), and the narrator repeated it (v.25a) in his description of Jesus' action at the crucial moment of exorcism, and was also indicated indirectly by the people (v.27). Jesus' authority and mission are also well emphasized by the people (vv.22,27) and the unclean spirit (v.24b) respectively. It will be our task to verify whether such importance is also noticeable of these themes throughout the entire Gospel of Mark. If so, this will then give us a partial prove of our pericope having a programmatic character in the Gospel.

Therefore, in this chapter we shall demonstrate in three sections, how «the Identity of Jesus», «the Authority of Jesus», and «the Mission of Jesus», programmatically develop throughout Mark's Gospel.

1. The Identity of Jesus

In this first section, the theme «the Identity of Jesus» will be treated in four parts: (a) the Presentation of Jesus, (b) the Question about Jesus' identity, (c) the Revelation of Jesus' identity, and (d) the direct relation of Jesus to God. These parts (a-c) show the presence of the theme in the principal parts of the Gospel, while part (d) shows the terms, ἅγιος - υἱὸς θεοῦ, etc., which concretely represent Jesus' relation with God.

In the demon's cry which calls Jesus, ὁ ἅγιος τοῦ θεοῦ (1:24), the theme of Jesus' identity is clearly present. Following the three main sections of Mark, we shall show the presence of this theme in the whole Gospel. In the Prologue (1:1-13), the evangelist Mark, John the Baptist, and God himself present it to the reader. The first half of the Gospel (1:14-8:26) strengthens the question about Jesus' identity through the cries of the demons, the questions and guesses of the human characters. In the second half of the Gospel (8:27-16:8), the trend changes from the questions of the human characters to the revelation of Jesus' identity to them. As the expression ὁ ἅγιος τοῦ θεοῦ deals directly with Jesus' relation with God, we shall therefore dedicate a special part of this section to the other expressions («my beloved Son», «Son of God», «Son», etc.), which indicate more precisely the same relation.

1.1 *The Presentation of Jesus (Mk 1:1-13)*

In the Prologue or Introduction (1:1-13), Jesus is presented to the reader, firstly, by the omniscient narrator (Mark) in the title of his Gospel: Ἀρχὴ τοῦ εὐαγγελίου Ἰησοῦ Χριστοῦ υἱοῦ Θεοῦ - «The beginning of the gospel of Jesus Christ, the Son of God» (1:1); which could also mean: the beginning of the good news that Jesus is the Christ, the Son of God. This not only gives the title but also the scope of Mark's work[1]. Secondly, John the Baptist, his precursor, describing Jesus as the one coming after him, called him, ὁ ἰσχυρότερός - «the mightier or stronger one» (1:7). He proved that designation by his relation with Jesus, and also by what Jesus will accomplish in his mission (esp. 3:27). Then, thirdly, at the Baptismal scene, the voice from Heaven (God) said of Jesus: σὺ εἶ ὁ υἱός μου ὁ ἀγαπητός, ἐν σοὶ εὐδόκησα - «You are my

---

[1] One observes that many scholars see Mk 1:1 as a title for the whole work of Mark, especially considering the anarthrousness of ἀρχή, its non-verbal nature and its scope in the Gospel. Cf. M.D. HOOKER, *St. Mark*, 33; H. ANDERSON, *Mark*, 66; V. TAYLOR, *Mark*, 152; J. GNILKA, *Markus* I, 42; C.E.B. CRANFIELD, *Mark*, 37; R. PESCH, *Markusevangelium* I, 74-75; J.G. COOK, *Structure and Persuasive Power*, 121-122, 126, 151-156, esp. 153-154 and n.38, sees it as a title, the «governing speech act» of Mark's Gospel, and an interpretation key to the whole Gospel. While some others limit it to Mk 1:1-8 (the Baptist's preaching) or the first section of the Gospel (introductory section: 1:1-15), but not the whole work. Cf. R.H. GUNDRY, *Mark*, 31; R.A. GUELICH, *Mark*, 7, 11-12; G. ARNOLD, «Mk 1,1 und Eröffnungswendungen», 123-127; W.L. LANE, *Mark*, 42. I would support those who regard Mk 1:1 as title of Mark's Gospel, because (a) it is Mark himself who placed it there for his work; (b) the whole account of the life and ministry of Jesus is the beginning or basis of the good news (cf. HOOKER, *Mark*, 33); (c) it is the gospel *about* Jesus (objective genitive); (d) the theme of Jesus, as the Christ, the Son of God, is dominant and at the heart of the gospel. Cf. GUELICH, *Mark*, 12; M. DE JONGE, *Christology in Context*, 54, 56. And this is clearly stated in this verbless heading or title.

beloved Son, with you I am well pleased» (1:11). With this initial presentation by three important characters in Jesus' story, the reader is armed with the key to the identity of Jesus in Mark's Gospel.

1.2 *The Question about Jesus' Identity (Mk 1:14-8:26)*

In the first half of Mark's Gospel (1:14-8:26), one meets with the question of the identity of Jesus, through the cries or confessions of demons, the questions of the people, the scribes, the disciples, Jewish public opinions, and Herod's judgement.

After the authoritative call of his disciples, Jesus made his first appearance in the synagogue of Capernaum (1:21-28). His presence stirred up the cry of a demoniac in the synagogue: τί ἡμῖν καὶ σοί, Ἰησοῦ Ναζαρηνέ; ... οἶδα σε τίς εἶ, ὁ ἅγιος τοῦ θεοῦ - «What have you to do with us, Jesus of Nazareth? ... I know who you are, the Holy One of God» (1:24). This demonic cry, beginning here in the pericope, dominates in the gospel, especially its first half[2]. And in their cry, the demons reveal the exact knowledge of Jesus' true identity, unlike the human characters[3]. This is clearly seen in a summary statement after his encounter in the synagogue, that Jesus did not allow them to speak because they knew him (1:34). In another summary statement, in Jesus' encounter with them, it is stated that whenever the unclean spirits beheld him, they fell down before him and cried out: σὺ εἶ ὁ υἱὸς τοῦ θεοῦ - «You are the Son of God» (3:11). All the same, Jesus imposed silence on them. At another encounter with Jesus at the country of Gerasenes, the demon cried out: τί ἐμοὶ καὶ σοί, Ἰησοῦ υἱὲ τοῦ θεοῦ τοῦ ὑψίστου; - «What have you to do with me, Jesus, Son of the Most High God?» (5:7). «These confessions of the demons are concentrated in the first part of the Gospel; in this part they are those who know truly Jesus, and have almost the function of keeping present the theme of the identity of Jesus»[4]. Thus, «the demons in Mark serve to keep Jesus' divine identity in the forefront of readers' minds. But even as compared to the demons' knowledge, theirs is more complete»[5].

---

[2] Cf. K. STOCK, «Die Machttaten Jesu», 199.

[3] K. STOCK, «La conoscenza dei demoni», 93-97, 111-112.

[4] K. STOCK, «Gesù è il Cristo», 247 (trans. is *mine*); Cf. J.D. KINGSBURY, *Christology of Mark*, 86.

[5] B.D. CHILTON, «Exorcism and History», 258.

On the part of the human characters, where the activity of Jesus among the people helped to prepare the ground for the question about Jesus' identity, this theme was raised through interrogations or questions[6]. In fact, this interrogation began in the same pericope of the synagogue of Capernaum, when the people in the synagogue questioned each other: τί ἐστιν τοῦτο; διδαχὴ καινὴ κατ'ἐξουσίαν·... - «What is this? A new teaching with authority...» (1:27). Or the scribes' questioning in their hearts in reproach to Jesus' healing words to the paralytic: τί οὗτος οὕτως λαλεῖ;... - «Why does this man speak thus? It is blasphemy! Who can forgive sins but God alone?» (2:7). These questions, as one can see, are done in an impersonal manner of wonder still vague; but the first determinate, personal interrogation was raised by the disciples[7] after Jesus had calmed the storm in the sea: τίς ἄρα οὗτός ἐστιν ... - «Who then is this, that even wind and sea obey him?» (4:41). On another occasion, those who were in the synagogue, who heard Jesus' teaching, in their astonishment asked many questions about Jesus, among which regards his identity: οὐχ οὗτός ἐστιν ὁ τέκτων, ὁ υἱὸς Μαρίας... - «Is not this the carpenter, the son of Mary ...» (6:3).

Relating the cries of the demons to the questions the human characters ask concerning the identity of Jesus, Kingsbury sees the relationship between them, in terms of the dynamics of Mark's story, as *contrapuntal*. He illustrates it thus:

> demonic cry (1:24), question (1:27), demonic cries (1:34), question (2:7), demonic cries (3:11), question (4:41), demonic cry (5:7), question (6:3). Also, it should be noted that the first demonic cry and the first question both occur in the first pericope that is not a summary- passage in which Mark portrays Jesus as being active in public (1:23-28 [vv.24,27])[8].

In effect, this exposes the reader, from the beginning of Jesus' public ministry, to a sustained sequence of utterances in which cries revealing the identity of Jesus alternate with questions about who he is[9].

---

[6] J.G. COOK, *Structure and Persuasive Power*, 162, notes that, Jesus'activities provoke four questions about his identity in 1:27; 2:7; 4:41; and 6:3. And that the demons answer this question several times in 1:24-25, 34, 3:11-12 and in 5:7. Cf. J.D. KINGSBURY, *Christology of Mark*, 88, 89.

[7] Cf. K. STOCK, «Gesú è il Cristo», 247.

[8] J.D. KINGSBURY, *Christology of Mark*, 86-87.

[9] J.D. KINGSBURY, *Christology of Mark*, 87.

On the other hand, Jesus' activity and the widespread of his fame, prompted the Jewish public and Herod to form their «evaluative points of view» about the identity of Jesus. In this case, some say he is John the Baptizer raised from the dead, «that is why these powers are at work in him»; others take him to be Elijah; while yet others take him to be a prophet. (6:14-16; cf. 8:27-28). Thus, «Mark himself illustrates how radical the misunderstanding of Jesus' person could be»[10]. However, the reader knows, from the beginning that these judgments are wrong and false, «because they do not square with what the reader knows is the "normative" understanding of Jesus in Mark's story»[11].

In this first half or second part of Mark's Gospel (1:14-8:26), one observes not only questions on the part of human characters but also wrong affirmations like the scribes saying that Jesus was possessed by Beelzebul (3:22), or his relatives, that he was insane (3:21). His disciples with their privileged position — sharing his own mission (3:14-15; 6:7-13, 30); experiencing the epiphanies (4:35-41; 6:45-52); the feeding miracles (6:34-44; 8:1-10), and many healing miracles and exorcisms, etc — even lacked the understanding of Jesus' identity[12]. Thus, their question, «who then is this?» remains an unanswered and open question. Since the human characters so far have exhibited no insight into Jesus' identity, the reader had to rely on the demons to be reminded of Jesus' identity.

1.3 *The Revelation of Jesus' Identity (Mk 8:27-16:8)*

In the second half of Mark's Gospel (8:27-16:8), a different pattern emerges. Here no longer do demons shout the identity of Jesus; on the contrary, Jesus' identity becomes a focal issue for the human characters, and some evince insight into it[13]. Thus it becomes a progressive revelation or disclosure of Jesus' identity to the human characters or rather to the reader. So «Mark guides the reader through a series of scenes in which he observes Peter confess Jesus to be the Messiah (8:29), Bartimaeus appeal

---

[10] L. SWAIN, «Mark's Christology», 704.

[11] J.D. KINGSBURY, *Christology of Mark*, 87-88.

[12] S.H. SMITH commenting on the anticipation and delay of the recognition scene (Jesus' identity) in Mark's Gospel with regard to the disciples, says: «Potentially, each such episode provides them with an opportunity to recognise who Jesus is, but they fail to do so, and Jesus becomes increasingly exasperated at their lack of understanding (4:13, 40; 7:18; 8:17-21)». Cf. «Structure of Mark», 214.

[13] Cf. J.D. KINGSBURY, *Christology of Mark*, 90.

to him as the Son of David (10:47-48), the Roman centurion declare him to be the Son of God (15:39), ...»[14] It is worth noting that the theme of identity of Jesus is also dominant in the account of his passion and death.

In the centre of Mark's Gospel (8:27-30)[15], Jesus himself took the initiative to present expressly and openly the problem of his identity to his disciples: «Who do men say that I am?» He received the same popular opinion of the Jewish public (8:28, cf. 6:14-16). Now he addressed the disciples directly: «But who do you say that I am?» Then it is here for the first time a human being - Peter, the leader and spokesman of the disciples - declares Jesus' identity: Σὺ εἶ ὁ Χριστός[16] - «You are the Christ» (8:29). After Peter's confession, Jesus begins to explain and announce to his disciples his passion, death and resurrection (8:31, cf. 9:31; 10:33-34), thereby correcting him that the Son of God, the Christ, the Son of man, must suffer, die and rise again (8:31). Thus, «as soon as he is recognised, however, he is compelled to teach what true messiahship means - suffering and death prior to glory, a fate which the followers are expected to share (8:34-38)»[17]. This teaching definitely was not easy for the disciples to understand (8:32-33). However, after six days, at the Transfiguration scene[18] on the mountain, a voice from the cloud (God) revealed to the three disciples: οὗτός ἐστιν ὁ υἱός μου ὁ ἀγαπητός, ἀκούετε αὐτοῦ - «This is my beloved Son; listen to him» (9:7). With this recognition scene and revelation, at the beginning of the second half of the Gospel, the progressive disclosure of Jesus' identity has begun for the human characters, and will continue.

---

[14] J.D. KINGSBURY, *Christology of Mark*, 91.

[15] Cf. I. DE LA POTTERIE, «De Compositione», 135-141; L. SWAIN, «Mark's Christology», 704; S. KUTHIRAKKATTEL, *The Beginning*, 37. For S.H. SMITH, «Structure of Mark», 215-217, this is the *recognition scene*, where recognition (ἀναγνώρισις) and reversal (περιπέτεια) coincide.

[16] Cf. S. KUTHIRAKKATTEL, *The Beginning*, 37; K. STOCK, «Gesú è il Cristo», 248; L. SWAIN, «Mark's Christology», 704.

[17] S.H. SMITH, «Structure of Mark», 216.

[18] On whether 8:27-30 and 9:2-8 are double recognition scenes, S.H. SMITH, «Structure of Mark», 216-217, clarifies, «the Transfiguration *is* a revelation - an epiphany of messianic glory - but it is not a recognition in the sense of a typical tragic ἀναγνώρισις; that has already occurred in 8:27-30. ... The Transfiguration is a manifestation of the true nature of the messianic identity which has just been recognised, and even then, Peter, with his peculiar comment in 9:5, seems unable to grasp it».

This disclosure of Jesus' identity began from the beginning for the reader[19], but for the human characters it comes in stages. Thus Kingsbury states:

If the first stage is Peter's correct and insufficient confession of Jesus to be Messiah (8:29), the second stage is Bartimaeus's appeal to Jesus as the Son of David (10:46-52). And if «Messiah» in 8:29 constitutes the «evaluative point of view» concerning Jesus' identity of Peter and the disciples, «Son of David» constitutes the «evaluative point of view» concerning Jesus' identity of Bartimaeus[20].

In fact, «the nub of the story is that Bartimaeus insistently appeals to Jesus as the Son of David to have mercy on him, and Jesus responds to his appeal by restoring his sight (10:47-52)»[21]. The Bartimaeus' story provides a sharp focus on the identity of Jesus, in other words, it prepares the christological focus of the story, since the narrative motifs employ four titles: Jesus, the Nazarene, son of David, rabbi. Thus, «the internal syntax of the story employs the need and the healing of Bartimaeus to focus the identity of Jesus: he is the son of David who draws near to his destiny in Jerusalem, ...»[22]

Jesus' triumphant entry (11:1-10) into Jerusalem riding on a colt created a symbolic action of a messianic manifestation (cf. Zech. 9:9). And the joyful cry out of those following him saw it so: «Hosanna! Blessed is he who comes in the name of the Lord! Blessed is the kingdom of our father David that is coming! Hosanna in the highest!» (11:9-10). Jesus is that messiah (8:29), they spoke about. In fact, this scene also touches on the identity of Jesus[23].

Concluding his teaching in the temple, after facing so many questions from the religious groups and authorities, Jesus took the initiative to raise the question of the relationship between the Christ and David before the people, by asking: πῶς λέγουσιν οἱ γραμματεῖς ὅτι ὁ χριστὸς υἱὸς

---

[19] On this, Quesnell observes that «in 8:27ff. the disciples recognize Jesus as the Christ for the first time. The reader has known that he is the Christ since at least 1:1. The reader knows more about him -that he is the Son of God (1:1, 11)». Q. QUESNELL, *The Mind of Mark*, 132.

[20] J.D. KINGSBURY, *Christology of Mark*, 102.

[21] J.D. KINGSBURY, *Christology of Mark*, 102.

[22] E.K. BROADHEAD, *Teaching with Authority*, 160.

[23] Cf. K. STOCK, «La conoscenza dei demoni», 108-110; J.D. KINGSBURY, *Christology of Mark*, 107-108.

Δαυίδ ἐστιν; - How can the scribes say that the Christ is the son of David? (12:35). Thus, this takes up the motif of Jesus' identity (the davidic lineage), as seen in the Bartimaeus' story. On how the Christ (Messiah) could be both the «son» of David and the «lord» of David, Kingsbury answers, «the Messiah is the "son" of David because he is descended from David; by the same token, the Messiah is also the "lord" of David because, as the Son of God, he is of higher station and authority than David»[24]. Hence, «in 12:35-37 Jesus challenges the simple davidic sonship of the Messiah, suggesting that he must be more than David's son»[25]. And this remains an open question (cf. v.37).

In the last part of the Gospel, the account of the passion and death of Jesus, the question of Jesus' identity is also very prominent. During Jesus' trial he was silent, but responded only to the questions that concern his identity[26]: the high priest asked him, σὺ εἶ ὁ χριστὸς ὁ υἱὸς τοῦ εὐλογητοῦ; - «Are you the Christ, the Son of the Blessed?»[27](14:61); and Jesus replied, ἐγώ εἰμι,... - «I am,...» (14:62). Pilate asked him, σὺ εἶ ὁ βασιλεὺς τῶν Ἰουδαίων; - «Are you the King of the Jews?»; and Jesus answered, σὺ λέγεις. - «You say so» (15:2). With this title, «King of the Jews», Jesus' trial continued until the inscription on the top of the cross (15:9,12,18,26). Even those mocking and insulting him did indicate his identity, ὁ χριστὸς ὁ βασιλεὺς Ἰσραὴλ καταβάτω νῦν ἀπὸ τοῦ σταυροῦ,... -«Let the Christ, the King of Israel, come down now from the cross, that we may see and believe» (15:32). Notwithstanding the insults, after Jesus' expiration (death) on the cross, a pagan centurion who was standing there present made a more adequate confession: ἀληθῶς οὗτος ὁ ἄνθρωπος υἱὸς θεοῦ ἦν. - «Truly this man was the Son of God!» (15:39). On the pivotal importance of the centurion's acclamation, Kingsbury affirms, «it constitutes for the first time in Mark's story the open confession of Jesus as the Son of God on the part of a human being and occurs precisely at the point where Jesus does attain to the end and culmination of his ministry»[28].

---

[24] J.D. KINGSBURY, *Christology of Mark*, 112-113.

[25] L. SWAIN, «Mark's Christology», 705.

[26] Cf. K. STOCK, «Gesú è il Cristo», 249.

[27] The sending of the «beloved son» in the parable of the wicked Tenants (12:6-8), refers to Jesus' identity as the Son of God.

[28] J.D. KINGSBURY, *Christology of Mark*, 132.

It is therefore not possible for one to negate the fact, that the theme of the identity of Jesus, the christological theme, is present and dominant in the whole work of Mark's Gospel[29]. And this identity motif was touched by the main characters in the story: the omniscient Narrator, God, John the Baptist, Jesus himself, the demons, disciples, the peoples, scribes (religious authorities), Herod, Bartimaeus, the High Priest, Pilate and the Centurion. So we can talk of a christological concentration in the Gospel of Mark; or one can even claim that the central and principal theme of this gospel is exactly the theme of the identity of Jesus.

1.4 *The Direct Relation of Jesus with God*

The expression «the Holy One of God» affirms the fact of a special and unique relation of Jesus with God; while the «Son of God» affirms the character of this relation, which is a personal and cordial relation of «son-father». We shall now trace how this designation, «Son of God», and other similar ones, «beloved Son», «Son of the Blessed One», and «Son» are present in Mark's Gospel. We simply present their occurrences in Mark.

1.4.1   Mark 1:1

Here Mark *introduces* this designation, «Son of God», in the title of his Gospel: Ἀρχὴ τοῦ εὐαγγελίου Ἰησοῦ Χριστοῦ υἱοῦ Θεοῦ.- «The beginning of the gospel of Jesus Christ, the Son of God» (1:1). The phrase, υἱοῦ Θεοῦ, has at least two problems: textual and grammatical. Firstly, it is omitted in some manuscripts (ℵ* Θ 28 *pc* sa^ms; Or) but present in ℵ¹ B D L W 2427 *pc* latt sy co; Ir^lat. The broad and strong external evidence favour the inclusion of the phrase[30]; it has also internal support[31]. There are other reasons for certifying the originality of the phrase: (a) As Mark is writing to Gentile audience, they will certainly respond to «Son of God» with thoughts of divinity[32]; (b) the identification

---

[29] Cf. K. STOCK, «Gesú è il Cristo», 249.

[30] Cf. B.M. METZGER, *Textual Commentary*, 73; R.H. GUNDRY, *Mark*, 33; R.A. GUELICH, *Mark*, 6; V. TAYLOR, *Mark*, 152.

[31] This title may have been omitted because of ugly sight of six genitives; or the abbreviation of a longer reading ΙΥΧΥΥΥΘΥ into a shorter one ΙΥΧΥ by homoioteleuton; or other reasons. Cf. R.H. GUNDRY, *Mark*, 33; R.A. GUELICH, *Mark*, 6; C.E.B. CRANFIELD, *Mark*, 38.

[32] Cf. R.H. GUNDRY, *Mark*, 34.

of Jesus as «Lord» in v.2 may lend some weight to the view that the divine
title «Son of God» belongs to the original text of 1:1[33]; (c) and moreover
«Son of God» is an important theme in Mark's Gospel, as we have already
seen. Secondly, we are faced with the anarthrousness of «Son of God» (cf.
also 15:39; and also the anarthrousness of «Christ»), which contrast with
the arthrousness of the same term/s elsewhere. Here Gundry prefers to
see the absence of the definite article as emphasizing the qualities of
divine appointment and divine sonship[34]. In fact, «the meaning of the
anarthrous phrase υἱὸς θεοῦ in the Gospel of Mark has to be assessed in
the context of the Gospel and its christology in its entirety»[35].

For us, the term, «Son of God» is very important for Mark's work;
indeed it sets the scope of his Gospel: to proclaim that Jesus is the Christ,
the Son of God. And it is the central and dominant theme that runs
through his Gospel. Thus, it introduces the theme of Jesus' identity right
here, at the beginning of the Gospel, and concludes it later with it too (cf.
15:39).

1.4.2   Mark 1:11

On the occasion of Jesus' baptism, God, the divine voice from heaven,
confirms that Jesus is his beloved Son: Σὺ εἶ ὁ υἱός μου ὁ ἀγαπητός, ἐν
σοι εὐδόκησα. - «You are my beloved Son; with you I am well pleased»
(1:11). And this is addressed to Jesus himself, adding audition on top of
vision to heighten Jesus' awareness. It is generally accepted that
ἀγαπητός («beloved») can also mean «only» or «sole» (יחיד in Hebrew),
and may be because an only son is naturally beloved[36]. Thus, «he is not
just Son of God in any way, but he is the only Son, whose relation with
God is unique in its kind, and to whom goes all the love of the Father.

---

[33] Cf. R.H. GUNDRY, *Mark*, 36.

[34] Cf. R.H. GUNDRY, *Mark*, 34.

[35] T.H. KIM, «Mark 15,39, 222.

[36] One would ask: what is the difference between υἱὸς θεοῦ and ὁ υἱός μου ὁ
ἀγαπητός? In the first place, «my beloved Son» is the way God addresses Jesus (1:11;
9:7; 12:6); while others (demons, the centurion and the evangelist) address him as «Son
of God» (1:1; 3:11; 5:7; 15:39). Both have to do with a quality of relation that is
personal. «Beloved» stresses the personal and cordial character of the relation; while
Jesus as the Son of God, as others testify, means a close and personal relation of Jesus
with God. As the beloved Son, Jesus is the unique or only Son of God.

God speaks from this relation»[37]. Here then we are not concerned about a function, but a relation; not about an event but a state. On the other hand, «"well pleased" corresponds with the Markan "only/beloved (ἀγαπητός) son" which underscores the primary motif of affection, delight and pleasure inherent in εὐδοκεῖν»[38]. There is thus a new and vital relationship to God which transcends Messiahship as it was understood in Jewish thought. In fact, «the fundamental note in the saying is the filial status of Jesus; and the words are best understood as an assurance, or confirmation, of this relationship, rather than a disclosure or revelation»[39]. Thus, the words of the divine voice in Mk 1:11 (as against Ps.2) stands on itself and expresses a state, a stable relation, the relation of Jesus to God, which one presents as the personal relation of «son-father»[40]. Hence God enters into Jesus' story, as a character, to confirm the special and unique relationship existing between himself and Jesus, before he begins his messianic mission.

1.4.3 Mark 1:24; 3:11; 5:7

The unclean spirits (demons) *identify* Jesus as the «Holy One of God» (1:24), «Son of God» (3:11), and «Son of the Most High God» (5:7). In this way the unclean spirits recognize and acknowledge Jesus, not as Messiah, but rather as the divine Son of God. «The fact that the demons are supernatural creatures gives them a supernatural knowledge; but beyond that the form of recognition in 3:11 is the most solemn in the entire work and brings to mind the solemn opening of the Gospel: Ἀρχὴ

---

[37] K. STOCK, «La conoscenza dei demoni», 106 (trans. mine).

[38] R.A. GUELICH, *Mark*, 34.

[39] V. TAYLOR, *Mark*, 162; C.E.B. CRANFIELD, *Mark*, 55; R.H. GUNDRY, *Mark*, 50.
     Often this saying is commonly traced to a combination of the phrases from Ps 2:7 and Isa. 42:1, which leads to its interpretation as an «adoption formula» - that is, that at this very point he was «made» Son of God, as is the king in Psalm 2. On the contrary, Mark interpretated these words simply as a declaration of Jesus' identity; and moreover for him «Jesus is by nature the Son of God and the voice at the Baptism declares him to be such». Cf. V. TAYLOR, *Mark*, 121; E. PINTO, «Son of God , 78; M.D. HOOKER, *St. Mark*, 48. Likewise «the advancement of σύ, "you", to the front shifts the point from adoption and enthronement (so Ps.2:7) to identification and acknowledgment». Cf. R.H. GUNDRY, *Mark*, 53, cf. 49.

[40] E. PINTO, «Son of God», 90, observes that the examination of the text of the Gospels shows that Jesus is constantly using the images of the Father and the Son to describe his relationship with God.

τοῦ εὐαγγελίου Ἰησοῦ Χριστοῦ υἱοῦ Θεοῦ. The connection cannot be overlooked. It represents the confession of the Gentile Church uttered in its most majestic form»[41]. However, these spirits acknowledge Jesus' superiority (1:24), and also worship him (3:11, cf. 5:6-7). The forward positions of τὰ πνεύματα τὰ ἀκάθαρτα and of αὐτόν emphasize this acknowledgement of Jesus as God's Son. Mark also emphasizes the repetitiveness and consistency with which the unclean spirits fall prostrate toward Jesus and shout to him that he is God's Son: «whenever they saw him» (ὅταν plus the imperfect indicative). Without exception they find themselves irresistibly drawn to acknowledge by gesture and outcry his divine sonship[42], because they know him (1:34).

The demoniac also addresses Jesus as «Son of the Most High God» (5:7). The term, (ὑψίστου - Heb. עליון), «the Most High God» is found in the Old Testament, mostly used by non-Israelites to denote the God of Israel. It is therefore appropriate in the mouth of one who was living in Gentile territory and was presumably himself a Gentile[43]. In this way, the unclean spirits in these three texts call out the true identity of Jesus, as the Son of God, which Mark introduced and was confirmed by God *in prima persona*.

1.4.4   Mark 9:7

In 9:2-8, the divine voice from the cloud (God) speaks, and once more enters into the story. Now God *reveals* to the three chosen disciples (Peter, James and John, 9:2) the mystery of Jesus' identity: οὗτός ἐστιν ὁ υἱός μου ὁ ἀγαπητός, ἀκούετε αὐτοῦ. - «This is my beloved Son; listen to him» (9:7). Here the divine voice addresses the disciples, not Jesus. Correspondingly, σὺ εἶ («you are», 1:11) changes to οὗτός ἐστιν («this is», 9:7). The disciples, on the mountain, had both visual and auditory experiences that overwhelmingly convinced them that Jesus was indeed the Son of God[44]. Thus, «the Transfiguration is seen by Mark as a revelation from God in which the three chosen disciples are allowed to behold the divine Glory of Jesus as well as to hear the voice of God lay

---

[41] C.R. KAZMIERSKI, *Jesus, the Son of God*, 102.
[42] Cf. R.H. GUNDRY, *Mark*, 158.
[43] Cf. M.D. HOOKER, *St. Mark*, 145; R.A. GUELICH, *Mark*, 279; C.E.B. CRANFIELD, *Mark*, 177.
[44] Cf. V. TAYLOR, *Mark*, 392.

claim to him as his Beloved Son»[45]. If one compares this scene with the Baptismal one, it will be observed that the new element is the exhortation to listen to Jesus. It is important because it connects the identity of Jesus with the disciples' obligation to listen to him. In fact, «the declaration of Jesus as God's beloved Son counteracts taking offence at his predicted passion and at the consequent command to take up one's cross and follow him (8:31-38)»[46]. Thus, the announcement of the passion, death and resurrection, and the revelation of the Son of God are strictly connected. And it is not a contradiction but a connection between the destiny of Jesus and his quality of Son of God. The divine and beloved sonship of Jesus, which was first confirmed to Jesus by God at the Baptismal scene, is here at the Transfiguraion scene, revealed to the disciples. We are not concerned here with, whether the disciples understood the revelation, or not; but rather here the emphasis is laid on the person or identity of Jesus, as the unique and beloved Son of God.

1.4.5 Mark 12:6

In 12:1-12, the parable of the Vineyard and the Wicked Tenants, we meet the *rejection* of Jesus, the Son of God. Jesus himself tells the story, where the owner of the vineyard is God. After sending many servants, whom the wicked tenants, either beat, wounded, or killed (12:3, 4, 5); he finally decided to send «υἱον ἀγαπητόν - a beloved son», saying, «They will respect τὸν υἱόν μου - my son» (12:6). Here we notice a three-step progression[47] in the use of «beloved son» in Mark (1:11; 9:7; 12:6), in contrast with Matthew and Luke. We observe the progressive revelation about the identity and destiny of Jesus: firstly, Jesus alone; secondly, a select group of apostles; thirdly and finally, even to Jesus' enemies[48]. In fact, the hearers of this parable are the true enemies of Jesus, the group of chief priests, scribes and elders (12:1,12; cf. 11:27), intimately

---

[45] C.R. KAZMIERSKI, *Jesus, the Son of God*, 125.

[46] R.H. GUNDRY, *Mark*, 461.

[47] The «three-step progression» is also seen in the triple repetition of the Passion predicitions - Mk 8:31; 9:31; and 10:32-34.

[48] Cf. J. SWETNAM, Review, 137; ID., «On the Identity of Jesus», 414; R.H. GUNDRY, *Mark*, 686; C.R. KAZMIERSKI, *Jesus, the Son of God*, 136-137. In the parable, Jesus brings to expression God's own «evaluative point of view» regarding him, as already shown in the baptismal and transfiguration scenes (1:11; 9:7 cf. 12:6), as «my beloved Son». Cf. J.D. KINGSBURY, *Christology of Mark*, 116-117.

connected with his trial (14:53) and death (14:64). And they were mentioned in the gospel for the first time really in the first prediction of Jesus' death (8:31; indeed, only in 8:31 and 12:10 occurs the verb ἀποδοκιμάζειν - to reject).

There is a great difference between the servants sent and the beloved Son in relation to the master or owner of the vineyard, and it consists on the quality of the one sent. There is no doubt that in this parable, Jesus speaks about his own mission, and also describes his relation with those who preceded him, sent by God, and his relation with God. Thus, Jesus establishes to be in personal and cordial relation of the beloved Son with God, in contrast with those who came before him. Hence this makes it abundantly clear that the term, «beloved son» does not designate a function of Jesus, but his unique and personal relation with God.

1.4.6   Mark 13:32

In his eschatological discourse, Jesus in 13:32 *refers* to himself as «the Son». It is significant, that this is the only place in Mark where ὁ υἱός is used absolutely. «It is an important piece of evidence against the view that Jesus could not have thought of himself as the unique Son of God (cf. Mt 11:27; Lk 10:22)»[49]. Here Jesus talks about «that day or that hour» of the coming of the Son of Man. In fact, «the astonishing thing is the inclusion of the Son with men and angels who know not the day or the hour»[50]. One would question, whether «the Son» at the level of Mark's story functions as an alternate to «Son of God» or to «Son of Man». To this, one could answer with Gundry that:

> In v.32 mention of «the Father» in the phrase immediately following «neither the Son» implies that we should understand «the Son» as God's, not man's. Indeed, anticipation of the reference to God in «the Father» causes «of God» to be omitted; for in referring to himself as «the Son» in relation to «the Father», Jesus does not need to include «of God» (cf. 1:11; 9:7)[51].

However, our concern here is not the authenticity of attributing ignorance of «that day or that hour» to Jesus, or whether «the Son» is «of God» or

---

[49] C.E.B. CRANFIELD, *Mark*, 411.

[50] V. TAYLOR, *Mark*, 522. The idea that the Day is known only to God is typically Jewish. cf. *ibid.*

[51] R.H. GUNDRY, *Mark*, 794-795; Cf. J.D. KINGSBURY, *Christology of Mark*, 138-139.

«of man»; but rather to highlight the unique relation of Jesus to God. Likewise, the bringing together «Son» and «Father» in the same verse puts in relief the «son-father»[52] relation. In fact, editorially, the divine sonship of Jesus has characterized Mark's Gospel from the beginning (1:1), and here is not excluded.

1.4.7 Mark 14:61-62

In the context of his trial (14:53-65), Jesus *confesses* or *confirms* his identity as the Christ and the Son of God (14:61-62). The high priest, before the assembly of the chief priests, the elders and the scribes (14:53), asked Jesus a double question, which he replied with silence (14:60-61a)[53]. Then, in defiance of justice, he put this incriminating question to Jesus: σὺ εἶ ὁ χριστὸς ὁ υἱὸς τοῦ εὐλογητοῦ; - «Are you the Christ, the Son of the Blessed?» (14:61c). Here σύ is emphatic and contemptuous[54]. The expression ὁ υἱὸς τοῦ εὐλογητοῦ (the Son of the Blessed) illustrates the Jewish tendency to avoid direct references to God[55]. However, unlike the preceding double question, Jesus' reply to this question on his identity is unequivocal and affirmative: ἐγώ εἰμι - «I am» (14:62)[56]. It should not surprise anyone, and I think it is entirely appropriate that at this point in Mark's story, Jesus should acknowledge his messianic status and true identity. «It is not something that he claims

---

[52] To add to the discussion, it is worth noting that God is addressed as Father of Jesus three times in Mark's Gospel, and in two contexts: (a) in the context of the coming of the Son of Man (8:38; 13:32); and (b) in the context of prayer of Jesus at Gethsemani. From the former context, it becomes a clear fact that the Son of Man is the Son of God.

[53] The double question is more in accord with Mark's style (8:17f) and its effect is vivid: first, an indignant query, «Have you no answer to make?», and then a demand, «What is it that these men testify against you?» Cf. V. TAYLOR, *Mark*, 567. Mark also doubles Jesus' refusal to answer — «but he was silent, and made no answer». This is also characteristic and effective. Cf. R.H. GUNDRY, *Mark*, 885; V. TAYLOR, *Mark*, 567.

[54] Cf. V. TAYLOR, *Mark*, 567; R.H. GUNDRY, *Mark*, 886.

[55] Cf. V. TAYLOR, *Mark*, 567; R.H. GUNDRY, *Mark*, 909. Matthew recasts the phrase in the form of «the Son of God».

[56] Jesus' affirmative answer here is surprising in view of the secrecy and silence about Jesus' identity that has reigned up to this point. Moreover, in comparison with the other Synoptic writers, one discovers that Mt 26:64 has σὺ εἶπας («you have said so»); and Lk 22:70: ὑμεῖς λέγετε ὅτι ἐγώ εἰμι («you say that I am»). Or the reply to Pilate, they all (Mk 15:2 = Mt 27:11 = Lk 23:3) have σὺ λέγεις («you say so»).

unwittingly declares his true identity as Messiah and Son of God»[57]. Furthermore, Jesus' reply, «I am» is a confession, «you will see ...» a prediction[58]; moreover, it is noteworthy that they appear here in v.62, the three important designations of Jesus - Christ, Son of God, and Son of Man - that relate to his mission, identity and destiny.

On the other hand, it is worth noting, that there is a strict connection between the parable of the vineyard and the wicked tenants (12:1-12) and the trial of Jesus (14:53-65)[59]. Not only that the group, who were the hearers of the parable, and the judges at the trial are identical (12:1,12; cf. 11:27; 14:53); it is also before them that the high priest puts his question (14:61), and in which they see in Jesus' response blasphemy, worthy of death (14:64)[60]. In fact, the high priest takes up in his question only what Jesus himself had said in this very revelatory parable. Thus, «Son of the Blessed» takes up the «beloved Son» of 12:6, and it is intended in this sense in order to distinguish it from the functional concept of the «Messiah». Indeed, «for Mark, Jesus will not be raised to divine Sonship at his exaltation, he is already Son of God as he stands before his accusers»[61]. Nevertheless, one must from the foregoing agree that, «it is because Jesus acknowledges that he is Messiah and Son of God that he is put to death, it is as Messiah that he is crucified, and it is through death that he is proclaimed as Messiah and Son of God (15:18,26,32,59)»[62].

I see the question and answer (14:61-62) in this pericope as the climax of the discussion on the identity of Jesus in Mark's story. This is because, faced with the challenge to defend his identity, Jesus himself confesses or confirms unequivocally his identity (even before his fatal enemies) which has remained secret. But the blindness of the religious authorities could not allow them to understand him, rather they saw his claim as blas-

---

[57] M.D. HOOKER, St. Mark, 361.

[58] Cf. R.H. GUNDRY, Mark, 910.

[59] Cf. R.H. GUNDRY, Mark, 908; J.D. KINGSBURY, Christology of Mark, 118-119; 150-151.

[60] After the departure of this group in 12:12, they appear again only in 14:1 planning to catch or arrest Jesus. Only in 12:12 and 14:1 can one find the combination of ἐζήτουν ... κρατῆσαι («seeking ... to arrest»), also in this way these texts are connected. It seems 14:1 took up their reaction and intention in 12:12, which was finally fulfilled in their condemning him to death in 14:64. Thus, this strengthens the link between the parable and the trial process.

[61] C.R. KAZMIERSKI, Jesus, the Son of God, 187.

[62] M.D. HOOKER, St. Mark, 361.

phemy. Hence they sentenced to death the Messiah and the Son of God, for claiming to be what he is.

1.4.8 Mark 15:39

Lastly, the centurion[63] *proclaims* in his confession that Jesus is truly the Son of God: ἀληθῶς οὗτος ὁ ἄνθρωπος υἱὸς θεοῦ ἦν. - «Truly this man was the Son of God» (15:39). The υἱὸς θεοῦ here forms *inclusio* with that in Mk 1:1. In fact, the centurion's word is the last statement on Jesus' identity in Mark's Gospel[64]; and forms not only the narrative climax but also the christological climax of this Gospel[65]. In Mark's Gospel it is neither the earthquake and the surrounding events (cf. Mt 27:54), nor the event in general (Lk 23:47), but rather the actual death of Jesus that caused the centurion's «confession». Thus the confession that Jesus is the Son of God is for Mark closely tied with the death of Jesus[66]. In order words, there is a close connection between Jesus' divine sonship and his death which reaches its climax in the passion narrative (cf. 14:62)[67].

The centurion, as the one charged with the execution of Jesus' crucifixion, took a strategic position[68] in order to report back to Pilate about Jesus' death (15:44, 45). His confession is based on what he saw about the person of Jesus: ἰδὼν... ὅτι οὕτως ἐξέπνευσεν - «he saw that he died thus (in this way)». In other words, he saw that Jesus died uttering a loud cry[69] (expired with a loud cry) — a wordless cry (15:37, cf. 15:34).

---

[63] This term κεντυρίων («centurion»), is a Latin loanword, which appears only here and in 15:44,45 within the NT; while ἑκατόνταρχος, -ης is found in Mt and Lk. «Mark's characteristic use of Latinism can be accounted for by Roman provenance or influence...» Cf. P.M. HEAD, *Christology*, 200; R.H. GUNDRY, *Mark*, 1044.

[64] Cf. K. STOCK, «Das Bekenntnis des Centurio», 289, 301.

[65] Cf. P.G. DAVIS, «Mark's Christological Paradox», 4, 14; M.D. HOOKER, *St. Mark*, 379.

[66] Cf. P.M. HEAD, *Christology*, 200; M.D. HOOKER, *St. Mark*, 378; K. STOCK, «Das Bekenntnis des Centurio», 290-293; 296-298.

[67] Cf. P.M. HEAD, *Christology*, 199.

[68] Mark gave a detailed description of his position: ὁ κεντυρίων ὁ παρεστηκὼς ἐξ ἐναντίας αὐτοῦ - «the centurion, who was standing facing (opposite) him» (15:39). In other words, he was in a position where he could observe everything about Jesus' death attentively. His observation and confession must have an important value in our discussion.

[69] A crucified person is normally exhausted, weaken bit by bit until he is at the end

So the centurion's declaration «is evoked and defined by the supernatural strength that enables Jesus at the moment of his death to shout with a superhumanly loud voice and with exhalant force so powerful that it rends the veil of the temple»[70]. Thus it is in this loud cry that the expiration (death) of Jesus took place. This loud wordless cry manifested an extraordinary power that one can see in it a revelatory character or an Epiphany event[71]. We know that the death cry and the confession are within the context of Jesus' trial which deals primarily with Jesus' identity. Thus «at the end of this trial, enlightened through the Epiphany of Jesus in his last cry, the centurion as the first human being confesses conclusively the identity of Jesus in the confession to his divine sonship»[72]. Likewise it is worth noting, that the consequent event of Jesus' death was that «the curtain of the temple was torn [rent] in two, from top to bottom» (15:38)[73]. And it has been observed that there is a connection between the temple and the identity of Jesus. Especially in Jesus' trial, each time the temple (ναός) is mentioned, Jesus' identity follows (three cases can demonstrate it: 14:58, cf. 14:61; 15:29, cf. 15:32; 15:38, cf. 15:39)[74]. One should not be surprised that when Jesus expired (breathed last; died), the temple's curtain was also torn in two.

The centurion attests «truly (ἀληθῶς) this man (human being)[75] was (ἦν) the Son of God (υἱὸς θεοῦ)». At the end of Jesus' trial, the centurion's confession takes up the question under consideration (Jesus'

---

of his natural power, and lapse into unconsciousness before dying. If Jesus died with a loud cry, then this cry must go back to the supernatural power (strength). This wonder contributed to the centurion's statement.

[70] R. H. GUNDRY, *Mark*, 974, cf. 947-948; K. STOCK, «Das Bekenntnis des Centurio», 291-293. «The centurion does not declare Jesus' divine sonship because he sees Jesus die on a cross, but because he sees Jesus die there in a way that defies naturalistic explanantion». Cf. GUNDRY, 974.

[71] Cf. K. STOCK, «Das Bekenntnis des Centurio», 293.

[72] K. STOCK, «Das Bekenntnis des Centurio», 293-294 (trans. mine).

[73] For the relation between the tearing (σχίζω) of the heavens in the Baptism of Jesus (1:10-11) and that of the temple's curtain (15:38), cf. P.M. HEAD, *Christology*, 195; R.H. GUNDRY, *Mark*, 949-950, 972. And these are the only occurrences of σχίζω in Mark.

[74] Cf. K. STOCK, «Das Bekenntnis des Centurio», 299-300.

[75] «This human being» makes a foil of Jesus' humanity against which his deity as indicated in «Son of God» stands out. Cf. R.H. GUNDRY, *Mark*, 951.

identity), and gives it a definite opinion, thereby ending the discussion without any more doubt. Therefore the matter is decided, this man is truly God's Son[76]. The imperfect tense ἦν implies that Jesus had been Son of God all along. As at the start (1:1) with regard to υἱὸς θεοῦ, its double anarthrousness stresses the quality of Jesus' divine Sonship[77]. However, following Colwell's rule, «a definite predicate nominative has the article when it follows the verb; it does not have the article when it precedes the verb»[78]. Hence υἱὸς θεοῦ can be translated as «the Son of God», instead of «a Son of God»[79]. «It seems plausible, therefore, that the absence of the definite article in Mark 15,39 was deliberate and not accidental on the part of either the centurion himself or the Markan author»[80].

When one compares the centurion with the Jewish leaders, one finds that his declaration contrasts sharply with them: be it with the high priest who charged Jesus with blasphemy for affirming to be «the Son of the Blessed One» (14:64, cf. 14:62)[81]; or the chief priests and scribes who wanted Jesus to come down from the cross, «that we may *see* and *believe*» (15:32). Thus the blindness of the chief priests places the belief (confession) of the centurion really in the light[82]. In fact, the apparent inappropriateness of the centurion (as a pagan) makes his confession itself that much more dramatic and remarkable[83]. Hence, «the centurion stands at this point as the representative of those who acknowledge Jesus as God's Son»[84].

---

[76] Cf. K. STOCK, «Das Bekenntnis des Centurio», 293-294, n.13.

[77] Cf. R.H. GUNDRY, *Mark*, 951.

[78] E.C. COLWELL, «Use of the Article, 13; P.G. DAVIS, «Mark's Christological Paradox», 11; E.S. JOHNSON, Jr, «Mark's Christology», 4; C.E.B. CRANFIELD, *Mark*, 460.

[79] Cf. P.H. BLIGH, «Note on Huios Theou, 52; T.F. GLASSON, «Son of God», 286, which states that grammatical usage supports the translation, «Truly this man was the Son of God».

[80] T.H. KIM, «Mark 15,39», 225.

[81] Cf. R.H. GUNDRY, *Mark*, 951.

[82] Cf. K. STOCK, «Das Bekenntnis des Centurio», 301.

[83] Cf. P.G. DAVIS, «Mark's Christological Paradox», 15; R.H. GUNDRY, *Mark*, 951, 975. Against this view, cf. E.S. JOHNSON, JR, «Mark's Christology», 3-22, especially 8-14.

[84] M.D. HOOKER, *St. Mark*, 379.

1.5 *Summary*

In this section, I have tried to dwell on the person of Jesus, highlighting the theme of his identity in Mark's Gospel. I tried to establish that this theme is central and dominant in the whole gospel: be it in the Prologue, as the presentation of Jesus; or in Jesus' ministry - activities and widespread fame - his identity was raised both by cries of the unclean spirits and the questions of the people. But Jesus, from the middle of the gospel, took the initiative to reveal his identity stage by stage to the human characters, until the centurion, the first human character, who proclaimed that Jesus is truly the Son of God. Departing from our pericope, we noticed that the unclean spirit identified Jesus' special relation with God, through confessing him as, «the Holy One of God» (1:24). But when compared with the more frequent designation, «Son of God», one discovers that the former affirms Jesus' special relation with God; while the latter affirms the character of this relation, which is personal (son-father relation).

Based on this result, I decided to trace this christological title, «Son of God» through the Gospel of Mark. Here I discovered that Mark, the omniscient narrator, introduced it as a scope of his work[85]; it was confirmed by God from heaven; the unclean spirits identified Jesus with it; God also revealed it to the three chosen apostles; the religious leaders rejected it; Jesus referred himself as such; and Jesus also confessed it before his enemies, who condemned him to death; and after his death the centurion proclaimed it saying: «truly this man was the Son of God». I would like to conclude this section with Hengel's comment, «more than any other title in the New Testament, the title Son of God connects the figure of Jesus with God»[86].

2. The Authority of Jesus

Another theme connected with the person of Jesus, which is very important for our discussion, is Jesus' ἐξουσία (his divine authority). As we observed in the analysis of the pericope in the Part 1, Jesus' authority created the first impression about Jesus' identity to the people (vv.22): it became the cause for wonder, and for the scribes, the root of contrasts or

---

[85] Cf. P.H. BLIGH, «Note on Huios Theou», 52, here G.B. CAIRD remarked that «the theme of the whole gospel right through to the declaration of the centurion is simply this: that Jesus is the Son of God».

[86] M. HENGEL, «The Son of God», 61.

conflicts with Jesus (especially in teaching). Jesus' exorcism of an unclean spirit from a man, through a simple command (v.25, cf. v.26), heightened this authority element in the pericope. And moreover this authority theme gave Jesus' teaching an element of newness (v.27). In fact, Jesus' authority is a consequence of his unique relation with God, as his beloved Son. So he has both the freedom or right and ability or power to act[87], because he is the Son of God. Having established the presence and weight of ἐξουσία in the pericope (1:21-28, esp. vv.22,27, cf. v.25), we shall now demonstrate its importance in Mark' Gospel.

Jesus' authority is the quality that characterized his public ministry in Mark's Gospel, that «left the most lasting impression on his followers and caused the greatest offense to his opponents...»[88] Jesus' authority is the central issue or the root cause of controversy or conflict with the religious authorities (especially the scribes) during his Galilean ministry[89]. This is what enhanced his person, especially his identity and mission, and attracted the attention of his followers, friends and antagonists alike. It will be our task to demonstrate how Jesus' authority is central or goes through the Gospel of Mark, taking cognizance of its explicit and implicit appearances. If we can verify our affirmation, then it will be nearer to justifying our pericope's function in Mark's Gospel as having a programmatic character.

In the first place, we shall examine how Jesus' authority was shown in his words and deeds or in his teaching and exorcism/healing. This will also give us the opportunity to delve into other aspects of miracles which Jesus performed in the course of his ministry. Then, we shall examine the force of Jesus' authority in the forgiveness of sins (2:1-12), and why the scribes had to react. Lastly, we shall engage ourselves with the preoccupation of the representatives of the Sanhedrin, towards the end of Jesus' ministry, about the origin or source of Jesus' authority.

---

[87] J. MARSH, «Authority», 319, states that «authority is closely connected with power, though usually, but not always, distinguished from it». Jesus has both the authority and the power to act, as it is well manifested in his ministry.

[88] J.R. EDWARDS, «The Authority of Jesus», 217; Cf. R.J. DILLON, «As One Having Authority», 98, n.21. E.G. SELWYN asks, what does one get by a continuous reading of the Gospel of Mark? And he answers it thus: «it is an impression of authority. This authority is demonstrated in deed as well as word». Cf. «The Authority of Christ», 84.

[89] Cf. R.J. DILLON, «As One Having Authority», 102; J.D. KINGSBURY, «The Religious Authorities», 46-47, 52-53, 60-61; ID., *Conflict in Mark*, 66-67, 86; P. GUILLEMETTE, «Un enseignement nouveau», 239-240.

2.1 *Jesus' Authority in Word and Deed (1:21-28)*

In our pericope (1:21-28), ἐξουσία appeared twice (vv.22, 27), and both are in the context of the astonishment or amazement of the people on Jesus' teaching and exorcism, as we mentioned above. The strategic position of this pericope, its composition, and being where Jesus made his first public appearance, makes one curious of what input it has for the concept of authority in Jesus' ministry and in Mark's Gospel. We all know that the first appearance of ἐξουσία (authority) v.22, was connected with Jesus' teaching. The lack of content to Jesus' teaching here highlighted the manner of his teaching, which he does with the quality of authority, and above all it contrasts Jesus' teaching with the scribes[90]. Thus the distinguishing element between Jesus' and the scribes' teaching is authority: «"the scribes" were brought forward at Mk 1:22 as teachers *without* "authority", not as "authorities" of lesser degree»[91]. Likewise Jesus' exorcism put in relief with greater emphasis Jesus' authority. Thus, «the effectiveness of Jesus' exorcism by word was taken to reinforce the *authority* of Jesus' teaching, which is characterised as "new" (1.27)»[92]. Here the element of newness in Jesus' teaching lies in his ἐξουσία (his divine authority)[93]. Hence this becomes a paradigmatic pericope to highlight Jesus' divine authority in his word and work: this is because the authority of his word and the authority of his action are united - and it lies and is stamped in the person of Jesus[94].

2.1.1 In Jesus' Teaching

Jesus began his mission by preaching (κηρύσσειν, 1:14, 38,39) the gospel of God with authority as seen in his double command: repent (μετανοεῖτε) and believe (πιστεύετε) in the gospel. Likewise he called his disciples with his divine authority: δεῦτε ὀπίσω μου - literally,

---

[90] Cf. D. LÜHRMANN, «Pharisäer und Schriftgelehrte», 182, n.41 observes that only in 3:15; 6:7 and 13:34 (Jesus' delegation of authority to his disciples) that ἐξουσία in Mark had nothing to do with scribes. In other words, the other 7x occurrences with Jesus, have always had connection with the scribes.

[91] R.J. DILLON, «As One Having Authority», 112.

[92] J. PAINTER, *Mark's Gospel*, 42.

[93] Cf. R.H. GUNDRY, *Mark*, 77, 85; K. SCHOLTISSEK, *Vollmacht Jesu*, 122, 123-124; R.T. FRANCE, «Teaching of Jesus», 106; R.A. HARRISVILLE, «The Concept of Newness», 77.

[94] Cf. M.Y.-H. LEE, *Autorität*, 102.

«come after me», or «follow me», v.17 (cf. v.20; 2:14). Thus, «Jesus assumes a commanding role in calling his disciples (1:16-20; 2:13-14; 3:13-19)»[95]. Then comes our pericope that is characterized by explicit appearance and manifestation of authority, which describes Jesus' actions as «teaching with authority». Coincidentally, in Mark's Gospel, «teaching» and «authority» are uniquely reserved only for Jesus, who delegates or authorizes his disciples also to exercise it. Scholtissek sees a programmatic character in the connection between both motives of teaching and authority: on the one hand, from now on wherever Jesus' teaching is mentioned, it will always be associated with «authoritative or powerful teaching»; on the other hand, this authority character of Jesus' teaching opens an immense conflict potential for Jesus' ministry[96]. Likewise the astonishment of the people is a clear sign of this authority in Jesus' teaching[97].

It is observed also that «Jesus' manner of speech is illustrative of his ἐξουσία»[98]. Unlike the OT prophets who used to communicate the divine message by beginning it with, «Thus says the Lord» as a guarantee of Yahweh's authority; Jesus assumes that authority himself, by introducing his message with: «Truly I say to you» (ἀμὴν λέγω ὑμῖν)[99]. In fact, many scholars, especially J. Jeremias, «have traced one essential element in the authority of Jesus to the christological claim implicit in his linguistic usage, especially his address to God as Abba and his placing of "amen" as a solemn asseveration at the beginning of a sentence»[100]. Likewise there is a sign of authority in Jesus' use of ἀκούω («listen» or «hear»), often as a command to listen to his teaching (especially in parables) or his message (cf. 4:3,9,23,24; 7:14,16). This reminds us of God's authoritative heavenly command to the disciples on the mountain: ἀκούετε αὐτοῦ - «listen to him» (9:7). So Jesus' teaching or speaking is always character-

---

[95] J.R. EDWARDS, «The Authority of Jesus», 229.

[96] Cf. K. SCHOLTISSEK, *Vollmacht Jesu*, 121-122.

[97] Cf. M.Y.-H. LEE, *Autorität*, 100. One can observe, apart from 1:22, 27, other instances where Jesus' teaching astonished either the crowd or the disciples: Mk 6:2; 10:24,26; 11:18; (cf. Mt 7:28; 13:54; 19:25; 22:33; Lk 4:32).

[98] J.R. EDWARDS, «The Authority of Jesus», 229.

[99] This usage characterized Jesus' speeches throughout the whole Gospel of Mark: Mk has 13x (cf. Mt 32x; Lk 6x; in Jn it is always ἀμὴν ἀμὴν λέγω ὑμῖν): 3:28; 8:12; 9:1,41; 10:15,29; 11:23; 12:43; 13:30; 14:9,18,25,30.

[100] H. ANDERSON, «Question of His Authority», 298; Cf. J. JEREMIAS, *New Testament Theology*, 35-37; H. SCHLIER, «ἀμήν», 337-338.

ized by this authority element, which is often highlighted by astonishment, whether in the synagogue (1:22,27; 6:2), or outside with the crowds (4:2ff), or privately with his disciples (10:24,26), or even in the temple (11:18). And this authority is rooted in his person as the beloved Son of God.

2.1.2 In Jesus' Exorcism

As Jesus' authority is manifested in teaching, so it is also in Jesus' exorcism of the unclean spirits or demons. It is made more manifest through the audible and visible signs exhibited by the unclean spirits. Thus in our text (vv.23-24), «Jesus' authority was challenged by the power of evil manifest in a person with unclean spirit»[101]. Jesus did not waste time in casting it out with a double command (cf. v.25), as we saw in Part I. And immediately the unclean spirit responded (v.26, cf. v.27de). That Jesus exorcized the unclean spirit with a simple command, and not with the normal exorcistic techniques emphasizes his divine authority. Therefore, Jesus exercizes his authority especially in exorcism so that the kingdom of God will break in into the world[102]. And this authority, which Jesus possesses as the Son of God, he also gave to his disciples to have authority over unclean spirits or demons (3:15; 6:7), and it is an important aspect of his and their mission (13:34)[103]. As Jesus demonstrated his authority in driving away the unclean spirit from the possessed man in the synagogue (1:23-26), and thereby restoring him to his health, so also he does in other cases of the sort (5:1-20; 7:24-30; 9:14-29). Hence showing that Jesus is the «stronger one» (3:27) who has come to bind Satan and his agents (demons), in order to liberate man and inaugurate God's kingdom.

From the foregoing, one can definitely say that Jesus' divine authority is felt both in his word and action.

---

[101] J. PAINTER, *Mark's Gospel*, 42.

[102] Cf. M.Y.-H. LEE, *Autorität*, 104; C.E.B. CRANFIELD, *Mark*, 80. Likewise S.H.T. PAGE, *Powers of Evil*, 140, also adds «it is in exorcism that the nature of Jesus' ministry as the bringing of God's rule to a world fallen under Satan's sway comes to most explicit expression».

[103] Cf. M.Y.-H. LEE, *Autorität*, 105; J. COUTTS, «The Authority of Jesus», 111-112.

2.2 *Jesus' Authority and Forgiveness of Sins (2:1-12)*

After seeing how Jesus' authority is manifested in his word and deed, especially in 1:21-28, and how it extended to his entire ministry, we want to treat here an important aspect of his divine authority: this is in «forgiveness of sins». It occurs in the context of the healing of the paralytic (2:1-12). And we observe that there is a close connection between these pericopes (1:21-28 and 2:1-12), especially in the integration of Jesus' word and action, and above all, the demonstration of Jesus' authority in both of them, in word and deed[104]. So Jesus' authority that was very much highlighted in the former, is deepened and widened in the latter. This pericope (2:1-12) is also the first of a group of five stories involving conflict (2:1-3:6). However, it «is not simply a collection of "conflict stories", but a demonstration of Jesus' authority and the refusal of the Jewish religious leaders to recognize it»[105]. And this divine authority of Jesus[106] will once more be manifested here.

Jesus, while preaching at home in Capernaum, saw four men who breaking through a roof, laid down a paralytic before him for healing, because they could not pass through the crowd. Seeing their faith[107], Jesus

---

[104] Cf. K. SCHOLTISSEK, *Vollmacht Jesu*, 171-172; M.D. HOOKER, *St. Mark*, 84; K. STOCK, «Die Machttaten Jesu», 203. Furthermore, Scholtissek affirms that the close, narrative and thematic connection between 1:21-28 and 2:1-12 serves for the Evangelist to strengthen further the Exousia-christology founded in 1:21-28: Jesus' messianic mission, his divine sonship (1:9-11,24), reveals itself beyond the authoritative exorcism even in the authoritative forgiveness of sins. Cf. *Ibid*, 172.

[105] M.D. HOOKER, *St. Mark*, 83.

[106] In fact, the basic issue in all controversy stories mediated by the Synoptic traditions had to do with the authority of Jesus, and this authority was signified by references to Jesus in his earthly activity as Son of Man. Cf. D.J. DOUGHTY, «The Authority», 178; H. TÖDT, *The Son of Man*, 113-125, 138. And according to N. PERRIN, as cited by D.J. DOUGHTY, *ibid.*, 161, this section of Mark's Gospel (2:1-3:6) was «composed by Mark in order to exhibit the authority of Jesus... It is to Mark that we owe the actual use of ἐξουσία in connection with the earthly Jesus... Mark intends both to stress the authority of Jesus and to claim that he exercized that authority as Son of Man». (quoted from «The Creative Use of the Son of Man Traditions by Mark», *USQR* 23 (1967/68) 357-365, 361).

[107] For the first time Mk refers to faith, but is it the faith of the bearers rather than the paralytic? However, most scholars rightly include the faith of the paralytic himself. Cf. M.D. HOOKER, *St. Mark*, 85; K. STOCK, «Die Machttaten Jesu», 202; C.E.B. CRANFIELD, *Mark*, 97; V TAYLOR, *Mark*, 194. On the contrary, R.H. GUNDRY, *Mark*, 112, opined that «their faith» may refer to the faith of the four, not including

says to the paralytic: τέκνον, ἀφίενταί σου αἱ ἀμαρτίαι - «My child[108], your sins are forgiven» (2:5). The historical present tense of λέγει, «he says», highlights Jesus' authority in pronouncing this statement; while the passive voice of ἀφίενται, «are being forgiven», could imply God's forgiveness[109], which Jesus knows about and reports to the paralytic[110]. But «the present tense of ἀφίενται most naturally means that Jesus pronounces the forgiveness as taking place at this very moment and therefore as effected by his pronouncement (cf. Acts 9:34). So we do not have a miracle - at least not yet - but a word, an authoritative word of sins being forgiven on the spot»[111]. This authoritative statement of Jesus did really stir up reactions from the scribes, to question in their hearts[112]: τί οὗτος οὕτως λαλεῖ; βλασφημεῖ· τίς δύναται ἀφιέναι ἁμαρτίας εἰ μὴ εἷς ὁ θεός; - «Why does this man speak thus? It is blasphemy! Who can forgive sins but God alone?» (2:7). In fact, the issue here is the forgiveness of sins, which is the exclusive prerogative of God in OT thought or Jewish tradition[113]. «In other words, Jesus was not being accused of claiming to be God but of blaspheming against God by claiming to do what God alone could do»[114]. And the penalty or punishment for blasphemy according to Lev.24:15f is death by stoning[115], and

---

faith on the part of the paralytic.

[108] Τέκνον (my child) is an affectionate or familiar form of address used of those with whom there is a personal relationship (cf. 10:24). Cf. S. KUTHIRAKKATTEL, *The Beginning*, 187; V. TAYLOR, *Mark*, 195; K. STOCK, «Die Machttaten Jesu», 205, adds that «this address, "child", refers to the helplessness and dependence of the one spoken to and to the fatherly loving care, mercy and the power of the speaker» (trans. mine).

[109] This is the so called theological passive, which means, «God forgives your sins». Cf. K. STOCK, *ibid*.

[110] Cf. R.H. GUNDRY, *Mark*, 112; K. STOCK, «Die Machttaten Jesu», 202.

[111] R.H. GUNDRY, *Mark*, 112; Cf. S. KUTHIRAKKATTEL, *The Beginning*, 187; V. TAYLOR, *Mark*, 195.

[112] Mark, as an omniscient narrator, informs his reader about what the scribes were questioning «in their hearts»; thereby showing that he can read their hearts. Cf. R.H. GUNDRY, *Mark*, 112.

[113] Cf. J.R. EDWARDS, «The Authority of Jesus», 222; K. STOCK, «Die Machttaten Jesu», 203; C.E.B. CRANFIELD, *Mark*, 99. Cf. Exod 34:6-7; Ps 103:3; Is 43:25; 44:22; Mic 7:18. And Jewish sources did not attribute forgiveness of sins to any eschatological figure, like the Messiah, prophet or high priest. Cf. R.J. DILLON, «As One Having Authority», 105, n.50.

[114] R.A. GUELICH, *Mark*, 87.

[115] Cf. V. TAYLOR, *Mark*, 196.

blasphemy is the very charge they will use to secure Jesus' death sentence in Mk 14:64[116].

But Jesus immediately perceived in his spirit what they questioned within themselves[117]. In fact, «to perceive the inward reasoning of the scribes requires divine power»[118]. So Jesus made it categorically clear to the scribes: ἵνα δὲ εἰδῆτε ὅτι ἐξουσίαν ἔχει ὁ υἱὸς τοῦ ἀνθρώπου ἀφιέναι ἁμαρτίας ἐπὶ τῆς γῆς - «But that you may know that the Son of man[119] has authority on earth to forgive sins...» (2:10). The use of ἐξουσία here contrasts with δύναται in v.7. Thus, «the shift from *dynatai* to *exousia* means that the Son of Man not only has the power but the right to forgive sins»[120]. In other words, «the pronouncement in v.10 means that the One who has authority to forgive sins in heaven is present in the Son of Man to forgive sins "on earth"»[121]. Hence, «authority to remit sins *on earth* is set over against the divine prerogative exercised *in heaven*»[122].

Then Jesus said to the paralytic: σοὶ λέγω, ἔγειρε ἆρον τὸν κράβαττόν σου καὶ ὕπαγε εἰς τὸν οἶκόν σου. - «I say to you, rise,

---

[116] Cf. R.J. DILLON, «As One Having Authority», 105; K. SCHOLTISSEK, *Vollmacht Jesu*, 171; D.J. DOUGHTY, «The Authority», 165; F. LANG, «Kompositionsanalyse», 1-24, esp. 11.

[117] Here again, «Mark writes as an omniscient narrator: he knows what Jesus knows without Jesus' having said what the scribes are thinking ... Hence, it is an important point to Mark that among Jesus' other powers is the power of clairvoyance which characterizes God himself (see 1 Sam 16:7; 1 Kgs 8:39, ... etc)». Cf. R.H. GUNDRY, *Mark*, 113.

[118] R.H. GUNDRY, *Mark*, 113.

[119] The term, «Son of Man», which occurs 14x in Mk, is exclusively used by Jesus to describe his function, which is manifested in his authority (2:10,28), destiny (8:31; 9:9,12,31; 10:33,45;14:21[bis],41) and coming (8:38;13:26; 14:26). It is not used in apposition, or as nominal predicates, or to express Jesus' identity, but often in dialogues, it is used as subject of communication with regard to Jesus. The most striking thing, is that its first appearance in Mark's Gospel, and even its employment is intimately associated with the motif of authority.

[120] J.R. EDWARDS, «The Authority of Jesus», 222. Likewise J.D.G. DUNN says that «it is impossible to soften the Christological force of 2:7 and 10: Jesus is able and has the authority to forgive sins, not merely to declare them forgiven». Cf. *Jesus, Paul, and the Law*, 27.

[121] J.R. EDWARDS, «The Authority of Jesus», 223. D.J. DOUGHTY, «The Authority», 179, observes that «the issue for Mark is not whether Jesus is rightly regarded as the Son of Man, but whether, as Son of Man, Jesus has divine authority on earth».

[122] V. TAYLOR, *Mark*, 198.

take up your pallet and go home» (2:11). Here, «σοὶ λέγω is emphatic, and together with the asyndetic construction (cf. i.44) gives the command a decisive, if not a peremptory, tone»[123]. Jesus is in fact here effecting both forgiveness of sins and healing, through his healing of the paralytic. Thus, «his power to forgive, no less effective because of its invisibility, will be proved by the healing of the paralytic»[124]. And «the present tense of the imperative in ἔγειρε (vv.9, 11), περιπάτει (v.9), and ὕπαγε lends emphasis to the paralytic's rising, walking, and going home as a demonstration of Jesus' power»[125]. The immediate obedience of the paralytic, who was brought by four people (v.3), going home carry his pallet by himself in v.12, shows that he has been completely healed. So, «the fact that Jesus heals the paralytic is for the eye of faith a sign that he also can and does forgive sinners. The miracle is a visible sign confirming and sealing for faith Christ's authority to forgive»[126].

The amazement of the people on Jesus' power and authority in word and deed (forgiveness of sins and healing) is comprehensive. It involves all, πάντας, v.12: «"all" stresses undoubtedness - even the sceptical scribes see the evidence»[127]. So all were amazed and glorified God. As we have already seen earlier that amazement is a sign of Jesus' authority, so it is also here. Hence this brief discussion shows us how Jesus' authority, which was introduced in 1:21-28, is further strengthened in 2:1-12 through Jesus' word and deed.

2.3 *The Question about Jesus' Authority (11:27-33)*

In this section, we shall come to the climax[128] of our discussion on Jesus' authority in Mark's Gospel. Here the chief priests, the scribes and

---

[123] V. TAYLOR, *Mark*, 198; R.H. GUNDRY, *Mark*, 114-115. Hence, «the staccato-like effect of the resulting asyndeton sounds a note of authority that stresses the miracle-working power of the command». Cf. GUNDRY, 115.

[124] J.R. EDWARDS, «The Authority of Jesus», 223. T.L. BUDESHEIM, «Jesus and the Disciples», 191, affirms that «it is the act of healing the paralytic which verifies Jesus' ἐξουσία to forgive sins».

[125] R.H. GUNDRY, *Mark*, 115.

[126] C.E.B. CRANFIELD, *Mark*, 100; K. STOCK, «Die Machttaten Jesu», 203; V. TAYLOR, *Mark*, 197.

[127] R.H. GUNDRY, *Mark*, 115; V.TAYLOR, *Mark*, 198.

[128] I call it a highpoint of our discussion, because the 7x ἐξουσία for Jesus in Mk's Gospel appears in three pericopes (1:21-28 = 2x; 2:1-12 = 1x; 11:27-33 = 4x). That we have 4x of these concentrated here, shows the weight the term ἐξουσία exacts in this pericope.

the elders (the representatives of the Sanhedrin)[129] confront Jesus in the temple[130] about the authority of his actions. They put before Jesus a double question about the nature and source of his authority (v.28)[131], which he replies with a counter-question (vv.29-30). In replying to Jesus' counter-question, the Jewish religious leaders meet a dilemma (vv.31-33a). Since Jesus makes his answer depend entirely on the reply to the counter-question[132], he gives them the response they deserve (v.33b). However, Jesus continues this confrontation with them in the next pericope (12:1-12)[133], where he indirectly answers their question.

2.3.1 Jesus' Authority questioned

When the chief priests, the scribes and elders came to Jesus (v.27), they put this question to him: ἐν ποίᾳ ἐξουσίᾳ ταῦτα ποιεῖς; ἢ τίς σοι

---

[129] These three groups also appeared together at 8:31; 14:43,53; 15:1. C.E.B. CRANFIELD, *Mark*, 362, observes that «the fact that all three groups were represented indicates the importance of the occasion».

[130] In Jesus' Jerusalem ministry, the Temple (ἱερόν) has a focal point, and becomes also a link between chapters 11, 12 and even 13. Cf. K. STOCK, «Gliederung», 481-515; F.G. LANG, «Kompositionsanalyse», 1-24; R. PESCH, *Markusevangelium I*, 32-40; I. DE LA POTTERIE, «De Compositione», 135-141. The word ἱερόν (temple) appears 9x in Mk (Mt 11x; Lk 14x; Jn 11x), and almost all occur in these three chapters (11:11,15[bis],16,27; 12:35; 13:1,3; cf. 14:49). With this word ἱερόν, the whole temple hill is meant, while the temple house accessible to only Priests is named ναός. Cf. C. MARUCCI, «Die Implizite Christologie», 294. Likewise G.S. SHAE, «The Authority of Jesus», 16, n.1 observes that «in Matt. and Mk. the word ἱερόν is used in the Temple-cleansing tradition and the word ναός is used in the statement about the destroying and rebuilding of the Temple».

[131] Cf. D. LÜHRMANN, *Markusevangelium*, 197; K. SCHOLTISSEK, *Vollmacht Jesu*, 218.

[132] Cf. J. KREMER, «Jesu Antwort», 131.

[133] Many scholars think that the authority debate between the Sanhedrin representatives and Jesus extended beyond 11:27-33, and as such includes 12:1-12; thereby bringing the two pericopes into a unit. This is considered especially as no change of location, time or audience is indicated. Moreover, the Sanhedrin's coming (ἔρχονται - 11:27) and going away (ἀπῆλθον - 12:12) form an inclusion that frames the entire unit. Cf. S. LÉGASSE, *L'Évangile de Marc*, II,700; J. PAINTER, *Mark's Gospel*, 160; J.G. COOK, *Structure and Persuasive Power*, 128; R.J. DILLON, «As One Having Authority», 101, n.32; R.H. GUNDRY, *Mark*, 656; K. SCHOLTISSEK, *Vollmacht Jesu*, 183-188, 206-215; W. WEISS, *Eine neue Lehre*, 162; J.D. KINGSBURY, *Conflict in Mark*, 79-80; M.Y.-H. LEE, *Autorität*, 36, 65-74, 158-60; K. STOCK, «Gliederung», 492, 504-506, 509.

ἔδωκεν τὴν ἐξουσίαν ταύτην ἵνα ταῦτα ποιῇς; - «By what authority are you doing these things, or who gave you this authority to do them?» (v.28). Some scholars think that there is no difference between the two questions; in other words, that the content of the second question is basically the same as the first - the source of Jesus' authority[134]. But that is not so because there is really a difference[135]. In fact, the first question deals with the nature or quality of Jesus' authority[136], in other words, his identity is set in question[137]. While the second deals with the source (*Herkunft, Ursprung*) of Jesus' authority[138], or who gave him the authority, in other words, referring to his mission (*Sendung*)[139]. If one considers Jesus' entry into Jerusalem (11:1-11) and his cleansing of the Temple (11:15-18), one can observe that the first question indicates two rights: the official right of the Sanhedrin over the temple, and Jesus' right to do what he is doing: thus there is a conflict of two authorities (rights)[140]. And therefore who gave Jesus the authority (right) to act that way? «The question asked shows a tempting intention: if Jesus says that God has given him this special authority, then he is threatened with the death penalty on the charge of "blasphemy"»[141]. In view of this, «the authority question in 11:28 brings therefore the christological fundamental question about Jesus' person and mission to the spot»[142].

---

[134] Cf. C. MARUCCI, «Die implizite Christologie», 296; J. KREMER, «Jesu Antwort», 130-131.

[135] G.S. SHAE, «The Authority of Jesus», 11, affirms that there are two different questions: «The first question deals with the dynamic force behind an act, whereas the second question has to do with authorizing person behind the act». Cf. M.Y.-H. LEE, *Autorität*, 120-121, n.1.

[136] Cf. R.J. DILLON, «As One Having Authority», 99-100; R.H. GUNDRY, *Mark*, 657; K. SCHOLTISSEK, *Vollmacht Jesu*, 218; ID., «Nachfolge und Autorität», 67; A.J. HULTGREN, *Jesus and His Adversaries*, 70; C.E.B. CRANFIELD, *Mark*, 362.

[137] Cf. M.Y.-H. LEE, *Autorität*, 115, 118, 121. Thus, «by what (ποίᾳ) authority» focuses attention on the nature of the authority, which should be personal, like prophetic, priestly, royal, or messianic authority.

[138] Cf. R.J. DILLON, «As One Having Authority», 99-100; R.H. GUNDRY, *Mark*, 657; K. SCHOLTISSEK, *Vollmacht Jesu*, 218; ID., «Nachfolge und Autorität», 67; M.Y.-H. LEE, *Autorität*, 120; A.J. HULTGREN, *Jesus and His Adversaries*, 69-70.

[139] Cf. R.J. DILLON, «As One Having Authority», 99-100; M.Y.-H. LEE, *Autorität*, 121.

[140] Cf. M.Y.-H. LEE, *Autorität*, 114-115.

[141] M.H.-Y. LEE, *Autorität*, 118 (trans. mine).

[142] K. SCHOLTISSEK, *Vollmacht Jesu*, 218 (trans. mine); Cf. R.J. DILLON, «As One

Another important point in the question is, «...ταῦτα ποιεῖς» - «are you doing these things?» This phrase appears in the two questions (v.28ab, cf. vv.29, 33). What does *these things* (ταῦτα) mean? On the one hand, in the context in which Mark places the encounter of the questions clearly refers to Jesus' actions in the temple (cleansing of the temple) on the previous day (11:15-17, cf. Jn 2:13-22)[143]. And ταῦτα (plural) therefore refers to the stoppages of selling, buying, money-changing, transport[144], and even Jesus' teaching (v.17). On the other hand, some scholars see the word ταῦτα being connected with ἐξουσία, in order to have a larger context in Mark's Gospel[145]: therefore, Mark seems to make room for *these things* to refer to the entire ministry of deed and word which is now coming to its climax, rather than any single moment thereof[146].

In my opinion, I would say that contextually, «these things» refers to the temple symbolic and prophetic actions of Jesus. But we should not limit its meaning to this single but recent event of Jesus' authority. This is because as ταῦτα is connected with ἐξουσία, we must remember that: (a) authority (ἐξουσία) has its climax and greatest concentration in this pericope; (b) «authority» has been the root cause of conflict and offence between Jesus and the religious leaders right from the beginning (cf. 1:22; 2:1-3:6; 3:22-30; 7:1-13; 8:11-13; 10:2-9; 11:15-18)[147]; (c) the scribes, who came down from Jerusalem to challenge his authority in Galilee,

---

Having Authority», 99-100, n.27; M.Y.-H. LEE, *Autorität*, 116-118, 120-121.

[143] Cf. R.H. GUNDRY, *Mark*, 657, 666, 681; L.W. HURTADO, *Mark*,189; C.S. MANN, *Mark*, 456; A.J. HULTGREN, *Jesus and His Adversaries*, 71-72; K. STOCK, «Gliederung», 487, 504; W. GRUNDMANN, *Markus*, 317; V. TAYLOR, *Mark*, 469-470; R. PESCH, *Markusevangelium II*, 210; C.E.B. CRANFIELD, *Mark*, 362; W.L. LANE, *Mark*, 413; E. TROCMÉ, «L'expulsion des marchands», 1-22, esp. 10f.

[144] Cf. R.H. GUNDRY, *Mark*, 657.

[145] Cf. G.S. SHAE, «The Authority of Jesus», 26.

[146] Cf. S. LÉGASSE, *L'Évangile de Marc*, II, 703; R.J. DILLON, «As One Having Authority», 100; J.R. EDWARDS, «The Authority of Jesus», 226; K. SCHOLTISSEK, *Vollmacht Jesu*, 215-218; M.D. HOOKER, *St. Mark*, 271; J.D. KINGSBURY, *Conflict in Mark*, 79; D. LÜHRMANN, *Markusevangelium*, 198; M.Y.-H. LEE, *Autorität*, 113-116; E. SCHWEIZER, *Markus*, 130; J. ERNST, *Markus*, 336; J. GNILKA, *Markus II*, 138; G.S. SHAE, «The Authority of Jesus», 18, 26-27, 28-29; J. KREMER, «Jesu Antwort», 131.

[147] Cf. R.J. DILLON, «As One Having Authority», 102; J.D. KINGSBURY, «The Religious Authorities», 46-47, 52-53; ID., *Conflict in Mark*, 66-67, 86; M.Y.-H. LEE, *Autorität*, 113-114; P. GUILLEMETTE, «Un enseignement nouveau», 239-240.

form part of the Sanhedrin questioning him now (3:22; 7:1; also 2:6; cf. 11:18,27; 12:12)[148]; (d) and they will also form the panel of his accusers to death (14:1,43,53; 15:1,31; cf. 8:31; 10:33)[149]; (e) here is the climax of the challenge to Jesus' exercise of authority in word and deed; because not only the scribes, but in fact, the highest council of the Jews (Sanhedrin) are involved through their representatives. Therefore, we should not underestimate this confrontation, because its outcome will continue until Jesus' trial in the Passion narrative (Mk 14-15)[150].

2.3.2 Jesus' Reaction

In Jesus' reply, he uses a counter-question[151] to posit his own question to them. Even in Jesus' question, he demonstrates his authority also here: (a) by answering their question with a counter-question[152], he shows his superiority over them[153]; (b) he uses two imperatives, ἀποκρίθητέ μοι (answer me) at the beginning and end of his question (vv.29, 30)[154]; (c) he conditions his answer to their reply (v.29)[155], and also gives them two alternatives (either/or), v.30; (d) likewise his refusal to answer them later (v.33b) adds to his authority[156]. However, Jesus asks the religious authorities whether the baptism of John came *from heaven* (ἐξ οὐρανοῦ)[157] or *from men* (ἐξ ἀνθρώπων), v.30. In Jesus' counter-

---

[148] Cf. R.J. DILLON, «As One Having Authority», 102; D. LÜHRMANN, «Pharisäer und Schriftgelehrte», 172; W. WEISS, *Eine neue Lehre*, 80, 172, 342.

[149] Cf. R.J. DILLON, «As One Having Authority», 102.

[150] L.W. HURTADO, *Mark*, 190, notes that «from this point in the narrative, there is only growing tension between Jesus and the Jewish authorities, which eventually leads to his arrest, trial and execution».

[151] One observes that the device of countering one question with another was fairly common in rabbinic discussions (cf. 10:2-9; 12:14-17). Cf. R.H. GUNDRY, *Mark*, 668; M.D. HOOKER, *St. Mark*, 271; W.L. LANE, *Mark*, 413; G.S. SHAE, «The Authority of Jesus», 13-14; V. TAYLOR, *Mark*, 470; J. KREMER, «Jesu Antwort», 131; STR.-B., *Kommentar zum Neuen Testament*, I, 861-62.

[152] J.R. EDWARDS, «The Authority of Jesus», 226, affirms that «his counterquestion demonstrates the authority about which he is questioned».

[153] Cf. J. KREMER, «Jesu Antwort», 132.

[154] Cf. M.Y.-H. LEE, *Autorität*, 126, 133; J. KREMER, «Jesu Antwort», 131-132.

[155] Cf. M.Y.-H. LEE, *Autorität*, 126; J. KREMER, «Jesu Antwort», 131.

[156] M.D. HOOKER, *St. Mark*, 272, confirms that «Jesus' refusal to answer is typical of the way in which he claims authority throughout Mark's Gospel».

[157] The word οὐρανός (heaven) is a typical Jewish circumlocution for God or the

question and reply to these Sanhedrin representatives, one observes that he takes up their first question in v.29 and v.33, and their second question in v.30.

The forward position of «the baptism of John» calls attention to the whole activity of the Baptist: his word (Mk 1:7f, cf.6:18) and his action (Mk 1:4f,9; cf. 1:6). In other words, John's baptism covers his entire ministry, that is, «a baptism of repentance for the forgiveness of sins» which he administered, and the witness which he gave about Jesus[158]. It was in Jesus' participation of John's baptism that he received the confirmation of his divine Sonship and mission[159], which manifested or opened up his public ministry, characterized by his authoritative word and deed. Thus, the baptism event, not only established Jesus' relation with John[160], but also confirmed Jesus' identity, mission and authority.

With regard to the provenance of John's baptism, Jesus posed the alternative, thereby delimiting the question and allowing only two possible conclusions: «from heaven (God)» or «from men». «The placement of "from heaven" before "was" and thus away from the alternative "from human beings" hints at the correct but self-damaging answer that the Sanhedrin ought to give»[161]. Thus, the counter-question clearly implies

---

divine name. Cf. R.H. GUNDRY, *Mark*, 657; M.Y.-H. LEE, *Autorität*, 131; G.S. SHAE, «The Authority of Jesus», 6, 17; STR.-B., *Kommentar zum Neuen Testament*, I, 862-865.

[158] Cf. M.Y.-H. LEE, *Autorität*, 128-129. M.D. HOOKER, *St. Mark*, 271, asserts, «Jesus answered a question about his own authority by pointing back to the activity of John must have seemed a clear claim to be the mightier one whom John foretold».

[159] J.R. EDWARDS, «The Authority of Jesus», 226-227, 232, observes that «it was at the baptism by John that the heavens were parted, the Spirit of power descended into Jesus (*eis auton*, 1:10), and the voice from heaven declared him God's Son. The baptism of Jesus, in other words, was the event that inaugurated his *exousia*, his conscious oneness with the Father, and his sovereign freedom and empowerment for ministry». Cf. B. VAN IERSEL, *Reading Mark*, 148; M.Y.-H. LEE, *Autorität*, 130-131, 134; G.S. SHAE, «The Authority of Jesus», 27.

[160] The Baptist was Jesus' precursor both in the ministry (Mk 1:4, 7-8) and in death at the leaders' hands (Mk 1:14; 9:13). Cf. R.J. DILLON, «As One Having Authority», 101-102. And Mark understands the fate of John and the fate of Jesus to be woven together. Cf. M.D. HOOKER, *St. Mark*, 272. Hence, J. GNILKA, *Markus II*, 141, observes that «the overarching character of the pericope is strengthened by the parallelism between the Baptist and Jesus, which runs through the whole gospel» (trans. mine). Cf. K. SCHOLTISSEK, *Vollmacht Jesu*, 211; J. ERNST, *Markus*, 338.

[161] R.H. GUNDRY, *Mark*, 658.

that Jesus' authority, like that of the baptism of John, is grounded in a commission from God (cf. 9:37)[162].

2.3.3 The Religious Authorities' Response

Jesus' counter-question placed his adversaries in a state of embarrassment; and they recognized their dilemma[163]: «if they acknowledged John's prophetic authority they would expose themselves to the charge of unbelief. They also realized they would be compelled to acknowledge that Jesus' authority comes from God»[164]. In fact, «their perplexity in deciding what answer to give is due, not to a desire to give the correct reply, but to a concern to preserve their own position»[165]. However, the Sanhedrin representatives cannot answer Jesus' counter-question without exposing themselves to either the reproach of unbelief, or setting themselves in contradiction to the view of the people[166]: «for all held that John was a real prophet» (v.32). So they decided to answer Jesus, «we do not know»[167] (v.33a). But this answer is really motivated through unbelief, fear and insincere diplomacy[168].

As a matter of fact, Jesus, in referring to John's baptism (of repentance for the forgiveness of sins, 1:4), calls to mind the fact, that those who accepted it, testified that they were in need of, and have the willness for, repentance; while those who refused it placed themselves against a divine mission of John, and place themselves against repentance - and the Jewish authorities did just that[169]. With the reference to John's baptism, Jesus takes up the theme of his previous day's action in the temple, which is a unique appeal for repentance. And the Jewish authorities, by calling Jesus to account for the authority of his actions, still show their lack of

---

[162] Cf. W.L. LANE, *Mark*, 414; C.S. MANN, *Mark*, 456.

[163] Cf. W.L. LANE, *Mark*, 414; K. STOCK, «Gliederung», 504; R.H. GUNDRY, *Mark*, 657, 658.

[164] W.L. LANE, *Mark*, 414.

[165] M.D. HOOKER, *St. Mark*, 272.

[166] Cf. J. KREMER, «Jesu Antwort», 133; M.Y.-H. LEE, *Autorität*, 148, 150.

[167] W.L. LANE, *Mark*, 414, opined that «the group sought to evade the issue with a confession of ignorance, implying that they had suspended their judgment». Likewise, R.H. GUNDRY, *Mark*, 658, asserts that «"they say" stresses the embarrassment evident in the Sanhedrin's answer, "We don't know"».

[168] Cf. J. KREMER, «Jesu Antwort» 133; M.Y.-H. LEE , *Autorität*, 149-150.

[169] Cf. K. STOCK, «Gliederung», 505.

readiness for repentance as in the case of John's baptism[170]. Now the Sanhedrin, by their indecision, insincerity and opportunism to evade answering Jesus' counter-question, have repeated their action towards John, with Jesus. However, «if John's baptism was of God — as the crowds believed and the Sanhedrin evidently feared — then Jesus' authority is the authority of God»[171].

2.3.4 Jesus' Answer

Since the Sanhedrin representatives have really not fulfilled Jesus' stated condition, therefore he refuses to answer their question about his authority. Kremer observes that «just in this refusal of the answer, which implies a condemnation of the high council, brings to expression the unsusual self-confidence of Jesus»[172], especially his authority[173]. However, Jesus' answer did not end here; but rather he continued his argument with his interlocutors (αὐτοῖς; αὐτούς [them], 12:1,12), in the parable of the vineyard and tenants, where he gave a complete and elucidated answer.

In this parable, Jesus placed himself (with his activity) and his interlocutors within the history of God with his people: where the prophets were sent first, and he is the last one sent by God. Jesus, as the beloved son, came on behalf of God, to demand for the payment of the fruits of the vineyard. So he shares with the prophet, not only the task (mission) but also the fate: the fruits were refused him and he is killed, but he will be rehabilitated by God[174]. So Jesus, continuing the mission of the prophets (cf. Jeremiah, John the Baptist), has both this mission and his

---

[170] Cf. K. STOCK, «Gliederung», 505; G.S. SHAE, «The Authority of Jesus», 23.

[171] J.R. EDWARDS, «The Authority of Jesus», 227. R.J. DILLON, «As One Having Authority», 102, states that «the two held mandates "from heaven" which an unbelieving officialdom could not recognize».

[172] J. KREMER, «Jesu Antwort», 133 (trans. mine).

[173] Cf. R.H. GUNDRY, Mark, 658; M.D. HOOKER, St. Mark, 272; M.Y.-H. LEE, Autorität, 152-153; J. KREMER, «Jesu Antwort», 133. W. GRUNDMANN, Mark, 318, affirms that «in the counter-question as well as in the refused information lies a challenge (provocation), in which Jesus' authority becomes evident» (trans. mine).

[174] Cf. K. STOCK, «Gliederung», 505-506. In this parable, God is to be understood as the owner of the vineyard; while the tenants are the leaders of Israel. The servants represent the prophets, sent by God and abused and killed by Israel's leaders; and last of all, the owner sent his beloved son. Mark understood him to be Jesus. Cf. J. PAINTER, Mark's Gospel, 162.

authority from God, as he is the beloved Son of God[175]. Thus, his mission and identity (as the beloved Son of God) make his authority from God (heaven) most authentic and conclusive. The rejection of the prophetic and messianic mission of Jesus by the Jewish leaders is very graphically presented in this parable. Hence «the Jewish Authorities understood Jesus, but then their understanding of his claims encourages (strengthens) them in their destructive will (12:12)»[176]. From now on, the momentum resulting from this debate leads to the passion and death of Jesus, as exemplified in the parable, which its cause is not far from Jesus' authority. Even Pilate was able to perceive the Jewish Authorities' envy during Jesus' trial (15:10).

2.4 *Summary*

We have tried in this section, to demonstrate how Jesus' divine authority, through his person, has manifested itself in every aspect of his mission in the whole of Mark's Gospel. This we have shown both in his words and actions. We also experienced his authority, as the Son of Man, to forgive sins, in spite of the opposition of the scribes. Lastly, we observed that this authority, which created astonishment and amazement among the people, became also the root cause of offence and conflict between Jesus and the Jewish Authorities, which began in Jesus' Galilean ministry and had its climax in Jesus' confrontation with the Sanhedrin representatives in the Temple of Jerusalem. The result of the question and counter-question between Jesus and Jewish Authorities was not positive: it ended in their determination to arrest, try him and kill him. This they succeeded when they accused him of Blasphemy (cf. 2:7; 14:64), whose penalty is death. The envy of the Jewish Authorities against Jesus, which Pilate perceived during Jesus' trial (15:10), is surely the effect of Jesus' authority, which began earlier (1:22,27; 2:10; cf.3:22-30; 7:1-13). However, what the Sanhedrin did not recognize, is that Jesus' authority is a consequence of the authority of the Son of God: therefore the ἐξουσία of Jesus is in fact the εξουσία of God[177].

---

[175] Cf. K. STOCK, «Gliederung», 506; K. SCHOLTISSEK, *Vollmacht Jesu*, 210-211.
[176] K. STOCK, «Gliederung», 506 (trans. mine); Cf. R.J. DILLON, «As One Having Authority», 101.
[177] Cf. J.R. EDWARDS, «The Authority of Jesus», 227.

3. The Mission of Jesus

The third theme for our consideration in this chapter, which still relates to the person of Jesus, is his mission. In our pericope, we have already established in Part 1, that through the unclean spirit's words spoken through his victim, Jesus' mission was highlighted: ἦλθες ἀπολέσαι ἡμᾶς; - «Have you come to destroy us?» (1:24b). Thus Jesus' mission is well expressed with a word about his «coming» (which some scholars call the ἦλθον-sayings). The above ἦλθον-saying[178] is the first, and one of the four sayings in Mark's Gospel (with an infinitive, it forms a «statement of purpose», thereby identifying an aspect of Jesus' mission). The others are: 1:38; 2:17; and 10:45. And these correspond to four important aspects of Jesus' mission as they stand in the Gospel.

The relation between Jesus and God, confirms his divine sonship, and gives rise to his authority and mission. So, just as Jesus' authority is consequent of his identity (as the beloved Son of God), so also is his mission. And likewise in Jesus' public ministry, it is well demonstrated in words and actions, how the authority of Jesus is very closely connected with his mission[179].

We shall therefore try to show in this section how Jesus' mission, identified in our pericope, ran through the whole Gospel, especially through this ἦλθον-sayings. Firstly, we shall recall how Jesus liberated men from demonic powers that enslaved them, as indicated in the words of the unclean spirit (1:24); secondly, we shall examine how Jesus began his mission, by proclaiming the gospel of God (1:38, cf. 1:14-15); thirdly, we shall highlight Jesus' effort to call sinners (2:17); and finally, we shall find out how Jesus shows an example of service by giving his life for all (10:45). In this way, we can demonstrate that Jesus' mission is, not only indicated in our pericope, but also an important theme in the Gospel of Mark. And this will surely help us to prove that our pericope is programmatic in Mark's Gospel.

3.1 Jesus breaks the Demons' Power (Mk 1:24)

As Jesus entered for the first time into the synagogue of Capernaum, he is reminded of his mission through the cry of the demoniac, «Have you

---

[178] For the ἦλθον-sayings in the Synoptic Gospels, see: E. ARENS, The HΛΘON-Sayings ; W. CARTER, «Jesus' "I have come"», 44-62.

[179] Cf. K. STOCK, «Die Machttaten Jesu», 203.

come to destroy us?» (1:24b). Thus, «the reference to Jesus' coming
surely relates, not to his coming to the Capernaum synagogue, but to his
coming to earth with a special mission, which includes laying waste the
demonic kingdom»[180]. In other words, in the word of the demon it is
established that Jesus' action is not an episodic event, but rather has a
fundamental meaning: through Jesus' coming the power of the demons is
broken[181].

Jesus' proclamation of the coming of the kingdom of God is, not only
in word, but also in deed. In fact, there is a close connection between
«proclaiming» and «casting out demons» as seen in Mk 1:39; 6:12. «For
Jesus finds himself as "proclaiming" (1:14,38,39) and also as "casting out
demons" (1:34,39) only in the first chapter of Mark»[182]. Indeed, «Mark
seems to see in proclaiming and casting out demons the principal elements
of the beginning of Jesus' activity»[183]. We shall now examine what the
unclean spirits/demons do to man, and what Jesus' coming or mission
signifies for man, and for the demons.

In Mark's Gospel, the demons are characterized in three ways[184]: (a)
they have a damaging power over man; (b) they know who Jesus is (that
he is their enemy); (c) and they belong to the power realm of Satan (3:22-
26), who tempted Jesus in the desert (1:13) and wants to hinder the
success of Jesus' work (4:15). However, one can observe what demons
can do to man in the three exorcisms reported in Mark's Gospel (1:23-28;
5:1-20; 9:14-27). Everything they do is geared to torment people and to
harm them[185]. This is demon possession, whose nature «is such that the
evil spirits overrides the personality of the individual he possesses, so that
he can control what the person says and does»[186]. By this the individual's

---

[180] S.H.T. PAGE, *Powers of Evil*, 142; R.H. GUNDRY, *Mark*, 76; E. ARENS, *The*
HΛΘON-*sayings*, 209, 220; E. LOHMEYER, *Markus*, 37.

[181] Cf. K. STOCK, «Die Machttaten Jesu», 198. This reflects the destruction of evil
powers/demonic world in the messianic age, as widely characterized Jewish
expectation. Cf. R. H. GUNDRY, *Mark*, 75; R. KAMPLING, «Dämonismus und
Exorzismus», 310; V. TAYLOR, *Mark*, 174.

[182] K. STOCK, *Boten*, 24 (trans. mine); D. TRUNK, «Jesus, der Exorzist», 9. With
regard to the other Synoptics, there exists no connection between «proclaiming» and
«casting out demons» (compare Mk 1:39 with Mt 4:23; 9:35; Lk 4:44).

[183] K. STOCK, *Boten*, 24; ID., «La conoscenza dei demoni», 93 (trans. mine).

[184] Cf. K. STOCK, «Die Machttaten Jesu», 198; ID., «La conoscenza dei demoni», 95.

[185] Cf. K. STOCK, «Die Machttaten Jesu», 198; «La conoscenza dei demoni», 96.

[186] S.H.T. PAGE, *Powers of Evil*, 141; R. KAMPLING, «Dämonismus und

personality is completely destroyed.

What is then the meaning of Jesus' coming for man? Jesus came to liberate men from the power of these demons/evil spirits: he gives back to the tormented man, a restored identity of himself, the free disposal of himself and the company with other people[187]. Jesus' coming signals the elimination of all powers hostile to God, so that «human beings should no more be subjected to strange, destructive powers, but rather should enjoy the revealed reign of God»[188]. In fact, Mark sees in the liberation (of man) from the power of the demons an essential part of Jesus' mission. This is evident, when he reports exorcism as Jesus' first miracle[189].

On the other hand, for the demons and evil spirits' world, Jesus' coming «(ἦλθες cf. Mk 1:24/Lk 4:34 and Mt 8:29) undoubtedly refers to the presence of Jesus which the demons see in itself as a menace to their security»[190]. With regard to the demons, Jesus knows only command (cf. 1:25; 9:25): the command to depart and to be silent. He treats them as he treats the natural forces of wind and water (ἐπετίμησεν, «he rebuked» cf. 1:25; 4:39). In fact, the verb, ὑπακούειν («to obey»), is used by Mk only for expressing the reaction of the demons, of the storm and of the sea, to Jesus' command (1:27; 4:41). «Jesus engages himself with the demons only to liberate men from their influence. Before them, he stands in a fundamental opposition, since they personify the forces (powers) that must not dominate men»[191]. Jesus, in fact, describes his action of exorcism thus: it is the stronger man who binds the strong one

---

Exorzismus», 308.

[187] Cf. K. STOCK, «Die Machttaten Jesu», 198; W. GRUNDMANN, *Markus*, 42-43. R. KAMPLING, «Dämonismus und Exorzismus», 310-311, states that exorcism has two aims: the demon, who is deprived of his power and cast out; and man, who is liberated again to himself. Thus exorcism becomes a special proof character of the reality of the kingdom of God.

[188] K. STOCK, «Die Machttaten Jesu», 199. (trans. mine)

[189] Cf. K. STOCK, «Die Machttaten Jesu», 198; D. TRUNK, «Jesus, der Exorzist», 9; ID., *Der messianische Heiler*, 205, among other things, observes that the exposed position of exorcism in the beginning of Jesus' public ministry is programmatic.

[190] E. ARENS, *The* ΗΛΘΟΝ-*sayings*, 219; M.D. HOOKER, *St. Mark*, 64, affirms that the destruction of demons is the purpose of Jesus' coming, and in its significance for Mark: «we see the one who has already overcome Satan waging war against God's enemies».

[191] K. STOCK, «La conoscenza dei demoni», 96 (trans. mine).

(3:27). And he claim to do this through the power of God's spirit (3:28-30)[192].

Mark, therefore, understands the mission of Jesus as most urgent, especially in the powerful announcing and pushing through the reign of God against any opposing/hostile power[193]. Thus, in the exorcism «the deprivation of the power of evil and the restitution of man takes place in the concrete present action of Jesus on men, to whom is made possible to experience in the liberating act, what the completion of the inbreaking salvation means»[194]. Jesus' action in word and deed, through the proclamation of the kingdom of God and the casting out of demons shows that his word is not an empty one; but is rather confirmed with an authoritative exorcism, healing and power over cosmic powers. Hence, the kingdom of God comes in word and deed in Jesus' person and work.

3.2 Jesus proclaims the Gospel of God (Mk 1:38)

In Mk 1:38, Jesus highlights κηρύσσειν («to proclaim» or «to announce»)[195], as an important aspect of his mission. He said to his disciples: «Let us go to the next (neighbouring) towns, that I may preach there also; for that is why I came out» (1:38). This saying of Jesus brings us back to Jesus' first act (after his Baptism, Temptation, and the arrest of John the Baptist), when he came to Galilee preaching the gospel of God. As the one coming from God, «the proclamation of the ultimate intention of God with his people is the real meaning of the mission of Jesus»[196]. What is proclaimed, is εὐαγγέλιον («gospel» or «good news»)[197] from God, which has unlimited (boundless), universal aim - to reach all men, nations and to the ends of the earth (cf.1:14; 13:10;

---

[192] Cf. K. STOCK, «Die Machttaten Jesu», 198; E. ARENS, The ΗΛΘΟΝ-sayings, 217, attests that Jesus «is the ἰσχυρός (Mk 3:26f.) who came to ἀπολέσαι the demonic powers». Cf. A. FRIDRICHSEN, «Conflict of Jesus», 128-129.

[193] Cf. K. STOCK, Boten, 25; S.H.T. PAGE, Powers of Evil, 142.

[194] R. KAMPLING, «Dämonismus und Exorzismus», 310 (trans mine); S.H.T. PAGE, Powers of Evil, 140.

[195] This word κηρύσσειν (to proclaim) appears 12x in Mark's Gospel: 3x for Jesus (1:14,38,39), 2x for the Baptist (1:4,7), and 2x for the disciples (3:14; 6:12), etc. It is worth noting that for Jesus, all appeared in the first chapter.

[196] K. STOCK, «Die Machttaten Jesu», 203 (trans. mine).

[197] The word εὐαγγέλιον («gospel») appears 7x in Mark (1:1,14,15; 8:35; 10:29; 13:10; 14:9) 4x in Matthew (4:23; 9:35; 24:12; 26:13) but none in Luke.

14:9)[198]. To achieve this, Jesus also called his disciples (1:16-20; 2:14) to join him in this mission of proclamation (3:14; 6:12), when he said to his first disciples: «Follow me and I will make you become fishers of men» (1:17). Thus, this establishes the relation between Jesus and his disciples, who will be the future bearers of the proclamation of the gospel[199].

In Mark's Gospel, Jesus' coming into Galilee is closely linked with his proclamation of the Gospel there (cf. 1:14, unlike Mt 4:12 or Lk 4:14). Likewise in Mk κηρύσσειν is used with the direct object τὸ εὐαγγέλιον τοῦ θεοῦ[200] exclusively in reference to Jesus' first proclamation in 1:14-15. The good news (gospel) from God that Jesus proclaims is: «The time is fulfilled, and the kingdom of God is at hand; repent, and believe in the gospel». The time (καιρός)[201] which God himself fixed, has been fulfilled in God's intervention into human history through Jesus Christ. In fact, «the message of Jesus takes up and answers the whole Old Testament expectation of the kingdom of God»[202]. According to our text, the kingdom of God[203] is at hand (ἤγγικεν): does it mean that it is near

---

[198] Cf. D. RHOADS, «Mission in Mark», 340; K. STOCK, «Mission bei Markus», 131; E. ARENS, The ΗΛΘΟΝ-sayings, 205.

[199] Cf. K. STOCK, «Mission bei Markus», 133-144, esp. 132, shows that formation of the missionaries (disciples) is one of the principal themes in Mark's Gospel, especially when one considers the space dedicated to the disciples, their relation with Jesus, and their formation. In this sense, one can say that Mark's gospel is characterized as missionary.

[200] Here τοῦ θεοῦ (about or from God), is genitive of person: but is it objective genitive (about God) or subjective genitive (from God)? Most scholars see the genitive as subjective: that is, the gospel from God. Cf. M.D. HOOKER, St. Mark, 54; S. KUTHIRAKKATTEL, The Beginning, 92; R.A. GUELICH, Mark, 43; C.S. MANN, Mark, 205; C.E.B. CRANFIELD, Mark, 62; V. TAYLOR, Mark, 166; but R.H. GUNDRY, Mark, 68 is for objective genitive («about God»).

[201] The word καιρός (appointed or fixed time), unlike χρόνος (period of time), is determined by God. «It is God's decision that makes a particular moment or period of time into a καιρός, a time filled with significance». Cf. C.E.B. CRANFIELD, Mark, 63; C.S. MANN, Mark, 205; S. KUTHIRAKKATTEL, The Beginning, 93-94; M.D. HOOKER, St. Mark, 54.

[202] K. STOCK, «Mission bei Markus», 133 (trans. mine); Cf. M. GRILLI, Comunità e Missione, 182-183; C.E.B. CRANFIELD, Mark, 63-64; W.L. LANE, Mark, 64.

[203] The term, kingdom of God (ἡ βασιλεία τοῦ θεοῦ [kingdom of Heaven, mostly used by Mt]), occurs 14x in Mk (Lk 32x; Jn 2x; Mt 4x/34 = kingdom of God / Heaven): 1:15; 4:11,26,30; 9:1,47; 10:14,15,23,24,25; 12:34; 14:25; 15:43. The kingdom of God certainly constitutes the key message of Jesus, yet he never attempts to define it. «Instead he explains it in metaphors, parables and short sayings, offers

(imminent) or that it has come (arrived)?[204] In other words, Jesus spoke about the kingdom of God as something *present* or as something in the *future*? This tension between the present and future dimension, may be intentional and inherent in Jesus' proclamation of the kingdom: not a wholly realized or a purely future eschatology[205]. This is because «Jesus spoke of the kingdom as future (14:25, cf. Lk 11:2) but also proclaimed that the kingdom was present in his own person and mission»[206]. Thus, the kingdom of God has come near in the person of Jesus. And in fact, the response demanded from people is given by the two imperatives in the text (v.15): «repent, and believe in the gospel». The call to repent within a proclamation context (1:4,14-15; 6:12) suggests that «repent», μετανονεῖν most likely carries the OT prophetic import שׁוּב («to turn back» or «to return»), that is, a profound and personal conversion; and not

---

personal and experiential insights into this polyvalent symbol and enables people to experience it personally». Cf. S. KUTHIRAKKATTEL, *The Beginning*, 97.

[204] The key to what Jesus proclaimed about «the kingdom of God» lies in the verb, ἤγγικεν. Some see it meaning «has come» based on the Semitic terms (נגע [Heb], מטא [Aram]) behind ἐγγίζειν and φθάνειν in the LXX. Cf. C.H. DODD, *The Parables*, 43-45. While some see the meaning as «nearness» based on their examination of NT use of ἐγγύς and ἐγγίζειν. Cf. W.G. KÜMMEL, *Promise and Fulfillment*, 19-25; J.Y. CAMPBELL, «The Kingdom of God», 91-94; K.W. CLARK, «Realized Eschatology», 367-383. However, R.H. FULLER, *The Mission*, 20-35, concurred with Kummel but suggested with M. BLACK, «The Kingdom of God», 289-290, that another Semitic term (קרב) might underlie ἐγγίζειν, a term that has both the meaning of «nearness» (qal stem) and «arrival» (hiphil stem). Cf. K.W. CLARK, «Realized Eschatology», 370; A.M. AMBROZIC, *The Hidden Kingdom*, 16. In the context of 1:15, ἐγγίζειν has a staightforward statement about something having happened, and several scholars have followed Dodd's conclusion, even if for different reasons. Cf. M. BLACK, «The Kingdom of God», 289-290; K.-G. REPLOH, *Markus - Lehrer der Gemeinde*, 20; A.M. AMBROZIC, *The Hidden Kingdom*, 21-23; W. KELBER, *The Kingdom in Mark*, 7-11; R.H. GUNDRY, *Mark*, 64-65. «Thus one is left with a context denoting "arrival" and a Greek verb which generally denotes "nearness" - an apparent syntactical contradiction». Cf. R.A. GUELICH, *Mark*, 44.

[205] Cf. R. SCHNACKENBURG, *God's Rule and Kingdom*, 141-142; R.F. BERKEY, «ΕΓΓΙΖΕΙΝ, ΦΘΑΝΕΙΝ», 177-187; A.M. AMBROZIC, *The Hidden Kingdom*, 23; R.A. GUELICH, *Mark*, 44.

[206] C.S. MANN, *Mark*, 206; Cf. M.D. HOOKER, *St. Mark*, 56-57; C.E.B. CRANFIELD, *Mark*, 65-68; V. TAYLOR, *Mark*, 167; W.L. LANE, *Mark*, 65. The fulfilment of time insures a *temporal* meaning for the kingdom's drawing near, while one sees the *spatial* nearness in the person of Jesus. Cf. R.H. GUNDRY, *Mark*, 65-66.

נחם («to change one's mind» or «to feel remorse»)²⁰⁷. This unconditional personal conversion creates the opportunity to entrust oneself to Jesus and the gospel. To believe ἐν τῷ εὐαγγελίῳ²⁰⁸ (in the gospel) means a total surrender to God by believing in God's rule. In short, «believe in the gospel» primarily «implies personal relationship: faith in Jesus Christ who is not only the herald of the Gospel but also its content»²⁰⁹.

From the very beginning onwards the message of the kingdom of God is essentially connected with its messenger or herald (Jesus), and the proclamation happens not only in *word* but also in *deed*, especially in the exorcisms/healings, in the forgiveness of sins, in the critique of the false understanding of the Law, in the admission of the company with sinners and tax collectors²¹⁰. Jesus' first day in Capernaum (1:21-34) was a concrete manifestation of his proclamation, which was exercised in authority both in word and action. Jesus did not want to confine his mission to one particular place, but rather he wanted to go beyond Capernaum (vv.35-39, esp. v.38).

Jesus left Capernaum for the neighbouring towns with the aim ἵνα καὶ ἐκεῖ κηρύξω· εἰς τοῦτο γὰρ ἐξῆλθον - «that I may preach there also; for that is why I came out» (v.38). It is clear from the context, and the γάρ-explanation construction, that Jesus' purpose is to preach, because «κηρύσσειν is the mission Jesus was entrusted with by God and is the fundamental reason for his "going out of Nazareth" (1:9) and into Galilee at large»²¹¹. This, he fulfilled in v.39. But some scholars base their

---

²⁰⁷ Cf. R.A. GUELICH, *Mark*, 45; M.D. HOOKER, *Mark*, 55; S. KUTHIRAKKATTEL, *The Beginning*, 99. R.H. GUNDRY, *Mark*, 66, states that «the call to repent links up with John's baptism of repentance (v.4) to provide continuity in the carrying of God's plan». In Mk μετάνοια occurs once (1:4; but Mt 2x; Lk 5x) and μετανοεῖν 2x (1:15; 6:13; but Mt 5x; Lk 9x). In Mk 1:4 μετάνοια is part of the content of John's preaching; while in 1:15 and 6:13 μετανοεῖν forms part of the object of Jesus' and the Twelve's preaching respectively.

²⁰⁸ This is the only place in Mark and rest of the NT where the verb «to believe» takes ἐν. Cf. V. TAYLOR, *Mark*, 167; W. EGGER, *Frohbotschaft und Lehre*, 49; C.S. MANN, *Mark*, 207. In fact, it is only here in the NT that the good news is made the explicit object of belief. Cf. R.H. GUNDRY, *Mark*, 70.

²⁰⁹ S. KUTHIRAKKATTEL, *The Beginning*, 101.

²¹⁰ Cf. K. STOCK, «Mission bei Markus», 133; S. KUTHIRAKKATTEL, *The Beginning*, 97; E. ARENS, *The ΗΛΘΟΝ-sayings*, 202; W.L. LANE, *Mark*, 66.

²¹¹ E. ARENS, *The ΗΛΘΟΝ-sayings*, 206; R.H. GUNDRY, *Mark*, 101; R.A. GUELICH, *Mark*, 70, 71; Z. KATO, *Die Völkermission*, 21-23.

interpretation of v.38 on ἐξῆλθον («I came out»): does it mean that Jesus came out from Capernaum[212], or from God[213], to fulfill this mission? As I have already indicated, the motive for Jesus movement is what matters - to preach. So he has to widen «the sphere of his powerful activity outside Capernaum rather than his concentrating that activity in Capernaum»[214]. Thus Jesus' missionary activity has just begun its march towards universalization. For Mark, «there are no longer boundaries to be guarded... the only boundary left is the extremity of the earth, which the disciples are to reach before the end comes»[215]. However, we must remember that Jesus' proclamation of the gospel of God continues in his teaching.

3.3 Jesus calls Sinners (Mk 2:17)

Jesus' authoritative word and deed in inaugurating the kingdom of God, is not only to destroy the demonic powers, but also to bring sinners back to their relation with God, those who have distanced themselves from God's will[216]. Thus, Jesus addresses his mission to such people when he said: οὐκ ἦλθον καλέσαι δικαίους ἀλλὰ ἁμαρτωλούς - «I came not to call the righteous, but sinners» (2:17). In Jesus' proclamation of the gospel, μετανονεῖν (to repent) is a requirement in God's kingdom, and man's response to Jesus' message (1:14-15), which is, a profound and personal conversion of man, in order to regain his relation with God. The call to repent also links up Jesus' proclamation with John's preaching «a

---

[212] Cf. M.D. HOOKER, St. Mark, 77; C.S. MANN, Mark, 217; V. TAYLOR, Mark, 184.

The occurrence of ἐξέρχεσθαι in v.35 (for praying) and in v.38 (for preaching) may support this view. Cf. C.E.B. CRANFIELD, Mark, 90; R.H. GUNDRY, Mark, 100.

[213] Cf. R.A. GUELICH, Mark, 70; E. LOHMEYER, Markus, 43. May be Luke's use of the verb, ἀπεστάλην (Lk 4:43) - «for I was sent for this purpose»- gives them the support. On the other hand, some support both, with the reason that the ambiguity may be intentional. Cf. C.E.B. CRANFIELD, Mark, 90; W.L. LANE, Mark, 82.

[214] R.H. GUNDRY, Mark, 94.

[215] D. RHOADS, «Mission in Mark», 345.

[216] E.P. SANDERS, «Sin, Sinners», 43, states that «while the verb "to sin" usually refers to an individual transgression, the noun "sinner" often (not always) indicates a worse state: a life which is not orientated around obedience to the will of God, but which is rather lived apart from him entirely. The cure for this condition is a change of one's life, sometimes indicated by the word "repentance" in the sense of "conversion"».

baptism of repentance for the forgiveness of sins» (1:4), and also continues it in his mission[217]. Jesus demonstrated his interest in restoring sinners to their wholeness (both in themselves and with God), in his authoritative healing and forgiveness of the sins of the paralytic (2:1-12). Therefore, in this section, we shall examine how Jesus called, Levi, a tax collector (a sinner) to be a disciple, and how Jesus also dined with him and his collegues. And we shall see what effect this had in his mission.

3.3.1 Jesus dines with Tax Collectors and Sinners

Like the first four disciples (1:16-20), Jesus passed (the sea), saw and called Levi the son of Alphaeus[218], to follow him; and he rose immediately and followed him (2:14)[219]. This Levi's call was the occasion and the context in which Jesus dined with many tax (toll) collectors and sinners (2:15-17). But who hosted the meal (feast)[220] and in whose house (v.15)?[221] In view of the reason for the feast, it is most likely that Levi

---

[217] Cf. R.H. GUNDRY, *Mark*, 66.

[218] On the problem of the name Levi, son of Alphaeus (Mk 2:14) or Matthew (Mt 9:9), cf. R.A. GUELICH, *Mark*, 99-100; V. TAYLOR, *Mark*, 202-203; C.E.B. CRANFIELD, *Mark*, 101-102; R.P. MEYE, *Jesus and the Twelve*, 140-142; R. PESCH, «Levi-Matthäus», 40-56; M.J. LAGRANGE, *Saint Marc*, 42.

[219] If one compares 2:14 (the call of Levi) with 1:16-18 (the call of Simon and Andrew), it will be observed that the former satisfied the basic and essential elements of the call. (a) Jesus' initiative: καὶ παράγων ... εἶδεν Σίμωνα// καὶ παράγων εἶδεν Λευὶν; (b) Daily Task: ἀμφιβάλλοντας ἐν τῇ θαλάσσῃ// καθήμενον ἐπί τὸ τελώνιον; (c) Jesus speaks: καὶ εἶπεν αὐτοῖς ...// καὶ λέγει αὐτῷ,; (d) Jesus calls: Δεῦτε ὀπίσω μου// Ἀκολούθει μοι; (e) Detachment from Task: καὶ εὐθὺς ἀφέντες τὰ δίκτυα// καὶ ἀναστὰς; (f) Following Jesus: ἠκολούθησαν αὐτῷ// ἠκολούθησεν αὐτῷ. M.D. HOOKER, *St. Mark*, 94, opined that «the call of a notorious sinner to be his (Jesus') disciple must have seemed to Mark an act of forgiveness parallel to that in the preceding story».

[220] Cf. M.D. HOOKER, *St. Mark*, 95, suggests that the verb, κατακεῖσθαι (to recline at table), refers to a feast rather than an ordinary meal. Cf. R.A. GUELICH, *Mark*, 101.

[221] Many scholars favour that Levi gave the great feast, in the company of his collegues, for Jesus and his disciples in his own house (cf. Lk 5:29; 19:1-10), as an expression of his joy. In other words, αὐτόν refers to Jesus, while αὐτοῦ refers to Levi (v.15). Cf. R.H. GUNDRY, *Mark*, 124; S. KUTHIRAKKATTEL, *The Beginning*, 203; E. ARENS, *The ΗΛΘΟΝ-sayings*, 20; C.E.B. CRANFIELD, *Mark*, 103; W.L. LANE, *Mark*, 103; J.R. DONAHUE, «Tax Collectors and Sinners», 56; E. KLOSTERMANN, *Markusevangelium*, 25. On the other hand, E.S. MALBON, «Mark 2:15 in Context», 282-292, argues that v.15 refers not to Levi's but Jesus' house. However, I agree with

hosted Jesus in his house. There were many «tax collectors and sinners» (not many disciples)[222] who participated in this feast. One may ask, what does the term, τελῶναι καὶ ἁμαρτωλοί («tax collectors and sinners») mean?[223] To this, Arens states, «in the eyes of official Judaism the tax-collectors were classed as sinners because of their profession, which was associated with robbery, and were despised because they worked for the pagan oppressor»[224]. Thus, they are not considered as two classes of people, but one (cf. there is only one definite article in v.16); and moreover, «sinners» is inclusive of «tax collectors»[225]. In fact, «that Jesus consorted with such people, and ate with them, was to the scribes a deep

---

the former, because there is a connection between 2:14 and 2:15-17; and moreover, if it were in Jesus' house, may be the Pharisees' scandal would have been avoided.

[222] Although this is the first time the word, μαθητής occurs in Mk, yet here it talks about «many tax collectors and sinners» and not «many disciples». This is because the *subject* of the verb συνανέκειντο (sit at table with), in the phrase v.15b is πολλοὶ τελῶναι καὶ ἁμαρτωλοὶ («many tax collectors and sinners»); and the γάρ-explanatory construction takes it up (ἦσαν γὰρ πολλοὶ... «for they were many who followed him» v.15c). Moreover, τῷ Ἰησοῦ καὶ τοῖς μαθηταῖς αὐτοῦ (with Jesus and his disciples) is the *object* of v.15b. Cf. R.H. GUNDRY, *Mark*, 128; M.D. HOOKER, *St. Mark*, 95; R.P. MEYE, *Jesus and the Twelve*, 142-145, esp. 144-145. Some thought about the verb, ἀκολουθεῖν («to follow») technically, and attributed the phrase «for there were many who followed him» to «many disciples». Cf. R.A. GUELICH, *Mark*, 102; C.E.B. CRANFIELD, *Mark*, 104; E. ARENS, *The* HΛΘON-*sayings*, 32-34; V. TAYLOR, *Mark*, 205.

[223] «Tax (toll) collector» is a profession; while «sinner» is a moral condition of a person. They are not two different «classes» of people. The two terms, «tax collector» and «sinners» are often in the synoptic tradition together (Mt 9:10,11; 11:19; Mk 2:15,16[bis]; Lk 5:30; 7:34; 15:1). The importance of this term in our text is clear: it occurs 3x (vv.15b,16b,d), and concentrates only here in Mark's Gospel. The term «sinners» denotes either those who do not observe the Law according to the Pharisaic ideal (in full sense), that is, «the people of the land»: עם הארץ. Cf. S. KUTHIRAKKAT-TEL, *The Beginning*, 204-205; R.A. GUELICH, *Mark*, 102; E. ARENS, *The* HΛΘON-*sayings*, 30. Or those who, on account of their way of life, were shunned by ordinarily respected people, and as such treated as religious and social outcasts. Cf. M.D. HOOKER, *St. Mark*, 95; C.E.B. CRANFIELD, *Mark*, 103; W.L. LANE, *Mark*, 103. See further, E.P. SANDERS, *Jesus and Judaism*, 174-211. While the term «tax (toll) collectors» earned contempt and bad reputation from the people, because those in this profession were known for their rapacity and dishonesty. Cf. J. JEREMIAS, *Jerusalem*, 303-312; ID., «Zöllner und Sünder», 293-300; J.R. DONAHUE, «Tax Collectors and Sinners», 49-61; F. HERRENBRÜCK, «Die Zöllner», 178-194.

[224] E. ARENS, *The* HΛΘON-*sayings*, 30.

[225] Cf. S. KUTHIRAKKATTEL, *The Beginning*, 206.

ground of offence»[226]. This brings us to the next point: Jesus encounter with the religious leaders.

3.3.2 Jesus' Action questioned

Jesus' eating with the tax collectors and sinners attracted the attention of the «scribes of the Pharisees»[227] to ask Jesus' disciples this question: «Why does he eat with tax collectors and sinners?»[228] (v.16). But why did they not ask Jesus directly? May be «their fear to ask Jesus directly makes another tribute to the awesomeness of his authority»[229]. However, «since Mark does not mention the Pharisaic scribes among those who eat with Jesus and his disciples, one presumes that he portrays the Pharisaic scribes as onlookers»[230]. All the same, Jesus did hear their question, and this sets the stage for his response.

3.3.3 Jesus' Response

Jesus' answer in v.17 had two sayings in a synonymous parallelism, with οὐ(κ) ... ἀλλά construction[231], which concern the healthy-sick, and the righteous-sinners respectively: οὐ χρείαν ἔχουσιν οἱ ἰσχύοντες ἰατροῦ ἀλλ᾽ οἱ κακῶς ἔχοντες· οὐκ ἦλθον καλέσαι δικαίους ἀλλὰ ἁμαρτωλούς («Those who are well have no need of a physician, but those who are sick; I came not to call the righteous, but sinners» v.17). While the first is a proverb, the second contains the «ἦλθον-saying». It is also observed that the second saying has a «dialectical negation»[232] structure,

---

[226] V. TAYLOR, *Mark*, 205.

[227] The «scribes of the Pharisees» is really an unusual combination that appears only here in Mark. Cf. R.A. GUELICH, *Mark*, 102; V. TAYLOR, *Mark*, 206. As a matter of fact, these are the scribes who belong to the party of the Pharisees (Acts 23:9). Cf. R.A. GUELICH, *Mark*, 56; M.D. HOOKER, *St. Mark*, 96; C.E.B. CRANFIELD, *Mark*, 104; E. KLOSTERMANN, *Markusevangelium*, 25.

[228] Here ὅτι can be regarded as used interrogatively. Cf. R.H. GUNDRY, *Mark*, 126; M.D. HOOKER, *St. Mark*, 96.

[229] R.H. GUNDRY, *Mark*, 126.

[230] R.H. GUNDRY, *Mark*, 128; V. TAYLOR, *Mark*, 207. It is normal near eastern custom for people to stand around observing a banquet as the scribes do here (cf. Lk 7:37). Cf. R.H. GUNDRY, *ibid.*, 128-129; K.E. BAILEY, *Through Peasant Eyes*, 4-5.

[231] This construction is typical of Jesus' sayings in Mark, cf. M.D. HOOKER, *St. Mark*, 97; V. TAYLOR, *Mark*, 207. But A. PLUMMER, *Mark*, 90, points to this frequency in Mk 3:26,29; 4:17,22; 5:39; 6:9; 7:19; 9:37; 10:8, etc.

[232] In a dialectical negation one statement, often the first, is placed in the negative

which is Semitic in keeping with OT counterparts as is the contrast «righteous» and «sinners»[233]. Indeed, «the negative statement in 2:17b is not a categorical, all-inclusive negative but a Semitic way of strengthening the positive. Hence it is not said that the righteous are excluded; in fact, the decisive point is that the call is directed towards sinners»[234]. Jesus has really come to call (καλέσαι)[235] sinners (Lk 5:31 adds «to repentance» - εἰς μετάνοιαν). And unless there is a profound personal conversion, there will be no disposition for the forgiveness of sins, which prepares one for God's rule. Thus, «by using a pericope that concludes with a reference to the "sick" and the "sinners", the evangelist picks up the theme of healing and forgiveness in 2:1-12»[236]. By calling Levi, the tax collector-sinner, to be one of his disciples; and moreover by identifying himself with him, and dining with the tax collectors and sinners (his collegues), Jesus has indeed demonstrated that he really came for them. Hence «for Jesus to refuse to have dealings with the disreputable would be as absurd as for a doctor to refuse to have to do with the sick; he has come on purpose to call sinners, and the disreputable people he is associating with are obvious members of that class»[237].

As Jesus' coming demonstrates his mission in proclaiming the gospel of the coming of the kingdom of God, initiating the battle on breaking the power of the hostile forces against man and in opposition to God, so also it is Jesus' task to bring back to the company of God, all those who have

---

in order to accentuate the other. Therefore, the import of the saying is found in the second statement about Jesus' coming to call sinners. Cf. R.A. GUELICH, Mark, 104; H. KRUSE, «Die dialektische Negation», 386.

[233] Cf. R.A. GUELICH, Mark, 104; E. ARENS, The ΗΛΘΟΝ-sayings, 44; R. PESCH, Markusevangelium I, 166; H. KRUSE, «Die dialektische Negation», 385-400.

[234] S. KUTHIRAKKATTEL, The Beginning, 209; R.A. GUELICH, Mark, 105; E. ARENS, The ΗΛΘΟΝ-sayings, 44, 54; J. GNILKA, Markus I, 109; W. GRUNDMANN, Markus, 84; R. PESCH, «Das Zöllnergastmahl», 74-75. On the righteous (δικαίους), some take it ironically to mean «all who think themselves righteous» (like the scribes or Pharisees). Cf. C.S. MANN, Mark, 231-232; W.L. LANE, Mark, 105.

[235] The verb καλέσαι («to call») here in Mk is not specific: it could mean a call to discipleship; or in the sense of «to invite» - in which case, Jesus becomes the host of the feast (messianic banquet). But with Lk's addition of «to repentance», the picture becomes clearer: a call to repentance. Cf. S. KUTHIRAKKATTEL, The Beginning, 209; C.S. MANN, Mark, 232; C.E.B. CRANFIELD, Mark, 106.

[236] R.A. GUELICH, Mark, 106.

[237] C.E.B. CRANFIELD, Mark, 107; Cf. D. RHOADS, «Mission in Mark», 344; S. KUTHIRAKKATTEL, The Beginning, 208; M.D. HOOKER, St. Mark, 97.

distanced themselves through sin, or refused to do God's will. To this people, Jesus came not as a judge, but as a doctor (2:17)[238].

3.4 *Jesus gives His Life for Many (Mk 10:45)*

After Jesus' third prediction of his death and resurrection (10:32-34), James and John (sons of Zebedee) approached Jesus with a request of being on his right and left hands, in his glory (10:35-40). When the other ten disciples heard it they were indignant, and Jesus addressed them all (10:41-45)[239]. It is in this context, that Jesus made this statement: καὶ γὰρ ὁ υἱὸς τοῦ ἀνθρώπου οὐκ ἦλθεν διακονηθῆναι ἀλλὰ διακονῆσαι καὶ δοῦναι τὴν ψυχὴν αὐτοῦ λύτρον ἀντὶ πολλῶν. - «For the Son of man also came not to be served but to serve, and to give his life as a ransom for many» (10:45).

This request of the Zebedees (10:35f) is parallel to the persuasion of Peter (8:32) and to the disciples' struggle for rank (9:33f); each of them follow immediately after Jesus' prediction of his destiny. And this parallel is really an indication that in this request, it concerns a sign of incomprehension and of opposition to the way of Jesus[240], and moreover, of ignorance[241]. Likewise, «the indignation of the ten against James and John, whose request they have heard, sets the stage and may imply that they share James and John's ambition and ignorance»[242]. In Mk through καὶ γάρ v.45 is connected with the preceding verses (vv.43-44), while in

---

[238] Cf. K. STOCK, «Die Machttaten Jesu», 204.

[239] In Mk and Mt this section (Mk 10:35-45/Mt 20:20-28) is almost identical, while in Lk it is absent. However, Lk has the discourse about service as a means to true greatness immediately after the Last Supper (Lk 22:25-27).

[240] Cf. K. STOCK, *Boten*, 135; R.P. MEYE, *Jesus and the Twelve*, 77, affirms that «the fact that the disciples do not understand even after the thrice-repeated teaching regarding Jesus' destiny is clearly illustrated by 10:35-45 (cf.10:32-34)».

[241] Jesus, in fact, reproached the two brothers with ignorance (cf. v.38). They do not know that Jesus' right and left positions are actually the right and left places of the cross. Thus «their ignorance lies in the fact, that they pass by and over the passion prediction and push their own person in the foreground and request for places in the glory». Cf. K. STOCK, *Boten*, 136 (trans. mine).

This is not the first time the disciples were reproached with ignorance or incomprehension, cf. Mk 4:13,40; 7:18; 8:17-18,21.

[242] R.H. GUNDRY, *Mark*, 579, 586; K. STOCK, *Boten*, 137, adds that through this Hearing and Indignation (of the ten) is 10:41-45 very closely connected with 10:35-40, and 10:32-45 is joined together as a unit.

Mt with ὥσπερ[243]. This verse (v.45) treats about the mission and task of the Son of Man; and of it was also spoken at the beginning of this section in 10:33. Our whole section 10:33-45 is therefore united through these words about the Son of Man. And it seems, that with 10:45 not only is the demand on the Twelve established, but also the meaning of the prediction of 10:33f is pointed at. On the other hand, 10:45 proves to be the closing words to the whole section 10:32-45, and probably also for 9:30-50, where also the prediction, struggle for rank, demand for service are together, but where such a united causal word is lacking[244]. Likewise 10:45 is one of Jesus' sayings that state the purpose of his coming (mission), cf.1:38; 2:17.

3.4.1   Jesus came to Serve

In response to the request of the Zebedees, Jesus advised the Twelve not to imitate the worldly power holders who dominate and exercise their authority over their subjects (10:42), «but whoever would want to become great among you must be your servant (ἔσται ὑμῶν διάκονος), and whoever would want to be first among you must be slave for all (ἔσται πάντων δοῦλος)»: 10:43b-44. To conclude this teaching (demand on the Twelve), Jesus used once more the Semitic, οὐκ...ἀλλά construction in the first part, v.45a, where «what is first said negatively serves only to

---

[243] The introductory connective, καὶ γάρ does not occur often in the Gospels (Mt 3x; Mk 2x; Lk 7x; Jn 2x; cf. Mk 10:45; 14:70; Mt 8:9; 15:27; 26:73), while ὥσπερ never used in Mk, is found 10x in Mt. Normally καὶ before γάρ means «even» or «also»; therefore καὶ γάρ means «for even» or «for also» («denn auch»; and in Latin «nam etiam»). Cf. R.H. GUNDRY, Mark, 581; C.E.B. CRANFIELD, Mark, 341-342; V. TAYLOR, Mark, 444; E. LOHMEYER, Markus, 223. K. STOCK, Boten, 141, suggests that since in Mk 10:43-45 continuously Serving is handled, the meaning «for even»/«for also» is surely here to be preferred. While E. ARENS, The ΗΛΘΟΝ-sayings, 123, n.21, observes that «Mk's καὶ γάρ implies that here the basis for that on which the exhortation of v.43f rests is given. It is causal, while Mt's ὥσπερ is comparative». Cf. M.D. HOOKER, St. Mark, 247-248.

[244] Cf. K. STOCK, Boten, 142. It is also observed that 10:45 is related to the whole section, which begins with 8:27, and can also be the closing words (Schlußwort). Cf. J. DELORME, «Aspects doctrinaux», 93; STOCK, Boten, 142, n.421. Likewise E.R. KALIN, «Christology and Ecclesiology», 450, attests that «the section (8:27-10:45) that begins by asking who Jesus is ends with a reference to his mission and his fate: "For the Son of Man came not to be served but to serve, and to give his life a ransom for many"».

underline what then is added positively»[245]. And he said: «For the Son of man also came not to be served but to serve…» Thus, while the paradox presented in this first part of the verse (v.45a) is parallel to that presented in vv.43b-44; indeed, v.45a provides the basis for vv.43b-44[246]. Jesus demonstrates here by example of his life and mission, what he has just demanded from his disciples.

To serve, διακονεῖν, means originally and primarily, «to wait at table»[247] (Mk 1:31; Lk 10:40; 12:37; 17:8; 22:27); then «to care for someone's living (livelihood)» (Mk 1:13; 15:41; Lk 8:3); and finally «to serve» in general[248]. In other words, διακονεῖν «has the special quality of indicating very personally the service rendered to another»[249]. Thus, in Jesus' demand of the Twelve, διάκονος connotes the personal character of service, while δοῦλος connotes its obligatory character[250]. In this way, Jesus taught his disciples that the only way to greatness is humility, which manifests itself in the personal attention and service to each other, as servant and slave of all. And this personal character in service has characterized Jesus' mission, both in his words and actions.

3.4.2 Jesus gives His Life

The second part of this verse (v.45b) also speaks of a form of service: the Son of Man is to give his life in order to bring redemption to others[251]. The ἦλθον-saying concluded thus: καὶ δοῦναι τὴν ψυχὴν αὐτοῦ λύτρον ἀντὶ πολλῶν. - «… and to give his life as a ransom for

---

[245] E. ARENS, The ΗΛΘΟΝ-sayings, 130; Cf. V. TAYLOR, Mark, 444.

[246] Cf. M.D. HOOKER, St. Mark, 250.

[247] Cf. R.H. GUNDRY, Mark, 589; E. ARENS, The ΗΛΘΟΝ-sayings, 132; K. STOCK, Boten, 119; H.W. BEYER, «διακονέω», 81-86.

[248] Cf. K. STOCK, Boten, 119.

[249] H.W. BEYER, «διακονέω», 81; K. STOCK, Boten, 119, 140; C.E.B. CRANFIELD, Mark, 341.

[250] Cf. R.H. GUNDRY, Mark, 581; E. BEST, Following Jesus, 126-127; K. STOCK, Boten, 140. In διάκονος the nature of this service expresses itself: it occurs in the personal care (attention) to the other. While in δοῦλος is the obligation to this service underlined: they cannot choose, whether they want to serve or not, they are «enslaved» to this service (cf. STOCK, ibid.).

[251] Cf. M.D. HOOKER, St. Mark, 250; W.L. LANE, Mark, 383, affirms that «in verse 45, which subsumes verses 43-44, the death of Jesus is presented as his service to God and as a vicarious death for many in virtue of which they find release for sin».

214   PART II: SYNTHETIC-THEOLOGICAL ANALYSIS

many»[252]. As we observed a semitic construction in v.45a, so also are further Semitisms in v.45b[253].

The expression δοῦναι τὴν ψυχὴν («to give one's life») is traditional for the death of martyrs among the Jews and soldiers among the Greeks[254]. The most important word is λύτρον (ransom)[255], which in the NT occurs only here and its parallel in Mt 20:28[256]. Outside the Bible is used of the ransom of a prisoner of war or a slave. But «the prevailing notion behind the word is that of deliverance by purchase»[257]. Likewise in ἀντὶ πολλῶν the preposition (ἀντί), which means «for», not in the sense of «instead of» or «on behalf of» but «in the place of»[258], and used only here in Mark[259]. It is worth noting that «the position of ἀντὶ πολλῶν shows that it is dependent on λύτρον and not δοῦναι»[260]. According to v.45b the ransom is paid with Jesus' voluntary self-sacrifice for many, and πολλῶν (many) here «does not exclude the meaning, "all"»[261]. Thus,

---

[252] K. STOCK, *Boten*, 143, observes in the ἦλθον-sayings, that while the other programmatic words (e.g. Mk 2:17; Mt 5;17; 10:34) only consist of antithetical phrase (expression), here the word is still continued «and to give his life as a ransom for many». With it is stated, how wide (broad) the service of the Son of Man goes: it knows no boundaries because he risks his own life.

[253] R.H. GUNDRY, *Mark*, 588, noted three Semitisms in v.45b: (a) the use of τὴν ψυχὴν αὐτοῦ as reflexive, «himself», including the larger meaning, «his life»; (b) the use of «in substitution for many» (ἀντὶ πολλῶν) for the beneficiaries; and (c) the paratactic «and» used epexegetically to mean «*by* giving his life...»

[254] F. BÜCHSEL, «δίδωμι», 166; Cf. V. TAYLOR, *Mark*, 444.

[255] For further information concerning λύτρον, cf. F. BÜCHSEL, «δίδωμι», 340-349.

[256] Cf. C.E.B. CRANFIELD, *Mark*, 342; R.H. GUNDRY, *Mark*, 590, observes that though this word, λύτρον, does not appear elsewhere, but the closely related words ἀντίλυτρον, ἀπολύτρωσις, and λυτρόω appear in this connection at Rom 3:24-25; 1 Cor 1:30; Eph 1:7; Col 1:14; 1 Tim 2:6; Titus 2;14; Heb 9:15; and in 1 Cor 6:20; 7:23 «you have been bought with a price» explains the notion of ransom.

[257] V. TAYLOR, *Mark*, 444; ID., *Jesus and His Sacrifice*, 99-105, esp. 104. He added that in the saying it is used metaphorically but forcibly to describe an act of redemption.

[258] F. BÜCHSEL, «ἀντί», 372; Cf. C.E.B. CRANFIELD, *Mark*, 343; V. TAYLOR, *Mark*, 444; *Jesus and His Sacrifice*, 103-104.

[259] Although it occurs only here in Mark, it is found in the other Gospels in Mt 2:22; 5:38; 17:27; 20:29; Lk 1:20; 11:11; 12:3; 19:44; Jn 1:16, and in the rest of the NT 11x. Cf. V. TAYLOR, *Jesus and His Sacrifice*, 103-104.

[260] F. BÜCHSEL, «ἀντί», 373; R.H. GUNDRY, *Mark*, 590; C.E.B. CRANFIELD, *Mark*, 343; E. ARENS, *The ΗΛΘΟΝ-sayings*, 139; V. TAYLOR, *Mark*, 445.

[261] V. TAYLOR, *Mark*, 444-445; E.C. MALONEY, *Semitic Interference*, 139-142,

«the many had forfeited their lives, and what Jesus gives in their place is his life. In his death, Jesus pays the price that sets men free»[262].

In 10:45 Jesus interpretes his whole way and the end of this way, the life-offering (self-sacrifice), as service, for the saving of many[263]. Thus, «this painful and glorious destiny of the Son of Man is something unique to his mission and in a definite sense is incommunicable: only he can accomplish this service»[264]. One can agree that in the final words of 10:45, that there is an inner logic which holds together the ideas of the Son of man, service, the giving of one's life, and a ransom[265]. And I think that the inner logic is Jesus' mission, that motivated his coming into the world.

3.5 Summary

We have so far tried to show how the ἦλθον-saying, which programmatically initiated Jesus' mission, was realized in Jesus' action of casting out of demons, healing of diseases and sicknesses, and also breaking other cosmic powers hostile to God, and enslaved men. This is also seen in Jesus' proclaiming the gospel of God, which announced the coming of the kingdom of God, that is not limited to any geographical location. He also called people to personal conversion for the forgiveness of their sins, even to the extent of associating with the social and religious outcasts, in order to restore them to their relation with God. Lastly, Jesus concluded his mission by his voluntary self-offering on the cross for our salvation. Thus, «with a word, that speaks from his own mission (cf. 1:38; 2:17), Jesus characterizes the spirit of his work as *Dienen* - "to serve" (10:45)»[266].

---

indicates the Semitic use of «many» for «all». J. JEREMIAS, «πολλοί», 543-545, states that the Hebrew *rabbîm* («many») in Is.53 (to which both Mk 10:45 and 14:24 refer to) is interpreted inclusively as «all» not only by later Judaism but also by Paul and John. Thus, «it is taken to refer to the whole community, comprised of many members, which has fallen under the judgment of God. There is no support for the idea that Jesus interpreted Is.53 differently». Cf. ID., *The Eucharistic Words*, 181-182.

[262] W.L. LANE, *Mark*, 384.

[263] Cf. K. STOCK, *Boten*, 143; R.H. GUNDRY, *Mark*, 581.

[264] W.L. LANE, *Mark*, 385; E. ARENS, *The ΗΛΘΟΝ-sayings*, 130, affirms that «while Jesus' life of service is an aspect that may be imitated, his redemptive death is not».

[265] Cf. M.D. HOOKER, *St. Mark*, 251.

[266] K. STOCK, «Mission bei Markus», 137 (trans. mine).

4. Conclusion

I would like to conclude this chapter here. So far we have tried to highlight that these three important themes seen in our pericope, Jesus' identity, authority and mission, have programmatic character in Mark's Gospel. In Jesus' identity we tried to show that it is really a central question or theme in the Gospel, because it involved the main characters of Jesus' story. We established that the true identity of Jesus is, «the Son of God» (or other related designations that express Jesus' relation with God). and it was evident from the beginning to the end of the Gospel. Likewise Jesus' authority was evident in his words and actions, especially in casting out demons with only commands, and not with exorcistic rites; his power over sicknesses and diseases, even cosmic and hostile supernatural powers. This divine authority especially in teaching, became for him a root cause of hostility and conflict with the Religious Authorities, which led to his condemnation and death. Jesus' authority was also very effective throughout his mission, especially in proclaiming of the gospel, whose content was the kingdom of God. Jesus inaugurated this reign of God, in word: through his proclamation and teaching; in deed: when Jesus broke the power of the demons or evil/hostile spirits who enslaved and overpowered men. Jesus' call of sinners to repentance, coming to them as a doctor, and not as a judge, is made evident in his last service of giving his life as a ransom for many and for all. Hence, these themes are not only dominate, but also demonstrate their programmatic character in the Gospel of Mark.

CHAPTER VI

The Deeds of Jesus

In Part 1, we discovered in our pericope, that the main activities which opened Jesus' public ministry in the synagogue of Capernaum, were his Teaching and Exorcism. «Teaching is, in fact, the principal activity of Mark's Jesus, for his personal work of proclaiming is spoken of in ch.1 only, whereas reference to his teaching occur throughout the Gospel down to the Passion narrative, the last one being 14:49»[1]. Even, Jesus' teaching activity is seen as the general framework (*Gerüst*) of his ministry in Mark's Gospel[2]. On the other hand, it has also been observed that both quantitatively and qualitatively Exorcism has the most dominant and largest single category of healing story in Mark's Gospel[3]. So in this chapter, it will be our task, to demonstrate in two sections that Jesus' Teaching and Exorcism, which were main themes in our pericope, were also Jesus' dominant activities in his entire ministry, and therefore programmatic in Mark's Gospel.

1. The Teaching of Jesus

In our pericope (1:21-28), as shown in our analysis in Part 1, there is a concentration of didactic (teaching) vocabularies, especially διδάσκειν and its cognate noun, διδαχή (4x: vv.21, 22a,b, 27; two each). Mark's repeated use of these didactic terms in this pericope, which describes Jesus' first appearance, is most striking because it emphasizes teaching

---

[1] A.M. AMBROZIC, «New Teaching», 132.

[2] Cf. R. PESCH, «Ein Tag», 126.

[3] Cf. G.H. TWELFTREE, «ΕΚΒΑΛΛΩ», 364; P.W. HOLLENBACH, «Jesus, Demoniacs», 568.

without its content. This emphasis on teaching is extended in the Gospel through references to other didactic terms, like διδάσκαλος, ῥαββεί, more than other synoptic writers[4]. He also uses some related terms and expressions to describe Jesus' teaching activity: for example, λέγειν («to speak», «to say», or «to tell»)[5], or λάλειν («to speak»)[6], and ἀκούειν («to hear»)[7]. Thus in this way, Mark emphasizes the teaching activity of Jesus in his narration more than the others.

Jesus taught in *Galilee*: in the synagogues, in houses, in the open air/beside the sea/in the desert/on the way; and in *Jerusalem*: in the temple. The beneficiaries of his teaching were the people (ὁ ὄχλος, the crowd) and his disciples[8]. Jesus' teaching is especially highlighted in the summary statements[9]. In fact, «the Marcan emphasis is strikingly summarized in the *Marcan* note that Jesus taught them "as his custom was" (Mark 10:1)»[10]. Hence «Mark leaves us with the impression that the main activity of Jesus was teaching»[11].

In view of the vast teaching material in Mark[12], we shall limit ourselves to Jesus' teaching of the people (crowd), as seen in our pericope (1:21-

---

[4] Cf. R.P. MEYE, *Jesus and the Twelve*, 35-39, 44-45, esp. 37, 39; H. FLENDER, «Lehren und Verkündigung», 704-713.

[5] The term λέγειν (with the noun λόγος) plus αὐτοῖς, is most often used by Mk to describe Jesus' ministry of the word, even relatively more frequent than does either Mt or Lk. Cf. R.P. MEYE, *Jesus and the Twelve*, 48-49. For example: 3:23; 4:2,13,21; 7:14,18; 9:35; 10:24,32,42, etc.

[6] Likewise Mark uses the term, λάλειν, with some frequency. «to speak the word (to them)» - ἐλάλει (αὐτοῖς) τὸν λόγον - is a typically Markan expression: cf. 2:2; 4:33; 8:32. Cf. R.T. FRANCE, «Teaching of Jesus,» 129, n.5; R.P. MEYE, *Jesus and the Twelve*, 49; E. BEST, *Temptation and the Passion*, 70.

[7] Apart from repeated instances of hearing about Jesus' activity (cf. 2:1; 3;8,21; 5:27; etc); there is another type of hearing (ἀκούειν), in which Jesus directs the attention of his audience to his word. (cf. 4:3,9,23; 7:14; etc. Cf. R.P. MEYE, *Jesus and the Twelve*, 49-51.

[8] Cf. E.S. MALBON, «Markan Characters», 113-116; R.T. FRANCE, «Teaching of Jesus», 105-106.

[9] Cf. C.W. HEDRICK, «Summary Statements», 289-311; W. EGGER, *Frohbotschaft und Lehre*, 111-119, 121-131; 143-156.

[10] R.P. MEYE, *Jesus and the Twelve*, 40.

[11] E. BEST, *Temptation and the Passion*, 72; R.T. FRANCE, «Teaching of Jesus», 106.

[12] For the teaching material in Mark, one can also consult, cf. R.T. FRANCE, «Teaching of Jesus», 112-123; R.P. MARTIN, *Evangelist and Theologian*, 111-117; C.F. EVANS, *The Beginning of the Gospel*, 49-54.

28). Therefore, we shall demonstrate in three parts, how Jesus taught the people: (a) as highlighted in the summary statements (1:21-22; 2:1-2; 2:13; 4:1-2; 6:6b; 6:30-34; 10:1); (b) as seen through the Parables (4:3-34; 7:14-15); and (c) Jesus' teaching in the temple (11:17-18; 12:35-37; 12:38-40; 14:49). In this way, we shall partially verify how our pericope is programmatic in Mark's Gospel.

1.1 *Jesus teaches the Crowd (Summary Statements)*

One of the striking ways in which Mark stressed how Jesus taught the crowd in his Gospel is through the Summary Statements (*Sammelberichte* - «Summary Reports»). And these are narrative units, which summarize several ones and generalize certain aspects of Jesus' ministry, while emphasizing what is for him (Jesus) typical[13] (for example: teaching and healing)[14]. The peculiarity of these summary reports (statements) is that through summary and generalization they indicate a broader time and geographical extent of Jesus' activity. To achieve this, it is observed, on the one hand, the preference for the use of Imperfect tense and Participle; and on the other hand, the frequent use of expressions like: πάντες (all), πολλοί (many), πάλιν (again), thereby expressing the repetitive, continuous or customary activity (e.g. 1:21-22; 2:13; 6:6b; 10:1)[15]. There is also the frequent absolute use of the verb, in which the fact of teaching is mentioned, without the content (the verb has no direct object)[16]. The summary statement could also be a literary introduction[17] to the following

---

[13] Cf. W. EGGER, *Frohbotschaft und Lehre*, 1.

[14] W. EGGER, *Frohbotschaft und Lehre*, 2, identified 13 of these: Mk 1:14f; 1:21f; 1:32-34; 1:39; 1:45; 2:1f; 2:13; 3:7-12; 4:1f; 6:6b; 6:30-34; 6:53-56; 10:1; - These include the teaching summaries as: 1:21f; 2:1f; 2:13; 4:1f; 6:6b; 6:30-34; 10:1. Cf. C.W. HEDRICK, «Summary Staments», 291-292; K.L. SCHMIDT, *Der Rahmen*, 320.

[15] Cf. C.W. HEDRICK, «Summary Statements», 292-293; W. EGGER, *Frohbotschaft und Lehre*, 1, 143.

[16] Cf. R.T. FRANCE, «Teaching of Jesus», 111-112; W. EGGER, *Frohbotschaft und Lehre*, 144-145. Likewise E.S. MALBON, «Markan Characters», 113, observes that «the Markan narrator frequently refers to Jesus as teaching without giving — or even suggesting — the content of his teaching; this is especially the case in those scenes in which Jesus teaches the crowd (ὄχλος: 2:13; 4:1-2; 6:34; 10:1; cf. 11:18; πᾶς: 1:21-27[1:27,πᾶς]; πολλοί: 6:2; τάς κώμας κύκλῳ: 6:7)».

[17] Cf. C.W. HEDRICK, «Summary Statements», 298, 301; W. EGGER, *Frohbotschaft und Lehre*, 143, 149-150, observes that such summary introduction could be valid for: Mk 1:21f (2x διδάσκειν, 1x διδαχή): introduction for the «Day at Capernaum»; 4:1f

pericope or a literary conclusion[18] to a preceding pericope. When all is said and done, the significance of the summary statements for the overall Gospel is «that they broaden, widen or expand the ministry of Jesus beyond the borders of the individual particularized narratives which constitute the dominant feature of Mark's Gospel»[19]. Hence, we shall observe through the summary statements, the extent and variety of Jesus' teaching to the people, in the synagogues, houses, beside the sea, in the villages or desert, and on the way to Jerusalem.

1.1.1 Mark 1:21-22

It is striking to observe that our pericope satisfies the criteria of the summary statements: for instance, the summarizing and generalizing quality of the narrative, the use of Imperfect tense and/or Participle, the absolute use of the verb, and also the literary introduction, not only for our pericope, but also beyond it. Thus, «the statement itself relates a general response to a generally described activity. It seems to imply more than one occasion on which Jesus taught in the synagogue»[20]. In this connection, Mark, in this summary statement about Jesus' first act of teaching in his public ministry, shows both its *programmatic character* and the dominant role «teaching» is going to play in his Gospel. Now we shall examine other summary statements to see how Jesus' teaching is reflected elsewhere.

1.1.2 Mark 2:1-2

This summary statement is the literary introduction to the story of the Paralytic (2:1-12)[21]. We are told that Jesus entered again (πάλιν)[22], or

---

(2x διδάσκειν, 1x διδαχή): introduction for the Parable narrative; 6:30-34 (6:30 - teaching of the disciples; 6:34 - teaching of Jesus): introduction to the pericope of the multiplication of bread. Likewise 2:1f is treated as the summary introduction for the following miracle account of the healing of the paralytic.

[18] C.W. HEDRICK, «Summary Statements», 301-302, sees 4:33-34 functioning as a literary conclusion to the Markan chapter on parables. Cf. K.L. SCHMIDT, *Der Rahmen*, 126-128.

[19] C.W. HEDRICK, «Summary Statements», 293, 303-304, 310, 311; W. EGGER, *Frohbotschaft und Lehre*, 1; K.L. SCHMIDT, *Der Rahmen*, 13.

[20] C.W. HEDRICK, «Summary Statements», 295; W. EGGER, *Frohbotschaft und Lehre*, 146-149; K.L. SCHMIDT, *Der Rahmen*, 50.

[21] Cf. W. EGGER, *Frohbotschaft und Lehre*, 149-151; V. TAYLOR, *Mark*, 193; K.L.

returned to Capernaum after some days. It was heard that Jesus was at home, means that he entered *incognito*[23]. And «many were gathered together» (συνήχθησαν πολλοί): «even though entering Capernaum incognito, Jesus attracts people so magnetically that he cannot stay hidden very long (cf. 1:33; 2:13; 3:7-8; 4:1-2; 5:21; 6:34; 8:1)»[24]. This really created a problem, «so that there was no longer room for them (ὥστε μηκέτι χωρεῖν), not even about the door (πρὸς τὴν θύραν)». Here «Jesus' magnetic power has increased the size of the crowd. Not as before, they fill the house or courtyard. They also fill the area outside the door, which by itself held the whole city on the previous occasion»[25]. Before now, Jesus' popularity motif had progressed from his fame spreading «everywhere» (πανταχοῦ) in 1:28 to the «whole city» of 1:33, and then to «everyone» (πάντες) searching for him in 1:37, then his preaching in synagogues throughout Galilee (1:39), and finally to 1:45, where people come to him from «everywhere» (πάντοθεν)[26]. Hence, one can say that here culminates the Markan emphasis on Jesus' growing popularity among the people so far, thereby intensifying Jesus' magnetism, and preparing for v.4[27].

In spite of this overcrowding of people, Jesus was speaking (teaching/preaching) the word to them (ἐλάλει αὐτοῖς τὸν λόγον). This once

---

SCHMIDT, *Der Rahmen*, 78-79.

[22] R.A. GUELICH, *Mark*, 84, notes that Mark frequently uses πάλιν at the outset of a pericope to refer to a previous place or event (e.g. 2:13; 3:1,20; 4:1; 5:21; 7:31; 8:1; 10:1,10,32). In fact, mentioning Capernaum here recalls Mk 1:21.

[23] R.H. GUNDRY, *Mark*, 110, observes that this might seem to disagree with Mark's emphasis on Jesus' magnetic power by allowing that Jesus can enter Capernaun and stay there for a while without immediately drawing a crowd (contrast 7:24-25; also 1:35-37; 3:20; 6:32-33, 54-55). On the other hand, Jesus does succeed in staying hidden for some days in Capernaum because he does not enter it openly.

[24] R.H. GUNDRY, *Mark*, 110.; E.S. MALBON, «Markan Characters», 110-112, 115, remarks that the crowd continually comes to Jesus.

[25] R.H. GUNDRY, *Mark*, 111; C.S. MANN, *Mark*, 223; C.W. HEDRICK, «Summary Statements», 301; V. TAYLOR, *Mark*, 193.

[26] Cf. G.R. OSBORNE, «Structure and Christology», 153, 155, 157, 161, 163; C.W. HEDRICK, «Summary Statements», 301.

[27] Cf. R.H. GUNDRY, *Mark*, 111; E.K. BROADHEAD, *Teaching with Authority*, 75-76. In v.4, we meet for the first time ὄχλος, which occurs 38x in Mk (Mt 49; Lk 41x). B. CITRON, «The Multitude», 408-411, states that there are three words in the Synoptic Gospels (πλῆθος, λαός, ὄχλος) which have been rendered multitude, people, crowd or throng.

more highlights Jesus' teaching activity, through using related didactic
term (λάλειν). Jesus is once more in Capernaum, but now he teaches the
crowd in the courtyard of the house, and not in the synagogue. However,
in this summary statement (introduction), the general popularity of Jesus
and the consequent attraction/response of the crowd are very much
highlighted, and these set the stage for Jesus' teaching and healing.

1.1.3 Mark 2:13

Here the summary statement[28] seems fragmentary and abrupt, but it
includes the distinctive and important Markan themes: Jesus by the sea,
crowds coming to him, his teaching them (cf. 1:21; 4:1)[29]. That Jesus
went out again (ἐξῆλθεν πάλιν) to the sea side[30], changes his geographical location from Capernaum and a house there (cf. 2:1-12). This verse
(v.13) does not belong to 2:1-12 or 2:14-17, but it could be a general
transition for what follows[31], including a background for the calling of
Levi[32].

The two Imperfects (ἤρχετο - «was coming»; ἐδίδασκεν - «was
teaching») indicate the coming and going of successive groups of hearers
to Jesus, and he successively teaches them. However, the forward position
of πᾶς ὁ ὄχλος, «all the crowd», intensifies once more Jesus' magnetic
power, thereby showing that wherever he goes he always draws the
crowd, and he also uses such occasion to teach them. Thus, «Mark 2:13
describes Jesus' change of location and characterizes the ministry of Jesus
as a teaching ministry that draws crowds»[33]. Here, Jesus' teaching of the
people changes its location again, neither in the synagogue nor about the
door/house, but at the sea side/shore.

---

[28] Cf. C.W. HEDRICK, «Summary Statements», 295-296; W. EGGER, *Frohbotschaft
und Lehre*, 151-153; K.L. SCHMIDT, *Der Rahmen*, 82.

[29] Cf. R.A. GUELICH, *Mark*, 99; W. EGGER, *Frohbotschaft und Lehre*, 152.

[30] Here «again» (πάλιν, Markan term) modifies the rest of the predicate including
«to the sea side», and this recalls 1:16, which started the story of Jesus' call of his first
four disciples beside the Sea of Galilee (1:16-20). Cf. R.H. GUNDRY, *Mark*, 123; K.L.
SCHMIDT, *Der Rahmen*, 82; A. PLUMMER, *Mark*, 87.

[31] Cf. C.W. HEDRICK, «Summary Statements», 295; R.A. GUELICH, *Mark*, 99; A.
PLUMMER, *Mark*, 87; E. KLOSTERMANN, *Markusevangelium*, 24.

[32] Cf. W. EGGER, *Frohbotschaft und Lehre*, 151; W.L. LANE, *Mark*, 100; V.
TAYLOR, *Mark*, 202.

[33] C.W. HEDRICK, «Summary Statements», 295.

The nearness of 2:13 to 2:14-17 also reveals Mark's style of narrative succession of the summary statement and calling narrative[34]. In fact, this summary report (2:13) also gives an interpretation of the whole section 2:1-3:6, for Mk through the summary reports 2:1f. and 2:13 sets the section under the theme «Word» and «Teaching»[35]. And this section (2:1-3:6) is one of the sections in which Jesus taught through debates and controversies[36]. Hence, this summary statement adds to the emphasis of Jesus' teaching, not only for the section, but also for the whole Gospel.

1.1.4 Mark 4:1-2

This summary statement has an important role in the chapter (on parables) because it gives it a literary (editorial) introduction. While Mk 4:1-2 is the literary introduction to the Parable stories (4:1-34), 4:33-34 is its literary conclusion[37]. The scene here of Jesus beside the sea with the gathering of the crowd and the presence of a boat seem to take up a similar scene in 3:7-12[38]. However, it makes a difference when Mk repeats Jesus' teaching (3x), the crowd (2x) and the sea (3x)[39], and these reflect the frequent themes we have met previously. He, thus, emphasizes the importance of these themes in Jesus' Galilean ministry.

Jesus began to teach again (πάλιν) beside the sea. Here πάλιν refers to 2:13 and 3:7. But in 2:13 «again» referred more to Jesus' going out to the sea side; here, it refers to his teaching. The lack of a verb of motion, the forward position of «again», Mk's use of compound expression, ἤρξατο διδάσκεν («he began to teach»), even the repetitiveness of «teaching» (2x διδάσκειν, 1x διδαχή), all put emphasis entirely on

---

[34] W. EGGER, *Frohbotschaft und Lehre*, 153, noticed that both stories of Mk 2:14-17 and 1:16-20 agree, due to the fact, that in both times there are the same narrative succession of *summary report* and *calling narrative*: the summary report of Jesus' preaching (Mk 1:14f) is followed by the story of the calling of the first disciples; the summary report of Jesus' teaching (2:13) is followed by the story of the call of Levi (cf. 3:7-12 + 3:13ff; 6:6b + 6:7ff). Cf. K.L. SCHMIDT, *Der Rahmen*, 82.

[35] Cf. W. EGGER, *Frohbotschaft und Lehre*, 153.

[36] Cf. R.P. MARTIN, *Evangelist and Theologian*, 113; C.F. EVANS, *The Beginning of the Gospel*, 49-50.

[37] Cf. C.W. HEDRICK, «Summary Statement», 301-302.

[38] Cf. R.A. GUELICH, *Mark*, 190; W. EGGER, *Frohbotschaft und Lehre*, 118; W.L. LANE, *Mark*, 152; V. TAYLOR, *Mark*, 251.

[39] Cf. M.D. HOOKER, *St. Mark*, 122; W. EGGER, *Frohbotschaft und Lehre*, 111; F. NEIRYNCK, *Duality in Mark*, 77, 86, 98, 102.

Jesus' teaching and also connote his authority (cf. especially 1:22,27)[40]. Jesus' seated position also befits his teaching the crowd[41], and emphasizes his exercise of didactic authority. Jesus is once more teaching the crowd beside the sea, not only in summary statements, but concretely in parables. In fact, Jesus was teaching a very large crowd that gathered about him, that he taught them from the boat, and this only gives the impression of the increase of the crowd coming to Jesus[42]. Here, Jesus was teaching the crowd «many things», πολλά[43] in parables (ἐν παραβολαῖς). Hence, this summary statement, not only does it emphasize Jesus' teaching activity, but also highlights its content (in parables), and the largeness of the crowd that is attracted to Jesus' ministry.

1.1.5 Mark 6:6b

This is one of the shortest summary statements[44] in Mark's Gospel, that emphasizes the teaching activity of Jesus[45]. The verse shows the peculiarity of a summary statement: the act of Jesus is described in the Imperfect (περιῆγεν) and Participle (διδάσκων)[46]. Despite the brevity of these short statements, «they cover even a longer period of time than

---

[40] Cf. R.H. GUNDRY, *Mark*, 189, 190; W. EGGER, *Frohbotschaft und Lehre*, 112, 118.

[41] This fits in well with the teaching section (4:1-34), and is also the normal position for teachers in antiquity. In Mark, Jesus adopts this «magisterial» position rarely, and only in cases of important and prolonged teaching (cf. 9:33-50; 13:3-37). Cf. V. FUSCO, *Parola e regno*, 151-152; J. MARCUS, *The Mystery*, 14; C. SCHNEIDER, «κάθημαι», 440-444, esp. 443.

[42] Cf. R.H. GUNDRY, *Mark*, 190; R.A. GUELICH, *Mark*, 190; W. EGGER, *Frohbotschaft und Lehre*, 112, 118. This increase is seen from πολὺ πλῆθος (3:7) and πλῆθος πολὺ (3:8) - «a great multitude», - to the superlative ὄχλος πλεῖστος («a very large crowd», 4:1) with πᾶς ὁ ὄχλος («the whole/all the crowd», 4:2).

[43] In the reference to teaching πολλά is not adverbial (1:45), but accusative meaning «many things». Cf. V. TAYLOR, *Mark*, 251; R.A. GUELICH, *Mark*, 191.

[44] Cf. C.W. HEDRICK, «Summary Statements», 296-297; W. EGGER, *Frohbotschaft und Lehre*, 153-155; K.L. SCHMIDT, *Der Rahmen*, 158-160.

[45] Cf. R.A. GUELICH, *Mark*, 313. This part of the verse is neither included in Mt 13:53-58 nor in Lk (cf. 4:16-30), but is peculiar to Mark; therefore, no one emphasized the teaching motif like him.

[46] Cf. W. EGGER, *Frohbotschaft und Lehre*, 153-154; R.A. GUELICH, *Mark*, 314, observes three of these short statements that use the Imperfect tense and a participial construction to describe Jesus' activity over a period of time (2:13; 6:6b; 10:1).

the stories that surround them»[47]. Here in Mk 6:6b Jesus was going (moving) around (κύκλῳ) among the villages teaching. Thus, Jesus continues his teaching activity, not beside the sea now, but within and around the villages.

If «6:6b seems actually only to serve the function of expanding the breadth of the ministry of Jesus»[48]; is this area not smaller than the earlier offered description of the crowd movement around Jesus (cf. 1:45; 3:7-12)[49]? The only reasonable answer, I think, is that this summary statement, like the others, helps to emphasize and put in relief the importance of Jesus' teaching ministry in the Gospel.

1.1.6 Mark 6:30-34

This is also regarded as a summary statement[50]. In this passage we meet once more two important themes of our discussion so far: the gathering of the crowd and Jesus' teaching activity. One observes an accumulation of literary motives and themes in this passage: the return of the apostles (from their mission activity), the invitation for rest because of the crowd, the departure in the boat, the flocking of the crowd, the compassion of Jesus, the shepherd motif, and the teaching activity[51]. From the foregoing, it is comprehensible to regard this passage as a separate narrative unit[52], though it could also be an introduction to the following pericope (6:35-44)[53]. Thus, «Mk 6:30-34 offers a detailed and complicated transition and introduction to the pericope of the Multiplication of Bread (Mk 6:35-44)»[54]. However, what interests us most in this text, is Jesus' teaching activity and the crowd element in the story.

---

[47] R.A. GUELICH, *Mark*, 314.

[48] C.W. HEDRICK, «Summary Statement», 297.

[49] Cf. W. EGGER, *Frohbotschaft und Lehre*, 153.

[50] Cf. C.W. HEDRICK, «Summary Statements», 297-298; W. EGGER, *Frohbotschaft und Lehre*, 121-131. But for K.L. SCHMIDT, *Der Rahmen*, 188, it is 6:30-33.

[51] W. EGGER, *Frohbotschaft und Lehre*, 121.

[52] Cf. C.S. MANN, *Mark*, 301; W. EGGER, *Frohbotschaft und Lehre*, 121; V. TAYLOR, *Mark*, 320.

[53] Cf. C.S. MANN, *Mark*, 301; C.W. HEDRICK, «Summary Statements», 297; W. EGGER, *Frohbotschaft und Lehre*, 121-123.

[54] W. EGGER, *Frohbotschaft und Lehre*, 121 (trans. mine); Cf. E.K. BROADHEAD, *Teaching with Authority*, 118, opines that the narrative description of the crowd in this passage provides an irreplaceable element for the story which follows.

In this passage the importance of the crowd is very much highlighted. In fact, the cause of both Jesus' withdrawal with his disciples «to a lonely place» (cf. 1:35,45)[55], and the lack of the leisure to eat (cf. 3:20), was the pressure from the crowd (the many)[56]. Likewise the crowd (πολλοί) are those who saw (εἶδον) Jesus and the disciples going, then recognized them (ἐπέγνωσαν), ran together (συνέδραμον), and then come ahead of (before) them (προῆλθον), v.33. Those Jesus saw when he came out of the boat were «a great throng» (πολύν ὄχλον)[57], and they (αὐτούς) were the object of his compassion (ἐσπλαγχνίσθη)[58], (v.34, cf. 8:2; Mt 9:36; 14:14). The emphasis on the presence of the crowd sets the stage, not only for Jesus' teaching (v.34d) which follows, but also for the feeding of the multitude (vv.35-44).

When Jesus saw a great throng of crowd, he had compassion on them because they were «like sheep without a shepherd»[59]. Then he began to teach them πολλά («many things»/«at length»)[60]. Jesus' compassion on the

---

[55] Cf. R.H. GUNDRY, *Mark*, 322; E.K. BROADHEAD, *Teaching with Authority*, 118; R.A. GUELICH, *Mark*, 339.

[56] Cf. M.D. HOOKER, *St. Mark*, 162; W. EGGER, *Frohbotschaft und Lehre*, 127; R.H. GUNDRY, *Mark*, 322, adds that «the present traffic of people is causing the need for privacy if the rest is to be gotten. The huge amount of the traffic revives emphasis on Jesus' magnetism, shown now through the thronging of people to the apostles, whom he empowered, as well as to him».

[57] Some scholars see two groups of the crowd that were merged together in this text: one group was there at the beginning of the story (v.31b) and saw Jesus and his disciples departing with a boat, and went «on foot» (πεζῇ, «on foot» or «by land», as contrasted to «by boat»), and were there before them (v.33); while the other group came «from all the cities» (ἀπὸ πασῶν τῶν πόλεων), and ran together (συνέδραμον) with the former to be there earlier. So Jesus was able to see a large crowd when he landed. Cf. R.H. GUNDRY, *Mark*, 323; W. EGGER, *Frohbotschaft und Lehre*, 129; V. TAYLOR, *Mark*, 320.

[58] Cf. C.E.B. CRANFIELD, *Mark*, 216; R.A. GUELICH, *Mark*, 340, remarks that «Jesus reacts with "compassion" when he sees the crowds rather than with agitations at not being able to get away from the public (cf. 6:30-31)».

[59] C.E.B. CRANFIELD, *Mark*, 217, underlines that «the characteristic of the multitude which is stressed here as calling forth Jesus' pity is its helplessness and bewilderment, its likeness to shepherdless sheep». While M.D HOOKER, *St. Mark*, 165, suggests that «the description implies criticism of the nation's leaders who are failing to guide the people». Cf. W. TOOLEY, «The Teaching of Jesus», 16.

[60] Many scholars agree that πολλά is adverbial, that is, «at length»: that Jesus taught the crowd at length (cf. v.35). Cf. M.D. HOOKER, *St. Mark*, 166; W. EGGER, *Frohbotschaft und Lehre*, 130, n.50; W.L. LANE, *Mark*, 226; V. TAYOR, *Mark*, 320.

crowd grew out of their being shepherdless, «not out of their hunger and lack of food (as in 8:2), and leads him to teach them. Thus, by teaching them he shepherds them;...»[61] Therefore, «by replacing the expected miracle activity with emphasis on Jesus' teaching, the import of the story becomes clear: it is the teaching of Jesus which properly satisfies the need of these shepherdless people»[62]. Hence this text «points to Mark's perception of the didactic role of Jesus' total ministry»[63]. Once more this summary statement has shown its own emphasis on the teaching theme[64]. Here Jesus teaches the people, not in the villages or beside the sea, but in the desert.

1.1.7 Mark 10:1

This is our last summary statement dealing with Jesus' teaching of the people. Here, Jesus left Galilee (ἐκεῖθεν «from there» - from the house in Capernaum [cf.9:33]) journeying towards Jerusalem («the region of Judea and beyond the Jordan»), «so we have here a major shift in both setting and location of the ministry of Jesus»[65]. It is also worth noting that «Mark 10:1 does not appear to be only a summary report ..., but it seems also to function as the literary introduction to the compiled narrative of the trip from Galilee to Jerusalem»[66]. In fact, this verse is the bridge between the Galilean and Jerusalem activity of Jesus[67]. It can also form a title for the following instructions (or teaching materials)[68]. In this case,

---

R.H. GUNDRY, *Mark*, 323-324, notes that the adverbial πολλά typifies Mark's style and stresses Jesus' didactic authority by indicating that he holds the crowd under his sway till late in the day (cf. 4:2 with 4:35; as well as 6:35).

[61] Cf. R.H. GUNDRY, *Mark*, 323.

[62] E.K. BROADHEAD, *Teaching with Authority*, 118-119; J. GNILKA, *Markus I*, 259; W. EGGER, *Frohbotschaft und Lehre*, 130; B. CITRON, «The Multitude», 416.

[63] R.A. GUELICH, *Mark*, 340.

[64] The teaching theme is well emphasized in this passage (Mk 6:30-34): beginning with 6:30 (the teaching of the Apostles/Disciples) and ending with 6:34 (Jesus' teaching of the crowd out of compassion). Cf. W. TOOLEY, «The Teaching of Jesus», 16.

[65] C.W. HEDRICK, «Summary Statement», 298.

[66] C.W. HEDRICK, «Summary Statement», 298, 299; W. EGGER, *Frohbotschaft und Lehre*, 156; V. TAYLOR, *Mark*, 416, notes that 10:1 is a summary statement which connects the two sections, 8:27 - 9:50 and 10:1-52 and is not simply a local setting for 10:2-9.

[67] Cf. K.L. SCHMIDT, *Der Rahmen*, 238; K.-G. REPLOH, *Markus*, 178.

[68] C.W. HEDRICK, «Summary Statement», 298, enumerates the following teaching

this summary statement qualifies as a literary introduction to the following narrative units or pericopes.

«And the crowds gathered to him again». This is the only place in Mark, where the crowds (ὄχλοι) is used in plural[69]. The vividness of their coming together (συνπορεύονται, «travel together»)[70] is shown in the historical present of the verb. The crowd flocking to Jesus «again» could refer to the pericope 9:14-29 (especially vv.14,15,25,26). However, this adds to the emphasis of the powerful attraction of crowds to Jesus. Thus, this sets the stage for Jesus' teaching activity.

In this verse, the second «again» clearly indicates that Jesus resumes his public teaching ministry. To emphasize the primary, habitual and continuous activity of Jesus' teaching, Mark not only used the adverb, πάλιν («again»), the expression, ὡς εἰώθει («as was his habit»), but also puts the verb, διδάσκειν, in Imperfect tense. The forward position of the clause concerning this habit, shows that Jesus has been in the habit of teaching crowds and emphasizes his authority[71]. Since Jesus is on the way (ὁδός) to Jerusalem, for Mk this teaching activity is one of the important stages of the Way[72]. Here, Jesus teaches the people again, neither in the synagogue nor beside the sea, in the desert, etc, but on the way.

One can see how Mk has so far used these summary statements to demonstrate the general image of Jesus' teaching in Mark's Gospel. He made teaching, Jesus' primary and habitual activity, and broadened its

---

topics as: «on marriage and divorce (10:2-12); on entering the Kingdom (10:13-16); on the danger of possessions (10:17-31); the teaching on the cross (10:32-34); the teaching on the nature of discipleship (10:35-45). Mark 10:46-52 may be intended to function as an example of the importance of faith».

[69] Cf. R.H. GUNDRY, *Mark*, 529; C.E.B. CRANFIELD, *Mark*, 318; V. TAYLOR, *Mark*, 417. May be the plural ὄχλοι is intended to suggest the different crowds which collected on different occasions (so CRANFIELD, *ibid.*); or perhaps the doubling of place names leads to plural, crowds coming together in both Judea and Transjordan (so GUNDRY, *ibid.*). I prefer the latter reason to the former.

[70] R.H. GUNDRY, *Mark*, 529, suggests that Mark uses -πορεύονται probably because the crowds are travelling to Jerusalem for the Passover Festival as Jesus is. But where Jesus is stationary, a crowd «comes together» (συνέρχεται - 3:20), «gathers together» (συνάγεται - 4:1), or «runs together» (ἐπισυντρέχει - 9:25; and I also add: συνέδραμον - 6:33; προστρέχοντες - 9:15).

[71] Cf. R.H. GUNDRY, *Mark*, 529.

[72] Cf. W. EGGER, *Frohbotschaft und Lehre*, 156. It is worth noting that ὁδός forms an *Inclusio* of the section Mk 8:27-10:52 (cf. ἐν τῇ ὁδῷ, «on the way»: 8:27; 9:33,34; 10:32,52).

temporal and geographical sphere without limitations, made the crowd the constant object of Jesus' public teaching ministry. Thus, Mark's peculiarity in emphasizing teaching in his Gospel, is clearly established when one compares these summary statements with their synoptic parallel texts: either they are absent (cf. Lk), or linked to healing (cf. Mt), or weakly expressed. Hence, Mk uses the summary statements, not only to demonstrate the dominance of the teaching theme, but also to confirm its programmatic character in Mark's Gospel. Now we shall turn to another aspect (the parables) that manifests Jesus' teaching ministry in the Gospel.

1.2 *Jesus teaches the Crowd: through Parables*

In the summary statements, as we saw above, Jesus' teaching had no content but only summarized and generalized; while in parables, as we shall see now, Jesus' teaching has its content or material (cf. 3:23-27; 4:3-9, 21-32; 12:1-12; 13:28f, 34-37). In Mk 4:33-34, it was clearly stated that Jesus taught the people with many parables, as they were able to hear; while he privately explained everything to his disciples. These verses (vv.33-34) also function as a literary conclusion to the chapter on parables (4:1-34)[73]. That Jesus taught the people «with many such parables» implies, on the one hand, that he taught them more parables than Mark records[74]; on the other hand, it emphasizes the abundance of Jesus' powerful teaching[75]. That Jesus speaks in accordance with the huge crowd's ability to hear «implies a superabundance of words full of life-force. He had more to say»[76]. Here Mk demonstrates his interest in the power of Jesus' teaching. We shall now examine how Jesus taught the crowd in parables, which will help to portray Mk's programmatic presentation of the teaching theme in his Gospel.

The key to the understanding of παραβολή (parable)[77] in the Gospels (Synoptic), and likewise in Mark, takes its significance from the LXX

---

[73] Cf. C.W. HEDRICK, «Summary Statements», 301-302; K.L. SCHMIDT, *Der Rahmen*, 126-132.

[74] Cf. R.H. GUNDRY, *Mark*, 234; M.D. HOOKER, *St. Mark*, 137; V. TAYLOR, *Mark*, 271.

[75] Cf. R.H. GUNDRY, *Mark*, 234.

[76] R.H. GUNDRY, *Mark*, 234.

[77] The first appearance of παραβολή (parable) was in Mk 3:23-27, where the «scribes who came from Jerusalem» challenged Jesus on his exorcistic activities, which he replied in parables.

rendering of the Hebrew מָשָׁל, *māšāl* (Aramaic, *mathla*). Thus, παραβολή can have variety of meanings, like proverb, similitude, wisdom
sayings, story, fable, comparison, riddle, or allegory as well as enigmatic
utterances[78]. Thus, the term «parable» (מָשָׁל/ παραβολή) is complex in
meaning, and serves to designate all expressions which contain a
comparison[79]. The purpose or aim of parabolic teaching is to elucidate
truth and not to obscure or conceal it. In fact, «parables are meant to
stimulate thought, to provoke reflection, and to lead men to a decision»[80].

In this section, we shall examine four parables, where Jesus explicitly
taught the crowd (people). Since Jesus gives the purpose and explanation
of the parables to the disciples privately in 4:10-20, 21-25[81], in response
to their question in v.10, we shall not enter into that. We shall, therefore,
limit ourselves to these four parables: (a) the parable of the sower (4:3-9);
(b) the parable of the growing seed (4:26-29); (c) the parable of the
mustard seed (4:30-32); (d) the parable about defilement (7:14-15).

1.2.1 The Parable of the Sower (Mk 4:3-9)

This is one of the three seed-parables in the chapter (4:3-9, 26-29, 30-
32). And each of these three parables mentioned above, «reflects upon
sowing, growth and harvest-elements which illumine the character of the
Kingdom of God»[82]. After the introduction of Jesus' teaching in parables
(vv.1-2), then comes the parable (vv.3-9, cf. Mt 13:1-9; Lk 8:4-8). The
parable is framed at the beginning and end by the verb, ἀκούειν: thus,

---

[78] Cf. C.E.B. CRANFIELD, *Mark*, 148; W.L. LANE, *Mark*, 150; J. JEREMIAS, *The
Parables*, 16, n.22; F. HAUCK, «παραβολή», 745-746.

[79] Cf. J.D. CROSSAN, «Parable», 147; M.D. HOOKER, *St. Mark*, 121; R.A.
GUELICH, *Mark*, 189; M. BOUCHER, *The Mysterious Parable*, 12-13, 86-89; J.
JEREMIAS, *The Parables*, 20; F. HAUCK, «παραβολή», 747.

[80] V. TAYLOR, *Mark*, 250, 252; W.L. LANE, *Mark*, 153, n.14.

[81] In 4:21-25 (the parables of the Lamp and Measure), people are divided over the
audience of this double parable: either the disciples or the crowd. Many scholars
attribute these parables (sayings) to Jesus' disciples. Cf. M.D. HOOKER, *St. Mark*, 133;
R.A. GUELICH, 228; C.S. MANN, *Mark*, 265; K. STOCK, *Boten*, 79-80, cf. 72. While
R.H. GUNDRY, *Mark*, 211; W.L. LANE, *Mark*, 164 think of the crowd. I would agree
with those for the disciples, because these are neither explained parables, nor presented
as story, but rather they are in direct address formulated as questions (v.21) or as
demand (v.24, cf. v.23), to which are followed by reason-backed sentences (vv.22,25).
Therefore, these features make them difficult to fit in with vv.26-32 (cf. STOCK, *ibid.*).

[82] W.L. LANE, *Mark*, 149.

ἀκούετε («hear»), v.3 and the closing command, ὃ ἔχει ὦτα ἀκούειν ἀκουέτω («he who has ears to hear, let him hear»), v.9, together form an *inclusio*[83]. In the parable story, one observes both binary structure[84] and triadic pattern[85] in the narration.

In the course of Jesus' teaching, he said to the people: ᾿Ακούετε. ἰδοὺ ἐξῆλθεν ὁ σπείρων σπεῖραι. - «Listen! A sower went out to sow» (v.3). «Listen» (ἀκούετε) emphasizes the importance of the teaching to follow; but to combine it with «see» (ἰδού) which calls for attention, signifies that this strange combination of two introductory imperatives calls for «attentive listening»[86]. Some scholars see this command «to listen» as pointing to *Shema*« (שְׁמַע, Deut 6:4: «Hear, O Israel»)[87]. The «sower» (ὁ σπείρων) is for many the focal point of the parable (hence, «the Parable of the Sower»)[88]. If Jesus is regarded as «the sower» then the «going out», ἐξῆλθεν, echoes the verb used by Jesus himself of his mission in 1:38 (2:13; 2:17)[89]. Thus, «the sower went out to sow» sets the stage for sowing the seeds.

As the sower makes his first act, «some seed fell along the path, and the birds came and devoured it» (v.4). Most scholars regard ὃ μὲν (subject of the verse) as meaning «a part of (the seed)»; while the following ἄλλο in

---

[83] Cf. R.H. GUNDRY, *Mark*, 191; J. MARCUS, *The Mystery*, 20; W.L. LANE, *Mark*, 153.

[84] Cf. J. MARCUS, *The Mystery*, 21, 22; J.D. CROSSAN, «The Seed Parables», 246.

[85] Cf. R.A. GUELICH, *Mark*, 190, 194, 195; A.N. WILDER, «The Parable of the Sower», 139-140.

[86] Cf. R.A. GUELICH, *Mark*, 192; C.E.B. CRANFIELD, *Mark*, 149. V. TAYLOR, *Mark*, 252, notes that the imperative ἀκούετε is peculiar to Mark's account (absent in Mt or Lk). Even the double imperative is also peculiar to him. While R.H. GUNDRY, *Mark*, 191, sees the introductory command as Mk's emphasis on Jesus' exercise of didactic authority.

[87] Cf. M.D. HOOKER, *St. Mark*, 122; C.E.B. CRANFIELD, *Mark*, 149; M. BOUCHER, *The Mysterious Parable*, 45; V. TAYLOR, *Mark*, 252. On the contrary is R.A. GUELICH, *Mark*, 192.

[88] Cf. R.A. GUELICH, *Mark*, 192; J. GNILKA, *Markus I*, 155; J. JEREMIAS, *The Parables*, 11-12; C.H. DODD, *The Parables*, 181. Some also call it «the Parable of the Seeds» (GUNDRY, 186; GUELICH, 186), «the Parable of the Various Soils» (CRANFIELD, 148), or «Das Gleichnis vom Viererlei Acker», Cf. E. LINNEMANN, *Gleichnisse Jesu*, 120.

[89] Cf. M.D. HOOKER, *St. Mark*, 123; R.A. GUELICH, *Mark*, 192; J. MARCUS, *The Mystery*, 37-39.

vv.5,7 as «another portion (of the seed)»[90]. That some seed fell «on/along the path» (ἔπεσεν παρὰ τὴν ὁδόν), is debated: whether the seed fell «on the path» or «by/beside/along the path»[91]. Since the sower did not consciously decide to sow the seed on or along the path, any of the alternative could be valid. But I think, what is more important, is not where it fell, but the fact that the birds devoured it (κατέφαγεν), thereby ending the life of the seed. In the next act, the other/another (portion of the) seed fell on rocky soil (πετρῶδες), scorched by the sun it withered away (vv.5-6). The description of the seed sown here contrasts sharply with the simple statements of vv.4,7 in its length and redundancy: (a) Three phrases (vv.5a,b,6b) having to do with the lack of ground or rootlessness, two of which begin with *dia to*, «on account of»; (b) Two forms of the verb, ἐξανέτειλεν/ἀνέτειλεν («to spring up»); (c) «Scorched» and «withered»[92]. These repetitions emphasize the failure of the seed to survive, attacked from under (lack of soil) and above (the scorching of the sun). Then the third act, some seed fell among thorns (εἰς τὰς ἀκάνθας), who grew up and choked it[93]. The last phrase in this verse, καὶ καρπὸν οὐκ ἔδωκεν («and it yielded no grain or fruit»), seem to break the symmetry of the triadic style, but it has an important role in the parable. Some commentators think that this concluding statement offers a summary for the three previous examples (vv.4-7) rather than for only the seed sown among thorns[94]. Likewise this phrase could mark a

---

[90] Cf. R.A. GUELICH, *Mark*, 193; V. TAYLOR, *Mark*, 252. One observes that the direct word for «seed» was lacking (cf. σπόρος, vv.26,27; σπέρμα, v.31).

[91] Cf. *BAGD*, 611, III, 1.d. On the problem of παρὰ τὴν ὁδόν, cf. R.H. GUNDRY, *Matthew*, 253; P.B. PAYNE, «Parable of the Sower», 123-129; J. DRURY, «Mark's Parables», 367-371; J. JEREMIAS, *The Parables*, 11-12; ID., «Palästinakundliches zum Gleichnis», 48-53.

[92] J. MARCUS, *The Mystery*, 23; cf. R.A. GUELICH, *Mark*, 193, 194; J.D. CROSSAN, «The Seed Parables», 245-246. Both Mt and Lk shorten the description, thereby avoiding the repetitions.

[93] Some scholars observe parallelism, almost rhythmic structure, and triadic pattern in this parable. Cf. J. MARCUS, *The Mystery*, 22; H.-J. KLAUCK, *Allegorie*, 187. While the triadic pattern of the verbs are seen in v.4 (ἔπεσεν, ἦλθεν, κατέφαγεν), vv.5-6 (ἔπεσεν, ἀνέτειλεν, ἐκαυματίσθη), v.7 (ἔπεσεν, ἀνέβησαν, συνέπνιξαν), v.8 (ἔπεσεν, ἐδίδου, ἔφερεν); on the violent destruction of the seeds (κατέφαγεν, ἐκαυματίσθη, συνέπνιξαν). Cf. R.A. GUELICH, *Mark*, 194; J.D. CROSSAN, «Seed Parables», 249.

[94] Cf. R.A. GUELICH, *Mark*, 194; R. PESCH, *Markusevangelium I*, 233; J.D. CROSSAN, «The Seed Parables», 246. However, H.-J. KLAUCK, *Allegorie*, 187 refuting

transition point from negative to positive in the parable[95]. In the last act, other seeds (ἄλλα) fell into good soil (εἰς τὴν γῆν τὴν καλὴν) and produced fruits (grains), thirtyfold, sixtyfold and hundredfold (v.8)[96]. The «other seeds» turn out to be individual seeds[97] (three in number) - «three seeds that fell into good soil to match the three seeds that fell on poor soils»[98]. Thus, there is a shift from ὃ μεν/ἄλλο (singular) in vv.4-7 to ἄλλα (plural) in v.8[99], thereby emphasizing the contrast between the destroyed seeds and the fruitful ones.

The focal point of the parable, I think, lies in this last verse (v.8). Although the amount of attention and space given to failures is surprising and emphatic; yet this progressive, threefold failure is overmatched by a threefold success[100]. Thus, the climax of the parable strongly emphasizes the glorious character of the harvest, the last of which would be an unusually large harvest: «the unexpectedly larger yield of "a hundredfold" stresses a productivity that more than compensates for the failures»[101]. Since this harvest «is seen against the background of many obstacles, it is clear that the emphasis does not fall on the enormity of the waste, but on the enormity and splendour of the harvest»[102]. Hence this parable calls for a reflection on the diversity of response to the proclamation of the Word of God, and above all, on the coming (in-break) of the Kingdom of God.

As Jesus began the parable with calling attention «to hearing» so he ended it (vv.3,9). Thus, the parable is enclosed in a framework calling

---

CROSSAN (*ibid.*, 246, 249) points to the singular verb *ed ken*, and may be also the singular seed (*auto*), in order to show that the phrase does not refer to the three seeds but one. However, I share with V. FUSCO, *Parola e regno*, 312, n.19 that it may not be directly, but *indirectly* the phrase *kai karpon ouk ed ken* refers to all three bad soils.

[95] Cf. J. GNILKA, *Markus I*, 159; J. MARCUS, *The Mystery*, 22; R.A. GUELICH, *Mark*, 194-195.

[96] One observes again the triadic pattern in the three verbs of bringing forth: ἀναβαίνοντα, αὐξανόμενα, ἔφερεν (growing up, increasing, yielding); and the three degrees of increament: τριάκοντα, ἐξήκοντα, ἑκατόν (thirtyfold, sixtyfold, one hundredfold). Cf. A.N. WILDER, «The Parable of the Sower», 139.

[97] Cf. C.E.B. CRANFIELD, *Mark*, 150; V. TAYLOR, *Mark*, 253.

[98] R.H. GUNDRY, *Mark*, 192; R.A. GUELICH, *Mark*, 195.

[99] Cf. R.A. GUELICH, *Mark*, 193; J. MARCUS, *The Mystery*, 42, n.98; F. HAHN, «Das Gleichnis», 134-136.

[100] Cf. R.H. GUNDRY, *Mark*, 192; J. MARCUS, *The Mystery*, 21.

[101] R.H. GUNDRY, *Mark*, 192; R.A. GUELICH, *Mark*, 195; V. TAYLOR, *Mark*, 254.

[102] W.L. LANE, *Mark*, 154; J. JEREMIAS, *The Parables*, 149-151; C.D. DODD, *The Parables*, 182-183.

for attentive hearing[103]. And «He who has ears ...» (v.9) is clearly a characteristic expression by which Jesus impressed on His hearers the need to give close attention to His words[104]. This makes it clear that Jesus teaches the people with authority. However, at the end of our first parable, we observe that seeds were sown, some could not survive because of many obstacles against them; while some were abundantly fruitful thereby compensating for the failure of the others. Therefore, one could relate this parable to Jesus' mission of proclaiming the word of God, and above all, to his entire ministry of inaugurating the kingdom of God. Thus, «Mark uses the parable of the seeds as a parable about parables to explain the rejection of Jesus by some people and the acceptance of him by others»[105]. Hence, in this parable, Jesus sets the stage for his teaching ministry.

1.2.2 The Parable of the Growing Seed (Mk 4:26-29)

Jesus continues his teaching activity with the second of the three seed-parables, which is here referring explicitly to the kingdom of God. Since it has to do with sowing, growth and harvest, it invites comparison with the parable of the sower[106]. This parable is only found in Mark (4:26-29). «Since only good growth and fruitful harvest occur, there is no thought of contrasting the fates of individual seeds»[107] (cf. vv.3-8).

The «kingdom of God», which is Jesus' central message in Mark[108], is here seen as seed scattered by «someone» or «a man» (ἄνθρωπος) upon the ground. And this reference gives this parable its uniqueness. The ὡς in v.26 governs the five subjunctives in vv.26-27, and signifies «as if»[109]. So, the kingdom of God is as if a man should scatter (βάλη) the seed, and

---

[103] Cf. R.A. GUELICH, *Mark*, 195, 197; C.E.B. CRANFIELD, *Mark*, 151.

[104] Cf. V. TAYLOR, *Mark*, 254. In slightly different forms this expression, «He who has ears» appears frequently in Jesus' sayings, cf. Mk 4:9,23; (7:16); Mt 11:15; 13:9,43; Lk 8:8; 14:35.

[105] R.H. GUNDRY, *Mark*, 191.

[106] Cf. W.L. LANE, *Mark*, 168.

[107] R.H. GUNDRY, *Mark*, 219; R.A. GUELICH, *Mark*, 244-245.

[108] Cf. R.A. GUELICH, *Mark*, 240; W. KELBER, *Kingdom in Mark*, 10-11; A.M. AMBROZIC, *Hidden Kingdom*, 1-2.

[109] The subjunctive after ὡς favours the translation «as if». Cf. R.H. GUNDRY, *Mark*, 224; M. ZERWICK – M. GROSVENOR, *A Grammatical Analysis*, 113; M. ZERWICK, *Biblical Greek*, 109-110, #321.

should be about his routine business[110], that is, «should sleep and rise night and day»[111], and the seed (ὁ σπόρος) «should sprout and grow long». Indeed, «the daily round of sleeping at night and rising at day not only provides the passage of time necessary to growth, but also distances the man from the growth;...»[112] Although the man has accomplished his task in the sowing, and is doing his day to day activity, yet he is unable to explain the mystery of life and growth of the seed[113], for «he knows not how» (ὡς οὐκ οἶδεν αὐτός). In fact, ὡς most likely introduces an indirect question («how it grows»)[114], which is answered by the next statement in v.28a.

In v.28, we meet the phrase, «the earth produces of itself» (αὐτομάτη ἡ γῆ καρποφορεῖ), which gives reason for man's ignorance or incomprehensibility of the process of growth[115]. The forward position of αὐτομάτη and the absence of a connecting-link add to its force[116]. Man's ignorance and the earth producing of itself, point to God's role behind the seed's growth, that is, God's miraculous activity in contrast to human activity[117]. This phrase (v.28a) is specified in «first the blade, then the ear, then the full grain in the ear» (v.28b)[118]. Thus, «by matching the threeness

---

[110] There is a change from aorist subjunctive (βάλῃ) to present subjunctives in v.27 (e.g. καθεύδῃ, ἐγείρηται), which means that, once the seed is sown, the man continues his ordinary daily life. Cf. R.A. GUELICH, *Mark*, 241; M.-J. LAGRANGE, *Saint Marc*, 115; A. PLUMMER, *Mark*, 131.

[111] The expression, νύκτα καὶ ἡμέραν, is semitic. The mention of night before day reflects a Jewish method of reckoning the twenty-four hour day from sunset to sunset. Cf. R.H. GUNDRY, *Mark*, 224; M.D. HOOKER, *St. Mark*, 135; V. TAYLOR, *Mark*, 267.

[112] R.H. GUNDRY, *Mark*, 220.

[113] Cf. V. TAYLOR, *Mark*, 267; R.A. GUELICH, *Mark*, 241.

[114] Cf. R.A. GUELICH, *Mark*, 241; C.E.B. CRANFIELD, *Mark*, 168; V. TAYLOR, *Mark*, 267.

[115] Cf. R.H. GUNDRY, *Mark*, 220, 221; R.A. GUELICH, *Mark*, 241; A.M. AMBROZIC, *Hidden Kingdom*, 115-116; V. TAYLOR, *Mark*, 267.

[116] Cf. R.H. GUNDRY, *Mark*, 221; V. TAYLOR, *Mark*, 267; C.E.B. CRANFIELD, *Mark*, 168, observes that the adjective, αὐτομάτη, is here used almost as an adverb.

[117] Cf. R.A. GUELICH, *Mark*, 241; C.S. MANN, *Mark*, 270; K. STOCK, *Jesus die Frohe Botschaft*, 60; J. ERNST, *Markus*, 142; R. PESCH, *Markusevangelium I*, 256; J. JEREMIAS, *The Parables*, 151-152; W. GRUNDMANN, *Markus*, 131.

[118] J.D. CROSSAN, «The Seed Parables», 251, rightly points out that v.28 is a more detailed specification of v.27.

of the man's throwing, sleeping, and rising the threeness of blade, ear, and full grain in the ear highlights the element of progression»[119].

The fourth stage of growth comes up in v.29 with the ripeness. The adversative δέ shifts the parable from growth to fruit, thereby bringing it to its climax[120]. In other words, «when the grain is ripe» (παραδοί, in the sense of permits or allows), means that «the time of the harvest is determined by the readiness of the fruit rather than attributed to the decision of man»[121]. At the harvest time, the sower takes up his role again which he began at the sowing[122]. So «at once he puts in the sickle» (ἀποστέλλει τὸ δρέπανον, literally, «he sends the sickle»)[123], means that the sower harvests the riped grains.

We have seen so far in this parable the growth of the seed, which portrays the kingdom of God. While the parable of the sower stressed different ways of hearing the word, the parable of the growing seed stresses the marvellous process of fruition resulting from the well heard and consequently explained word[124]. In this foregoing parable, man's ignorance of the process of growth was stressed, thereby highlighting God's role behind the seed's growth which «points to God's role in effecting his kingdom and, thus, giving assurance that God would bring it all to "harvest" apart from human efforts»[125]. Hence, in Jesus' teaching in parables, an element of God's kingdom is always stressed.

---

[119] R.H. GUNDRY, *Mark*, 220; R.A. GUELICH, *Mark*, 242, adds that both details sketch «life as usual» respectively.

[120] Cf. R.A. GUELICH, *Mark*, 242; C.S. MANN, *Mark*, 270; V. TAYLOR, *Mark*, 268.

[121] R.H. GUNDRY, *Mark*, 220; E. LOHMEYER, *Markus*, 86-87.

[122] The sower (farmer) who scatters (sows) the seed brings it to its culmination by being the reaper who harvests the seed. Cf. R.A. GUELICH, *Mark*, 242, 244.

[123] Some scholars see this reference to «sickle» as having an echo of Joel 4 (3):13, in which the harvest motif may refer to eschatological or final judgement. Cf. M.D. HOOKER, *St. Mark*, 136; R. PESCH, *Markusevangelium I*, 257; J.D. CROSSAN, «The Seed Parables», 253; J. JEREMIAS, *The Parables*, 151-152; V. TAYLOR, *Mark*, 268. While others, and I agree with them, hold that the emphasis falls more on harvesting fruit (connoting the final stage of the growth of the seed), not on the coming harvest as such. Cf. R.H. GUNDRY, *Mark*, 222; R.A. GUELICH, *Mark*, 244; J. ERNST, *Markus*, 142; J. GNILKA, *Markus I*, 184.

[124] Cf. R.H. GUNDRY, *Mark*, 221.

[125] R.A. GUELICH, *Mark*, 241; J. MARCUS, *The Mystery*, 172-173; R. PESCH, *Markusevangelium I*, 256; W. GRUNDMANN, *Markus*, 131; C.E.B. CRANFIELD, *Mark*, 167.

1.2.3 The Parable of the Mustard Seed (Mk 4:30-32)

This parable, like the preceding one, deals explicitly with the kingdom of God, and is the third seed-parable. It is recorded by the three synoptics[126], though the synoptic comparison is very complicated[127], we shall highlight some when necessary. Mark changes from «throwing» (βάλλειν) seed of the preceding pericope (cf. v.26) to «sowing» (σπείρειν) here (vv.31,32), thereby recalling the series of sowing in the first seed parable (vv.3-9), in order «to make an inclusion that stresses Jesus' teaching in parables the mystery of God's rule»[128]. Another inclusion and emphasis on Jesus' teaching in parables could be the phrase «on/upon the ground» (ἐπὶ τῆς γῆς, cf. vv.1,26,31; ἐπὶ τὴν γῆν, cf. vv.8,20)[129]. Mk opens the parable with a double question or introductory formula (v.30), then the antithetical parallelism which contrasts the smallness of the seed with the largeness of the plant (vv.31,32), and emphasizes «sowing» (repeated twice, vv.31,32; the second is resumptive). The three elements of sowing, growing and producing are present, but I think, in this parable the important point is the contrast between the almost invisible seed and the enormous bush[130].

The parable of the mustard seed in Mk's Gospel begins with a double question, or an introductory formula, which is both personal and plural[131]. Thus Jesus said: «how shall we compare (ὁμοιώσωμεν) the kingdom of God, or by what parable shall we represent (θῶμεν) it?»[132] (v.30). To answer the double question, it is introduced with ὡς («like»,«as»): «it is

---

[126] In Mt 13:31-33 and Lk 13:18-21 there are twin parables of the Mustard Seed and the Leaven, which is absent in Mk. Lk also puts this parable in another context.

[127] Cf. R.H. GUNDRY, Mark, 226-227; R.A. GUELICH, Mark, 247; J.D. CROSSAN, «The Seed Parables», 254-258; H.K. MCARTHUR, «The Mustard Seed», 198-201.

[128] R.H. GUNDRY, Mark, 228. In fact, «all three parables concerning seed and growth are expressly tied to God's rule (contrast vv.21-23, 24-25)». Cf. Ibid., 227.

[129] Cf. R.H. GUNDRY, Mark, 228.

[130] Cf. M.D. HOOKER, St. Mark, 136; C.E.B. CRANFIELD, Mark, 169; W.L. LANE, Mark, 171; C.-H. HUNZINGER, «σίναπι», 290; H.K. MCARTHUR, «The Mustard Seed», 201, 210.

[131] J.D. CROSSAN, «The Seed Parables», 254-255, observes that while in Mk the questions are personal and plural (ὁμοιώσωμεν ... θῶμεν), in Lk it is rather impersonal (τίνι ὁμοία) and singular (τίνι ὁμοιώσω).

[132] The two verbs (ὁμοιώσωμεν... θῶμεν) are aorist subjunctives; and the subjunctives are deliberative. Cf. M. ZERWICK – M. GROSVENOR, A Grammatical Analysis, 114; C.E.B. CRANFIELD, Mark, 170; V. TAYLOR, Mark, 269.

like a grain of mustard seed» (κόκκῳ σινάπεως, v.31)[133]. The mustard seed, when sown (ὅταν σπαρῇ) upon the ground (ἐπὶ τῆς γῆς)[134], is very small. And this smallness is emphasized thus: «is the smallest (μικρότερον)[135] of all the seeds on earth»[136]. To this emphasis, Gundry highlights:

> the forward position of μικρότερον, «smaller», adds further emphasis; and the use of the comparative «smaller» in a superlative sense, the modification of the «seeds» with «all», and the addition of ἐπὶ τῆς γῆς, which echoes the first part of the parable, absolutize the smallestness of the mustard seed. A shift in the meaning of ἐπὶ τῆς γῆς from «on the soil» to «on the earth» underscores this absolutization[137].

After this stress on the size of the mustard seed, there is need for a new start; therefore in v.32 ὅταν σπαρῇ is repeated, which is resumptive[138]. However, when the seed is sown, it grows/springs up (ἀναβαίνει)[139] and becomes the greatest of all shrubs (μεῖζον πάντων τῶν λαχάνων)[140]. The phrase, «the greatest of all shrubs» antithetically parallels the

---

[133] Mustard seed was proverbial in Palestine for its smallestness. Cf. R.H. GUNDRY, *Mark*, 229, 233; M.D. HOOKER, *St. Mark*, 136; C.-H. HUNZINGER, «σίναπι», 288; H.K. MCARTHUR, «The Mustard Seed», 201. Though mustard seed is used proverbially as the smallest seed, but in reality (botanically) it is not so. Cf. R.A. GUELICH, *Mark*, 249; C.S. MANN, *Mark*, 271; C.E. CARLSTON, *The Parables*, 158, n.8; V. TAYLOR, *Mark*, 270.

[134] Mk's mustard seed was sown «upon the ground», while Lk's and Mt's are «in his own garden» and «in his field» respectively.

[135] The comparative is here used as superlative. Cf. M. ZERWICK, *Biblical Greek*, 49, #147; M. ZERWICK – M. GROSVENOR, *A Grammatical Analysis*, 114; C.E.B. CRANFIELD, *Mark*, 170.

[136] V. TAYLOR, *Mark*, 270, calls this phrase, μικρότερον... ἐπὶ τῆς γῆς, an «explanatory parenthesis».

[137] R.H. GUNDRY, *Mark*, 229.

[138] Cf. R.A. GUELICH, *Mark*, 250; C.E.B. CRANFIELD, *Mark*, 170.

[139] The word, ἀναβαίνει, is considered strange to describe growth (in Mt and Lk is αὐξάνειν, «to grow»). Cf. C.S. MANN, *Mark*, 271; V. TAYLOR, *Mark*, 270. However, it links this parable to the first one (cf. vv.7,8), which describes the «springing up» of a sown seed.

[140] In Mt and Lk, both speak of the seed becoming a tree, while Mk has shrubs/vegetable plant. As Mk emphasized the smallest of the seed so he did to the largestness/greatestness of the plant.Thus, R.H. GUNDRY, *Mark*, 230, adds, «again a use of the comparative for the superlative and an addition of "all" to the noun absolutize the thought».

statement of smallness in v.31, «the smallest of all seeds on earth»[141]. This «greatest of all shrubs/vegetable plants» produces large branches (followed by a result clause, ὥστε + Inf.), «so that the birds of the air can make nests in its shade». This clause may echo OT imagery of branches and birds. In fact, the symbol of a tree in whose shade birds take shelter is found in Ezek. 17:23 and 31:6; while in Dan 4:12,14 and 21 the birds nest in the branches (cf. Mt 13:32 and Lk 13:19)[142]. This OT allusion can enhance the idea of the plant's size: the branches are large enough for the birds to nest in its shade. On the other hand, implicitly it can refer to a great kingdom that encompasses other nations[143]; but it is not clear whether «birds of heaven» refers to the Gentiles[144].

As we conclude this parable of the mustard seed, it is worth noting that «for Mark, the Kingdom of God is displayed in the life of Jesus, but it is displayed like seed thrown on the earth... Just as the harvest comes from the grain sown in the earth, and the mustard bush springs from the almost invisible seed, so the Kingdom will follow from the ministry of Jesus»[145]. Thus, the ministry of Jesus corresponds with the sowing of the mustard seed, with the promise of a future glorious fulfilment[146].

These three seed-parables, we have seen so far, concretely refer and correspond to Jesus' teaching ministry, and indeed his entire mission, because as Jesus teaches the crowd in parables, so he sows the seed of the Word and Kingdom of God. And this continues to widen the scope and variety of his teaching mission. Now we shall examine another aspect of parable (on defilement), which Jesus taught the people.

---

[141] Cf. R.H. GUNDRY, *Mark*, 230; R.A. GUELICH, *Mark*, 249, 250.

[142] Cf. M.D. HOOKER, *St. Mark*, 136; R.H. GUNDRY, *Mark*, 230; R.A. GUELICH, *Mark*, 251; C.S. MANN, *Mark*, 271-272; C.E.B. CRANFIELD, *Mark*, 170; W.L. LANE, *Mark*, 171, n.78; H.K. MCARTHUR, «The Mustard Seed», 202-203; V. TAYLOR, *Mark*, 270; C.H. DODD, *The Parables*, 190.

[143] Cf. R.A. GUELICH, *Mark*, 251.

[144] Some hold that the Gentiles are under consideration here. Cf. C.S. MANN, *Mark*, 272; W.L. LANE, *Mark*, 171, n.78; J. JEREMIAS, *The Parables*, 147; V. TAYLOR, *Mark*, 270; C.H. DODD, *The Parables*, 191. On the contrary are, cf. R.H. GUNDRY, *Mark*, 230; R.A. GUELICH, *Mark*, 251.

[145] M.D. HOOKER, *St. Mark*, 137.

[146] Cf. H.K. MCARTHUR, «The Mustard Seed», 209.

1.2.4 The Parable about Defilement (Mk 7:14-15)

The parable about defilement (7:14-15) is the most important saying in the defilement pericope (7:1-23)[147]. When the Pharisees gathered together to Jesus, with some scribes from Jerusalem, they observed that some Jesus' disciples were eating with defiled hands (unwashed hands), v.2. Based on this observation, they raised their question (v.5). After commenting on their attitude to God's law (vv.6-13), Jesus decided to address the people directly, on the matter (v.14-15), though later on he explained the parable to his disciples, on their request (vv.17-23). Our concern here will be limited to Jesus' teaching of the people in the parable.

Jesus summoned (προσκαλεσάμενος, «to call to oneself», or «to summon»)[148] the people again. We saw in the summary statements, that generally the crowd spontaneously gathers around Jesus, but here he called the crowd to himself, as he normally does to his disciples: in fact the Markan Jesus calls to himself both the disciples and the crowd[149]. On summoning the crowd «again» there is no clear antecedent for πάλιν, since this is the first time the term, προσκαλεῖσθαι, applies to the crowd. It may be a reminiscent of 4:1-2, the setting of Jesus' last extensive teaching «in parables» (4:1-34)[150]; or refers to the crowd motif in 6:45, where Jesus dismissed «the crowd»[151]. However, summoning the crowd again, Jesus said to them: «hear me, all of you, and understand» (v.14). The command to listen recalls the introduction to the parable of the sower (4:3, cf. 4:9,23,24; 9:7)[152]. There, the imperative was in

---

[147] This defilement pericope is found only in Mt 15:1-20 and Mk 7:1-23, but absent in Lk.

[148] The use of προσκαλεσάμενος is especially characteristic of Markan style, cf. V. TAYLOR, *Mark*, 343. This word occurs 9x in Mk; 6x in Mt and 4x in Lk. In Mk, it was used 8x for Jesus (1x for Plate, 15:44), which he addressed: 5x to the disciples: 3:13; 6:7; 8:1; 10:42; 12:43; to the crowd and the disciples: 8:34; to the crowd alone: 7:14; and to the scribes: 3:23. Likewise in Mt 5x it is used for Jesus, while in Lk only once (18:16).

[149] Cf. E.S. MALBON, «Markan Characters», 105-107; J. PAINTER, *Mark's Gospel*, 111-112, suggests that Jesus' calling the crowd as he did to those whom he chose the twelve (3:13), «implies a positive relationship to the crowd that responded to his call».

[150] Cf. R.A. GUELICH, *Mark*, 374; C.E. CARLSTON, «The Things That Defile», 92.

[151] Cf. R.H. GUNDRY, *Mark*, 353; R.A. GUELICH, *Mark*, 374.

[152] Cf. J. PAINTER, *Mark's Gospel*, 112; R.H. GUNDRY, *Mark*, 353; M.D. HOOKER,

present tense, and no object; but here the imperative is aorist, and has an object μου, «me», to stress the authority inherent in Jesus' person[153]. The further command to understand echoes the pairing of hearing and understanding in 4:12 (cf. 8:17-18), and doubles the emphasis on Jesus' didactic authority[154]. However, the combination of the command «to hear and understand» is unique to 7:14 (cf. Mt 15:10), and emphasizes the fact, that what Jesus is about to say is very important[155].

Jesus said to the people: «there is nothing outside a man which by going into him can defile him; but the things which come out of a man are what defile him» (v.15). In this verse lies the central message of this pericope. The structure of Jesus' saying is that of Semitic antithetical parallelism (οὐδέν ... ἀλλά)[156]. The important word in this pericope, κοινόω, which occurs twice in v.15[157], means in classical Greek. «to make common» or «to communicate or share», while in NT it means «to defile» or «to profane»[158]. Thus, Jesus tries to answer in public his antagonists' question: Why do the disciples eat with defiled hands? (v.5). Here, there is an assumption that eating with «defiled hands» could through contact «defile» one's food, and eating «defiled food» would «defile» the person[159]. But «Jesus' saying marks a progression from the question *how* to eat to *what* to eat»[160]. «Nothing outside a man which by going into him (εἰσπορευόμενον εἰς αὐτον) can defile him» ultimately applies to food, though the food eaten by «defiled hands» and not directly to the question

St. Mark, 178; R.A. GUELICH, Mark, 374; C.E.B. CRANFIELD, Mark, 239; V. TAYLOR, Mark, 343.

[153] Cf. R.H. GUNDRY, Mark, 353.

[154] Cf. R.H. GUNDRY, Mark, 353.

[155] Cf. W. HENDRIKSEN, Mark, 280; C.E.B. CRANFIELD, Mark, 239; E.P. GOULD, Mark, 130.

[156] Cf. R.H. GUNDRY, Mark 354; M.D. HOOKER, St. Mark, 179; R.A. GUELICH, Mark, 375; J. GNILKA, Markus I, 284; R. PESCH, Markusevangelium I, 379; V. TAYLOR, Mark, 342.

[157] This verb occurs 14x in NT: 5x in Mk (7:15[bis],18,20,23), 5x in Mt, 3x in Acts, and 1x in Heb.

[158] Cf. C.S. MANN, Mark, 316; C.E.B. CRANFIELD, Mark, 239; V. TAYLOR, Mark, 343.

[159] Cf. R.A. GUELICH, Mark, 375; M.D. HOOKER, St. Mark, 178.

[160] R. H. GUNDRY, Mark, 354; M.D. HOOKER, St. Mark, 178, affirms that the question in v.5 concern the condition of the eater, while the saying here concerns the character of the food itself.

of unclean foods or the food laws of Leviticus 11 and Deuteronomy 14[161]. But «things coming out of a person» (τὰ ἐκ τοῦ ἀνθρώπου ἐκπορευόμενα) can refer generally to all that comes from within someone including thoughts, actions and words[162]. Thus, Jesus introduces «the question of food laws for the purpose of denying defilement from without in favor of affirming defilement from within, i.e. for the purpose of redefining defilement as moral rather than cultic»[163]. Indeed, «the distinction between the relatively unimportant outward acts of eating, drinking and washing, on the one hand, and the vitally important acts of will, desires and emotions, on the other, could not be more forcibly expressed»[164]. In essence the saying enunciates the principle that only *persons* can be defiled (unclean), not *things*[165]. Hence in Jesus' parabolic teaching, he «prophetically» summons his hearers to do God's will from the whole person. «Instead of attacking the ritual or ceremonial law of purity, Jesus calls for a total purity, the sanctification of the whole person, as anticipated for the age of salvation»[166].

The programmatic teaching theme of Jesus is progressively marching on. The seed-parables have shown that as Jesus teaches the people, so he sows parabolically both God's Word and Kingdom. Jesus' parabolic teaching brought out different aspects of growth, its problems and prospects, failures and successes; man's ignorance and God's role; and above all, the miraculous jump from small seed to a great tree. Likewise, Jesus' emphasizes that the real defilement is not in physical but moral and spiritual, involves the whole person, and issues from the heart. Hence, in the parabolic teaching, Jesus concretizes the programmatic character of his teaching ministry.

---

[161] Cf. R.A. GUELICH, *Mark*, 375; V. TAYLOR, *Mark*, 343.

[162] Cf. R.A. GUELICH, *Mark*, 375; J. GNILKA, *Markus I*, 284; J. NEUSNER, «First Cleanse the Inside», 494, n.2, affirms that one's purity or acceptability before God involved one's entire person, one's «heart», as seen reflected in one's thoughts and conducts.

[163] R.H. GUNDRY, *Mark*, 354.

[164] A.W. ARGYLE, «"Outward" and "Inward"», 198. Therefore, what Jesus is saying, is that the real defilement is not physical (or material) but moral and spiritual: defilement issues from the heart. Cf. W. HENDRIKSEN, *Mark*, 280; E.P. GOULD, *Mark*, 130.

[165] Cf. C.S. MANN, *Mark*, 316; V. TAYLOR, *Mark*, 343.

[166] R.A. GUELICH, *Mark*, 376; R. PESCH, *Markusevangelium I*, 379.

1.3 *Jesus teaches the Crowd: in the Temple*

Jesus' teaching activity, which programmatically began in Galilee (in our pericope), continues to the end of his ministry in the temple of Jerusalem. In the summary statements, we saw already the emphasis on Jesus' teaching of the crowd in a summary and generalized form, and in absolute sense. But in the parables we experienced the teaching content itself. Towards the end of his ministry, Jesus also taught in the temple. We shall now examine what he taught the people in the temple: (a) 11:17-18, (b) 12:35-37, (c) 12:38-40, (d) 14:49.

1.3.1 Mark 11:17-18

On Jesus' first day in Jerusalem[167] he entered the temple, and having looked round at everything, he went back to Bethany in the evening (11:11). On the second day[168], he returned to Jerusalem with his disciples, and entering once more into the temple, he began to drive out those who sold and bought in the temple; and would not allow anyone to carry anything through the temple (vv.15-16). And it is in this context, that Jesus taught them saying: «Is it not written, "My house shall be called a house of prayer for all the nations"? But you have made it a den of robbers» (v.17). The first part of this quotation is from Is. 56:7 (LXX), both Mt and Lk omitted πᾶσιν τοῖς ἔθνεσιν («for all the nations»); while the second part is from Jer.7:11. The audience is not clear, however, they are most likely everyone in the temple precinct — not excluding those selling and buying (v.15), and even the standing crowd (v.18)[169]. After Jesus' teaching, there were different reactions (v.18): (a) the chief priests and the scribes, «sought a way to destroy him», and «they feared him»; and the reason for this fear is given by two γάρ; (b) the people, «were astonished at his teaching».

In Jesus' activity in the temple, one observes that «Mark's use of ἐδίδασκεν, "he was teaching", alongside ἔλεγεν, "he was saying", puts the emphasis on Jesus' exercise of authority in what he says as well as in

---

[167] From the text, one can say that Jesus spent three days in Jerusalem (temple), going into and coming out of it: first day (11:1-11), second day (11:12-19) and third day (11:20-12:44, or even till 13:37).

[168] On this day, as Jesus was going to Jerusalem, he cursed the fig tree without fruits (11:12-14).

[169] Cf. R.H. GUNDRY, *Mark*, 640; M.D. HOOKER, *Mark*, 268.

what he does»[170]. However, when Jesus said, «My house shall be called (κληθήσεται)[171] a house of prayer for all the nations», he thus cites literally Is.56:7 LXX, thereby highlighting the destiny and function which God has designed for his house: it is a house of prayer and is for all the nations[172]. As a matter of fact, «what makes the temple a "house of prayer for all peoples" is the fact that this present regulation now opens access to it and to its worship to members of other races»[173]. This quotation occurs in the midst of promises which describe God's generous purposes for his people Israel and for all the nations (Is.56:3-8)[174]. In order words, «the opening of the community to eunuchs and foreigners, too, is made in the context of the promise that Yahweh is to gather the dispersed of Israel — he "gathers" Israel also from those who hitherto have not been able to belong to her»[175].

The adversative δέ puts the divine intention in sharp contrast with the people's behaviour: «But you have made (πεποιήκατε)[176] it a den of robbers». The phrase «a den of robbers» (σπήλαιον λῃστῶν) is found in Jer.7:11, in a denunciation of those whose moral behaviour was repugnant to God, but who nevertheless came to the temple[177]. In our text, the

---

[170] R.H. GUNDRY, *Mark*, 640. One can notice that in vv.15-17, the first two verbs (ἤρξατο ἐκβάλλειν, κατέστρεψεν) are in aorist; while the following three (ἤφιεν, ἐδίδασκεν, ἔλεγεν) are in imperfect, thus durative and continous action/s.

[171] This word, κληθήσεται (shall be called), future passive is used by both Mt and Mk, while Lk used ἔσται (shall be).

[172] Cf. W.L. LANE, *Mark*, 406. It is worth noting that the designation of the Temple as a house of prayer is ancient (cf. 1 Kgs 8:28-30; Is. 56:7(bis); 60:7 LXX), but the clause «for all the nations» is found only in Is.56:7 and Mk 11:17. Cf. C.S. MANN, *Mark*, 449; W.L. LANE, *ibid.*

[173] C. WESTERMANN, *Isaiah 40-66*, 315.

[174] Cf. W.L. LANE, *Mark*, 406.

[175] C. WESTERMANN, *Isaiah 40-66*, 315.

[176] Mark alone used the perfect tense (cf. Mt 21:13: ποιεῖτε [historical present]; Lk 19:46: ἐποιήσατε [aorist]), which expresses a definitive, durative effect in the present. Cf. *BDF*, 176-177, #342.

[177] Cf. M.D. HOOKER, *St. Mark*, 268; R.P. CARROLL, *Jeremiah*, 208-211. Considering its context (Jer.7:1-15), v.11 «suggests that the temple acquires its status from the quality of the worshippers who gather there. It is but a suggestion, a question raised: "a cave of robbers has this house become?" But it makes the connection between the worshippers' lives and temple service work in the other direction. The holy place does not save people, but how they live outside the temple gives the holy place its real quality» (cf. CARROLL, *ibid.*, 209-210).

merchants are described as «robbers», «not so much because they were involved in fraudulent practices but because they were insensitive to the holiness of the area where they practiced their trade»[178]. By citing this text, Jesus gives a definitive negative judgement on the temple: it does not correspond anymore to its nature (divine intention), they have indeed profaned it. In other words, Jesus' action is a clear condemnation of the priestly authorities who have permitted these practices[179], which resulted to different reactions.

When the chief priests and scribes heard it, they sought for his death (cf. 3:6), because of their fear of his powerful hold on the people. «So strong is the effect of his teaching that hearing, plotting, and fearing run simultaneously with the other and with the crowd's being astonished. Seeking to destroy him sets going the fulfilment of his passion predictions (8:31; 9:12,31; 10:33-34) and thus begins to revive emphasis on his predictive power»[180]. While the chief priests' and scribes' fear (ἐφοβοῦντο) led them to plot against Jesus' death[181], the crowd, on the other hand, was as usual «astonished (ἐξεπλήσσετο) at his teaching» (cf. 1:22; 6:2). Just as Jesus' first teaching in the synagogue of Capernaum astonished the people then, so also his first teaching in the temple now (cf. 11:18).

1.3.2 Mark 12:35-37

This pericope falls within Jesus' third day visit to the Temple (cf. 11:27), which witnessed a series of controversies or conflicts with the different religious groups[182]. The narrator concluded these debates with the statement: «And after that no one dared to ask him any question» (12:34). In the course of Jesus' teaching in the temple, after answering

---

[178] W.L. LANE, *Mark*, 407; C.S. MANN, *Mark*, 449.

[179] Cf. M.D. HOOKER, *St. Mark*, 268.

[180] R.H. GUNDRY, *Mark*, 640.

[181] The chief priest, the scribes and the elders are those connected with Jesus' death (cf. 8:31; 10:33; 11:18,27; 14:1,43,53; 15:1,31); and from now on they will be preoccupied on how to put Jesus to death (cf. 12:12; 14:1, 55).

[182] These debates or controversies began with the chief priests, the scribes and the elders, who questioned about Jesus' authority (11:27-33, 12:1-12); some of the Pharisees and some of the Herodians set a trap for Jesus on the payment of taxes to Caesar (12:13-17); the Sadducees also questioned about the Resurrection (12:18-27); and one of the scribes asked him about the Great Commandment (12:28-34).

other peoples' questions, Jesus took the initiative to raise before the
people his own question, which contains a double question[183]: «How can
the scribes say that Christ is the son of David?» (v.35). To answer this
question, Jesus cited Psalm 110:1, which heavily emphasized the
designation of the Christ as Lord. This leads then to the challenging
question: «so how is he his son?» (v.37). One could say that this question
asks for the source of the designation «Son of David»: «In view of Jesus'
noting the divine inspiration of David and citing of Ps.110:1, the question
asks for an inspired scriptural source. There is none»[184]. In fact, Jesus'
question here is about his true identity: what is his origin?

This is not the first time that Jesus had taken the initiative to ask people
question about his identity (cf. 8:27, 29). In 8:27, Jesus asks his disciples:
«Who do men say that I am?» And in v.29, he asks them too: «But who
do you say that I am?» Then Peter answered him, σὺ εἶ ὁ χριστός («You
are the Christ»). Jesus still modified Peter's correct answer by revealing
that he will be a suffering Messiah (cf. 8:31; 9:31; 10:33f). There, the
identity question was raised for the sake of the disciples; but here, in
12:35-37, it was raised for the first time to the people by Jesus[185]. There
was no response to the question, and therefore it remains an open question
(cf. 4:41). Thus, in this pericope, «its point is not to deny the Davidic
descent of the Messiah, but to suggest that a much higher view of his
origin is necessary since David calls him "lord"»[186]. The identity of Jesus,
which has always been present as a principal question during his ministry,
has surfaced again in Jesus' teaching in the temple.

One can observe that in 11:1-10, Jesus made a messianic manifestation,
that was a conscious realization of the prophetic announcement of Zech
9:9. Through this symbolic action, Jesus reveals in what role he
approaches near to the city of Jerusalem: as a true messianic king. The
global reaction of the people (11:8-10) confirmed this Jesus' symbolic
action. Every other following activity of Jesus in Jerusalem is illumined

---

[183] Cf. R. PESCH, *Markusevangelium* II, 251, observes that Jesus' speech established
in double-question (vv.35bc, 37ab; the question-phrases present the whole teaching as
rounded question, in the beginning and at the end: πῶς ... καὶ πόθεν), is given in the
Form of a Syllogism.

[184] R.H. GUNDRY, *Mark*, 718.

[185] This Jesus' teaching is not directed to a limited group (the Pharisees) as in Mt
22:41 (cf. Lk 20:41) but to a great throng of the crowd (Mk 12:37b).

[186] V. TAYLOR, *Mark*, 492.

and placed under this programmatic beginning: he had shown concretely how one should understand his messianic task. But here, in our present text, it is no more the question of the task of the Messiah, but of his origin, of his personal relation with God[187]. The Messiah cannot be simply the Son of David: for him, one must attribute a transcendental origin, he is the Son of God (cf. 12:6; 14:61f; 15:39)[188].

The powerful effect of Jesus' exposing of the scribes comes out clearly in the impression of the crowd, πολὺς ὄχλος[189] on his teaching, whose listening Mk describes with ἡδέως («gladly»), to emphasize the extent and power of Jesus' grip on the crowd.[190] It is, therefore, clear that in his teaching in the Temple, though here in question form, Jesus sets in the fore-front, his identity question, which is going to feature prominently in the Passion Narrative. Hence, on the one hand, Jesus criticizes the scribes' teaching about the Messiah's origin; on the other hand, he raises the question of his identity.

1.3.3 Mark 12:38-40

Jesus continues his teaching in this pericope. One can observe the uniting elements between this pericope and the preceding one: (a) there is an explicit reference to 12:35, where it was said that «Jesus taught in the temple»; in v.38, it reads, «and in his teaching he said», (cf. 1:22,27; 11:18; and esp. 4:2). Thus, this indicates the unity of this teaching, and serves to tie vv.38-40 to vv.35-37[191]. (b) In vv.35-37, Jesus criticizes what the scribes «say» (their teaching), while in vv.38-40, he criticizes what they «do» (their comportment or behaviour)[192]. (c) Jesus has not changed his audience, the enthusiastic crowd, who heard him gladly, cf. v.37c. Therefore, the same crowd heard both Jesus authoritative denouncement of what the scribes «say» and what they «do».

---

[187] One can observe that in Jesus' activity in Jerusalem, the messianic question was present at the beginning (11:1-10), in the centre (12:1-12), and at the end (12:35-37).

[188] Cf. R. PESCH, *Markusevangelium* II, 254, adds that, the unpronounced remains: the Messiah, as David calls him Lord, must be more than David's Son (cf. Mt 12:41f), an another Son: the Son of Man = the Son of God.

[189] Mark characteristically describes the crowd as πολύς, «large» or «great» (cf. 4:1; 5:21,24; 6:34; 8:1; 9:14; cf. 3:7,8).

[190] Cf. R.H. GUNDRY, *Mark*, 719; R. PESCH, *Markusevangelium* II, 255.

[191] Cf. R.H. GUNDRY, *Mark*, 719.

[192] Cf. R.H. GUNDRY, *Mark*, 719; M.D. HOOKER, *St. Mark*, 294; V. TAYLOR, *Mark*, 492.

In Mk's Gospel, Jesus' criticism of the scribes is addressed to the crowd, who were his audience in the temple (v.37); while in Lk 20:45-47, it is addressed to the disciples in the hearing of the crowd. In Mt 23:1-12, Jesus speaks to the crowds and to his disciples, but continues in 23:13-36 attacking directly the scribes and the Pharisees in 7 «woes» (such an attack is also found in Lk 11:37-52, though not in the temple, but during a meal in the house of a Pharisee).

Jesus' denunciation of the scribes in Mk 12:38-40 has two parts: the first, which starts with an imperative (βλέπετε ἀπὸ)[193], warns against the scribes' negative characteristics (behaviour); while the second, with a future indicative, speaks of an imminent sentence (judgment) on them[194]. The scribes love: (a) parading themselves in long robes (their sabbath/religious garment); (b) and being greeted in the market places, which lead to ostentation and awesome respect[195]. They also love: (c) the best (first) seats in the synagogues; and (d) the chief couches (places of honour) at feasts, which lead to admiration and honour[196]. They are also described as: (e) those who devour widow's houses; and do so (f) under the pretext of long prayers, which lead to exaction, hypocrisy and false piety[197]. These negative descriptions and designations are crowned with a severe judgement or «a forceful prediction (cf. Jas 3:1; Wisd 6:6)»[198].

Jesus' attack on the scribes must have shocked the crowd[199]. But does Jesus' criticism mean to discredit these authorized doctors of Law before the people, or to keep the people on guard against their behaviour? The

---

[193] In Mk 8:15 (the only other passage with βλέπειν ἀπό), an admonition is directed against the conduct of another group, Jesus' adversary: the Pharisees and the Herodians (cf. 3:6; 12:13).

[194] Cf. R.H. GUNDRY, *Mark*, 719; C.S. MANN, *Mark*, 492.

[195] R.H. GUNDRY, *Mark*, 719, notes that the forward position of ἐν στολαῖς, «in long robes», emphasizes the scribes' ostentation. Cf. V. TAYLOR, *Mark*, 494.

[196] Cf. M.D. HOOKER, *St. Mark*, 295; R. PESCH, *Markusevangelium* II, 258.

[197] Cf. M.D. HOOKER, *St. Mark*, 294, 295; V. TAYLOR, *Mark*, 495; E.P. GOULD, *Mark*, 239.

[198] R.H. GUNDRY, *Mark*, 720. This harsh judgement may be connected with the ill treatment of the widows by those (the scribes), who should help and protect them, instead they exploit them. Cf. M.D. HOOKER, *Mark*, 295; R. PESCH, *Markusevangelium* II, 259.

[199] R.H. GUNDRY, *Mark*, 719, suggests that since the crowd are those who fawningly greet the scribes and otherwise pay them honour and admiration, the denunciation must shock them.

indication of their imminent condemnation is caused by their comportment, which demonstrates that the crowd must guard themselves from/against such a behaviour (cf. 8:15). In Mt 23:3, Jesus speaks explicitly against the tendency to follow the scribes (and the Pharisees) in what they do. Here there seems to be a link between «teaching» and «behaviour». In fact, Jesus' teaching in the temple is not to destroy the scribes, who are secretly seeking to destroy or kill him, but to alert the people, to beware of their hypocrisy and false piety; and to open their eyes to seek the truth, and not to allow themselves to be deceived by misleading religious leaders, who exploit their ignorance and gain their respect.

As a matter of fact, this pericope ends Jesus' public teaching ministry, both to the people, and in the temple; because the next pericope is Jesus' private teaching to his disciples (12:41-44). The contrast between Jesus and the scribes introduced at the beginning of his public ministry in the synagogue of Capernaum (cf. 1:22), is exposed here in the temple before the people, by Jesus' attack on the scribes' teaching and behaviour (12:35-40), at the end of his public teaching ministry.

1.3.4 Mark 14:48-49

The last reference of Jesus' teaching, and also that of his teaching in the temple, was made in the context of Jesus' arrest. In Mk 14:43-50, Judas (one of the 12) led «a crowd with swords and clubs», from the chief priests and the scribes and the elders, in order to arrest Jesus. Jesus protests against the manner of his arrest[200], and addressing the crowd, said: «Have you come out as against a robber (ὡς ἐπὶ λῃστὴν), with swords and clubs to capture me (συλλαβεῖν με)?» (v.48, cf. v.43)[201]. He went further, «Day after day (καθ'ἡμέραν)[202] I was with you in the

---

[200] Cf. R.H. GUNDRY, *Mark*, 860; M.D. HOOKER, *St. Mark*, 352; R. PESCH, *Markusevangelium* II, 401; V. TAYLOR, *Mark*, 560.

[201] R.H. GUNDRY, *Mark*, 860, suggests that the question foreshadows the crucifixion of two bandits with him (15:27) and exposes the injustice of his arrest by indirectly and ironically calling to mind his beneficial healings and exorcisms instead of banditry. While M.D. HOOKER, *St. Mark*, 352, opines that possibly Mark sees irony in the fact that those whom Jesus accused of behaving like robbers (cf. 11:17) now treat him as though he were a robber. And I think, both suggestions bring out the many-sidedness of the irony.

[202] «Day after day» (καθ'ἡμέραν) could mean «in the daytime», that is, as opposed to the night time raids of a bandit, and his being arrested at night. Cf. R.H. GUNDRY,

temple teaching, and you did not seize me (οὐκ ἐκρατήσατέ με)»[203]. This surely refers in its Markan context to the last week of Jesus' public ministry, especially his teaching in the temple (cf. 11:15-18; 12:12,14,-35,38)[204].

Jesus closed his public ministry in the temple teaching the people. He has always done his teaching activity for the people *in public* (expect for his disciples' instructions he does in private) and *during the daytime*. Thus, Jesus' reference to his daily teaching in the temple coincidently concludes his teaching mission in Mark's Gospel. Here, Jesus addresses the crowd[205], whom he is accustomed to teaching. The irony is that this same crowd, who are now hostile and armed with swords and clubs in order to arrest Jesus, may be the same crowd, who used to come together (1:33; 2:13; 3:7-8,20; 4:1-2; 6:34; 8:1), gather together (2:2; 4:1; 5:21), run together to (6:33; 9:15,25), or travel together with (10:1) Jesus, and were feared (11:18,32; 12:12) by the religious leaders. This is no more Jesus' audience but have been bought off by the religious authorities for the accomplishment of their purpose. Hence, they have become more-orless a mob, who have no sense of direction, but to be guided by Judas to achieve a common objective: to arrest and put Jesus to death.

Jesus concluded his speech by resigning himself to the will of God: «but let the scriptures be fulfilled»[206]. In other words, they would not have

---

Mark, 860; M.D. HOOKER, *St. Mark*, 352. On the other hand, it could refer to Jesus' daily teaching in the temple, which implies, for many scholars, a longer Jerusalem ministry than the three days described by Mark. Cf. M.D. HOOKER, *ibid.*; V. TAYLOR, *Mark*, 560; C.S. MANN, *Mark*, 598.

[203] When one compares the use of κρατεῖν («to seize», cf. vv.44,46, and also v.49) and συλλαμβάνειν («to take with», v.48) in the pericope, the force of the latter becomes clearer. Cf. R. PESCH, *Markusevangelium* II, 401, notes that συλλαμβάνειν is only here in Mark's Gospel. R.H. GUNDRY, *Mark*, 860, adds that, this word suits the arresters' coming out, for now they will have to take Jesus with themselves back to the Sanhedrin (who sent them). The irony and discrepancy increases, because Jesus was so close to them in the temple teaching, freely and peacefully ministering to the people, and therefore easy apprehensibility, and yet they could not arrest him; but now they come with weapons to arrest the defenceless Jesus.

[204] Cf. R.H. GUNDRY, *Mark*, 860.

[205] In Mk 14:48 and Mt 26:55, Jesus addresses the crowd and also refers to the teaching theme, but in Lk 22:52, he addresses the chief priests and the officers of the temple and the elders, who had come out against him, and nothing about teaching was mentioned.

[206] This quotation is elliptic. Cf. R.H. GUNDRY, *Mark*, 860; R. PESCH, *Markusevan-*

succeeded in arresting him, as they failed several times, if it were not so ordained by God. Thus, their success is only to fulfill the scriptures, as God wills it. One can see how important these verses are to us in the discussion about Jesus' teaching mission. In fact, Jesus' teaching in the temple had content, and was characterized by Jesus' critique of the words and actions of these Religious Leaders, who were in charge of the Jerusalem temple. In spite of Jesus' daily activities in the temple, they ended his ministry by arresting him. This also ended Jesus' teaching ministry in Mark's Gospel.

1.4 *Summary*

In our pericope we discovered that Jesus taught the crowd (people). We were therefore encouraged to examine the theme of teaching in Mark's Gospel. We studied Jesus' teaching of the people, in the summary statements, through the parables, and in the temple. In the summary statements, we saw the summarized, generalized and broadened scope of Jesus' teaching, which also demonstrated its variety in different geographical locations. In fact, Jesus taught at any opportunity and anywhere: in the synagogue, before the house (door), beside the sea, in the desert, on the way, and in the temple. In all these cases, the crowd was always with Jesus, and he used these opportunities to teach them. He also went to them in the villages around, and to the regions and beyond, in order to teach them.

If Jesus' teaching lacked content in the summary statements, it is not so with the parables. It was demonstrated here that in Jesus' teaching, he did not speak to the people without a parable (cf. 4:33-34). These parables played an important role in the explanation of the inauguration of the kingdom of God in Jesus' teaching ministry, especially the seed-parables. The parable about defilement clarifies that defilement is not physical but moral and spiritual; implies not the body, but the heart. The teaching in these parables gives the people the time to reflect and make their own decisions.

The climax of Jesus' teaching ministry was in the temple. Here he attacked the religious authorities before the people on the profanation of the temple, both in his actions (the cleansing of the temple), and in his

---

gelium II, 401. M.D. HOOKER, *St. Mark*, 352, adds that this quotation emphasizes once more Mark's conviction that everything that takes place is part of God's plan.

teaching. He wanted to restore the status and dignity, the destiny and function of the temple: that the temple is the house of God and for all nations. He also attacked publicly the scribes, the learned doctors of the Law, both in their teaching and in their behaviour. In this connection, he raised before the people the question of his identity (his origin, as the Messiah); and predicted a hard judgement for their ostentatious and hypocritical behaviour, which led them to exploitation and earned them honour and awesome respect before the people. This undoubtedly may have impressed, and at the same time, shocked the people.

Therefore, in Jesus' teaching, he touched different aspects of the life of the people, and led them to the truth, but leaving them to reflect and make their own decisions. In this way, Jesus' teaching runs through the Gospel, and confirms our thesis, that it is a dominant theme, and helps to prove the programmatic character of our pericope.

2. The Exorcism of Jesus

Exorcism was among the two actions Jesus performed in the Synagogue of Capernaum. It will be our task in this section to find out whether this Capernaum exorcistic experience is unique, or whether it is a verifiable phenomenon in other parts of the Gospel: hence has it a programmatic character in the Gospel?

Already, in discussing about «the Authority of Jesus»[207], we focused on exorcism by highlighting that with Jesus' simple and authoritative command he casts out demons from their victims. And in «the Mission of Jesus»[208], we saw among other aspects, that the meaning of Jesus' coming for man was: to liberate him from the power of these demons/evil spirits, and restore him to his identity and liberty; while for the demons, Jesus' presence is a menace to their security, and to destroy their kingdom and inaugurate the kingdom of God. Now we shall concentrate on the frequency of the exorcistic event in order to demonstrate its dominance in Mark's Gospel.

The terms usually connected with exorcism are: πνεῦμα ἀκάθαρτον («unclean spirit») often associated with the verb, ἐξέρχεσθαι («to go or come out»), and δαιμόνιον («demon») also often associated with the

---

[207] Cf. Chapter V, sec. 2.1.2.
[208] Cf. Chapter V, sec. 3.1.

verb, ἐκβάλλειν («to cast out») and also ὁ δαιμονιζομένος[209] («the demon-possessed»). In Mark's Gospel, the terms «unclean spirits» and «demons» are synonymous and are interchangeably used. This leads us to the discovering of where the materials for exorcism in the Gospel are.

We shall discover that not only Jesus performed exorcism. His disciples whom he gave authority to cast demons (6:7, cf. 3:15) also did so (6:13). Likewise the disciples (especially John) reported of a man casting out demons in Jesus' name, and they wanted to forbid him, but Jesus advised them not to do so (9:38-40). Nevertheless, we shall concentrate in our discussion only on Jesus' exorcism. Therefore, following the Gospel, we shall find this, after 1:21-28, in two summary statements (1:32-34; 1:39), in two reactions to this activity of Jesus (3:11-12; 3:22-30), and in three detailed pericopes (5:1-20; 7:24-30; 9:14-29).

2.1 Jesus' Exorcism in Summary

We have already seen the effect of the summary statements in Jesus' teaching: that they summarize Jesus' activity and also generalize it, thereby broadening its temporal and geographical spheres, and underlining its importance. The generalizing summaries of Jesus' ministry in Mark, do not only affect Jesus' teaching activity, but also his exorcism. We shall now go forward to examine such summary statements.

2.1.1 Mark 1:32-34

After Jesus' exorcism in the synagogue (public) of a man with unclean spirit, and healing in Simon's house (private) of a woman (Simon's mother-in-law) having fever, the effect of these Jesus' actions on the people was immediate. That evening, at sunset (that is, after the Sabbath), the people brought to Jesus all who were sick or possessed with demons (v.32). One can observe that in this pericope, «the healing activity of Jesus is clearly summarized, introducing new information in a general and non-specific fashion»[210]. In this summary statement, Mark brings together, pairs and repeats[211] Jesus' actions in the synagogue and Simon's house, in

---

[209] The expression, δαιμονιζομένος, occurs only in 1:32 and at the end of the Gerasene demoniac narrative in 5:15,16,18. Cf. R.A. GUELICH, *Mark*, 65.

[210] G.H. TWELFTREE, *Jesus the Exorcist*, 128.

[211] In Mt 8:16-17 and Lk 4:40-41 both separated the healing and exorcism without repeating them. Mark's repetition forms an inclusion (cf. vv.32 and 34) which

the people bringing the sick and the demon-possessed to him for healing and exorcism, which Jesus eventually effected. This summary «plays up the healing and exorcistic power of Jesus»; «points to the broad reach of Jesus' power»[212]; and above all, the exorcism and healing in vv.23-28 and 29-31 are thus seen as typical, not unique[213].

The mention of demon-possessed people recalls the man with an unclean spirit (vv.23-26). And «the shift from "unclean spirit" (πνεύματα ἀκάθαρτα) of 1:23-28 to the terminology here may reflect the consistent use of "demon" (δαιμόνιον) in conjunction with "to cast out" (ἐκβάλλειν)»[214]. However, Jesus healed many who were sick and cast out many demons; but he did not permit the demons to speak, because they knew him (cf. v.34). Once more Jesus would not allow the demons to speak (cf. v.25; 3:12) and the reason is clearly stated: because they know who he is: it is Jesus' identity which must not be publicly proclaimed[215]; and moreover, he does not want to be recognized through them[216]. The demons have already affirmed of having this knowledge, «I know who you are, the Holy One of God» (cf. 1:24), and it was not contested by Jesus, but rather recognized as valid (1:34, cf. 3:12)[217].

We can then observe here that the immediate reaction of the people to Jesus' public exorcism in the synagogue and the private healing in Simon's house, was to bring to him, the sick and demon-possessed people for healing and casting out. Jesus responded without hesitation. The demons would like to defend themselves against Jesus' menacing presence, but Jesus' powerful silencing does not allow it. So Jesus' divine power (authority) is so great that it heals the sick, silences the self-defence of the demons (revealing his identity), and cast them out.

---

emphasizes Jesus' power. Cf. GUNDRY, 89.

[212] R.H. GUNDRY, *Mark*, 87, 88.

[213] Cf. M.D. HOOKER, *St. Mark*, 71. In fact, the echo of the earlier scene reminds us that Jesus' activity now fulfils the words spoken by the unclean spirit in v.24; that first exorcism in the synagogue was not an isolated event, but demonstrated the overthrow of all demonic powers. Cf. *Ibid.*

[214] R.A. GUELICH, *Mark*, 66. Furthermore, he adds that all ten occurrences of «demon» in Mk come either directly with «to cast out» - ἐκβάλλειν - (1:34,39; 3:15,22; 6:13; 7:26; 9:38) or in the immediate context (1:34b; 7:29,30). *Ibid.*

[215] Cf. R.H. GUNDRY, *Mark*, 88; M.D. HOOKER, *St. Mark*, 71.

[216] Cf. K. STOCK, «La conoscenza dei demoni», 94.

[217] Cf. K. STOCK, «La conoscenza dei demoni», 93.

2.1.2 Mark 1:39

Here Jesus went throughout all Galilee, preaching in their synagogues and casting out demons (v.39). «Along with Jesus' preaching go exorcisms, just as an exorcism went along with his authoritative teaching in vv.21-28»[218]. This very short summary statement demonstrates that just as Jesus had rescued one man from the power of a demon in the synagogue at Capernaum, so now he casts out demons from many people throughout the whole area. «In this sense what Mark describes as having happened in Capernaum is typical of what happens elsewhere»[219].

Jesus takes the initiative to go the synagogues to cast out demons. The idea of Jesus' going out throughout the whole area of Galilee to cast out demons from people in the synagogues, is only emphasized by Mark[220]. This shows that not only do people come to Jesus for healing and exorcism (vv.32-34), Jesus also goes to them, so that what he does in the synagogue of Capernaum (vv.21-28), he also does in other synagogues (v.39). And this also becomes a typical and programmatic action of Jesus throughout the Gospel. «As in v.28, the addition of the "whole" to "Galilee" underscores the breadth of Jesus' powerful activity. So also does the asyndetic pairing of "in the whole of Galilee" with "in their synagogues"»[221].

Again this summary statement has a connection with and parallel with our pericope (vv.21-28). Here Jesus responds to the reaction of the people, who are longing for the kingdom of God through his presence. Now we turn to the reactions to Jesus' exorcisms.

2.2 *Reaction to Jesus' Exorcism*

The phenomenon of exorcism is also present in the reaction of the demons to Jesus' exorcism, likewise the accusation or criticism of the

---

[218] R.H. GUNDRY, *Mark*, 94; R.A. GUELICH, *Mark*, 70, affirms that both Jesus' teaching and his preaching declare the fulfillment of time; the presence of the kingdom, as seen in his ministry of healing (1:29-31, 32-34) but particularly of exorcism (1:21-28, 39a,b).

[219] M.D. HOOKER, *St. Mark*, 77; R.A. GUELICH, *Mark*, 70.

[220] In Mt 4:23, Jesus went about all Galilee, teaching, preaching and healing (exorcism was not mentioned). But in v.24, because of Jesus' fame people brought him those sick of various diseases, including demoniacs and he healed them. While in Lk 4:44, Jesus was preaching in the synagogues of Judea (exorcism was also not mentioned).

[221] R.H. GUNDRY, *Mark*, 95.

scribes with regard to Jesus' exorcism. We shall examine these reactions briefly to highlight the element of Jesus' authoritative and superior power over the unclean spirits.

2.2.1 The Demons' Attitude (3:11-12)

These verses, that have to do with Jesus' exorcism, occur within the summary statement of 3:7-12. In this summary statement we meet again the crowd motif (vv.7-9), Jesus' healing of the sick (v.10) and Jesus' exorcism (vv.11-12). The sick and the possessed people are brought together again (cf. 1:32-34).

The reactions of the demons/unclean spirits towards Jesus is described in 3:11: whenever they beheld (ἐθεώρουν) him, they fell down or prostrated (προσέπιπτον) before him, and cried out (ἔκραζον). «Without exception they find themselves irresistibly drawn to acknowledge by gesture and out cry his divine sonship. He has a magnetic hold on them just as he has on the large multitude»[222]. Here the demons demonstrate once more of knowing Jesus' identity: they cried out, «You are the Son of God» (v.11, cf. 1:24; 5:7). This, without doubt, represents Mark's christological designation for Jesus (1:1,11; 9:7; 15:39). But apart from God himself (1:11; 9:7), the demons are the only ones to refer to Jesus by this title before the centurion in 15:39[223].

Jesus also reacted to the unclean spirits' revelation (provocation), by a strong rebuke (πολλὰ ἐπετίμα), not to make him known[224]. This rebuke or silence of the demons, is Jesus' normal reaction to them (cf. 1:25, 34). Jesus' reason for subduing them is given in 3:12, because they who have correct knowledge of who Jesus is (cf. 1:24, 34; 3:11), may make him known (3:12); and he does not want to be known through them[225]. «Accordingly, Jesus appears in 3:11-12 to have power over the unclean

---

[222] R.H. GUNDRY, *Mark*, 158. He also observed that the word play of προσέπιπτον (v.11) and ἐπιπίπτειν (v.10) enhances the point: as the sick «were falling *on*» Jesus *to touch him*, so the unclean spirits «were falling *toward*» him *to acknowledge his divine Sonship*. *Ibid.*

[223] Cf. R.A. GUELICH, *Mark*, 148; K. STOCK, «La conoscenza dei demoni», 94.

[224] R.H. GUNDRY, *Mark*, 159, notes that the imperfect tense of ἐπετίμα indicates that Jesus has to issue his rebuke time after time. The emphatic forward position of the adverb (πολλά) makes the rebuke even stronger. This emphasis on the strength of the rebuke reinforces the point of Jesus' magnetism.

[225] Cf. K. STOCK, «La conoscenza dei demoni», 94-95.

spirits as seen in their prostration and recognition of him»[226]. In other words, «this pericope portrays a strong Jesus before whom unclean spirits fall every time they see him and whose true identity they shout out. Their testimony to Jesus is visible, audible, and invariable»[227]. Hence Mark uses the opportunity in such a summary setting to identify again for the reader who Jesus is, namely, the Son of God[228].

One can observe that here the evangelist presupposes that Jesus has the power to cast out the demons, however he highlights explicitly that the unclean spirits know the identity of Jesus, and that Jesus rebukes or impedes them from divulging this knowledge among the people[229]. Here we meet once more the typical motif of our pericope: the demons' crying out of Jesus' identity (1:24, 34; 3:11), Jesus' rebuking or silencing them (1:25, 34; 3:12), and the crowd motif (1:22,27, 33; 3:7-9). We shall see another reaction to Jesus' exorcism, now from the scribes.

2.2.2 The Scribes' Criticism (3:22-30)

In 3:22-30, we meet the scribes, who came down from Jerusalem, accusing Jesus of being possessed by Beelzebul, and that he casts out demons by the prince (ruler) of demons (v.22). The scribes' criticism of, or objection to Jesus' activity is not new. Right from our pericope, we see a contrast between Jesus and the scribes (in teaching, cf. 1:22). Thus, the narrator gave us a foreshadow of those who would be Jesus' arch-enemies in the whole Gospel. Immediately, in 2:6-7, the scribes objected to Jesus having authority to forgive sins (and healing), but Jesus replied in the affirmative. Likewise they criticized him for eating with tax collectors and sinners (cf. 2:16), Jesus also replied to their criticisms. It is not surprising, at this stage, when Jesus' fame is spreading throughout the whole area, that the scribes' interpretation of Jesus' exorcistic activity (cf. 3:22), should be so; however, Jesus did not hesitate to clarify the scope of his mission. Hence, in this pericope, we see: the charge (v.22), Jesus' reply (vv.23-26), parable of exorcism (v.27), and Jesus' warning on the misinterpretation of his activity (vv.28-30).

In Mark's Gospel, he does not use an exorcism story as a setting for the pericope, while both Mt and Lk precede the controversy with an exorcism

---

[226] R.A. GUELICH, *Mark*, 148.

[227] R.H. GUNDRY, *Mark*, 159.

[228] Cf. R.A. GUELICH, *Mark*, 149.

[229] Cf. K. STOCK, «La conoscenza dei demoni», 94.

(cf. Mt 12:22-23; Lk 11:14)[230]. The charge (Mk 3:22, cf. Mt 12:24; Lk 11:15) that Jesus has Beelzebul also explains how it comes about that he is able to cast out demons by their ruler. Thus, «Beelzebul» and «the ruler of the demons» (and in vv.23, 26, «Satan» as well), are the same[231]. In fact, «the emphatic positions of Βεελζεβούλ, "Beelzebul" and of ἐν τῷ ἄρχοντι τῶν δαιμονίων, "by the ruler of the demons", stress the seriousness of the charge»[232].

Jesus, in replying to the scribes' charges, began with the second accusation that he casts out the demons by their ruler, and he demonstrated the absurdity of their thinking in the parables of «a kingdom» and «a house» divided (vv.23-26, esp. 24,25). So, «it is impossible for Jesus to be casting out demons by Beelzebul/Satan for that would mean Satan was divided»[233]. The absurdity is evident, because Satan wants to conserve and not to put an end to his dominion; and likewise in Jesus' adversaries' affirmation, that Jesus cast out Satan by means of Satan[234]. However, «even if he were exorcising by Satan, even if Satan were divided against himself, Jesus' exorcisms would still mark the destruction of Satan and his kingdom»[235].

In 3:27 Jesus explains, in a parabolic language, that something effectively happens when he casts out demons, because Satan's house is plundered[236]. Since it is not easy to enter a strong man's house and plunder it, unless he is bound, then his house can be plundered. In effect, Jesus is the Stronger Man, the superior power, that overpowers Satan, the strong man, in order to plunder him. Thus, «what we have is a *parable of exorcism*. Satan, the Strong Man, is bound and his house, the possessed person, is taken from him»[237].

---

[230] Cf. G.H. TWELFTREE, *Jesus the Exorcist*, 102.

[231] Cf. R.H. GUNDRY, *Mark*, 172; J.A. FITZMYER, *Luke X-XXIV*, 920-921; H. KRUSE, «Das Reich Satans», 39-41.

[232] R.H. GUNDRY, *Mark*, 172.

[233] G.H. TWELFTREE, *Jesus the Exorcist*, 106.

[234] Cf. K. STOCK, «La conoscenza dei demoni», 98-99. He went further to show that in the realm of power, be it small or great, it divides and disappears when its members are against each other.

[235] G.H. TWELFTREE, *Jesus the Exorcist*, 106.

[236] Cf. K. STOCK, «La conoscenza dei demoni», 99.

[237] G.H. TWELFTREE, *Jesus the Exorcist*, 112; K. STOCK, «La conoscenza dei demoni», 99, affirms that Jesus, the Stronger Man and Superior Power plunders Satan (the Strong Man), in order to liberate men from his influence and power. And Jesus

The scribes, in their double charge against Jesus (of being possessed by Beelzebul and of casting out demons by his power), place Jesus on the part of Satan (3:22,30); while the demons place Jesus on the part of God (cf. 1:24; 3:11). If this liberating (exorcistic) action of Jesus, that happened under the eyes of all and is fulfilled by the power of the Spirit of God, is attributed to the ruler of demons (Satan), it is a question of an effective absurdity and of a very grave sin (blasphemy against the Holy Spirit, vv.28-29)[238]. This concerns sin and salvation, the participation in the communion with God or the exclusion from it. Jesus is on the part of salvation and communion with God; while Satan is on the part of sin and exclusion from God's communion. The scribes, having the boldness to reject Jesus' salvific action through the Holy spirit, and attributing it to Satan (the chief of demons), therefore place Jesus on the part of Satan; and in this way they set themselves on the part of the chief of demons, and exclude themselves from the communion with God[239].

Hence, the scribes' interpretation of Jesus' exorcism, demonstrates the absurdity of their thought, the obduracy in their rejection of the evident truth of Jesus' salvific action, and the grave sin of blasphemy by attributing God's action to that of Satan. However, the scribes' accusation did not deter Jesus from continuing his exorcistic activity. Having performed exorcism in the Jewish zone, Jesus now turns to the Gentile zone, by means of a boat he arrives in the country of the Gerasenes.

2.3 Jesus exorcizes a Gerasene Demoniac (5:1-20)

This is Jesus' second detailed exorcism story, which took place in the Gentile country of the Gerasenes, as narrated in Mark's Gospel. It falls in within the four miracles of Jesus (4:35-5:43): the calming of the storm (4:35-41), the exorcism of the Gerasene demoniac (5:1-20), the healing of the woman with flow of blood (5:25-34), and the raising of Jarius' daughter (5:21-24, 35-43). The pairing of this pericope (5:1-20) with the calming of the sea (4:35-41), demonstrates that Jesus, as the Son of God, has power and authority not only to subdue the chaotic forces of nature, but also has power over the demonic forces that defy all human control[240].

---

does this with the power of God through the Holy Spirit (v.29).

[238] Cf. K. STOCK, «La conoscenza dei demoni», 99.

[239] Cf. K. STOCK, «La conoscenza dei demoni», 100.

[240] Cf. M.D. HOOKER, St. Mark, 141; R.A. GUELICH, Mark, 288.

Although, this exorcism story has several common features of Mark's earlier references to demoniacs (cf. 1:23ff; 3:11)[241], yet it is unique, because in comparison with other exorcism stories of Jesus, no other story has such a dramatic ending as this one[242]. This pericope could be divided into: the setting (1-5), Jesus and the demon(s) (6-10), the swine scene (11-13), the witnesses' reaction (14-17), the healed man's response (18-20)[243].

2.3.1 The Setting of the Exorcism Story

It is said: «Settings represent that aspect of narrative that provides context for the actions of the characters»[244]. In this connection, we see the geographical setting (where they landed), which has Markan duality[245]: «to other side of the sea, to the country of the Gerasenes» (v.1). It introduces the characters: Jesus (v.2a) and the demoniac (vv.2b-5): the long portrayal of the demoniac took care of the description of his difficult situation and spatial location (tomb). The demoniac met (ὑπήντησεν)[246] Jesus (v.2), and this meeting will be developed in vv.6-7. The inability of anyone to bind the demoniac with chains or fetters stresses the power of the unclean spirit. Thus, «the man's uncontrollable nature, his incredible strength to shatter all attempts to chain him, his tormented mind and self-destructive behaviour all points to the superhuman forces and their numbers (5:3-5,9)»[247]. This elaborate description of the power of the demon(s) sets the stage for Jesus' exorcism to be uniquely masterful[248].

---

[241] These characteristic features are: crying out with a loud voice (cf. 1:23), to prostrate (cf. προσέπιπτον, 3:11), the question, «What have you to do with me?» (cf. 1:24), the confession of Jesus, as «Son of the Most High God» (cf. 1:24, ὁ ἅγιος τοῦ θεοῦ; 3:11, ὁ υἱὸς τοῦ θεοῦ), the fear of torment (cf. 1:24, ἦλθες ἀπολέσαι ἡμᾶς). Cf. V. TAYLOR, *Mark*, 280; C.S. MANN, *Mark*, 279.

[242] Cf. G.H. TWELFTREE, *Jesus the Exorcist*, 75-76.

[243] Cf. R.A. GUELICH, *Mark*, 274; R. PESCH, *Markusevangelium* I, 282; V. TAYLOR, *Mark*, 277.

[244] M.A. POWELL, *Narrative Criticism*, 69.

[245] Cf. F. NEIRYNCK, *Duality in Mark*, 45-53, 94-96; R.H. GUNDRY, *Mark*, 248.

[246] The verb, ὑπαντᾶν, occurs only here in Mk (Mt 2x; Lk 3x; Jn 4x).

[247] R.A. GUELICH, *Mark*, 288, cf. 278; R.H. GUNDRY, *Mark*, 248-249. One observes five *hapax legomena* in vv.3-5: κατοίκησις (dwelling), ἅλυσις (chain), πέδη (fetter), διασπᾶν (tear apart), δαμάζειν (tame). Cf. R.A. GUELICH, *Mark*, 277; C.S. MANN, *Mark*, 278; V. TAYLOR, *Mark*, 279.

[248] Cf. R.H. GUNDRY, *Mark*, 249; M.D. HOOKER, *St. Mark*, 141.

2.3.2 Jesus and the Demon(s)

The attitude and gesture of the demoniac in vv.6-10 changes from what we saw in vv.3-5: the demoniac's running and worshipping Jesus, his recognition of him as the Son of God, his fear of being tormented, and even his begging eagerly not to be cast out from the region, all shows «that he has met his match and simply desires to negotiate a settlement»[249]. Thus he «betrays his recognition and acknowledgement of Jesus as his superior (cf. 3:11). And this submissive gesture of recognition stands in stark contrast to the previous description of one totally uncontrollable (5:3-4) and accents Jesus' power to do what none before had accomplished»[250]. «My name is Legion; for we are many», gives us the reason why no one was able to bind or tame the demoniac (he has the strength of over six thousand unclean spirits). Therefore, «Mark wants to impress on his audience how many unclean spirits Jesus is about to exorcise»[251].

2.3.3 The Swine Scene

The beseeching of the demons in v.10, not to be cast out of the region, was specified in v.12, with the presence of a great herd of swine feeding there on the hillside (v.11). So they begged Jesus: «Send us to the swine, let us enter them». When Jesus permitted them, they came out of the man and entered into them, rushed into the sea, there the two thousand swines were drowned in the sea (v.13). The destruction of the swines, perhaps indicates the destruction of the unclean spirits and certainly underlines the cure of the demoniac[252]. It gives also «visible evidence that the spirits have come out of the man and fulfilled their urge to destroy life (cf. v.5; 9:22; Rev.9:5)»[253]. This dramatic end of the unclean spirits, therefore, «illustrates Jesus' authority over Satan and his forces by delivering a man possessed by an unclean spirit»[254], and a dramatic fulfillment of the demoniac's cry in 1:24: «Have you come to destroy us?»[255] This exorcism story can also be read against the background of the dispute between Jesus

---

[249] R.A. GUELICH, *Mark*, 279.

[250] R.A. GUELICH, *Mark*, 278.

[251] R.H. GUNDRY, *Mark*, 251; R.A. GUELICH, *Mark*, 282, sees the «legion» as demonstrating the immense power of the forces that had taken control of their victim.

[252] Cf. M.D. HOOKER, *St. Mark*, 141; G.H. TWELFTREE, *Jesus the Exorcist*, 75.

[253] R.H. GUNDRY, *Mark*, 252.

[254] R.A. GUELICH, *Mark*, 283.

[255] Cf. M.D. HOOKER, *St. Mark*, 141.

and the scribes over his exorcisms in 3:22-30. Hence, Jesus is vividly described as the one, who binds the «strong man» (3:27), who through Legion had so powerfully controlled a man that no one else could successfully bind with human fetters (5:3-5)[256].

2.3.4 The Witnesses' Reaction

The fate of the swines made the herdsmen to flee, and also resulted in a crowd coming to see what had happened. They saw the reality and completeness of the cure of the ex-demoniac: he was «sitting there clothed and in his right mind»[257]. And the effect upon the witnesses was that «they were afraid» (ἐφοβήθησαν). This indicates the people's standing in reverential awe of Jesus, as his disciples did at 4:41[258]. The witnesses (those who had seen it) told their story about the demoniac and the swine (v.16). The «separate mention of the demoniac and of the pigs emphasizes the double victory of Jesus over Legion. The emphasis now lies, not on "what" (τί) has happened (as in v.14), but on "how" (πῶς) it has happened»[259]. The request for Jesus to leave the region follows naturally from the people's fear of him: in view of what they have experienced, Jesus was for them a public danger[260].

2.3.5 The Healed Man's Response

On Jesus' departure from the Gentile zone, the healed man (ex-demoniac) pleaded that he might be with him (ἵνα μετ'αὐτοῦ ἦ, v.18). This aspiration to be with Jesus matches the very purpose for which he appointed the Twelve in 3:14, ἵνα ὦσιν μετ'αὐτοῦ, «that they might be

---

[256] Cf. R.A. GUELICH, *Mark*, 289; R.H. GUNDRY, *Mark*, 249; M.D. HOOKER, *St. Mark*, 141.

[257] Cf. G.H. TWELFTREE, *Jesus the Exorcist*, 77,78; V. TAYLOR, *Mark*, 283, notes that the three participles, καθήμενον, ἱματισμένον, and σωφρονοῦντα, describe features which must immediately have struck the attention of the beholders.

[258] Cf. R.H. GUNDRY, *Mark*, 253; V. TAYLOR, *Mark*, 284, adds that the fear mentioned (ἐφοβήθησαν, cf. 4:41) is awe in the presence of the supernatural.

[259] R.H. GUNDRY, *Mark*, 254.

[260] Cf. G.H. TWELFTREE, *Jesus the Exorcist*, 78; V. TAYLOR, *Mark*, 284; R.H. GUNDRY, *Mark*, 254, observes that as the unclean spirits besought Jesus not to send them away (ἀποστείλη, v.10), so now these people beseech Jesus himself to go away (ἀπελθεῖν). This twist underscores his authority: whether sending away or going away, Jesus can only be besought, not ordered about.

with him»[261]. However, «here μετ'αὐτοῦ moves ahead of the verb for emphasis on Jesus: the ex-demoniac wants to be with him, his great and powerful deliverer, rather than with his compatriots»[262]. Jesus, on the contrary, asked him to go home to his dear ones and tell them what they Lord has done for him and his mercies towards him. Instead he began to proclaim what Jesus had done for him in the Decapolis, and all marvelled (ἐθαύμαζον).

In this dramatic exorcism story, we have seen how Jesus' power and control over a man tormented and controlled by the forces of evil is vividly depicted. The man's reaction to Jesus' presence (vv.2b,6), the unclean spirit's recognition of Jesus (v.7), the response of the local inhabitants (vv.14-17) and the healed man (vv.18-19) to Jesus, all bear witness to his power[263]. And I would add that Jesus' authority was also emphasized by the four occurrences of παρακαλεῖν («to beg» or «to beseech» - vv.10,12,17,18) in the pericope. Jesus exercizes this authority by granting the unclean spirits' request (v.13, cf. v.12), and by refusing the healed man to be with him (v.19, cf. v.18)[264]. Hence, this exorcism story not only emphasizes Jesus' power and authority over Satan and his evil forces, but also adds to the variety of the reality of exorcism in Mark's Gospel. We shall now go to the next exorcism story.

2.4 *Jesus exorcizes a Greek Woman's Daughter (7:24-30)*

This exorcism story also took place in the Gentile territory of the region of Tyre. A Syrophoenician woman came to plead with Jesus for help on behalf of her daughter, who is possessed by unclean spirit. This short story has its uniqueness in comparison with other exorcism stories. Here the exorcism is done at a distance: there is no direct act or word of exorcism of Jesus to the demon. There is no report of astonishment, and even the faith of the woman is not explicitly mentioned (cf. Mt 15:28). This is the only exorcism story, where the terms of exorcism with their

---

[261] Cf. R.H. GUNDRY, *Mark*, 254; G.H. TWELFTREE, *Jesus the Exorcist*, 79; R.A. GUELICH, *Mark*, 284; K. STOCK, *Boten*, 15-27, esp. 17-19; V. TAYLOR, *Mark*, 284.

[262] R.H. GUNDRY, *Mark*, 254.

[263] Cf. R.A. GUELICH, *Mark*, 288.

[264] Cf. R.H. GUNDRY, *Mark*, 252, 254. About the unclean spirits, he says, «not only does Jesus have power to cast them out. He also has authority to tell them where they may go next - and they acknowledge that he does. His permission displays an exercise of that authority and stands in place of a renewed command to come out» (*ibid.*, 252).

verbs are all mentioned (cf. πνεῦμα ἀκάθαρτον, v.25; δαιμόνιον, vv.26,29,30; ἐκβάλλειν, v.26; ἐξέρχεσθαι, vv.29,30). Remarkably, one observes a concentration of diminutives[265] in this passage (eg. θυγάτριον, v.5 [cf. vv.26,29]; κυνάριον, vv.27,28; ψιχίον, v.28; παιδίον, vv.28,30 [cf. τέκνον, v.27a,b]). This pericope can be divided thus: Jesus' change of location (v.24), the Syrophoenician woman and her request (vv.25-26), the dialogue between Jesus and the woman (vv.27-29), and the woman's confirmation of Jesus' exorcism (v.30).

2.4.1 Jesus and the Syrophoenician Woman

Jesus went from there (ἐκεῖθεν, most likely, from a house, v.17)[266] to the Gentile region of Tyre, trying to hid himself in a house without success, because of his fame even in this foreign land (cf. 3:8)[267]. A Gentile (Greek) woman, Syrophoenician by birth[268], who heard about Jesus' presence in the house, came and fell on Jesus' feet[269], and requested for his help on behalf of her daughter. She begged Jesus to cast out the demon that hold her daughter victim. Jesus made a figurative saying, as if to divert attention from the woman's desperate need. Thus, Jesus said to her, «Let the children first be fed, for it is not right to take the children's bread and throw it to the dogs» (v.27). Here the «children» would refer to «the Jews»[270], while «the dogs», «the Gentiles»[271]. «Be

---

[265] Cf. R.H. GUNDRY, *Mark*, 375; R.A. GUELICH, *Mark*, 386.

[266] It is most likely from the house in 7:17, as Mark consistently uses ἐκεῖθεν in contexts where one leaves a house (6:1, 10-11, 9:30; 10:1). Cf. R.H. GUNDRY, *Mark*, 372; R.A. GUELICH, *Mark*, 383-384. V. TAYLOR, *Mark*, 348, thinks of Gennesaret (cf. 6:53-56).

[267] R.H. GUNDRY, *Mark*, 372, observes that Jesus not being able to escape notice even though he enters another house in order that no one might recognize him (cf. v.17; 2:1-2; 3:7-8, 20; 6:30-33; 9:30) exhibits his power of attraction, a favourite theme of Mark (cf. esp. 1:45).

[268] The definition of the woman as «Greek», could connote both her culture, religion and language; while «Syrophoenician» specifies her origin, in contrast to «Libophoenician». Cf. R.H. GUNDRY, *Mark*, 372; R.A. GUELICH, *Mark*, 385; V. TAYLOR, *Mark*, 349.

[269] She prostrated or fell on Jesus' feet (προσέπεσεν), as a sign of deep respect and need or desperation (cf. 5:22, also in the context of Jarius' daughter's need). Cf. R.H. GUNDRY, *Mark*, 372.

[270] Cf. R.A. GUELICH, *Mark*, 386.

[271] Gentiles are sometimes described as «dogs» by Jewish writers, generally with reference to their vices. Cf. V. TAYLOR, *Mark*, 350; Str.-B. I, 724-726; M.D. HOOKER,

filled, or fed, or satisfied» (χορτασθῆναι) refers to Israel's place in salvation history and her claim to God's blessings[272]. This saying recognized the distinction which God demands between Jews and Gentiles. In fact, this distinction creates problem and hesitation in the scope of Jesus' mission: is this primacy of the Jews exclusive or only temporary? However, the woman replied, «Yes, Lord; yet even the dogs under the table eat the children's crumbs» (v.28). The word, κύριε, could mean the English «Sir», but the woman's evident belief in Jesus' supernatural power favours a higher meaning, «Lord»[273]. This witty and persistent answer of the woman shows that she accepts and recognizes that salvation belongs to Israel[274], but she pleads for Jesus' help, which knows no boundary. Thus, her reply sets the stage for Jesus' exorcism.

2.4.2 Jesus' Exorcism at Distance

Then Jesus said to her, «For this saying you may go your way; the demon has left your daughter» (v.29). Jesus is pleased with the woman's wit and persistence, and sent her home assuring her that the demon has gone out of her daughter[275]. It is striking that no faith is mentioned (cf. Mt 15:28)[276], and Jesus does not go with her to confront the demon and speak a word of exorcism[277]. Indeed, the perfect tense of ἐξελήλυθεν, «has gone out», emphasizes his power of accomplishing the exorcism at a distance and the supernatural knowledge displayed in his announcing the

---

St. Mark, 183; G.H. TWELFTREE, Jesus the Exorcist, 90. The κυνάριον, a diminutive of dog, could mean a «little dog», «puppy» or a «house dog». Cf. O. MICHEL, «κύων, κυνάριον», 1104.

[272] Cf. R.A. GUELICH, Mark, 386.

[273] Cf. R.H. GUNDRY, Mark, 374; J. ERNST, Markus, 213; J. GNILKA, Markus I, 293. Hence M.D. HOOKER, St. Mark, 183, adds, «certainly those who called Jesus Lord would soon come to feel that this woman, like the Gentile centurion in 15:39, showed true insight into the identity of Jesus».

[274] Cf. M.D. HOOKER, St. Mark, 182; R.A. GUELICH, Mark, 387; O. MICHEL, «κυνάριον», 1104; J. JEREMIAS, Jesus' Promise, 30, adds that the woman recognized the «divinely ordained division between God's people and the Gentiles».

[275] Cf. V. TAYLOR, Mark, 351.

[276] Cf. C.S. MANN, Mark, 321; R.A. GUELICH, Mark, 388, observes that Mark, whose stories have made so much of faith or its absence (cf. 2:1-12; 5:21-43; 6:1-6a), lets the story stand as evidence.

[277] Cf. R.H. GUNDRY, Mark, 375.

exorcism[278]. When the woman reached home she confirmed the exorcism (v.30), which has taken place according to Jesus' assuring word. «So great is Jesus' power that he has not needed to pronounce a word of exorcism in the presence of the demon»[279].

The story of the Syrophoenician woman placed in a broader context of Mark's Gospel (7:1-23, discussion of defilement), demonstrates the force of Jesus' redemptive ministry in removing the social/ritual boundaries between Jews and Greeks (Gentiles), clean and unclean (cf. 1:40-45; 5;1-20, 21-43; 7:1-23, 24-30)[280]. This woman offers a contrast not only with Jews (cf. 7:1-13), but also with the disciples (cf. 6:52; 7:18; and 8:14-21)[281]. Jesus' exorcism activity here once more demonstrates how unlimited Jesus' authority and power over Satan and demons can go, both near and far. We shall now go to Jesus' last exorcism activity in the Gospel.

2.5 *Jesus exorcizes a Boy with Unclean Spirit (9:14-29)*

In the foregoing exorcism story (7:24-30), we met a woman (mother) pleading for the exorcism of her daughter possessed by unclean spirit, and Jesus effected the healing at distance. Here, once more in the Jewish zone, we see a father pleading for his son in the same predicament, but the possessed boy is present: a very difficult demonic possession, because the unclean spirit is both deaf and dumb. It has been observed that there appears to be a definite heightening of demonic resistance to Jesus which can be traced in the sequence 1:23-27 > 5:1-20 > 9:14-29[282]. Our present exorcism story (9:14-29) is Jesus' last exorcism activity in Mark's Gospel. And one can observe some verbal connections with the first exorcism narrative (1:23-27)[283].

The peculiarity of this exorcism narrative is its detailedness, this is especially observed when compared with its parallels (cf. Mt 17:14-21;

---

[278] R.H. GUNDRY, *Mark*, 375.

[279] R.H. GUNDRY, *Mark*, 375.

[280] Cf. R.A. GUELICH, *Mark*, 386, 388.

[281] R.A. GUELICH, *Mark*, 389.

[282] Cf. W.L. LANE, *Mark*, 334-335.

[283] Some of the verbal connections are: γραμματεῖς (1:22; 9:14); συζητεῖν (1:27; 9:14,16); πνεῦμα ἀκάθαρτον (1:23,26,27; 9:25); ἀπολέσαι (1:24; 9:22); ἐπετίμησεν (1:25; 9:25); ἐξελθε ἐξ αὐτοῦ (1:25,26; 9:25,26); ἐπιτάσσειν (1:27; 9:25); σπαράξας [συνσπάραξεν] (1:26; 9:20,26); κράξας [ἀνέκραξεν, φωνῆσαν] (1:23,26; 9:26); ἐθαμβήθησαν [ἐξεθαμβήθησαν] (1:27; 9:15).

Lk 9:37-43a). It has doublets or progressive descriptions of some motifs within the pericope: the crowd motif (vv.14-15, 25), the boy's possession (vv.17-18, 20, 21-22), bringing the boy for exorcism (vv.17b, 19e-20a), request for exorcism (vv.18b, 22b), unbelief [belief] motif (vv.19, 23-24), Jesus' dialogue with the boy's father (vv.17-18, 21-24). In Markan style, often the second description clarifies or specifies the meaning. Some aspects of the story is peculiar to Mark (vv.14-16, 21-24, 26a-27). The astonishment of the crowd surprisingly opens and not ends the story (cf. Lk 9:43a)[284]. As a matter of fact, the disciples' inability to cast out the unclean (deaf and dumb) spirit was highlighted, in order to focus on Jesus' ability[285]: thus the disciples' inability forms an inclusion (vv.14-19, 28-29) for Jesus' authoritative and powerful exorcism (vv.20-27). Athough this pericope is difficult to divide because of the doublets, yet one can generally divide it thus: (a) Jesus and the disputing disciples/crowd (vv.14-19); (b) Jesus exorcizes a possessed boy (vv.20-27); and (c) Jesus and his disciples (vv.28-29).

2.5.1 Jesus and the disputing Disciples/Crowd

Jesus, on coming down from the mountain with his three disciples, noticed that the rest of the disciples were overwhelmed by a great crowd surrounding them, with the scribes leading a heated argument. Perhaps, the reason for the dispute was the disciples' inability to exorcize a dumb spirit[286], or what authority they have to attempt an exorcism[287]. However, all the crowd[288], immediately they saw Jesus, were exceedingly amazed[289],

---

[284] Cf. M.D. HOOKER, *St. Mark*, 222; V. TAYLOR, *Mark*, 401, adds that it is remarkable that no statement describes the effect produced on the eyewitnesses.

[285] Cf. G.H. TWELFTREE, *Jesus the Exorcist*, 97; R.H. GUNDRY, *Mark*, 487, notes that the disciples inability makes a foil against which Jesus' ability to perform the exorcism will stand out in powerful contrast (cf. TWELFTREE, 92).

[286] Cf. R.H. GUNDRY, *Mark*, 487.

[287] Cf. W.L. LANE, *Mark*, 330.

[288] The crowd motif is strong in this pericope (ὄχλος πολὺν, v.14; πᾶς ὁ ὄχλος, v.15; εἷς ἐκ τοῦ ὄχλου, v.17; ὄχλος, v.25): they were with the disciples and scribes, then greatly amazed (ἐξεθαμβήθησαν), they ran up (προστρέχοντες) to Jesus and were greeting him (ἠσπάζοντο); and then one of them (the boy's father) answered Jesus' question to the disputing crowd, and finally were running together to Jesus (ἐπισυντρέχει).

[289] The verb, ἐξεθαμβήθησαν, is the perfective of θαμβεῖν, which could connote awe so extreme as to cause emotional distress, bodily tremors, and psychological

ran up to him and greeted him. When Jesus asked the reason for the dispute, the boy's father related the health situation of his son, who has a dumb spirit: the spirit seizes him, dashes him down, and he foams and grinds his teeth and becomes rigid. The details of the spirit's hold over the boy, and the inability of the disciples to exorcize the spirit in Jesus' absence, set the stage to make Jesus' exorcism all the more impressive in its display of superior power[290]. The failure of the disciples, the disputing scribes and crowd, could have provoked Jesus' exasperated rebuke of this generation of unbelief (v.19, cf. Deut. 32:5)[291]. Jesus' calling for the boy to be brought to him prepares for his exorcistic act.

2.5.2 Jesus exorcizes a possessed Boy

The people brought the boy to Jesus. But when the spirit saw him, it immediately convulsed (συνσπάραξεν) the boy completely, and he fell on the ground and rolled about, foaming at the mouth (ἀφρίζων), v.20. Jesus found out from the boy's father that the illness has been from childhood, and that the spirit has often cast him both into the fire and water, to destroy him (vv.21c-22a). The demonic immediate convulsion of the boy is a demonstration of power designed to intimidate Jesus. And indeed, the progressive and elaborate description of the boy's possession in vv.20-22 confirms vv.17-18, and thus heightens the effect when Jesus demonstrates the superiority of his power[292]. Jesus' exorcism was

---

bewilderment (9:15, cf. 14:33; 16:5,6).

[290] Cf. R.H. GUNDRY, *Mark*, 488-489.

It says in v.18, that the disciples «lacked the strength» (οὐκ ἴσχυσαν, cf. οὐκ ἠδυνήθησαν [-μεν] v.28; Mt 17:16,19; Lk 9:40), in other words, «were not able». Does this not remind us of Jesus as the stronger one? (cf. 1:7; 3:27). And that is how Jesus interpreted his exorcism activity (cf. 3:27).

[291] Scholars are divided on whom Jesus' rebuke was directed: R.H. GUNDRY, *Mark*, 489, thinks that Jesus was condemning the crowd, including the boy's father and the scribes, who had made the disciples' failure a reason to dispute the power of Jesus himself. On the contrary, G.H. TWELFTREE, *Jesus the Exorcist*, 94; W.L. LANE, *Mark*, 332; C.E.B. CRANFIELD, *Mark*, 300, hold that it was directed to the disciples. Yet, M.D. HOOKER, *St. Mark*, 223; C.S. MANN, *Mark*, 370; V. TAYLOR, *Mark*, 398, think that not necessarily the disciples, the boy's father, or the crowd, rather the people (nation) among whom his ministry was exercised (cf. 6:6). I would say, that although it was directed to the disciples, yet it does not exclude others, who showed signs of unbelief.

[292] Cf. R.H. GUNDRY, *Mark*, 489.

interrupted by the dialogue (vv.21-24) between Jesus and the boy's father. Perhaps the man's faith was plagued by doubt and hesitation, when he said to Jesus, «if you can do anything, have pity on us and help us» (v.22b)[293]. Jesus, picking up his word, «if you can», assured him that all things can be done for one who has faith. Immediately he cried out, «I believe; help my unbelief»[294].

Jesus rebuked the unclean spirit: «You dumb and deaf spirit, I command you, come out of him, and never enter him again» (v.25). The spirit as deaf and dumb heightens the difficulty of the exorcism which Jesus is performing; on the other hand, «'Εγώ», «I» highlights the authority of his person in giving a command to come out, and sets him in contrast with the failed disciples[295]. The spirit, after crying out and convulsing the boy terribly came out, and the boy was like a corpse (v.26). «The spirit's shouting, convulsing the son severely, and leaving him resting on the ground so limp as to look dead give auditory and visible evidence of exit (cf. 1:25-26)»[296]. However, Jesus took the boy by the hand and lifted him up, and he rose (v.27). The same three Greek verbs (κρατήσας, ἤγειρεν, ἀνέστη) were used in 5:41-42[297].

2.5.3 Jesus and his Disciples

When Jesus and his disciples were alone in the house, they asked him, «why could we not cast it out?» (v.28). The disciples' private question to Jesus confirm their failure, and once again makes out of it a foil to magnify Jesus' ability to accomplish the exorcism. But Jesus replied them, that this kind could only be driven out through prayer (v.29). Thus, «the

---

[293] R.H. GUNDRY, *Mark*, 490, notes, «the question of Jesus' ability stems from the failure of the disciples: if their ability derives from his, their failure seems to imply the inadequacy of his ability».

[294] Apparently this man's faith in Jesus' ability to exorcize the spirit was crushed by the disciples' failure, but with Jesus' rebuke, his faith now revives. Cf. R.H. GUNDRY, *Mark*, 490-491.

[295] Cf. R.H. GUNDRY, *Mark*, 491; V. TAYLOR, *Mark*, 400, observes that compared with 1:25 and 5:8 the command is more peremptory, being expressed both positively and negatively.

[296] R.H. GUNDRY, *Mark*, 492.

[297] Cf. M.D. HOOKER, *St. Mark*, 27-28; W.L. LANE, *Mark*, 334, opines that the accumulation of the vocabulary of death and resurrection in vv.26-27, and the parallelism with the narrative of the raising of Jarius' daughter, suggest that Mark wished to allude to a death and resurrection.

exorcist is to make use of prayer; he is to rely, not on his own powers but on the power of God»[298]. But, «Jesus' power as the Son of God is so great that in performing the exorcism he did not need to pray»[299]. Once more Jesus demonstrates his authority and power over Satan and the evil and unclean spirits: he shows his superpower over the most difficult exorcism in the Gospel, that made a boy both deaf and dumb. Therefore, Jesus through exorcism, as we have so far seen, liberates man, and prepares him for the kingdom of God.

2.6 Summary

In this section, we have given a panoramic view of the reality of exorcism in Mark's Gospel. We saw that the phenomenon of exorcism did not begin and end in Jesus' first exorcism in the synagogue of Capernaum. Jesus' exorcism also existed in other parts of the Gospel. In the summary statements, we saw the people bringing their sick and demon-possessed to be healed and cast out (1:32-34); and Jesus going to their synagogues to liberate men from the unclean spirits as he did in Capernaum (1:39). Surely, there were reactions to Jesus' exorcism activity. The demons recognize and reverence Jesus, as the Son of God, they also would like to defend themselves from his menacing presence, but Jesus' powerful silencing does not allow them to speak, because they know him (3:11-12). While the scribes accuse Jesus of being possessed by unclean spirit, and casting out demons by the power of Beelzebul, the chief of demons (3:22-30). In this way, the scribes place Jesus on the part of Satan, while the demons place him on the part of God. The scribes, in boldly attributing Jesus' liberating action through the Holy Spirit to Satan, blaspheme and exclude themselves from God's communion.

Jesus continues his liberating ministry of exorcism by extending it beyond Galilee. In 5:1-20, we meet a demoniac who lived in tombs and defied all control, with incredible strength to shatter chains and fetters, and self-destructive behaviour; but when he met Jesus, the superior power, he bowed down, recognized him as the Son of the Most High God, submitted to his authority and negotiated for a settlement. The exorcism ended in a dramatic way through the drowning of the swines

---

[298] Cf. V. TAYLOR, *Mark*, 401; W.L. LANE, *Mark*, 335; M.D. HOOKER, *St. Mark*, 225.

[299] R.H. GUNDRY, *Mark*, 493.

(pigs) in the sea. Then, the ex-demoniac came back to his right mind healed. In 7:24-30, a Syrophoenician woman pleads for her daughter, possessed by unclean spirit, before Jesus. Her faith in the divine power of Jesus to heal her daughter; her wit and persistent, was rewarded. Jesus exorcizes her daughter at distance, without confronting the demon, or speaking a word of exorcism. Lastly, in 9:14-29, we come to the most difficult exorcism, a dumb and deaf, unclean spirit, who has tried many times to destroy the boy, its victim. Even the failure of the disciples in their attempt to cast it out, provoked dispute, doubt and hesitation on the crowd, the scribes and the boy's father. But Jesus' authoritative double command, and his raising him from the apparent death, restored the boy to his family.

In all these exorcism stories, we see the demons, submitting to the divine authority and super-power of Jesus, the stronger one, who has come to bind them, nay, to destroy them, and to liberate man for God's kingdom. Our discussion has demonstrated that the Capernaum experience (1:23-27) is not unique, but a typical, paradigmatic and programmatic event in Mark's Gospel.

3. Conclusion

At the beginning of this chapter, we set for ourselves the task to verify whether Teaching and Exorcism, which featured as the main activities of Jesus in the synagogue of Capernaum, were also main activities of Jesus in the whole Gospel. We saw that Jesus, not only taught his disciples, but above all the people (crowd) everywhere and at any opportunty: in the synagogues, in front of houses, beside the sea, goes about in the villages teaching, in the desert, on his way to Jerusalem, in the temple, and even made reference to his teaching activity during his passion (14:49). The evangelist, not only emphasized Jesus' teaching activity through didactic terms, more than other synoptic Gospels, but he even described it as the activity Jesus is accustomed to doing (10:1). This proves how Jesus' teaching activity runs through the Gospel, and shows itself as a dominant theme too.

On the other hand, we have seen also how Exorcism has both quantitatively and qualitatively the most dominant and largest single category of healing story in Mark's Gospel. In exorcism, Jesus exercized his power and authority over the unclean spirits or demons, as the stronger one (3:27), who came to destroy Satan's kingdom, to liberate man from its dominance, and to inaugurate God's kingdom. This, Jesus demonstrated throughout the Gospel: in the synagogues, outside or inside the house, beside the sea, in the open air, even at distance without frontal confrontation with the demons, or words of exorcism. He exorcized men and women, those brought to him, and especially a girl (daughter) and a boy (son) through the pleading of a mother and a father, both in the Jewish and Gentile zones. Jesus exorcized any type of evil/unclean spirit, be it the seeming harmless in the synagogue, or the uncontrollable and self-destructive one living among the tombs, or the deaf and dumb one with destructive intent. All this proves and confirms how important exorcism was in Jesus' ministry; and above all, how dominant a theme exorcism is in Mark's Gospel.

The importance of these themes of Teaching and Exorcism, and their position and dominance in the Gospel, give a partial demonstration that our pericope (1:21-28) has a programmatic character in Mark's Gospel.

CHAPTER VII

The Relation with Jesus

In the discussion of our pericope (1:21-28), we met many characters in the text, both explicit or implicit, present or absent: the presence of Jesus, the people, the man with unclean spirit were explicitly stated, while that of the disciples is implicitly mentioned; on the other hand, the scribes were not present in the scene. In the treatment of Jesus' exorcism, we saw how Jesus relates to the demonic world, that is, as fatal enemies. In Jesus' teaching, exorcism, and healing ministry, we observed how the people (crowd) come, gather around Jesus, but there is yet an important aspect of the people still to be noted: their reaction to Jesus' words and deeds. We have also already noticed the scribes' questions about Jesus' authority, or their criticism of his actions, but we shall still discover their relation to Jesus.

Therefore, in this chapter divided into three sections, we shall examine: firstly, how Jesus relates with the disciples both in the text and in the Gospel; secondly, how the people (crowd) reacted with wonder to Jesus' words and actions both in the text and the entire Gospel; and thirdly, what was the relation between Jesus and the scribes both in the text and the whole Gospel. In other words, can Jesus' relation with the disciples, the crowd's reaction (wonder) and the scribes' contrast with Jesus observed in our pericope, be verified in other parts of the Gospel; or so to speak, are they dominant themes in the Gospel?

1. Jesus in Company

In the analysis of v.21 of our pericope (1:21-28), we highlighted the importance of the verb εἰσπορεύονται as signifying the presence of the four fishermen (Simon, Andrew, James and John) with Jesus (cf. vv.18,20, 29). We also proposed that this verb fulfilled Jesus' first

intention for his disciples, «being with him» (cf. 3:14). It is our intention
in this section, therefore, to investigate more on the characteristics of this
verb and its significance for a wider narrative unit, the Gospel. We shall
then examine whether the phenomenon of indefinite plural or implicit
subject is verifiable, with the same connotation as seen in our text,
throughout the whole Gospel: whether this reality has a programmatic
character in Mark's Gospel?

1.1 *The Characteristics of Είσπορεύονται*

In the first place, this verb is in historical present, thereby introducing
a completely new significant situation in location, time, audience and even
theme[1]. This becomes clearer when we notice that v.20 ended with an
aorist (ἀπῆλθον). This is also in plural, a characteristic feature of Mark's
Gospel: «The first and perhaps of all the most significant distinction
between the three Synoptists in this sphere is the distinction between the
use of the plural and of the singular in the narrative of the movements of
Jesus and his disciples»[2]. However, this third person plural has no explicit
subject. Since a text or a pericope is not considered as an isolated unit,
but must be a part of a larger narrative unit, therefore the subject of the
indefinite/implicit plural must be found in the context. Hence, the text
must have a narrative connection with either its immediate or remote
context.

The verb, εἰσπορεύονται, as seen in the pericope, not only signifies
a verb of movement but also Jesus' moving together with his companions.
Almost all the other verbs of the same kind from 1:21 to 14:42[3] manifest
a continued movement together of Jesus with his disciples. Therefore, this
verb represents a beginning of a movement, which opens Jesus' public
ministry in Galilee and beyond. It is worth noting that what is normal for
verbs of movement is implicit subject, not only for the plural but also for
the singular. For instance, Jesus is the implicit subject in the following

---

[1] Cf. W. EGGER, *Frohbotschaft und Lehre*, 147; M. ZERWICK, *Markus-Stil*, 57.

[2] C.H. TURNER, «Marcan Usage», (1925) 225. He went further to say that, «twenty-
one instances are enumerated in #1 of these notes (cf. 228-231), in which the plural is
used by Mark, denoting the coming and going of Jesus and his disciples — in fifteen
of them the word is ἔρχεσθαι or one of its compounds — followed at once by the
singular in reference to Jesus alone» (*ibid.*).

[3] These verbs of movement appeared in these texts: 1:21,29,38; 4:35; 5:1,38;
6:32,53-54; 8:22; 9:9,14,30,33; 10:32,46; 11:1,12,15,19,20,27; 14:26,32,42.

verbs of movement: 1:21b,35,39; 2:1,13,23; 3:1,13; 6:1; 7:24,31; 9:28; 10:1,17; 11:11; 13:1. When one compares some cases like 3:7; 6:1; 8:10,27; 10:46b with the implicit plural under consideration, it becomes obvious that Jesus is the explicit subject, since it is in singular, and the connection with his disciples is only stressed in the companionship which is expressed by μετά and καί[4]. But they fail to represent the double element of «movement» and «being with» of Jesus and his disciples which εἰσπορεύονται stands for.

One would then ask, what does this say on the character of Jesus' activity, and on the relationship between Jesus and the disciples? The verb under consideration shows that there is a movement, and that in this movement Jesus is not alone, but with some companions, whom he called to follow him (vv.16-20). This brings to mind Jesus' intention for his disciples, whom he called and appointed: «to be with him, and to be sent out to preach and ... to cast out demons» (3:14-15). Jesus called them not only to form a community but also to accompany him and be his companions. He wants them to be near or close by, so that with their physical presence they will witness his word and deed[5], and be a part of his ministry. That is why they were always in movement with him wherever his activity takes him to. As I indicated earlier, «Jesus for Mark is always "on the move", and the disciple of Jesus is precisely the one who is on the move with him»[6]. Indeed this movement has been opened by εἰσπορεύονται. On the other hand, I have also earlier stated, that in our pericope, I see Jesus' intention for his disciples fulfilled in anticipation, because apart from being with Jesus represented by the verb, the two aspects of the mission of the twelve (cf. 3:14-15): preaching/teaching and exorcism (vv.21-22, cf. v.27; vv.23-28) are also fulfilled here. Thus, the disciples are with Jesus to learn from him, to learn about him[7]. Hence, as highlighted by the verb, Jesus is not only with his companions in all his movements, but also in his entire missionary activities.

---

[4] Cf. K. STOCK, *Boten*, 146, affirms that Jesus' companionship with his disciples can be expressed in different ways: often with μετά («with»), for instance, in 3:7; 8:10; 11:11; 14:17; or with καί («and») in 6:1; 8:27; 10:46b. It could also be expressed implicitly in plural, as Jesus' change of places were reported. The latter, in fact, is what will engage our attention in this section.

[5] Cf. K. STOCK, *Boten*, 18.

[6] C.M. MURPHY, «Discipleship in Mark», 306; K. STOCK, *Boten*, 18, n.23.

[7] S. FREYNE, *The Twelve*, 120 (cf. 120-128, 137); K. STOCK, *Boten*, 18, n.25.

We shall now see how Jesus' company is composed of in the Gospel, beginning from Galilee to Jerusalem.

1.2 *Jesus and His Disciples*

The indefinite plural verb, εἰσπορεύονται, has opened for us the discussion on Jesus' company and his movements with his companions (disciples) in Mark's Gospel. We shall find out from the context, who form part of Jesus' company in these movements. This task will be examined in three stages (three sections of the Gospel): in Galilee (1:14-8:26), on the Way to Jerusalem (8:27-10:52), and in Jerusalem (11:1-16:8).

1.2.1 In Galilee (1:14-8:26)

After the call of the four fishermen by the sea of Galilee (1:16-20), Jesus' first act was to come with them into *Capernaum* (εἰσπορεύονται, v.21). At the end of Jesus' teaching and exorcism in the synagogue, they left there (ἐξελθόντες ἦλθον, 1:29) for the House of Simon and Andrew, where Jesus cured Simon's mother-in-law of her fever sickness. Both in the synagogue and the private house, these Jesus' first four companions were present and witnesses of Jesus' teaching, exorcism and healing activities. When Jesus left the house very early to pray in a lonely place (1:35), Simon and those with him (Σίμων καὶ οἱ μετ'αὐτοῦ, v.36) pursued him. As they found him, they told him, «Every one is searching for you» (v.37). But Jesus replied them, «Let us go elsewhere to the neighbouring towns» (ἄγωμεν ἀλλαχοῦ εἰς τὰς ἐχομένας κωμοπόλεις, 1:38). Thus, Jesus invites his companions to accompany him to the neighbouring towns. In the context, I think that Jesus' companions here should be «Simon and those with him» (cf. v.36), who are apparently Andrew, James and John (cf. vv.16-20,29)[8], that is, the four fishermen. Therefore, Jesus moves in company from Capernaum (1:1-38) to all of Galilee (1:39, 40-45), in order to preach and continue his mission.

After teaching the crowd in parables and private explanation to his disciples (4:2-34, esp. 33-34), Jesus himself taking the initiative, said to his companions, διέλθωμεν εἰς τὸ πέραν, («let us go across to the other side», 4:35). Since he was teaching *on the Sea* from the boat, the disciples

---

[8] Cf. R.H. GUNDRY, *Mark*, 94; R.A. GUELICH, *Mark*, 69; K. STOCK, *Boten*, 134.

as the boatmen, took him with them just as he was[9]. This is the second time Jesus has used the first person plural, «let us» (cf. 1:38), thereby emphasizing, on the one hand, the binding relationship between him and his companions (disciples)[10]; and on the other hand, that he is not alone. But who are those with him? One can observe that he said «to them» (αὐτοῖς), v.35, which means «to his own disciples» (τοῖς ἰδίοις μαθηταῖς)[11], the ones most recently mentioned in v.34[12]. Here we meet the term for Jesus' companions: μαθηταί[13]. In this boat travel, Jesus' identity was also raised by his disciples (4:41).

Jesus and his disciples came to the other side[14] of the sea, the country of the *Gerasenes* (ἦλθον εἰς τὸ πέραν τῆς θαλάσσης, 5:1, cf. 4:35). The same group with Jesus in the boat accompanied him to this city of the Gentiles (cf. 4:34), who witnessed Jesus' authority and power over the cosmic powers of the sea (v.39); and will now be the eyewitnesses of another difficult exorcism scene. Here the exorcism ended in a dramatic way, with the unclean spirits drowning the pigs in the sea. Nevertheless, when Jesus had crossed again to the other side, Jarius, a ruler of the synagogue came to him to plead for his sick daughter (5:22). We are told, they came to *Jarius' House* (ἔρχονται εἰς τὸν οἶκον, 5:38). Here those

---

[9] It must be noted that this is the first boat travel Jesus will make with his companions. E.S. MALBON, «Sea of Galilee», 363, observes that Jesus crosses the sea freely (4:35; 5:1,18,21; 6:53,54; 8:10,13) and at one point commands his disciples to cross the sea before him (6:45).

[10] This cohortative first person plural also occurs in 1:38 (the first called, cf. 1:29), and in 14:42 (for the three disciples), and in the indicative in 10:33 (for the Twelve).

[11] Instead of using αὐτοῦ («his») with μαθηταί, which is Mark's favourite (see below), ἰδίοι, «own», which has a strong meaning, is used. Cf. R.H. GUNDRY, *Mark*, 237; V. TAYLOR, *Mark*, 271-272, sees the use of «his own disciples» as intentional, in this case, there is a note of intimacy in the passage.

[12] Cf. R.H. GUNDRY, *Mark*, 237.

[13] The word, μαθηταί («disciples») is a general term describing those who were associated with Jesus at any particular moment. Cf. C.H. TURNER, «Marcan Usage», (1926-27) 26. This appeared first in 2:15. C.H. TURNER, «Marcan Usage», (1924-25) 227-228, cf. 235-237, demonstrates that Mark's Gospel reveals its archaic and primitive character by its predominant use of the phrase «his disciples» (οἱ μαθηταὶ αὐτοῦ); whereas the other Gospels tend to introduce the absolute statement, «the disciples».

[14] «"The other side" ties this story to the previous one by indicating the arrival at the destination given in 4:35 for the boat trip». Cf. R.A. GUELICH, *Mark*, 275; E. MANICARDI, *Il Cammino di Gesù*, 28.

who entered the house with Jesus were the three disciples (Peter, James, and John, cf. v.37 and v.40 [τοὺς μετ'αὐτοῦ - «those with him»]), whom he only allowed to accompany him. This is the first time Jesus is taking with him only three disciples[15]. Hence, they were the witnesses of this great event, the raising of Jarius' daughter (vv.41-43).

In 6:7-13, Jesus accomplished his second intention for his disciples (cf. 3:14-15): «to be sent out to preach and have authority to cast out demons». Here in v.7, Jesus called to himself (προσκαλεῖται)[16] the Twelve and began to send them out (ἀποστέλλειν)[17] two by two, and gave them authority over unclean spirits. When the apostles (οἱ ἀπόστολοι)[18] returned, Jesus asked them to come to a lonely place for some rest, since the crowd's flow could not give them the opportunity even to eat (vv.30-31). We are told they went away in a boat (ἀπῆλθον ἐν τῷ πλοίῳ, 6:32) to *a lonely place*. Therefore, those who formed Jesus' company in this boat travel were «the Twelve», whom Jesus sent out for mission (6:7-13), and also «the apostles» who came back from their mission (6:30). Here I think that both «the twelve» and «the apostles» are one and the same, since the apostles were the twelve Jesus sent two by two in 6:7-13, cf. v.30[19].

After feeding the great crowd, that Jesus met in the desert, out of his compassion on them, «because they were like sheep without a shepherd» (6:34-44), Jesus made his disciples get into the boat and go ahead before him (6:45). Walking on the sea, Jesus joined them later, and got into the boat with them (6:51). When they had crossed over, they came to land at *Gennesaret* (διαπεράσαντες ... ἦλθον εἰς Γεννησαρέτ ..., 6:53,54). The four verbs, all in third person plural, with variety of moods (an aorist

---

[15] This is the first of the three of such occasions (5:37, cf. 9:2; 14:33). R.H. GUNDRY, *Mark*, 273, states that «the exception of the inner trio provides the miracle with a requisite number of discipular witnesses in addition to the parents (cf. Deut. 19:15). A miracle so stupendous as raising the dead benefits from such a number of witnesses».

[16] This verb is often used by Jesus for his disciples (5x out 9x of its occurrences): 3:13; 6:7; 8:1; 10:42; 12:43.

[17] Jesus is always sending his disciples (the Twelve) in twos, cf. 6:7; 11:1; 14:13.

[18] «The apostles» (οἱ ἀπόστολοι) occurs only here and in a disputed reading in 3:14. Contextually, it picks up the ἀποστέλλειν of 6:7 and designates those sent as the «sent ones» or «missionaries». It points primarily to their role rather than their status. Cf. R.A. GUELICH, *Mark*, 338.

[19] Cf. K.H. RENGSTORF, «ἀπόστολος», 425.

participle, aorist active, aorist passive, and a genitive absolute: διαπεράσαντες, ἦλθον, προσωρμίσθησαν, ἐξελθόντων αὐτῶν)[20], deliver one point: that Jesus did not land alone in this city. Those who form his companions must be sought in the context since these verbs are all implicit. Jesus' companions were his disciples (τοὺς μαθητὰς αὐτοῦ, 6:45, cf. vv.35,41). Jesus' disciples were not only witnesses of Jesus' miraculous feeding of the five thousand people, but also his miraculous walking on the sea, and the curing of many sick people in the present city.

After Jesus' feeding of the four thousand (8:1-10), he came to Dalmanutha with his disciples in a boat (8:10-13). But when he was embarrassed by the Pharisees' malicious question, he left again with them, and they came to *Bethsaida* (ἔρχονται εἰς Βηθσαιδάν, 8:22). Those in Jesus' company were those with him in the boat (8:13-21), who were with him in Dalmanutha, and assisted in the feeding of the four thousand: these were his disciples (οἱ μαθηταὶ αὐτοῦ, 8:1,4,6,10). Jesus' disciples were therefore present and experienced the feeding of the four thousand, his reproach of them for lack of understanding, and climaxed in the cure of the blind man (8:22-26).

One can observe that in Jesus' ministry and movements in Galilee he was never alone, but in company, and almost always with the boat. These boat travels offered Jesus and his disciples some privacy from the crowd, and becomes for them a place of communion, revelation, and teaching (4:35-41; 6:45-51; 8:14-21). This stresses the importance of the Sea of Galilee in Jesus' Galilean ministry and movement[21]. Now we go to the next section, on the way to Jerusalem.

1.2.2 On the Way to Jerusalem (8:27-10:52)

This movement towards Jerusalem began in Caesarea Philippi with Jesus and his disciples (cf. 8:27), where he asked them about his identity: «Who do men say that I am?» (v.27, cf. v.29). In fact, «from Caesarea Philippi to Jerusalem the record is one of almost continuous movement»[22].

---

[20] The four verbs say: they crossed over, they came (landed at) to Gennesaret, and they moored to the shore; and as they got out of the boat (disembarked) the people immediately recognized Jesus (vv.53-54).

[21] E.S. MALBON, «Sea of Galilee», 363, affirms that «the Sea of Galilee is the geographical focal point for the first half of the Gospel of Mark, the center of the Marcan Jesus' movement in space (7:31)».

[22] C.H. TURNER, «Marcan Usage», (1926-27) 26.

We shall therefore examine who were Jesus' companions as he moves towards Jerusalem.

After Jesus' Transfiguration scene *on the mountain*, as they were coming down the mountain (καταβαινόντων αὐτῶν ἐκ τοῦ ὄρους, 9:9), Jesus charged them not to tell anyone what they had seen, until the Son of man should have risen from the dead (cf. v.9). This means that Jesus was not alone, but was with companions. The question is: who form Jesus' company here? Indeed, those who were in Jesus' company, as he came down the mountain, were the three disciples (Peter, James and John), whom he took with him to the high mountain (cf. 9:2). They were privileged to witness Jesus' glory and God's revelation of Jesus' identity, as the beloved Son of God (9:2-8).

But when they came to the disciples, they saw a great crowd about them (ἐλθόντες ... εἶδον ὄχλος πολὺν περὶ αὐτοὺς, 9:14). Jesus was still in the same company (cf. 9:2, as seen above), and having left the mountain arrived here, and saw or met the other disciples (τοὺς μαθητὰς, v.14), who were arguing with the scribes, and had been asked to cast out the demon from the boy, but were unable (τοῖς μαθηταῖς σου, v.18), and also asked Jesus privately why they could not cast it out (οἱ μαθηταὶ αὐτοῦ, v.28). Hence, these three privileged disciples formed Jesus' company both during the Transfiguration experience and came down with him (from the mountain) to meet the rest of the disciples. And this is the second time, that Jesus has taken them for a special event (cf. 5:37,40 for 5:41-43).

Then they went out from there (cf. the house, v.28) and passed *through Galilee* (ἐξελθόντες παρεπορεύοντο διὰ τῆς Γαλιλαίας, 9:30) *incognito*. Here Jesus taught his disciples privately, by foretelling to them his death and resurrection for the second time (9:31, cf. 8:31). Those who accompany him in his present movement are surely the audience of his present teaching (τοὺς μαθητὰς αὐτοῦ, v.31), and those who were with him in the house (οἱ μαθηταὶ αὐτοῦ, v.28), from where he came out with them. Hence Jesus was with his disciples in this teaching activity.

And they came to *Capernaum* (ἦλθον εἰς Καφαρναούμ, 9:33). As Jesus was in the house he asked them, what they were discussing on the way? They were too ashamed to answer[23], so they were silent. But the omniscient narrator reveals to us, that they had discussed about who was the greatest (v.34). Here those who were in Jesus' company as he arrived

---

[23] Cf. V. TAYLOR, *Mark*, 404.

in Capernaum, are those to whom he directed his question; and they have remained implicit. And I think that Jesus' companion here were his disciples (cf. v.31)[24]. However, Jesus called the twelve (τοὺς δώδεκα, v.35), and said to them, «If any one would be first, he must be the last of all and servant of all». The question then is: could Jesus' disciples (cf. v.31), who formed Jesus' company here, not be the same as the Twelve (cf. v.35)?[25] Nevertheless, the disciples were Jesus' companions in his movement to Capernaum, but the twelve (the small group) were the beneficiaries of his teaching in this section (9:33-50).

They were *on the road* going up to Jerusalem (ἦσαν ... ἀναβαίνοντες εἰς Ἰεροσόλυμα, 10:32), and Jesus was walking ahead of them, and this provoked among them amazement, and those who followed him fear[26]. Since the subject of the verbs is implicit, one must have to look for it from the context. Jesus' companions here are most likely Jesus' disciples (τοῖς μαθηταῖς αὐτοῦ, vv.23,24, cf. vv.10,13)[27]. The text says that Jesus took the Twelve again (τοὺς δώδεκα, v.32) and began to tell them concerning his death and resurrection about to take place in Jerusalem

---

[24] Cf. R.H. GUNDRY, *Mark*, 508; C.E.B. CRANFIELD, *Mark*, 307; V. TAYLOR, *Mark*, 404.

[25] Some scholars see Jesus' mention of the twelve (v.35), after addressing the disciples (v.33) as strange, odd or unnecessary. Cf. M.D. HOOKER, *St. Mark*, 227; C.E.B. CRANFIELD, *Mark*, 307-308; V. TAYLOR, *Mark*, 404, suggests that it does not seem likely that Mark is drawing a distinction between them (the twelve) and the other disciples. On the contrary, R.H. GUNDRY, *Mark*, 509, cf. 167, affirms that Mark writes «the Twelve», which distinguishes the small group of apostles from the larger group of disciples, to provide a numerical framework for the upcoming contrast between first and last, i.e. between first and twelfth.

[26] Most scholars regard 10:32 as having two groups in mind: that the disciples, who were with Jesus, were amazed; while those following him (the people) were afraid. Cf. K. STOCK, *Boten*, 132; E.S. MALBON, «Markan Characters», 108, 116; C.E.B. CRANFIELD, *Mark*, 335; E. KLOSTERMANN, *Markusevangelium*, 105; V. TAYLOR, *Mark*, 437. However, R.H. GUNDRY, *Mark*, 570, 571; M.D. HOOKER, *St. Mark*, 244, agree with the two groups, but attributed amazement to the people, while fear to the disciples. On the other hand, some hold that there is only one indiscriminate group. Cf. T. DWYER, *Motif of Wonder*, 159-160; E. BEST, *Following Jesus*, 120; W.L. LANE, *Mark*, 373, n.60.

[27] Cf. R.H. GUNDRY, *Mark*, 569, 570, adds, that here, a reference to people in general who were going up to Jerusalem on the road would naturally contrast with Jesus and the disciples, recently said to be on the road. Mark's penchant for the indefinite third person plural supports this judgment.

(vv.33-34)[28]. Did Jesus reveal the third prophecy of his death and resurrection (which is more detailed) only to the twelve (vv.32-34), or to his disciples, whom he has done so twice (cf. 8:31; 9:31)? In other words, are the disciples who were Jesus' companions here, the same as the twelve, who were privileged to know what Jesus is about to experience in Jerusalem?[29]

And they came to *Jericho* (ἔρχονται εἰς Ἰεριχώ, 10:46). One would be inclined to think that those who accompanied Jesus to Jericho were the twelve (cf. v.32, 41)[30]. But those who were in Jesus' company as he went out of Jericho, were his disciples (τῶν μαθητῶν αὐτοῦ, v.46b) and a great multitude, who were explicitly stated. In our discussion, we confirm here that in Jesus' journey to Jericho, which is our concern, he was accompanied by the Twelve.

In this section dealing with Jesus' journey towards Jerusalem, we meet Jesus often teaching his disciples or the Twelve, whether in the prophecy of his death and resurrection (8:31; 9:31; 10:32-34), or in revelation (9:2-13), correction of some conducts (8:32-33; 9:33-37, 38-41; 10:13-16, 35-45), or other matters (8:34-38; 9:28-29, 42-50; 10:10-12, 23-31). The key term in this section (8:27-10:52) is *on the road/way* (ἐν τῇ ὁδῷ). The last section was characterized by boat trips, because of the Sea of Galilee; but here because they are «on the road», they travel on foot. Our next attention will be directed to Jesus' stay in Jerusalem.

1.2.3 In Jerusalem (11:1-16:8)

Jesus' movement in Jerusalem, has the city of Jerusalem, especially the Temple, as its focal point, on which his movements and ministry were centred[31]. In this section, we shall examine also whether Jesus' companionship with his disciples continued or not.

---

[28] R.H. GUNDRY, *Mark*, 571, states that «to anticipate James and John plus "the ten" (vv.35,41), Mark here writes that Jesus took along "the Twelve", rather than that he took along "his disciples"».

[29] This third foretelling of Jesus' death and resurrection was reserved, or was exclusively addressed to the Twelve, even though Jesus was accompanied by a larger group of his followers (disciples). Cf. K. STOCK, *Boten*, 132, 133. So, then, the taking along separates the Twelve from a larger group of followers. Cf. GUNDRY, *Mark*, 571.

[30] R.H. GUNDRY, *Mark*, 593, confirms that since Jesus took the Twelve aside in v.32e, «they» seems limited to Jesus and the Twelve (see also vv.35, 41).

[31] W.L. LANE, *Mark*, 413, affirms that Jesus apparently made the Temple the focal-point of his ministry throughout the duration of his final period in Jerusalem (cf. 11:11, 15-18, 27; 12:35, 41; 13:1-2; 14:49). Cf. K. STOCK, *Boten*, 145.

When they drew *near to Jerusalem* (ὅτε ἐγγίζουσιν εἰς Ἰερο-σόλυμα, 11:1), to Bethphage and Bethany, at the Mount of Olives, Jesus sent two of his disciples on an errand of bringing a tied colt to him (11:1-7a). Here initiates Jesus' entry into Jerusalem (11:7b-11), which the disciples and many people assisted in. Those who drew near to Jerusalem with Jesus as his companions were surely his disciples who left Jericho with him (τῶν μαθητῶν αὐτοῦ, cf. 10:46b), and the big crowd. We were told later that Jesus, after looking around on all things in the Temple, left Jerusalem in the evening for Bethany with the Twelve (μετὰ τῶν δώδεκα, 11:11).

On the following day, when they came from Bethany (ἐξελθόντων αὐτῶν ἀπὸ Βηθανίας, 11:12), Jesus was hungry. On seeing a fig tree in a distance, he searched for something to eat, but found nothing but leaves; he cursed the fig tree. And his disciples heard it (οἱ μαθηταὶ αὐτοῦ, 11:14). Then who formed Jesus' company in his journey from Bethany? One would think that the Twelve, who went to Bethany with Jesus, will come out with him on the following day, thereby forming his companions[32]. But to say that Jesus' disciples heard the curse of the fig tree, means that they were present, and should have come out from Bethany with him. I think Jesus' company here should be the Twelve, who are also his disciples[33].

And they came to *Jerusalem* (ἔρχονται εἰς Ἰεροσόλυμα, 11:15). Jesus then entered the temple and drove away those who were selling and buying there. When the chief priests and elders and the scribes heard it they sought to destroy him, but they were afraid of the multitude, who were all astonished at his teaching. In the evening they went out of the city (ἐξεπορεύοντο ἔξω τῆς πόλεως, 11:19). Who are then in Jesus' company here? These should be the disciples who heard Jesus' curse of

---

[32] K. STOCK, *Boten*, 148-149, establishes that immediate connection between 11:11 and 11:12 shows that the same person-circle who went to Bethany (Jesus with the 12), also returned back from Bethany to Jerusalem. Cf. J. COUTTS, «Authority of Jesus», 115, n.1. To the εἰς Βηθανίαν of 11:11 corresponds exactly the ἀπὸ Βηθανίας of 11:12. Cf. STOCK, *Boten*, 149; R.H. GUNDRY, *Mark*, 648.

[33] R.H. GUNDRY, *Mark*, 635, agrees that «though "his disciples" may include more than the Twelve, and often does, here the phrase appears to describe only the Twelve (cf. v.11) as those who learn by listening ("disciple" meaning "learner")». Cf. K. STOCK, *Boten*, 149, 150.

the fig tree (cf. 11:14), before they arrived in Jerusalem, and with whom Jesus also left the city (cf. 11:15, 19)[34].

In the morning, as they passed by (παραπορευόμενοι ... εἶδον, 11:20), they saw the fig tree withered. Jesus then taught his disciples the lesson from the fig tree. And they came again to Jerusalem (ἔρχονται πάλιν εἰς Ἰεροσόλυμα, 11:27). The «again» exactly marks the third entry into Jerusalem[35]. Here the chief priests, the scribes and the elders questioned Jesus about his authority to do what he has done. Jesus' company here remains the same, that is, his disciples who are the Twelve (cf. 11:11).

After *the Last Supper*, when they had sung a hymn, they went to the Mount of Olives (... ἐξῆλθον εἰς τὸ ὄρος τῶν ἐλαιῶν, 14:26). The subject of these two verbs remains implicit, which the context should resolve. Surely those who were at Supper with Jesus should form his company of movement here. We recall that, Jesus came for the Passover Meal with the Twelve (μετὰ τῶν δώδεκα, v.17, [cf. εἷς τῶν δώδεκα, vv.10,18,20]), likewise we observed earlier that, those who spoke to Jesus about the Passover and prepared it, were his disciples (οἱ μαθηταὶ αὐτοῦ, vv.12,13,14). Nevertheless, those who sang and went out with Jesus to Mount of Olives were the Twelve (cf. v.17)[36].

And they went to a place called *Gethsemane* (ἔρχονται εἰς χωρίον ... Γεθσημανὶ, 14:32); and Jesus said to his disciples, «Sit here, while I pray». There is no doubt that Jesus' company here were his disciples, whom he spoke to (cf. v.32). These could also mean those who were at the Last Supper[37]. But after Jesus' prayer, he said, «Rise, let us be going; see, my betrayer is at hand» (ἐγείρεσθε ἄγωμεν ..., 14:42)[38]. Who are in Jesus' company here? These are the three disciples (Peter, James and

---

[34] R.H. GUNDRY, *Mark*, 648, states that since v.19 builds on v.11, the designation of Jesus and the Twelve as the subjects of going out in v.11 eliminates the need for a similar designation here. Cf. STOCK, *Boten*, 149.

[35] Cf. R.H. GUNDRY, *Mark*, 656.

[36] When one compares 14:17 with 14:14 (Jesus' meal with his disciples) and with 14:15 («for us»), it shows that «my disciples» also means the Twelve. If now in 14:14 the name «disciples» is applied to them, and if in 14:17 only the Twelve as Jesus' companions were named, then it seems likely that with «my disciples» in 14:14 only the Twelve are meant. Cf. K. STOCK, *Boten*, 155-156.

[37] Cf. C.H. TURNER, «Marcan Usage», (1926-27) 29.

[38] One observes here another first person plural of verbs of movement used by Jesus (cf. 1:38; 4:35; 10:33; 14:42).

John), whom Jesus took (παραλαμβάνει)[39] with him (14:33). This is the last time we meet Jesus in company, either with the three disciples, the Twelve or his disciples.

Immediately after Jesus' address to the three disciples, Judas (one of the twelve) came with him a crowd with swords and clubs, from the chief priests and the scribes and the elders (14:43). In fact, they have come to arrest Jesus (14:44-49). Then we read that they all forsook him, and fled (ἀφέντες αὐτὸν ἔφυγον πάντες, 14:50). The implict subject of these verbs have changed. The word, ἔφυγον, initiates the separation between Jesus and his disciples. Therefore, the implicit subject does not represent Jesus' company any more: that is, «the three», «the four», «the twelve», or «his disciples», as the case may be. But here all the disciples left Jesus and fled, even the young man, who followed him (vv.51-52), or Peter who followed him at a distance (v.54). Jesus is now alone before the high priest, and the assembly of all the chief priests and the elders and the scribes (v.53).

This separation between Jesus and his disciples in 14:50 was foretold by Jesus himself, when he said to them, «You will all fall away; for it is written, «I will strike the shepherd, and the sheep will be scattered'» (14:27). He also promised them that they all will meet again: «But after I am raised up, I will go before you to Galilee» (14:28). Indeed, this promise was reaffirmed at the resurrection scene by the young man sitting in the tomb, as he spoke to the women, «But go, tell his disciples and Peter that he is going before you to Galilee; there you will see him, as he told you» (16:7).

In Jesus' movement, as in the other sections, he was never alone. He was always with his disciples (the Twelve). And Jesus' movement with his disciples in Jerusalem was centred on the Temple. His movement was almost always to and fro Bethany and Jerusalem. In fact, he never spent the night in Jerusalem but in Bethany, and the first night that he and the Twelve spent in Gethsemane the Jewish authorities arrested him. And after this his disciples left him and fled (14:50), and that ended Jesus being in company, from then onwards, he was alone.

---

[39] This verb, παραλαμβάνειν, occurs 6x in Mark, but used 4x for Jesus. Among the 4x, 3x are used for the three disciples, in 5:40 (cf. v.37, but in v.40, including the father and the mother of the child); 9:2; 14:33; while once for the Twelve, cf. 10:32.

1.3 *Summary*

In this section we have tried to show that εἰσπορεύονται which we discovered in our pericope, as demonstrating that Jesus was not alone as he came to Capernaum, is also a dominant motif in the Gospel. The characteristic of this verb of movement x-rayed in our discussion, that it combines both «movement» and «being together» with Jesus. Jesus travelled both on the land and on the sea, but always with his disciples, whether they are three, four, twelve or all of them. In Galilee, the sea played an important part that they travelled with boat; on the way to Jerusalem, it was on foot; while in Jerusalem it was also on foot. In all this moving and being together, Jesus never missed the opportunity to teach or instruct his disciples or the Twelve. Jesus was always with his disciples, not only in his movements, but also in his ministry; often they are the privileged eyewitnesses of his healing and exorcism, in short, his word and deed.

We can confidently say that Jesus in company, which we observed in 1:21a, is a dominant theme observed throughout the Gospel. Therefore εἰσπορεύονται, which is indefinite plural, with the significance of «Jesus in company» has a programmatic character in the Gospel. And this arms us to demonstrate the function of our pericope in the Gospel.

2. The People's Reaction of Wonder

The People's reaction to Jesus' word and deed was most evident in our pericope (1:21-28), as we saw in our analysis in Part I, especially in vv.22 and 27. After Jesus' teaching, the people reacted with astonishment (ἐξεπλήσσοντο); likewise after Jesus' exorcism of an unclean spirit, the reaction of the people was also heightened in amazement (ἐθαμβήθησαν). Thus, the whole idea or phenomenon of wonder, which began in our pericope with these two expressions of wonder (ἐξεπλήσσοντο, ἐθαμβήθησαν, vv.22,27)[40], introduced us to the motif of wonder in Mark's Gospel. We also observed in Part I, that the motif of wonder comprises all the narrative elements which express astonishment, fear, terror, and amazement. Thus these reactions of wonder may be expressed by a verb (ἐκπλήσσομαι, ἐξίστημι, θαμβέομαι [ἐκθαμβέομαι],

---

[40] Mark often uses «double expressions» (two reactions of wonder in a single pericope) in his narration, for instance, in 1:22,27; 5:15,20; 5:33,42; 6:2,6; 6:50,51; 10:24,26; 16:5,6,8. Cf. T. DWYER, *Motif of Wonder*, 21.

θαυμάζω [ἐκθαυμάζω], φοβέομαι), by a noun (ἔκστασις, θάμβος, φόβος), or by any description of a reaction or state of awe[41]. Since T. Dwyer[42] has made a detailed study of the motif of wonder in Mark's Gospel, we shall limit ourselve to the People's reaction, as seen in our pericope. Therefore, it will be our task in this section, to verify whether this motif of wonder observed here in the people's reaction to Jesus' word and deed, is unique to our pericope, or it is a dominant theme throughout the Gospel. In other words, has the people's reaction of wonder a programmatic character for Mark's Gospel?

To proceed in this verification process, we shall first of all examine the people's reaction to Jesus' teaching; secondly, their reaction to Jesus' exorcism and healing; and thirdly, their reaction to Jesus' himself.

2.1 *The People's Reaction to Jesus' Teaching*

The first reaction of the people, who were indefinite and implicit in our pericope, was to be astonished at Jesus' teaching. We shall now examine whether this reaction is also observed in the other parts of the Gospel. However, we shall begin briefly with our text, and then we can go to the others.

2.1.1 In Capernaum (1:22, 27)

Since we have already established that the people's reaction of amazement at Jesus' authoritative teaching during his first public appearance in Capernaum began in our pericope, especially in vv.22 and 27, we would like to concentrate on the verification of other parts of the gospel where this phenomenon is present. We shall now turn to the next text concerning the people's reaction to Jesus' teaching.

2.1.2 In Nazareth (6:2)

Jesus came to his native town or country (τὴν πατρίδα αὐτοῦ), Nazareth, with his disciples (6:1). And as it was on the sabbath, he entered in the synagogue and began to teach the people. Many who heard him were astonished (ἐξεπλήσσοντο), and asked some questions (vv.2-3). This is the second time a verb of wonder, ἐκπλήσσομαι, is associated

---

[41] Cf. T. DWYER, *Motif of Wonder*, 11; ID., «Motif of Wonder», 49; G. THEISSEN, *Miracle Stories*, 69; R. PESCH, *Markusevangelium* II, 150.

[42] Cf. T. DWYER, *Motif of Wonder*, 92-195.

with Jesus' teaching and the people (v.2, cf. 1:22). The setting of this pericope is very similar to 1:21-28, with the common themes of Jesus teaching, the synagogue, the sabbath, the people's amazement[43], the disciples being with Jesus in his movements and ministry, and questions leading to Jesus' identity. This pericope (6:1-6a) can be divided into four parts: Jesus' entry with his disciples into his home town (v.1); Jesus' teaching in the synagogue and the astonished and offended reaction of the townspeople (vv.2-3); Jesus' aphoristic response to their reaction (v.4); and Jesus' working of few miracles and marvels at the townspeople's unbelief (vv.5-6a)[44]. However, we shall concentrate on the people's reaction.

This seems to be the third time Jesus entered the synagogue on the sabbath, and most likely also taught the people and healed some of them (cf. 1:21-28; 3:1-6; 6:1-6). But it is also striking here, as in 1:22, that the content of Jesus' teaching was not stated. Thus, «that he (Mark) pays no attention to the content of Jesus' teaching, only to its effect, and that the townspeople will take offense at Jesus show the strength of Mark's desire to stress Jesus' authority: even offended astonishment serves the emphasis»[45]. In fact, it is Jesus' authoritative teaching which caused the people's wonder. «The people are overcome with a "shocked numbness" as they hear the authoritative new teaching, resplendent with divine power»[46]. The people's reaction is, therefore, described with the strong expression verb, ἐκπλήσσομαι (cf. 1:22; 7:37; 10:26; 11:18), which expresses always a moment of overwhelming, of ecstasy, of numbness caused by terror or shock[47]. Indeed, this is occasioned by Jesus' exercise of his authority in teaching.

The people's reaction of wonder was expressed in questions: πόθεν τούτῳ ταῦτα ..., «Where did this man get all this? ...» (vv.2-3)[48]. Thus

---

[43] Cf. T. DWYER, *Motif of Wonder*, 121.

[44] Cf. R.H. GUNDRY, *Mark*, 289.

[45] R.H. GUNDRY, *Mark*, 289.

[46] T. DWYER, *Motif of Wonder*, 122; E. GRÄSSER, «Jesus in Nazareth», 6, notes that in Nazareth the powerful teacher finds the situation he was right to expect - overwhelmed hearers. While R.H. GUNDRY, *Mark*, 289, observes, «that the astonishment was going on (imperfect tense) as the people were listening (ἀκούοντες, a present participle) brings it into the closest possible connection with Jesus' teaching».

[47] R. PESCH, *Markusevangelium I*, 317; Cf. E. GRÄSSER, *Jesus in Nazareth*, 9; ID., «Jesus in Nazareth», 6.

[48] T. DWYER, *Motif of Wonder*, 121, notes that the question πόθεν τούτῳ ταῦτα

«the reason for their reaction comes out to light in a series of five questions three aimed at Jesus' ministry and two at him personally»[49]. These questions contain three times a contemptuous demonstrative pronoun (τούτῳ ... τούτῳ ... οὗτός), «this one» or «this man». The first three questions are: «Where did this one get these things? What is the wisdom given to him? What mighty works are wrought by his hands!» (v.2). The second question concerning his wisdom and the third about his mighty deeds specify the general question, «where did this one get these things?»[50] Thus, these questions concern the source and nature of Jesus' teaching, wisdom and power; in other words, what was the source of his wisdom, and who had empowered him to speak and act with such authority?[51] In short, is it from Heaven or from men (11:30), or from Satan (3:22,30)?[52] The next two questions concern Jesus' personality and origin: «Is not this the carpenter, the son of Mary and brother of James and Joses and Judas and Simon, and are not his sisters here with us?» (v.3). Here the townspeople use Jesus' origin to argue against him. However, Mark has used wonder to lead to a discussion of the identity of Jesus or the source of his power[53]. These questions eventually led to offense at Jesus (ἐσκανδαλίζοντο ἐν αὐτῷ, v.3), and the people's unbelief (τὴν ἀπιστίαν, v.6), which amazed Jesus.

The people cannot deny the phenomena of Jesus' remarkable wisdom and stupendous miracles; they can only wonder where they came from and what they represent. Thus, «in addition to exorcism, Mark intends the miracles and wisdom to verify the authority of Jesus' teaching (cf. 1:21-

in 6:2 reminds us of the question, τί ἐστιν τοῦτο in 1:27 and τίς ἄρα οὗτός ἐστιν in 4:41, and the reader is directed to the progression «what is this?» followed by «who is this?» followed by «where did this one get these things?».

[49] R.A. GUELICH, Mark, 308; R. PESCH, Markusevangelium I, 317-318; R.H. GUNDRY, Mark, 290, has four questions.

[50] Cf. R.A. GUELICH, Mark, 308-309; R.H. GUNDRY, Mark, 290.

[51] Cf. W.L. LANE, Mark, 201; V. TAYLOR, Mark, 299.

[52] Cf. R.A. GUELICH, Mark, 309; R. PESCH, Markusevangelium I, 317; W.L. LANE, Mark, 201.

[53] Cf. T. DWYER, Motif of Wonder, 122; R.H. GUNDRY, Mark, 292, establishes that «for Mark, identifying Jesus as the carpenter misses his identity as the one stronger than John the Baptizer (1:7). Identifying him as Mary's son misses his identity as God's Son (1:1,11; 3:11; 5:7; 9:7; 12:6; 13:32; 14:61-62; 15:39). Identifying him as the brother of James, Joses, Jude, and Simon misses his identity as the one whom another Simon ... and another James ... dropped everything to follow (1:16-20)...».

28)»[54]. Hence the people's reaction of wonder not only highlights Jesus' teaching authority, divine wisdom, miraculous powers, but above all, Jesus' identity, as the Son of God.

2.1.3 In the Temple (11:18)

Jesus came to Jerusalem and entered the temple, where he drove out those who were selling and buying in the temple. He also taught the people and they were astonished, as usual. Thus, the people's reaction of wonder, observed in the first part of Mark's Gospel with regard to Jesus' teaching (cf. 1:22,27; 6:2), is also observed in the second part, here. This introduces us to the special relation between 11:15-19 and 1:21-28.[55] In both cases, Jesus has entered the city, and goes to the place of worship (the synagogue in 1:21-28, the temple here). He exercised his divine authority by casting out those who defile the temple as he exorcized the unclean spirit in the synagogue in 1:25-26. With the same wonder verb, ἐκπλήσσομαι, both in 1:22 and 11:18, the crowd marvels at Jesus' teaching. In 1:22 Jesus' teaching is contrasted by the scribes, while in 11:18 the scribes and other leaders confront him. Some differences also exist, especially in 1:22 Jesus' teaching lacked content, but here it has (cf. 11:17). Likewise the clause, πᾶς γὰρ ὁ ὄχλος ἐξεπλήσσετο ἐπὶ τῇ διδαχῇ αὐτοῦ, is almost identical to 1:22, but with the only change being the explicit or definite subject.

Jesus' word (teaching) and action (driving out people) in the temple provoked reactions both on the religious authorities and on the people. This is because through Jesus' action (vv.15-16) and teaching (v.17) he condemned, not only the buyers and sellers in the temple, but also the religious leaders, who allowed God's house to be profaned. When the chief priests and scribes heard it, they sought a way to destroy Jesus, «for they were afraid of him» (ἐφοβοῦντο γὰρ αὐτόν, v.18)[56]. «The prompting of the plot by fear of him confirms the strength of his exercise of authority»[57]. The second γὰρ-clause giving the reason for the leaders' fear, says, «because all the multitude were astonished at his teaching», v.18. Apart from what the religious authorities have heard, the crowd's

---

[54] R.H. GUNDRY, *Mark*, 291.

[55] Cf. T. DWYER, *Motif of Wonder*, 164.

[56] T. DWYER, *Motif of Wonder*, 165, observes that just as the holiness of John made Herod afraid (6:20), so the authority of Jesus made the leaders afraid.

[57] R.H. GUNDRY, *Mark*, 640-641.

astonishment heightens their fear. In fact, «it also prepares for the hierarchs' fear of the crowd themselves — because of the crowd's being in awe and support of Jesus (11:32; 12:12, 37; 14:1-2)»[58].

The crowd's astonishment attracts our attention. Just as those in the synagogue at Galilee were struck with wonder at Jesus' authoritative teaching (with the authority manifesting itself in the exorcism), so those in the temple in Jerusalem are also awe-struck at the (authoritative) teaching (manifesting itself in Jesus' taking authority over the temple)[59]. However, «the infelicity of stringing together two γάρ-clauses in succession and the parallelism further created by the imperfect tense in both ἐφοβοῦντο and ἐξεπλήσσετο, put great weight on his (Jesus') power over both the hierarchs and the crowd»[60]. This brings us to Mark's main point: that the awe-inspiring power of Jesus' teaching, backed up by his strong actions, strikes fear even in the hearts of the religious leaders, and astonishment on the crowd.

From the foregoing, we have demonstrated that the people's astonishment at Jesus' authoritative teaching is not unique to the Capernaum scene (1:22,27), but also verifiable in other parts of the Gospel, both in the synagogues of Galilee and in the temple in Jerusalem (6:2; 11:18, cf. 1:39; 3:1-6; 12:37). It is most striking that the same awe-inspiring expression verb, ἐκπλήσσομαι, was used for the three scenes of Jesus' teaching (1:22; 6:2; 11:18). It is then no surprise that Jesus' teaching could provoke fear or astonishment in different people, both related to the motif of wonder.

2.2 *The People's Reaction to Jesus' Exorcism/Healing*

The people's reaction to Jesus' ministry is not limited to his teaching. This is because Jesus acted in word and deed: Jesus taught and also performed many miracles. Among Jesus' miracles, we notice the people's reactions more often to Jesus' exorcisms and healings. We shall examine some of them now.

---

[58] R.H. GUNDRY, *Mark*, 641.

[59] Cf. T. DWYER, *Motif of Wonder*, 165-166; V. TAYLOR, *Mark*, 465. R.H. GUNDRY, *Mark*, 641, notes that by attaching «all» to the «crowd» and putting the phrase (πᾶς γὰρ ὁ ὄχλος) before the verb, Mark displays the effect of Jesus' didactic authority at its highest power (so also 2:13; 4:1; 9:15).

[60] R.H. GUNDRY, *Mark*, 641. This double expression of wonder in «fear», on the one hand, and «amazement/astonishment» on the other hand, featured also in 10:32 (ἐθαμβοῦντο, ἐφοβοῦντο), both in imperfect tense.

2.2.1 In the Synagogue (1:27)

The people's reaction of astonishment in v.27 was both for Jesus' teaching and his exorcism in the synagogue of Capernaum. This is shown through the ascensive καί («even»), which joins exorcism to the «new teaching with authority». Thus here also the people's wonder at Jesus' exorcism/healing began. We have now to verify other texts that exhibit this phenomenon in the gospel.

2.2.2 In the House (2:12)

Jesus returned to Capernaum unnoticed, but when the people heard he was at home, they gathered together, and he began to teach them (2:1-2). While Jesus was in the house teaching, they brought him a paralytic, whom he first of all forgave his sins (vv.3-5). This Jesus' act stirred up reaction from the scribes, who accused him of blasphemying (vv.6-7). Jesus perceived their reaction in his spirit, and asked them why such a question should be in their hearts (vv.8-9). Jesus then demonstrated to them that «the Son of Man has authority on earth to forgive sins» (v.10). Then Jesus said to the paralytic: «Rise, take up your pallet and go home» (v.11). The ex-paralytic immediately rose, took up his ballet and went out before all of them; so that they were all amazed and glorified God (v.12). Therefore, in this pericope (2:1-12), we want to examine the motif of wonder, as it relates to the people's reaction to Jesus' word and deed.

There is a close connection between 1:21-28 and 2:1-12, especially in the integration of Jesus' word and deed; likewise in Jesus' exercise of his divine authority. These realities are so evident in both pericopes. While on the one hand, the word (teaching, forgiveness of sins) are invisible; on the other hand, the deed (exorcism, healing) are visible and concrete. Just as Jesus' exercise of his ἐξουσία both in his teaching and exorcism caused the people in the synagogue to wonder (ἐξεπλήσσοντο, ἐθαμβήθησαν, 1:22,27), so also his exercise of it in forgiveness of sins and healing will cause them to be amazed (ὥστε ἐξίστασθαι)[61] and even to glorify God in 2:12.

Jesus' authoritative command and its immediate fulfillment struck those present (eye-witnesses) with amazement (vv.11-12), because this healing

---

[61] The verb, ἐξίστημι, could mean «being outside oneself» or of «being amazed or astonished». Of being amazed, this verb occurs 3x in Mk (Mt 1x; Lk 2x): 2:12; 5:42; 6:51; while the former meaning is only in Mk 3:21. Cf. J. LAMBRECHT, «ἐξίστημι», 7.

happen before them all (ἔμπροσθεν πάντων). Therefore the people's reaction was a as result of Jesus' authority in word and deed (cf. ὥστε ἐξίστασθαι πάντας)[62]. The people are amazed at *both* the healing and the forgiveness: «the healing of the paralytic, like exorcism of 1:23-28 vouches for the unprecedented "authority" which is claimed in the accompanying pronouncement»[63]. Thus, «the onlookers are all (πάντας) amazed, and since this interesting usage occurs (in contrast to the possible ὁ ὄχλος), it may well be that πάντας includes even the scribes»[64]. In fact, Mark does not limit amazement to only those sympathetic to Jesus in the rest of the gospel[65]. The people's reaction of wonder was expressed in doxology, so «the exclamation of the crowd gives voice to the uniqueness of the event: "We have never seen anything like this" (2:12)»[66]. Hence, all those who were present, thoroughly shaken by this extraordinary event, were amazed and glorified God, whose Son, Jesus has demonstrated his divine authority on earth as the Son of Man, by concretizing his word of forgiveness in healing the paralytic.

2.2.3 In the Country of the Gerasenes (5:15,20)

The people's next reaction of wonder is within the context of the pericope of exorcism (5:1-20). We meet again the double expressions of

---

[62] Cf. R.H. GUNDRY, *Mark*, 120, notes that, for ὥστε, «so that» as a Marcan introduction to the effect of Jesus' words and deeds, see 1:27,45; 2:2,12; 3:10,20; 4:1; 15:5.

[63] R.J. DILLON, «As One Having Authority», 104; Cf. W. WEISS, *Eine neue Lehre*, 141-142.

[64] T. DWYER, *Motif of Wonder*, 103; R.H. GUNDRY, *Mark*, 115; W.L. LANE, *Mark*, 99. J.A. KLEIST,*Mark*, 146, argues that that «all» gave glory to God, we need not infer that even the scribes who were present joined in the chorus of praise. But I agree with R.H. GUNDRY, *Mark*, 120, that since Jesus has addressed his questions and his authenticating miracle to the scribes in this passage (see vv.8a,10a), the scribes should be the last ones excluded. In fact, the doubling of «all» in v.12 favours their inclusion with everybody else.

[65] Cf. T. DWYER, *Motif of Wonder*, 103, n.50, observes that, it is an interesting feature of Mark that even opponents of Jesus can be amazed, as 12:17 and 15:5 show.

[66] J.R. EDWARDS, «Authority of Jesus», 223; R.H. GUNDRY, *Mark*, 115; W.L. LANE, *Mark*, 99. T. DWYER, *Motif of Wonder*, 100, observes that this is the only place in Mark where a doxology is joined with a reaction of amazement, and in fact the only place in the gospel where a doxology occurs (however note 7:37, an acclamation rather than a doxology).

wonder (ἐφοβήθησαν, ἐθαύμαζον, vv.15,20)[67]. There are common elements (including amazement) in this pericope (5:1-20) with our pericope (1:21-28)[68]. The people's motif of wonder took place after the exorcism. As a matter of fact, this exorcism took place in the Gentile territory. Here Jesus meets a man with an unclean spirit (named Legion, cf. v.9), which made his condition humanly uncontrollable (cf. vv.3-5). But when confronted by Jesus, the unclean spirits submitted to Jesus' superior power, as the Son of the Most High God (vv.6-7), and pleaded for their security (v.10), and they left the man and ended dramatically through the pigs around, who were drowned in the sea with them (vv.11-13). This event alarmed the herdsmen to flee, and they went into the city and in the country to tell their story (v.14). Indeed, «the fleeing of the herdsmen shows them awestruck at the display of Jesus' power»[69].

When the people heard the story of the herdsmen, they came to see what (τί) had happened (v.14b). So they came to Jesus, and saw the demoniac, the man who had had the legion, sitting there, clothed and in his right mind; and they were afraid (ἐφοβήθησαν, v.15). «The doubling of coming and seeing, the switch to the historical present tense, and the escalation from an infinitive to another main verb emphasize the awe-inspiring presence of Jesus and the saving effects of the exorcism he has performed»[70]. In fact, the saving effects of Jesus' exorcism are: the ex-demoniac's *sitting*, his *being clothed*, and his *sanity*, all contrast with his previous condition (cf. vv.3-5)[71]. The people, observing closely this contrast in the man through Jesus' healing, were afraid (ἐφοβηαθη-σαν)[72]. This means that the people were standing in reverential awe of

---

[67] The double expressions where φοβέομαι combine with another verb of wonder, are 5:15,20; 10:32; 11:18; but for others, see T. DWYER, *Motif of Wonder*, 21.

[68] These were mentioned while we analyzed this pericope (5:1-20, cf. Chapter VI, sec. 2.3, n.241), with regard to exocism. However one can still refer to T. DWYER, *Motif of Wonder*, 112.

[69] R.H. GUNDRY, *Mark*, 253.

[70] R.H. GUNDRY, *Mark*, 253.

[71] Cf. T. DWYER, *Motif of Wonder*, 114; R.H. GUNDRY, *Mark*, 253; C.E.B. CRANFIELD, *Mark*, 180. W.L. LANE, *Mark*, 187, puts these contrasts so: «The man whom neither chains nor men could restrain was sitting in a docile manner before Jesus; he who had terrified others as he ran naked among the tombs was now clothed; the one who had shrieked wildly and behaved violently was now fully recovered. So radical was the transformation that the townspeople were stunned and frightened».

[72] The verb, φοβέομαι, meaning among others «to be afraid», «become frightened»

Jesus, as his disciples did at 4:41[73]. Thus, in Jesus, God has brought a man under the dominion of evil back into society, and this is frightening to the locals[74]. But when the eyewitnesses told the people how (πῶς) it happened: what happened to the demoniac and to the pigs (v.16); they became afraid and requested Jesus to leave their town (v.17). Hence the people's reverential awe turned into fear, because of Jesus' supernatural powers[75].

When Jesus refused the ex-demoniac to be with him, he told him, «Go home to your friends, and tell them how much the Lord has done for you, and how he has had mercy on you», v.19[76]. But as the man proclaimed in the Decapolis how much Jesus had done for him; all men marvelled (v.20)[77]. This means that the healed man went beyond his home, and even region (Gerasenes) to reach the Decapolis. «This expansion serves Mark's purpose of showing the powerful effect of Jesus' action»[78]. So «all» marvelled (ἐθαύμαζον)[79] at Jesus' word and action. Hence, in 5:1-20 neither reaction of wonder by the people is directed at exorcism itself: one is the response to the power released in restoring the man (v.15), and the other responds to the testimony of the man (v.20)[80].

---

occurs 95x in NT. In the Gospels the motif of fear in the presence of an epiphany carries particular theological weight. In Mark it occurs about 12x (Mt 18x; Lk 23x; Jn 5x): 4:41; 5:15,33,36; 6:20,50; 9:32; 10:32; 11:18,32; 12:12; 16:8). Cf. H. BALZ, «φοβέομαι», 429-430; T. DWYER, *Motif of Wonder*, 113. We must remark that this is the first time φοβέομαι is associated with the people.

[73] Cf. R.H. GUNDRY, *Mark*, 253; R.A. GUELICH, *Mark*, 284; R. PESCH, *Markusevangelium* I, 292; V. TAYLOR, *Mark*, 284, affirms that the fear mentioned is awe in the presence of the supernatural.

[74] Cf. T. DWYER, *Motif of Wonder*, 114.

[75] Cf. R.A. GUELICH, *Mark*, 284, agrees that what may initially have been «awe» (5:15) turned to «fear» of what Jesus might do next.

[76] C.S. MANN, *Mark*, 280, observes that the injunction to spread the story contrasts strongly with the opposite injunctions in 1:25,44; 3:12; 5:43; and 7:36. Perhaps the best explanation is that this was outside of Galilean territory.

[77] Cf. R. PESCH, *Markusevangelium* I, 294, notes that the doubling of the expression v.19e (ὅσα ὁ κύριός σοι πεποίηκεν) and v.20b (ὅσα ἐποίησεν αὐτῷ ὁ Ἰησοῦς) means that in Jesus' deed, God's act, his mercy takes place.

[78] R.H. GUNDRY, *Mark*, 255.

[79] The verb θαυμάζω occurs 4x in Mark (5:20; 6:6; 15:4,44), all for reactions of wonder. Here alone in Mk it is combined with a form of πᾶς; but Mk uses πᾶς with amazement elsewhere in 2:12; 9:15 and 11:18. Cf. T. DWYER, *Motif of Wonder*, 115.

[80] Cf. T. DWYER, *Motif of Wonder*, 115.

2.2.4 Beside the Sea of Galilee (7:37)

In the pericope, 7:31-37, we observe another people's reaction of wonder: here it concerns Jesus' healing of the deaf and dumb man within the region of the Decapolis[81]. This pericope (7:31-37) is similar to the healing of the blind man at Bethsaida (8:22-26)[82], but only here is it concluded with the amazement of the people. Jesus' healing of the deaf and dumb man in this region of Decapolis, caused an intense reaction of the people, that «nowhere, even in Mark, is so great astonishment depicted»[83]. In fact, this is the only place in Mark where ἐκπλήσσομαι is used with a miracle or healing (cf. 1:22; 6:2; 10:26 and 11:18 - all relate to Jesus' teaching). We shall now examine how the people reacted to this Jesus' healing activity.

People brought to Jesus a man who was deaf and had an impediment in his speech (dumb), and besought him to lay hands on him (v.32). Jesus took him aside from the crowd, put his finger into his ears, and spat and touched his tongue (v.33). With his divine sigh, he said to him, «Be opened!» - ἐφφαθα = διανοίχθητι; and his ears were opened, his tongue released, and he spoke plainly (vv.34-35). Jesus charged them to tell no one, but they were overwehlemed that they zealously proclaimed it the more. They were astonished beyond measure, that they expressed their amazement in acclamation and praise of God (vv.36-37). It is this astonishment that attracts more our attention here.

The first reaction of the people (v.36) was the zealous proclamation of Jesus' action of healing. Jesus' deed cannot remain concealed, but must be made known, and is effusively proclaimed[84]. The second reaction of the people (ἐξεπλήσσοντο, v.37) is quite intense. The preceding adverb, ὑπερπερισσῶς («beyond all measure») is found only here in Greek

---

[81] R.H. GUNDRY, *Mark*, 383, observes that the proclamation of the ex-demoniac in Decapolis (5:20) prepared for Jesus' further ministry in this region. Cf. T. DWYER, *Motif of Wonder*, 135; R.A. GUELICH, *Mark*, 286; 397.

[82] Cf. T. DWYER, *Motif of Wonder*, 135; C.E.B. CRANFIELD, *Mark*, 253-254, also noted that both pericopes are absent in Mt and Lk. The common features in both pericopes (7:31-37; 8:22-26) are: touching the sick requested (7:32; 8:22); the sick taken apart (7:33; 8:23); spitting into the sick part (7:33; 8:24); placing hand on the sick (7:33; 8:23); and forbidding to let others know (7:36; 8:26).

[83] V. TAYLOR, *Mark*, 356.

[84] Cf. R. PESCH, *Markusevangelium* I, 398; R.A. GUELICH, *Mark*, 397; V. TAYLOR, *Mark*, 355.

literature[85]. Mark is, indeed, interested in the stupendousness of the miracle, which caused the crowd to proclaim the miracle «all the more» (μᾶλλον περισσότερον). But the emphasis on the stupendousness of the miracle reaches a climax in the crowd's second reaction: «And they were extremely abundantly astonished, saying, "He has done all things well; he even makes the deaf hear and the dumb speak"» (v.37)[86].

The acclamation of the crowd, «He has done all things well» echoes the words of Gen 1:31 (cf. Sir 39:16) regarding God's work at creation[87]. Likewise the reference to the healing of the deaf to hear and the dumb to speak, reminds us of the work of the Messiah in the delivery of Israel (cf. Is. 35:5f). Thus, in their excitement the people generalized the healing, or perhaps they were referring to what Jesus had done previously[88]. However, this Gentile crowd's wonder that led to acclamation is a positive response, a believing response[89], unlike that which led to offence (cf. 6:2). Therefore, just as the people were greatly astonished at Jesus' teaching (word), so also they were in his miracles, especially his exorcism and healing activity (deed).

2.3 *The People's Reaction to Jesus Himself*

The first part of the Gospel was characterized mainly by Jesus' authoritative teaching and miracles, but the second part focused mainly on Jesus' passion, death and resurrection. In other words, one should not be surprised if the amazement of the people here focuses on the person of Jesus, who is about to fulfill his redemptive mission in Jerusalem. The two cases we shall examine (9:15; 10:32), coincidentally took place on their way to Jerusalem.

---

[85] Cf. T. DWYER, *Motif of Wonder*, 136.

[86] Cf. R.H. GUNDRY, *Mark*, 385, also noticed that nearly everything in this verse is emphatic: (a) the forward position and strong meaning of ὑπερπερισσῶς; (b) the strong meaning and imperfect tense of ἐξεπλήσσοντο; (c) the first position of καλῶς; (d) the universal plural of πάντα; (e) the placement of πάντα before the verb πεποίηκεν; (f) the perfect tense of πεποίηκεν, (cf. 5:19); (g) the present tense of ποιεῖ; (h) the advancing of τοὺς κωφούς away from its infinitive ἀκούειν; (i) the plural of τοὺς κωφούς, τοὺς ἀλάλους; and (j) the cognatic assonance and wordplay of ἀλάλους λαλεῖν.

[87] Cf. R.A. GUELICH, *Mark*, 397; R. PESCH, *Markusevangelium* I, 398.

[88] Cf. W.L. LANE, *Mark*, 268; R. PESCH, *Markusevangelium* I, 398.

[89] Cf. T. DWYER, *Motif of Wonder*, 137; W.L. LANE, *Mark*, 268, calls it «the response of faith»; while W. GRUNDMANN, *Markus*, 202, adds that the praise was from deep amazement and full of belief.

2.3.1 Down the Mountain (9:15)

The people's reaction of wonder occurred also in this pericope (9:14-29), which deals with exorcism of a boy possessed by an unclean spirit. But the astonishment of the people occurs surprisingly at the beginning and not the end of the exorcism. This is the first time in Mark we meet this rare and intensive verb ἐκθαμβέομαι (cf. 14:33; 16:5,6), which is not used outside Mk in the NT[90]. Here the wonder verb is linked with sight (ἰδόντες, 9:15, cf. 16:5). Since we have treated this pericope in exorcism, we shall now concentrate on the people's reaction of great amazement.

When Jesus came down with his three disciples, he met a great crowd, who were distracted by the scribes arguing with the disciples. And immediately all the crowd saw Jesus, they were greatly amazed (ἐξεθαμβήθησαν), and ran up to him and greeted him (v.14-15). The difficulty here is the reason why the people were overwhelmingly and utterly amazed at seeing Jesus. There are different opinions to interpret the people's wonder, among which are: as a result of the effect of the transfiguration[91]; because of Jesus' unexpected and opportune appearance[92]; due to Jesus' arrival in the nick of time[93]; or simply the presence of Jesus himself that provokes astonishment[94]. To take a position on this matter, we shall consider the context of this episode, because «the immediacy (εὐθύς) of the crowd's extreme awe, the inclusion of "all" of them — large crowd though they are — and the placement of "all the crowd" before both the circumstantial participial phrase and the verb emphasize the impact which the sight of Jesus makes on the crowd»[95].

---

[90] Cf. T. DWYER, *Motif of Wonder*, 147. The simplex of this verb, θαμβέομαι, we have already seen in 1:27; 10:24,32. The preposition ἐκ has the function of intensification, so that the verb has the meaning here of «utterly astounded». Cf. *Ibid.*, 148.

[91] Cf. R.H. GUNDRY, *Mark*, 487-488; M.D. HOOKER, *St. Mark*, 222-223.

[92] Cf. V. TAYLOR, *Mark*, 396; C.E.B. CRANFIELD, *Mark*, 300; C.S. MANN, *Mark*, 370.

[93] Cf. B.H. BRANSCOMB, *Mark*, 166.

[94] Cf. T. DWYER, *Motif of Wonder*, 147, 149; J. GNILKA, *Markus* II, 46; W.L. LANE, *Mark*, 330; K. TAGAWA, *Miracles et Evangile*, 107; G. BERTRAM,«θαμβέω», 6.

[95] R.H. GUNDRY, *Mark*, 488. T. DWYER, *Motif of Wonder*, 148, adds that the emphasis here, as with 2:12, is that «all» including, one assumes, the scribes mentioned in v.14, are utterly astonished at the appearance of Jesus. The crowd's running and greeting Jesus emphasizes further the impact of Jesus' presence on the crowd. (cf.

In the first part of the Gospel, God intervened through Jesus' authoritative word and deed, especially in teaching, miracles, exorcism and healing, and this provoked the people's reaction of wonder. But in the second part, which Jesus introduced by foretelling his passion, death and resurrection (cf. 8:31), no miracles have yet featured. In fact, the two last miracles in this section are still to come (9:19-27 [exorcism]; 10:46-52 [healing]). Therefore, the people's amazement is not caused by miracles, because here wonder is at the beginning instead of the end of Jesus' exorcism. However, Jesus' forthcoming passion (which is emphasized in 8:31-9:1; 9:7; 9:9-13) puts his ministry in a different light[96]. With few miracles, reduced contact with the people, the demand to follow him with one's cross (cf. 8:34-38), Jesus' determined purpose on his way to the cross, the people began to evaluate the person of Jesus. Hence, in my opinion the most likely reason is that which concerns the person of Jesus himself, whose momentary absence has heightened the people's desire for him, and whose presence now provokes the great amazement among the people.

2.3.2 On the Road (10:32)

The next appearance of the people's wonder occurred in the pericope (10:32-34), where Jesus foretells for the third time his death and resurrection. Just before Jesus' announcement to the Twelve of his forthcoming passion, it was reported that «they (Jesus and his disciples, vv.23,24) were on the road, going up to Jerusalem, and Jesus was walking ahead of them; they (the disciples) were amazed (ἐθαμβοῦντο), and those who followed (the crowd) were afraid (ἐφοβοῦντο)», v.32a[97]. On the basis that there were two groups, and that the amazement is attributed to the disciples, while fear (being afraid) to those following Jesus (the crowd), as stated earlier, then we take our position here. In fact, «Amazement, astonishment, and fear are not unknown by — and not inappropriate for — the followers of Jesus, whether these followers are disciples or the crowd»[98]. Thus, the people's reaction to Jesus here is fear or awe. Our concern then will be limited to this people's reaction.

GUNDRY, *ibid.*)

[96] Cf. T. DWYER, *Motif of Wonder*, 149.

[97] Cf. sec. 1.2.2, n.26.

[98] E.S. MALBON, «Markan Characters», 116.

In a periphrastic construction, ἦν προάγων αὐτοὺς ὁ 'Ιησοῦς, we are told that «Jesus was walking (going) ahead of them (the disciples)». In Mark προάγειν occurs 5x (Mt 6x; Lk 1x), of which 3x belongs to Jesus (10:32; 14:28; 16:7)[99]. This movement of Jesus aroused amazement in the disciples and fear in the crowd. In Mark the word, φοβέομαι, is almost exclusively used by him for the human reaction to supernatural event[100]. In fact, here ἐφοβοῦντο is used absolutely[101]. The fear of those following Jesus is not directed to a determined or fixed object, but it is really the fact, that Jesus goes to Jerusalem, and the resolute manner in which he does it, provokes amazement and fear respectively[102]. Thus, «the ignorance out of which grow amazement and fear highlights Jesus' supernatural knowledge and determined confrontation of the fate awaiting him in Jerusalem»[103].

However, the person of Jesus is central in this little scene in v.32a. What awakens amazement in the disciples and fear in those who follow is not the way to Jerusalem, nor an awareness of what will be accomplished there, but Jesus himself[104]. Thus, the power of the Lord, who holds his own and their fate in his hands, is manifested for the Evangelist and his readers in the awe and dread which characterize the attitude of those around him[105]. We must also note that the people were not privileged to hear Jesus' third foretelling of his death and resurrection that could cause fear (cf. 9:32, especially for the disciples), but this came later (cf. vv.32b-34). Hence, the people's reaction of fear concerns Jesus himself and the resolute and determined manner, in which he confronts his divine mission.

---

[99] K. STOCK, *Boten*, 131, observes that the going ahead of Jesus in 10:32 is the counterpart of 14:28; 16:7: now Jesus will go ahead of them from Galilee to Jerusalem, then he will go ahead of them from Jerusalem to Galilee. Only in Mark is this counter-movement emphasized.

[100] K. STOCK, *Boten*, 132.

[101] This is the second time φοβέομαι is attributed to the crowd (people). The first was in 5:15, where they came to Jesus and saw the ex-demoniac sitting there, clothed and in his right mind; and they were afraid. The fear then is fixed on what they saw, but here it is not stated, thus the verb is used absolutely.

[102] Cf. K. STOCK, *Boten*, 132.

[103] R.H. GUNDRY, *Mark*, 571.

[104] Cf. W.L. LANE, *Mark*, 374; G. BERTRAM, «θαμβέω», 6.

[105] Cf. G. BERTRAM, «θαμβέω», 6; W.L. LANE, *Mark*, 374; K. TAGAWA, *Miracles*, 108-110; E. LOHMEYER, *Markus*, 220.

2.4 *Summary*

Jesus had a good rapport with the people (crowd) throughout his public ministry, except towards the end when the Religious Leaders prejudiced their minds against Jesus: They were always coming or gathering around Jesus to witness the power and authority of his word and deed. They are also moved with wonder when these events are beyond their expectations. This reaction of wonder, as we have shown, began in our pericope (1:21-28, esp. vv.22,27), and continued throughout the Gospel. There were other characters in the gospel who reacted with wonder, for instance, Jesus himself (6:6; 14:33); the disciples (4:41; 6:50,51; 9:6,32; 10:24, 32); the religious leaders (11:18,32; 12:12,17); the women at the tomb (16:5,6,8); Pilate (15:5,44); Herod (6:20); the woman with flowing blood (5:33). In spite of all these reactions, the people's reaction to Jesus' word and deed remains the dominant motif in the entire gospel. Is it not surprising to note, that among many miracles, which Jesus performed only *Exorcism/Healing*, and *Teaching*, which featured in our pericope as the object of the people's reaction of wonder (1:22,27), were the same phenomena that attracted the crowd's wonder throughout the Gospel? Why did we not notice amazement even in (nature) miracles like the multiplication of bread (6:35-44; 8:1-9)? Therefore, we are encouraged to say, from our proof, that the people's reaction of wonder is a dominant motif, and has a programmatic character for the Gospel. Hence this will help us to prove the function of our pericope in Mark's Gospel.

3. The Scribes' Contrast with Jesus

In studying Jesus' relation with the characters in the text, we have seen that Jesus was always in the company of his disciples, likewise the people (crowd) were attracted to Jesus by their response of wonder; now we want to examine Jesus' relation with the scribes, which is contrast. This contrast with the scribes, nay, with the religious leaders, was first discovered in Part I, when we analysized 1:22. We also observed in that analysis that the issue of authority underlied every controversy or conflict between Jesus and the scribes. It will be our task to investigate whether this contrast between Jesus and the scribes is unique to our pericope, or it can be verified in other parts of the Gospel.

The scribes as characters were active in Mark, so their contrast with Jesus opened the way to Jesus' conflict with other members of the Jewish religious authorities. Thus, the scribes, who are more often mentioned than the other religious groups, were almost always linked with these groups in their conflicts or contrasts with Jesus[106]. The scribes linked with Pharisees, together they see and ask about Jesus' disciples' eating «with hands defiled, that is, unwashed», (7:1-2,5). On the other hand, «the actions of the two-part subgroup (chief priests and scribes) do not differ significantly from the actions of the tripartite group (chief priests, scribes, and elders)»[107]. Jesus predicted he would be handed over to the chief priests and scribes (10:33); they seek to destroy him out of fear because of the astonishment of the crowd at his teaching (11:18); seek to arrest him by stealth and kill him (14:1); and mock him as he hangs on the cross (15:31). While Jesus also predicted he would be rejected by the chief priests, scribes and elders (8:31); they question him about his authority (11:27); send a crowd with swords and clubs to arrest him (14:43); assemble to examine him (14:53); and hold a consultation and bind him over to Pilate (15:1). Thus, in these conflicts or controversies, the scribes and Pharisees raise religious objections based on their interpretation of scripture and tradition; while the chief priests, scribes, and elders raise also what must be called political objections based on their struggle with Jesus for authority and influence over the people[108].

Jesus' contrast with the religious authorities, be it with only the scribes, or with the scribes linked with other groups, as we saw above, continues beyond our pericope. But we shall in our investigation limit ourselves to where the scribes were *alone*, since they were alone in our pericope. Thus, we shall try to verify whether this phenomenon of Jesus' contrast with the scribes is a dominant theme in the gospel. Hence we shall examine such texts as: 1:22; 2:6,16; 3:22; 9:11,14; 12:28,32,35,38, which will reflect, (a) on Teaching, (b) on Exorcism, and (c) on Forgiveness of Sins.

---

[106] In Mark's Gospel, these religious groups occur as follows: scribes, 21x; Pharisees, 12x; chief priests, 14x; and elders, 5x. However, the scribes are alone in 1:22; 2:6; 3:22; 9:11,14; 12:28,32,35,38; linked with the Pharisees (2:16; 7:1,5), with the chief priests (10:33; 11:18; 14:1; 15:31), and with the elders and chief priests (8:31; 11:27; 14:43,53; 15:1). For the scribes' link with the Pharisees, and with the chief priests and elders, see: J.D. KINGSBURY, «The Religious Authorities», 44-45, 46; E.S. MALBON, «Jewish Leaders», 265, 266, 267, 268, 271; D. LÜHRMANN, «Die Pharisäer und die Schriftgelehrten, 171-172.

[107] E.S. MALBON, «Jewish Leaders», 268.

[108] Cf. E.S. MALBON, «Jewish Leaders», 266-267; J.D. KINGSBURY, «Religious Authorities», 46; D. LÜHRMANN, «Die Pharisäer und die Schriftgelehrten», 181-185.

3.1 *On Teaching*

The contrast between Jesus and the scribes is most evident in teaching. In fact, the *tertium comparationis* (medium of comparison) between Jesus and the scribes is teaching[109]. We shall therefore examine briefly how the scribes' teaching contrasts with that of Jesus.

3.1.1 Jesus' Authority (1:22)

The scribes were referred to in our pericope by the narrator, even before they actually appeared on the scene. This reference was negatively presented. In fact, the only negative particle, οὐκ, in the pericope (1:21-28) refers to the scribes, who never functioned in the scene, which makes their appearance very curious. The reason for the astonishment of the people at Jesus' teaching, was because «he taught them as one having authority, and not as the scribes» (1:22). One can then observe that the basis of comparison between Jesus and the scribes is teaching, while the contrast is authority. Thus, «in characterizing Jesus in 1:22 as authoritative in contrast to the religious authorities (scribes) who are without authority, Mark identifies "authority" as the issue lying at the root of Jesus' conflict with the authorities»[110]. In other words, in featuring the scribes' teaching as betraying a lack of authority, Mark shows that only the contrast as such between authority and lack thereof interests him as a means of exalting the figure of Jesus[111]. Hence 1:22 x-rays three important elements or motifs, which will help us in our investigation on the relation between Jesus and the scribes, that is: «teaching», «authority», and «contrast». We shall now verify this phenomenon of contrast in the other parts of the gospel.

3.1.2 The Coming of Elijah (9:11)

We have seen the contrast between Jesus' and the scribes' teaching in *how* or the manner of doing so (cf. 1:22: with authority), but in 9:11 we

---

[109] Cf. R.J. DILLON, «As One having Authority», 103; J.D. KINGSBURY, «Religious Authorities», 46, adds that Mark presented the scribes, like Jesus, as typically teaching the people.

[110] J.D. KINGSBURY, «Religious Authorities», 52-53. On authority as the issue underlying every controversy or conflict Jesus had with the religious authorities, see, *ibid.*, 46-47, 51, 54, 59, 60; also KINGSBURY, *Conflict in Mark*, 66-67, 86; R.J. DILLON, «As one having Authority», 102, 103; D. LÜHRMANN, «Die Pharisäer und die Schriftgelehrten», 182; P. GUILLEMETTE, «Un enseignement nouveau», 239-240.

[111] Cf. R.H. GUNDRY, *Mark*, 74.

shall see the contrast in *what* the scribes teach[112]. Here the three disciples ask Jesus a question about Elijah's coming based on the scribes' teaching. We shall examine this scribal teaching within the context of the Transfiguration and its consequence (cf. 9:2-9, 10-13). As Jesus took the initiative to go up to the mountain with his three disciples, so also he came down with them, initiating a discussion, which raised their question to him. So we shall discuss the contrast between the scribes' and Jesus' teaching, by briefly examining Jesus' charge to his disciples (v.9), the disciples' reaction (vv.10-11), and Jesus' response (vv.12-13).

Jesus «charged them to tell no one what they had seen, until the Son of Man should have risen from the dead» (v.9)[113]. And this is the only instance in the Gospel where Jesus sets a limit to the silence enjoined (9:9, cf. 8:30; also 5:43; 7:36)[114]. The reaction of the disciples (vv.10-11) is linked to the preceding saying of Jesus in v.9: «so they kept the saying in mind, questioning among themselves, what the rising from the dead meant» (v.10)[115]. In spite of the transfiguration revelation, the death and resurrection of the Son of Man remains for the disciples something unexpected and incomprehensible (cf. 8:32f; 9:5f.,30,32)[116]. Then they asked Jesus the question, «why do the scribes say that Elijah must come first?» (v.11). This question regarding the coming of Elijah arises from his presence in the story of the Transfiguration[117].

---

[112] Cf. E.S. MALBON, «Jewish Leaders», 264.

[113] The content of «what they had seen», ἃ εἶδον, should be the vision (9:2b-4) and the revelation (9:7), which the three disciples have become eye-witnesses.

[114] Cf. W.L. LANE, *Mark*, 323.

[115] The problem here is whether πρὸς ἑαυτοὺς can be taken with ἐκράτησαν (with the meaning «they kept the matter to themselves») or with συζητοῦντες (meaning «they discussed or questioned among themselves, or one with another»). Many scholars favour the latter. Cf. M.D. HOOKER, *St. Mark*, 219; W.L. LANE, *Mark*, 322, n.25; C.E.B. CRANFIELD, *Mark*, 297; V. TAYLOR, *Mark*, 394. I also agree with the second option, that the disciples kept Jesus' saying and questioned among themselves what his saying meant, because συζητεῖν is linked with πρὸς ἑαυτοὺς in 1:27 (cf. Lk 22:23; Acts 9:29), and with πρὸς αὐτούς in 9:14,16; while κρατεῖν was never linked with these expressions.

[116] Cf. W.L. LANE, *Mark*, 323-324.

[117] Cf. V. TAYLOR, *Mark*, 394; C.E.B. CRANFIELD, *Mark*, 296. R.H. GUNDRY, *Mark*, 463, also notes that this question grows out of scribal teaching based on the statement in Mal 3:23-24 that God will send Elijah before the Day of the Lord, out of Jesus' recent mention of the scribes in his first prediction of the Passion and Resurrection (8:31), out of Elijah's appearance on the Mount of Transfiguration (cf.

In the teaching of the scribes, taken up by the disciples and based on Mal 3:23[118], it becomes manifest the order (πρῶτον) of the eschatological events and the fact that it is established by God (δεῖ). It is probable that this question actually masks the disciples' objection to Jesus' announcement of his suffering and death, for the restoration Elijah is to effect just prior to the end makes messianic suffering unnecessary. In fact, «the reference to scribal teaching sheds light on a polemic use of the biblical teaching concerning the return of Elijah before the day of the Lord to discredit the impression created by Jesus' authoritative word and deed»[119].

In Jesus' response to the disciples' question, he took up the scribal opinion, giving Malachi's prophecy his own deeper and fuller reason: Elijah must come first to restore all things[120]. «So Jesus affirms on the one hand indeed (μέν) that Elijah is going to effect a universal restoration, but denies on the other hand that this will take place before the passion of the Son of Man»[121]. To stress the denial he placed together the two scriptural tasks of both Elijah and the Son of Man: the coming of Elijah and the fate of the Son of Man (v.12)[122]. With ἀλλὰ λέγω ὑμῖν ... Ἡλίας ἐλήλυθεν («but I tell you that Elijah has come» (v.13a), Jesus contrasts his saying with that of the scribes: while the scribes say that Elijah must come (v.11), Jesus say that Elijah has come (v.13)[123]. Thus, while the scribes are still expecting the coming of Elijah, Jesus asserts that his coming is already verified (cf. v.13). In fact, Elijah has come, »and they did to him whatever they pleased, as it is written of him« (v.13b). Jesus in v.13

---

especially his having been mentioned first and chiefly in v.4), and out of the immediately foregoing mention of the Son of Man's resurrection from the dead (vv.9-10).

[118] In Mal 3:23-24 (LXX 3:22-23) we read, «Behold, I will send you Elijah, the prophet, before the day of the Lord comes, the great and terrible day. To turn the hearts of the fathers to their children, and the hearts of the children to their fathers, lest I come and strike the land with doom».

[119] W.L. LANE, *Mark*, 324-325.

[120] Cf. R.H. GUNDRY, *Mark*, 464.

[121] R.H. GUNDRY, *Mark*, 464.

[122] May be the disciples' intention is to eliminate the second (the fate of the Son of Man) through the first (the coming of Elijah). But Jesus requests that one should take into consideration both words of the scripture, and opposes an interpretation of the first that does not take account of the second.

[123] Cf. R.H. GUNDRY, *Mark*, 464-465; E.S. MALBON, «Jewish Leaders», 264-265. However, Elijah's having already come does not refer to his appearance on the Mount of Transfiguration.

affirms two facts, one next to the other (καὶ-καὶ): the coming of Elijah and the arbitrary manner in which he was treated, both in fulfilment of the scripture (καθὼς γέγραπται). The arbitrary treatment of Elijah implicitly identifies Elijah with John the Baptist[124]. Thus, what Jezebel failed to do in the OT (cf. 1 Kgs 19:2,10), Herodias has succeeded in doing to the second Elijah (John the Baptist, cf. Mk 6:14-29)[125]. Hence, in contrast to the scribal teaching of Elijah's yet to come, Jesus affirms that he has already come and also verifies this affirmation.

3.1.3 The Great Commandment (12:28,32)

Jesus' dialogue with a scribe is seen in this pericope (12:28-34), which is the first of a pair of pericopes dealing with scribes (cf. 12:35-37; 12:38-40). In our discussion on the contrast between Jesus and the scribes, we come to a peculiar case, an exception to the rule: here we meet a «friendly» scribe[126]. «This is surprising in view of the hostile attitude of the previous questioners; it is even more surprising when we remember the antagonism shown to Jesus by the scribes elsewhere in Mark»[127]. Thus, this pericope becomes an «oasis» in the midst of a desert of controversies. It will be our task, therefore, to highlight the peculiarity of this pericope, in view of our investigation on the contrast between Jesus' and the scribes' teaching.

One of the scribes came up and saw Jesus and the Sadducees disputing (cf. vv.18-27), and he was pleased with Jesus' answer, so he asked his

---

[124] Cf. V. TAYLOR, *Mark*, 395. The phrase, «and they did to him whatever they pleased (ὅσα ἤθελον)», probably refers to the fate of John the Baptist, since ἤθελον occurs several times in the story of John's martyrdom for the wishes of Herod, Herodias, and the Herodias' daughter (6:19,22,25,26). Cf. R.H. GUNDRY, *Mark*, 465.

[125] Cf. R.H. GUNDRY, *Mark*, 465; M.D. HOOKER, *St. Mark*, 221; W.L. LANE, *Mark*, 326; V. TAYLOR, *Mark*, 395. In addition Gundry observes that the scripturalness of Elijah's maltreatment parallels and supports John's maltreatment, which in turn parallels and supports the scripturalness of the Son of man's coming maltreatment (cf. *ibid.*).

[126] Cf. V. TAYLOR, *Mark*, 485. Unlike Mk, both Mt and Lk state specifically that the questioner's intention was to put Jesus to the test (cf. Mt 22:35; Lk 10:25).

[127] M.D. HOOKER, *St. Mark*, 286; Cf. J.D. KINGSBURY, «Religious Authorities», 48; K. STOCK, «Gliederung», 497. One observes that from the beginning to the end of the Gospel, except 12:28,32, the scribes are in contrast with Jesus, either alone or with other groups (cf. 1:22; 2:6,16; 3:22; 7:1,5; 8:31; 9:14; 10:33; 11:18,27; 12:35,38; 14:1,43,53; 15:1,31).

own question, «which commandment is the first of all?» (v.28)[128]. It is not clear whether the scribe's question is antagonistic, however, distinguishing it from the preceding controversies, there seem to be a «complete lack of animosity»[129].

In Jesus' response he cited Deut. 6:5, beginning with «Hear, O Israel»[130], and combined it with Lev. 19:18, and both express the love of God and the love of neighbour (vv.29-31). «For Jesus the whole Law is summarized in the will of God which calls for the love which is wholehearted response to God and to the neighbor»[131]. Nevertheless, «addition of the second commandment may also have the purpose of stressing that the scribe must not stop at thinking lovingly about God but must go on to act lovingly toward his neighbor»[132].

The scribe repeats affirmatively the response of Jesus and adds the comment that the observance of these two commandments is more valid than all holocausts and sacrifices (vv.32-33)[133]. Mark used the adverb καλῶς («well») to describe the scribe's impression of Jesus' answer to the Sadducees (v.28); here now the scribe himself uses the same adverb to describe Jesus' answer to his question (v.32)[134]. In fact, Jesus' prove of his didactic superiority again earned him the respectful address,

---

[128] K. STOCK, «Gliederung», 494, 495, notes that there is an immediate connection with the preceding discussion, in that the scribe was impressed by Jesus' answer to the Sadducees.

[129] Cf. J.D. KINGSBURY, «Religious Authorities», 47. Nevertheless, Kingsbury has earlier established that this pericope, in both form and position reveals itself to be a controversy (*Ibid.*). Likewise R.H. GUNDRY, *Mark*, 710, sees the scribe's approach to Jesus as antagonistic as that of the Pharisees or the Sadducees, since Mark used the same verb, ἐπερωτάω («ask, question»), to introduce the questions of both the Sadducees and the scribe (vv.18, 28, cf. 10:2); and moreover, with his question the scribe is daring to challenge Jesus antagonistically.

[130] W.L. LANE, *Mark*, 432, observes that Mark alone reports that Jesus introduced his answer with the opening words of the *Shema* (Deut 6:4). Cf. C.E.B. CRANFIELD, *Mark*, 377; V. TAYLOR, *Mark*, 486.

[131] W.L. LANE, *Mark*, 432; C.E.B. CRANFIELD, *Mark*, 378, notes that the scribe had asked which was the first commandment. Jesus adds a second, because he knows that these two are inseparable.

[132] R.H. GUNDRY, *Mark*, 711.

[133] The scribe has correctly affirmed the superiority of love of God and man over burnt-offerings and sacrifices. Cf. R.H. GUNDRY, *Mark*, 712; M.D. HOOKER, *St. Mark*, 289, W.L. LANE, *Mark*, 433; V. TAYLOR, *Mark*, 488.

[134] Cf. R.H. GUNDRY, *Mark*, 711.

διδάσκαλε («Teacher»), from the scribe (v.32, cf. v.28). It is really here in v.32 that the friendly attitude of the scribe is more clearly evident than in v.28.

Jesus says to this scribe to which reaction and response is expressly praised: «You are not far from the kingdom of God» (v.34). It seems that Jesus' saying refers to the scribe's response and not to his personal realization[135]. However, one can observe that this pericope is dominated by mutual agreement or approval between Jesus and this scribe[136]. Only after Jesus' encounter with the scribe does Mark signal the end of debate between Jesus and the religious authorities with the comment: «And after that no one dared to ask him any question» (v.34c)[137]. Since Jesus has passed every test, and the controversies ended (cf. 11:27-12:34), the initiative shifts back to him (cf. 11:1-19)[138]. Hence, Jesus has once more demonstrated the authority of his teaching, of which even one of his enemies' own expert — a scribe — has confessed its correctness and truth.

3.1.4 The Origin of the Christ (12:35)

In this pericope (12:35-37), we meet again *what* the scribes teach in 12:35 concerning Christ as the son of David. In fact, «"teaching" revives the contrast between Jesus' teaching with authority and the scribes' teaching without it (cf. 1:21-22)»[139]. Jesus' encounter with the scribe in the preceding pericope (12:28-34) was «friendly», but Jesus described him, as «not far from the kingdom of God». May be what the scribe lacked is developed in this pericope: that is, the right understanding of the Messiah. For the acceptance of Jesus' teaching and the right understand-

---

[135] Cf. K. STOCK, «Gliederung», 495-496.

[136] Cf. K. STOCK, «Gliederung», 495; M.D. HOOKER, *Mark*, 289; J.D. KINGSBURY, «Religious Authorities,» 47-48; ID., *Christology of Mark*, 109; D. LÜHRMANN, «Pharisäer und die Schriftgelehrten», 181.

[137] Cf. J.D. KINGSBURY, «Religious Authorities», 47; ID., *Conflict in Mark*, 82. While Mark concludes the phase of controversy here (12:34); Luke does so earlier (20:40), and Matthew later (22:46).

[138] Cf. R.H. GUNDRY, *Mark*, 712; K. STOCK, «Gliederung», 496-497; V. TAYLOR, *Mark*, 490.

[139] R.H. GUNDRY, *Mark*, 717. This pericope belongs to the teaching of Jesus, because during Jesus' activity in Jerusalem, the evangelist uses the verb, διδάσκειν, only in 11:17 and 12:35, and never used it for the controversies (cf. 11:27-12:34); likewise the crowd appears as Jesus' audience only in 11:18 and 12:37 (in 11:32; 12:12,41 it has another function).

ing of his person are necessary for the membership to the kingdom of God[140]. Thus, with the question about the Davidic sonship of the Messiah (Christ) in 12:35-37, the theme of the position of the person of Jesus enters once more in the forefront[141]. We shall verify here the contrasting views of Jesus and the scribes about the origin of the Messiah.

At the end of the debate between Jesus and the religious leaders, «no one dared to ask him any question» (cf. 12:34), so Jesus took up the initiative to pose his own question to the people (a great crowd, cf. v.37): «How can the scribes say that the Christ is the son of David?» (v.35, cf. 9:11-13). This question «presupposes not only general scribal agreement on this designation of the expected Christ, but also the lack of this designation in the OT. On the basis of this absence Jesus is challenging the scriptural accuracy of the scribal designation»[142]. However, Jesus cites Psalm 110:1, in which David himself emphasized the designation of the Christ as Lord (v.36). Then how can the Christ be his son? (v.37)[143]. Here the scribes stand exposed: «they pass for experts in Scripture, but their designation of the Christ does not even come from it»[144]. In other words, how is it possible for the Christ to be both the «son» of David and the «lord» of David? This question was not given a response. It remains open and suspended (cf. 4:41). In fact, these questions are calculated to provoke thoughtful reflection and decision[145]. Although, Jesus parabolically had already anticipated the answer to this question, that in his person the beloved son of the Lord of the vineyard came (12:6)[146]. Nevertheless,

---

[140] Cf. K. STOCK, «Gliederung», 508, 509. In 12:34-35, we meet a point of intersection which closes a section and opens another, at the same time, both are in many ways linked with each other, especially related to the kingdom of God. Here two themes related to the kingdom of God are treated: the person of Jesus and Jesus' mission (activity). Cf. STOCK, «Gliederung», 497, 508.

[141] Cf. K. STOCK, «Gliederung», 508.

[142] R.H. GUNDRY, Mark, 718; E.S. MALBON, «Jewish Leaders», 264. Likewise W.L. LANE, Mark, 435-436, n.60, observes that the formulation of v.35 invites comparison with 9:11f.: in both contexts Jesus does not question the accuracy of the scribal teaching but he probes the intention of the biblical texts undergirding that teaching.

[143] J. MARCUS, «Mark 14:61», 137, states that as David himself has acknowledged the Messiah's superior role; «Son of David», therefore, cannot express the fullness of Jesus' identity.

[144] R.H. GUNDRY, Mark, 718.

[145] Cf. W.L. LANE, Mark, 436, 437.

[146] Cf. K. STOCK, «Gliederung», 508.

«the Messiah is the "son" of David because he is descended from David; by the same token, the Messiah is also the "lord" of David because, as the Son of God, he is of higher station and authority than David»[147]. Hence, Jesus' Sonship is more than a matter of human origin or descent and his dignity is transcendent[148]: He is indeed the Son of God (cf. 12:6; 14:61f.; 15:39).

3.1.5 The Scribes' Conduct (12:38)

In this pericope (12:38-40), Jesus continues and concludes his teaching in the Temple (v.38), still with the same audience (v.37). As he has criticized what the scribes teach, he now warns the people against the scribes' conduct. Since Jesus emphatically demanded the thoughtful reflection and decision on the identity of the Christ (vv.35-37), so also he emphatically warns against the false conduct towards God and men (vv.38-40)[149]. In fact, Jesus' denouncement of the scribes' conduct, include pretence, exaction, avarice, hypocrisy and false piety. Thus, «the accusation that on the pretext of deep piety they made public prayers an opportunity to win the esteem of men indicates the peril in the loss of perspective in the service of God. This displacement of the honor of God from the center of concern is what distinguished the scribes from Jesus and exposed them to the searching judgment of God»[150]. With this stern denunciation of scribal practices, Mark concludes the account of Jesus' public teaching, both to the people and in the temple.

So far, we have observed that Jesus' contrast with the scribes, which began with teaching (cf. 1:22), is also dominant in teaching in the gospel, except in 12:28,32. This contrast is most evident in *how* and *what* both Jesus and the scribes taught, and moreover their general comportment. From our investigation, one can conclude that «the scribes in general — according to the Marcan narrator and the Marcan Jesus — teach without authority and without understanding and act with pride and without compassion»[151]. Now we shall turn to the next aspect of this contrast between Jesus and the scribes.

---

[147] J.D. KINGSBURY, *Christology of Mark*, 112-113.
[148] Cf. W.L. LANE, *Mark*, 438; V. TAYLOR, *Mark*, 492, 493.
[149] Cf. K. STOCK, «Gliederung», 509.
[150] W.L. LANE, *Mark*, 441.
[151] E.S. MALBON, «Jewish Leaders», 265.

3.2 On Exorcism

The contrast between Jesus and the scribes is not limited to teaching alone, but even extended to Exorcism, which was one of Jesus' deeds in the synagogue. We shall now find out how this contrast is also experienced here.

3.2.1 Jesus' Exorcistic Activity (3:22)

In this pericope (3:22-30), we are told that the scribes, who criticized Jesus' exorcistic activity, came down from Jerusalem (v.22, cf. 7:1). Thus, «from Jerusalem» distinguishes the scribes who lay the charges against Jesus from the scribes mentioned in 2:6,16 (1:22 refers to scribes in general)[152]. In fact, «Mark brands the scribes as prime movers of Jesus' passion and death by noting their provenance "from Jerusalem", which assures us that they are quite the same people as the constituents of the Sanhedrin who will inaugurate the final offensive with their challenge to Jesus' "authority" (11:27-28)»[153]. Hence, it is possible that they were the official emissaries from the Great Sanhedrin who came to examine Jesus' activity[154].

The scribes made two accusations or charges against Jesus: that «he is possessed by Beelzebul» and «he casts out demons by the ruler of the demons» (v.22). In fact, some scholars have observed that there is much in common between the sequence of the exchange over Beelzebul and the debate in the temple about «authority» (11:27-12:12)[155]. It is most likely that Jesus' «authority» is at stake in both passages, even if the word does

---

[152] Cf. R.H. GUNDRY, Mark, 172.

[153] R.J. DILLON, «As One Having Authority», 106; R.H. GUNDRY, Mark, 172, adds that the scribes in Jerusalem will help engineer Jesus' crucifixion (8:31; 10:33; 11:18,27-28; 14:1,43,53; 15:1,31; cf. also 7:1).

[154] Cf. W.L. LANE, Mark, 141.

[155] Cf. M.Y.-H. LEE, Autorität, 200-204; R.J. DILLON, «As One Having Authority», 106-107, observes as follows: In the first place, the two accusations of 3:22 («he is possessed by Beelzebul» and «he casts out demons by the ruler of the demons») matches the pair of questions posed in 11:28 («by what authority?» and «who has give you this authority»). The dual issue of Jesus' personal legitimacy (authority or identity) and his mission is joined in both passages, and really Jesus' «authority» is at stake in both. Secondly, the structure of Jesus' answer gives to the challenge, in both places a counterchallenge (3:23; 11:29-30) and an answer «in parables» (3:24-27; 12:1-11); and a reinforced judgment of the opponents' disposition concludes both arguments (3:28-30; 12:12).

not occur in the passage under discussion[156]. However, Jesus responds to their charges, beginning with the second charge, he asked them: «How can Satan cast out Satan?» (v.23). And with the parables of a divided «kingdom» and «house» (vv.24-26), he demonstrates the absurdity of their charges. With the parabolic indication in v.27 of the real reason for Satan's downfall, i.e. Jesus' exorcistic invasion of Satan's domain, Jesus completes his answer to their second charge[157]. As Jesus has shown the scribes the absurdity of their second charge that he casts out demons by the ruler of the demons (vv.23-27); now he shows them the seriousness of their first charge that he has Beelzebul (vv.28-29), by stressing it with, «Truly, I say to you».

To say that Jesus is possessed by Beelzebul or unclean spirit (cf. vv.22,30) is to raise the question of the source of his power or authority. «In the face of the claim that he is possessed by an unclean spirit Jesus affirms that he possesses the Spirit of God»[158]. The scribes exposed themselves to danger when they attributed to the agency of Satan the redemption brought by Jesus. Thus, «by assigning the action of God to a demonic origin the scribes betray a perversion of spirit, which, in defiance of the truth, chooses to call light darkness»[159]. And this is Blasphemy against the Holy Spirit which denotes «the conscious and deliberate rejection of the saving power and grace of God released through Jesus' word and act»[160]. In this way, we see once more that Jesus' contrast with the scribes is still strong, even in his exorcistic activity.

3.2.2 The Disciples' Inability (9:14)

When Jesus came down from the mountain of Transfiguration with his three disciples, they saw a great crowd about the other disciples, and the

---

[156] Cf. R.H. DILLON, «As One Having Authority», 107; M.Y.-H. LEE, *Autorität*, 201; D. LÜHRMANN, *Markusevangelium*, 75.

[157] Cf. R.H. GUNDRY, *Mark*, 173-174.

[158] W.L. LANE, *Mark*, 143.

[159] W.L. LANE, *Mark*, 145; J.D. KINGSBURY, *Conflict in Mark*, 73, confirms that to attribute to Beelzebul and not God exorcisms performed by divine authority is to slander the Holy Spirit.

[160] W.L. LANE, *Mark*, 145; Cf. K. STOCK, «La conoscenza dei demoni», 99; H. BEYER, «βλασφημία», 624; O.E. EVANS, «The Unforgivable Sin», 240-244, esp. 243-244. R.H. GUNDRY, *Mark*, 177, notes that the false accusation of some earlier scribes that Jesus had blasphemed (2:6-7) has given way to his true accusation that the present scribes have committed blasphemy.

scribes arguing with them (v.14). This dispute occurred within the context of the pericope on exorcism (9:14-29). Surely this contrast of the scribes with the disciples of Jesus, is indirectly with Jesus. In fact, this is not the first time the scribes contrast with Jesus' disciples: they are also implicated in 2:16; 7:1-5 in a controversy between Jesus and the scribes. On the other hand, the presence of the scribes here may probably indicate witnesses sent out by the Sanhedrin in Jerusalem to gather evidence against Jesus (cf. 3:22-30; 7:1-5)[161]. However, the inability of the disciples, whom the father of the possessed boy asked to exorcize the spirit in Jesus' absence (v.18, cf. v.28), may provide the reason behind this dispute[162]. Likewise, «the dispute undoubtedly concerned not only the failure of the disciples but the more basic question concerning their authorization to attempt an exorcism»[163]. That the disciples later asked Jesus in private why they could not cast out the spirit (cf. v.28), recollect and confirm their earlier failure. Hence this contrast of the scribes with Jesus' disciples, of which Jesus was the target, aims at the disciples' inability and/or their authority to exorcize.

3.3 On Forgiveness of Sins

After the mention of the scribes in 1:22, as a foreshadow of their antagonism and contrast with Jesus; they were present in the following pericopes we shall now discuss (2:6; 2:16), to challenge Jesus' *authority* (identity) and *mission*. So the contrast between Jesus and the scribes is not limited to teaching and exorcism, but also extended to the forgiveness of sins.

3.3.1 The Authority to Forgive Sins (2:6)

This pericope (2:1-12), which concerns the forgiveness and the healing of the paralytic, has already been considered, when we discussed the *Authority of Jesus*, and the *People's reaction of wonder*; so here we shall briefly concentrate on this element of contrast between Jesus and the scribes. However, we must remember that the scribes made their first

---

[161] Cf. W.L. LANE, *Mark*, 330.

[162] Cf. R.H. GUNDRY, *Mark*, 488.

[163] W.L. LANE, *Mark*, 330. This conclusion follows from his argument that the scribes came from Jerusalem, which I seem to share, since Jesus is on his way to Jerusalem.

appearance here (vv.6-7), after being mentioned in contrast with Jesus' authority in 1:22.

When a paralytic was brought to Jesus for healing, Jesus forgives the man his sins. Witnessing Jesus forgive the man's sins, some of the scribes sitting there considered «in their hearts» that he has made himself guilty of blasphemy, by arrogating to himself the authority of God (vv.6-7)[164]. This charge of blasphemy is also the charge for which the Sanhedrin finally condemns Jesus to death (14:64)[165]. To demonstrate that he does in fact possess the divine authority to forgive sins, Jesus utters a second word, instantly healing the paralytic. Thus, Jesus' power to forgive, no less effective because of its invisibility, is proved by the healing of the paralytic: the power to forgive and the power to heal are one[166]. In this pericope, therefore, Jesus demonstrated to the antagonistic scribes his divine authority both in word and deed. Hence, «the authority of Jesus transcends the immediate issue of forgiveness of sins»[167].

3.3.2 Eating with Sinners (2:16)

In considering the *Mission of Jesus*, we discussed this pericope (2:15-17), which followed the call of Levi, the tax collector. We shall, therefore, try to highlight here the scribes' contrast with Jesus. Those who challenged Jesus' action of eating with the tax collectors and sinners were the «scribes of the Pharisees»[168]. And I consider this pericope as belonging to the texts that refer to scribes alone, because the emphasis rests on the «scribes», while the Pharisees were merely referred to.

After Levi's call, he prepared a feast, in which Jesus and his disciples dined with many tax collectors and sinners. Observing Jesus recline at table with many tax/toll collectors and sinners, the scribes of the Pharisees quickly voiced their objection. This is because «to eat with toll collectors

---

[164] Cf. J.D. KINGSBURY, *Conflict in Mark*, 70.

[165] Cf. J.D. KINGSBURY, «Religious Authorities», 55; *Conflict in Mark*, 69; R.J. DILLON, «As One Having Authority», 105.

[166] Cf. J.R. EDWARDS, «Authority of Jesus», 223.

[167] D.J. DOUGHTY, «Authority of the Son of Man», 168.

[168] The «scribes of the Pharisees» is an unusual combination found only in Mark, which means that the «scribes» belong to the party or group of the Pharisees, like that of the Sadducees or Essenes. Cf. R.A. GUELICH, *Mark*, 56; M.D. HOOKER, *St. Mark*, 96.

and sinners is to make oneself ritually impure»[169]. Moreover, «by inviting such disreputable persons as toll collectors and sinners to have table fellowship with him, Jesus grants them forgiveness and invites them to live in the sphere of God's gracious rule»[170]. The scribes, offended at what they see, asked the disciples why Jesus eats with such people. When Jesus heard it, he retorts that the very purpose of his mission is to call, not the righteous but sinners. Hence, «for Jesus to refuse to have dealings with the disreputable would be as absurd as for a doctor to refuse to have to do with the sick; he has come on purpose to call sinners, and the disreputable people (tax collectors and sinners) he is associating with are obvious members of that class»[171]. In this way, Jesus concretizes the inauguration of the kingdom of God among the people.

3.4 Summary

We have seen from our discussion that the contrast between Jesus and the scribes is not a unique phenomenon limited to our pericope. It is rather what one can verify in other parts of the gospel. It was most evident from our investigation, especially in how and what both the scribes and Jesus teach the people. Since the scribes teach without authority and understanding, Jesus corrected them and warned the people against their conduct. In fact, it is worth observing that the mention of the contrast with the scribes immediately at the beginning of Jesus' teaching ministry (1:22) corresponds to its conclusion in 12:35-37,38-40, where this contrast manifests itself massively with regard to the teaching and conduct of the scribes. Thus this contrast and antagonism between the scribes and Jesus reigned throughout, except in 12:28,32 with the «friendly» scribe. Likewise in exorcism, the contrast was not less: the scribes from Jerusalem accused Jesus of being possessed by unclean spirit, and denied him the ability to cast out demons, but attributed it to Beelzebul, the prince of demons. Because of this, Jesus accused them of blasphemy against the Holy Spirit. On forgiveness of sins, the scribes accused Jesus of being guilty of blasphemy for arrogating to himself the duty of God. Jesus, on his part, demonstrated that as the Son of God, he can forgive sins as the Son of Man on earth. In all these contrasts, we

---

[169] J.D. KINGSBURY, *Conflict in Mark*, 70.

[170] J.D. KINGSBURY, *Conflict in Mark*, 71.

[171] C.E.B. CRANFIELD, *Mark*, 107.

observe that the issue of authority is at its root. Hence, the theme of Jesus' controversy with the scribes in Mark from the beginning (1:22; 2:6) until the bitter end in the trial (14:55-64) and the mocking of the crucified one (15:31f) is therefore the question of Jesus' ἐξουσία and with it the question of his Messiahness[172]. Therefore, without doubt we can establish that the contrast between Jesus and the scribes, as a phenomenon, is a dominant theme in Mark's Gospel.

4. Conclusion

At the beginning of this chapter, we set for ourselves an aim, to verify whether the relationships Jesus had with the main characters in the pericope are verifiable in the other parts of the gospel. Firstly, we saw from our pericope and the other parts of the gospel, that Jesus was always in the company of his disciples, whether they are three, four, twelve or all of them; they were together with him both in his movements and ministry, on both land and sea, and became the eyewitnesses of his word and deed. Secondly, the crowd was always attracted to Jesus, and became the object of his teaching, and benefitted in his word and deed. But they were always astonished at his teaching, exorcism and healing, and moreover the divine authority with which he executes his ministry. And thirdly, there was always contrast between the scribes and Jesus, especially in teaching, exorcism or forgiveness of sins, and the root issue of this conflict is Jesus' divine authority. This antagonism of the scribes towards Jesus, either alone or linked with the other religious groups, which led to Jesus' condemnation and death, had only one exception in 12:28,32, the praise of the «friendly» scribe.

In our discussion it becomes most evident that these three themes of Jesus in company of his disciples, the people's reaction of wonder, and the contrast between the scribes and Jesus, are not only verifiable in other parts of the gospel, but above all, they are dominant themes in the Gospel. Therefore, they are not unique themes limited to our pericope, as we have observed, but they are the principal themes in Mark's Gospel, and their presence during the first public activity of Jesus is programmatic for his whole ministry.

---

[172] D. LÜHRMANN, «Pharisäer und die Schriftgelehrten», 182.

GENERAL CONCLUSION

At the end of our investigation, it is time to give a general conclusion and evaluation to our Thesis. Since we have always given a summary conclusion at the end of each chapter, we shall now try to confirm the programmatic character of our pericope (our thesis), and say what significance this character has for Mark's Gospel.

1. The Programmatic Character of Mk 1:21-28.

We have so far tried to demonstrate in the two parts of our thesis, that our pericope has a programmatic character for Mark's Gospel, taking into consideration: (a) the position of the pericope in the Gospel, (b) the first appearance of important words and themes, (c) the concentration of many of the fundamental themes of Jesus' ministry in Mark's Gospel, and (d) Jesus' central position.

a) In the *Preliminary Observations* especially in the *Synoptic Comparison*, we saw that Matthew and Luke placed typical and important materials at the beginning of Jesus' Galilean public ministry. So also, Mark's placement of our pericope at Jesus' first appearance and activity gives a hint to its possible important and programmatic significance for his Gospel.

b) In addition to the position of our pericope, we also observed in the *Linguistic-Syntactic Analysis*, that many words which appeared for the first time in the pericope were also Mark's favourite terms. Therefore, the concentration of these Markan key-words and favourite terms at this point gives a good signal of its programmatic purpose for Mark's Gospel.

c) We also discovered in the *Semantic Analysis* a series of significant themes. We have then demonstrated in Part II, that each of these themes is often or frequently present through the whole Gospel of Mark. Hence, the concentration of these themes in the pericope, that initiates Jesus' Galilean public ministry, gives us a clear proof of its programmatic character for Mark's Gospel.

d) In both the *Narrative* and *Pragmatic (Reader-Response) Analyses*, we saw that Jesus was central as the protagonist of the story of our pericope. This was evident, in the narrative analysis, in how the author/narrator characterized Jesus: what he said and did, and how the other characters reacted to him; and also in the pragmatic (reader-response) analysis, in how the reader saw him. Just as Jesus is central to our pericope, so also he is for the whole Gospel. Hence, our pericope, in this sense, has a programmatic character for Mark's Gospel.

2. Its Significance for the Gospel

Finally we ask: the fact that these themes in this combination in our pericope have a programmatic character for Mark, what does it express, and what does it signify for the «nature» of this Gospel? To answer this question we shall compare Jesus' first public appearance in Mark with the other synoptic evangelists — Matthew and Luke. This is because the first public appearance and activity of Jesus in these three Gospels have important impact on their Gospel account. Moreover, Jesus at this initial point, so to speak, proclaims his programme: what he wants to do, what he wants to realize, what should and will characterize his action in his mission. Is his action at this beginning of his public ministry typical of his activity for these Gospels? Have they any orientation also to universal mission? We shall therefore briefly examine the main activity and themes of Jesus' inaugural appearance and its relationship with the concerned Gospels.

2.1 *Jesus' Programmatic Appearance compared*

The comparison of Jesus' first appearance is limited to the three Gospels, as stated above. Now we shall highlight Jesus' main activity and the main themes here, and see how they are taken up in the Gospel narratives. However, we shall try to identify the peculiarity of Mark in this comparison.

2.1.1 Jesus' Main Actitvity

The first important and common element in Jesus' inaugural appearance for the three synoptic evangelists is that all of them have *teaching* as their starting points. In Matthew, Jesus went up the mountain and taught his disciples (before the people), as seen in «the Sermon on the Mount» (5:1-7:29). Here *teaching* is Jesus' main activity because it is placed before his other activities (preaching and healing)[1]. Likewise in Luke 4:16-30, Jesus' first appearance which was his visit to Nazareth, focused on his *teaching* activity[2]. Jesus' visit to the synagogue of Capernaum in Mark 1:21-28 also initiated with *teaching*. In all these Gospels the people (crowd) were moved with astonishment at Jesus' divine authority with which he taught them. However, in Mark's account, apart from his teaching activity, Jesus also performed an exorcistic action. In fact, it is this Jesus' exorcistic action that distinguishes Mk from Mt and Lk.

Another important peculiarity one can also discover here about Mark, is that he combines Jesus' word and deed («teaching» and «exorcism») in his narrative. In Mt and Lk, Jesus' word and deed are separately found: it is in 8:1-9:38, that Mt reported about Jesus' deed, while his teaching is in 5-7[3]; and for Lk, Jesus' deed is found in the next pericope (4:31-37). Thus, in Mk one does not need to go to the next chapter or pericope for the combination of Jesus' word and deed.

2.1.2 The Main Themes

Apart from Jesus' teaching (and exorcism) in his programmatic appearance in the Gospels, one can observe other themes concentrated in these passages. For Matthew, one can see also: «mountain» as a setting; the astonished great crowd; the listening disciples; and Jesus as an authoritative teacher. While in Luke we see also, the fulfilment of Is 61;

---

[1] A. STOCK, *Method and Message*, 65, confirms that, «By citing teaching (didaskein) ahead of preaching and healing in the summary passages (4:23; 9:35; 11:1), Matthew gives it the position of stress and invites the implied reader to attach special importance to it». Cf. D.A. HAGNER, *Matthew 1-13*, 80, 82; L. MORRIS, *Matthew*, 91.

[2] Jesus' Nazareth's visit account exemplifies and introduces his public ministry with a focus on his teaching in the synagogues. Cf. D.L. BOCK, *Luke 1:1-9:50*, 394; J. NOLLAND, *Luke 1-9:20*, 184. J.B. GREEN, *Luke*, 207, highlighting its central importance for the whole narrative, says among other things, that «it stands as a concrete representation of the ministry of Jesus summarized in 4:14-15».

[3] D.A. HAGNER, *Matthew 1-13*, 195, confirms that between the framework of two summaries (4:23-25; 9:35) the evangelist has presented two major blocks of materials, the first concerning the teaching of Jesus (chaps. 5-7) and the section (8:1-9:38) concerning mainly the deeds of Jesus, who is thus presented as the Messiah of both word and deed.

the prophetic mission beyond Israel towards the pagans; the people's wonder and rejection of Jesus' words; and Jesus' anticipated violent death. But in Mk, apart from Jesus' «teaching» and «exorcism», we have also, Jesus being with his disciples; the contrast of the Scribes with Jesus; the question about his identity, authority, and mission; the astonishment of the crowd; and the spread of Jesus' fame everywhere. One can observe that in Mt and Lk the themes are poorly concentrated in their passages, while in Mk the concentration of the themes are richer and more versatile.

2.1.3 Their Relationship with the Gospels

The question is: how do the themes of the individual evangelist relate with his Gospel account? Are these themes taken up in these Gospels? In Matthew it is easy to observe that Jesus' inaugural activity of teaching was dominant in his Gospel. This is concretized in the long discourses of 5:1-7:29; 9:36-11:1; 13:1-53; 18:1-19:1; 23:1-26:1. But some themes like «mountain» as a setting for teaching was only in 5:1 and 24:3[4]; or the crowd's astonishment at Jesus' teaching was only twice (7:28; 22:33; in 13:54 was only generalized), just to mention a few. In Luke, it is also typical for Jesus to teach/preach, whether in the synagogues (4:15,31,44; 6:6; 13:10), in the temple (19:47; 20:1; 21:37; 23:5), or other places (5:3,17; 8:1; 13:22,26). Some of the themes are not dominant, like Jesus' «rejection»: in fact, «the rejection in Nazareth is a "dress-rehearsal" for the passion, and sets up theological categories which prepares the reader for Jesus' prophetic destiny in Jerusalem»[5]. But in Mark, apart from teaching, which is Jesus' principal and customary activity (cf. 10:1), other themes are also repetitive and dominant in his Gospel, as we have shown in Part II of our work. This is also another peculiarity of Mark against other synoptic evangelists: not only are the themes richer in concentration in the pericope, they are also dominant throughout his Gospel.

Another important element of this relationship with the Gospel is with regard to the disciples. In Matthew the disciples were commissioned by Jesus to preach (10:7,27), but his typical activity in Mt (teaching) is for them a future action, especially in their universal mission (Mt 28:16-20, esp. v.20). While in Luke, the main task is «preaching», both in their

---

[4] The «mountain» could be taken as a place of special event/revelation: 4:8 (for temptation); 14:23 (for prayer); 15:29 (for healing); 17:1 (for transfiguration); 28:16 (commission of the disciples for mission).

[5] J. NOLLAND, *Luke 1-9:20*, 200.

present ministry and future mission (Lk 9:2; 24:47). It seems teaching has no place in their mission. However, since Jesus' teaching is a fulfilment of the OT Scripture, he reminded his disciples of this fulfilment in himself (24:27,44, cf. 4:21), and enjoined them to preach the repentance and forgiveness of sins in his name to all nations (24:47). But in Mark, the disciples' preaching and teaching were both their present and future activities. In fact, the disciples performed the typical activity of Jesus during the course of his ministry. Thus, their missionary activity is anticipated in Jesus' own.

In this comparison of Jesus' main activity, the themes and their rapport with the Gospel, we discovered some peculiarities in Mark's Gospel account. We shall now find out the significance of this peculiarity for his Gospel.

2.2 The Significance of Mark's Peculiarity

After the above comparison we shall find out the significance of its results for Mark's Gospel: the exorcistic action; the combination of Jesus' word and deed; the richer concentration of the themes; their repetitiveness and dominance in his Gospel; and the disciples' performance of Jesus' typical activity.

2.2.1 Jesus' Exorcistic Action

Jesus' simple and authoritative command that cast out an unclean spirit from a man in the synagogue raised a christological question about his identity. On the one hand, the unclean spirit reveals Jesus' name, origin and true identity (1:24), of which Jesus did not spare time to silence it. On the other hand, the bystanders questioned among themselves about the authority of his word and deed: that he teaches with authority and commands the demons and they obey him (1:27). Their christological question remained unanswered among the human characters of the Gospel story until the centurion gave the right answer, after Jesus' death on the cross, saying: «Truly this man was the Son of God!», (15:39). In fact, characteristically, Mark in all, concentrates on the person of Jesus, or more precisely, on the question about his identity both in this pericope and the entire Gospel[6].

---

[6] The christological problem (Jesus' identity) is present and dominant in the whole of Mark's Gospel. This is touched by the main characters of the story: the omniscent

Exorcism is also an important aspect of Jesus' mission in proclaiming and inaugurating the kingdom of God. This means that Jesus has to break the power of evil and unclean spirits (demons), in order to liberate man from these demonic powers and restore him to God's creation and to his lost identity. Jesus' exorcistic activity, therefore, is a menace to the demonic world, which one of them also acknowledged in Jesus' coming (1:24b). Hence, Jesus' exorcistic activity, which is dominant in Mark's Gospel, not only raised the question about Jesus' identity, but also prepares the ground for the inauguration of God's kingdom (1:15).

2.2.2 The Combination of Jesus' Word and Deed

It is typical for Mk to combine Jesus' word and deed, which anticipates what follows in his ministry in the entire Gospel. This is clearly indicated by the summary statement, 1:39: «And he went throughout all Galilee, preaching in their synagogues and casting out demons». And it gives us the exact picture of what Jesus did in Capernaum synagogue. In fact, in Jesus' mission, the proclaiming of the coming of the kingdom of God, is not only in word (teaching) but also in deed (exorcism). Thus, the proclaiming and casting out demons are not only the principal elements of the beginning of Jesus' activity, but also his typical and characteristic activity in the whole Gospel, as we saw in Ch. VI. Moreover, the combination of teaching and exorcism in our pericope and elsewhere illumines each other, and emphasizes the unity of Jesus' word and deed. And the uniting element in this combination is Jesus' divine authority.

When one looks into Mark's Gospel, or the Part II of our Thesis, one will observe that this dominant activity of Jesus' teaching and exorcism, were: the aim of the disciples' being with Jesus; the reason for raising the question about Jesus' identity, authority and mission; the major causes of contrast, criticism and hostility of the Scribes towards Jesus; the main object of the bystanders' astonishment; the main content of the spread of Jesus' fame everywhere. Mark, therefore, makes Jesus' inaugural action in the synagogue both programmatic and paradigmatic for his mission.

---

narrator, God, John the Baptist, Jesus himself, the demons, the disciples, the people (crowds), the scribes (religious leaders), Herod, Bartimaeus, the High Priest, Pilate and the centurion.

2.2.3 The Richer Concentration of Themes

The concentration of many important and fundamental themes of Mark in Jesus' inaugural appearance, gives variety to his account. This is evident when one observes that not only is the pericope richly concentrated with these themes, but that they are repetitive and dominant in the whole Gospel. And it is interesting to note that these themes, in one way or the other refer to Jesus, and characterize him in the Gospel. This is because it has to do with what he «says» or «does», or how others «react» towards him.

2.2.4 The Disciples' Mission anticipated

Jesus' typical activity of preaching/teaching and exorcism was also performed and continued by his disciples. It means that in Jesus' Capernaum episode, his disciples' mission was anticipated. This is evident in Jesus' appointment and commission of his disciples: «And he appointed twelve, to be with him, and to be sent out to preach and have authority to cast out demons», (3:14-15, cf. 6:7, 12-13, 30). The «beginning» and «continuing» meaning of respectively κηρύσσειν («to proclaim/preach») and διδάσκειν («to teach») in Jesus' ministry, were also valid both for him and his disciples. Thus, the silent presence of the disciples in Mk 1:21-28, was preparing them to learn «being» with Jesus, and to «observe» his characteristic activity of word and deed, and to learn how to «act» like him in his movements and mission.

2.3 *The Gospel of Mark's Orientation to Mission*

After our comparison of Mark's Gospel with the other synoptic evangelists on Jesus' first appearance and activity in his Galilean public ministry, and after highlighting and discussing the peculiarities of Mark's account, it is now time to say what our programmatic pericope signify for Mark's Gospel. It is most obvious that Mark's Gospel is oriented to mission, because Jesus sets out from the very beginning of his ministry the typical activity that will characterize his mission both in his word and deed. The exorcistic activity of Jesus and its effect in his mission; the typical combination of Jesus' word and deed; the richer concentration of very important and fundamental Markan themes, which are also dominant in Jesus' ministry in the Gospel; and the disciples' anticipated mission in our pericope, all help to confirm this mission orientation. Therefore, Mk 1:21-28 introduces the reader, not only to the programmatic character of

Jesus' ministry, but also the mission programme of Jesus (and the Twelve/Apostles) for Mark's Gospel. Hence, this could even support Rhoads' assertion that «the Gospel of Mark has a radical approach to mission... No other New Testament document is so thoroughly oriented to mission»[7].

---

[7] D. RHOADS, «Mission in Mark», 340.

ABBREVIATIONS

1 QapGen	*Genesis Apocryphon* (from Qumran Cave 1)
1 QH	*Hôdāyôt* (Thanksgiving Hymns, from Qumran Cave 1)
1 QM	*Milhāmāh* (War Scroll, from Qumran Cave 1)
AncB	Anchor Bible
ABD	D.N. FREEDMAN, ed., *The Anchor Bible Dictionary*, I-VI, New York 1992
AnBib	Analecta Biblica
ASeign	*Assemblées du Seigneur*
ASV	American Standard Version
AV	Authorised Version
BAGD	W. BAUER – W.F. ARNDT – F.W. GINGRICH – F. DANKER, *A Greek-English Lexicon of the New Testament & Other Early Christian Literature*, Chicago – London 1979².
BDF	F. BLASS – A. DEBRUNNER – R.W. FUNK, *A Greek Grammar of the New Testament and Other Early Christian Literature*, Chicago – London 1961.
BEThL	Bibliotheca ephemeridum theologicarum Lovaniensium
Bib	*Biblica*
BiLe	*Bibel und Leben*
BiTod	*Bible Today*
BTB	*Biblical Theology Bulletin*
BWANT	Beiträge zur Wissenschaft vom Alten und Neuen Testament
BZ	*Biblische Zeitschrift*
BZNW	Beihefte zur Zeitschrift für die neutestamentliche Wissenschaft
CBQ	*Catholic Biblical Quarterly*
CBQ.MS	Catholic Biblical Quarterly Monograph series
cf.	confer
CGTC	Cambridge Greek Testament commentaries
ch.	chapter
CThMi	*Currents in Theology and Mission*
ed.	editor/editors

EDNT	H. BALZ – G. SCHNEIDER, ed., *Exegetical Dictionary of the New Testament*, I-III, Grand Rapids 1990-1993.
e.g.	exempli gratia (for example)
EHPhR	Études d'histoire et de philosophie religieuses
EHS.T	Europäische Hochschulschriften: Reihe 23, Theologie
EKK	Evangelisch-Katholischer Kommentar zum Neuen Testament
esp.	especially
ET	*Expository Times*
EtB	*Études bibliques*
etc.	et cetera
EThL	*Ephemerides theologicae Lovanienses*
EvTh	*Evangelische Theologie*
f./ff.	and the following
Fs.	Festschrift
FTS	Frankfurter theologische Studien
FzB	Forschung zur Bibel
GNT	Greek New Testament
HNT	Handbuch zum Neuen Testament
HThK	Herders theologischer Kommentar zum Neuen Testament
HThR	*Harvard Theological Review*
HUCA	*Hebrew Union College Annual*
ibid.	*ibidem*
ICC	International Critical Commentary
ID.	Idem
IDB	*The Interpreter's Dictionary of the Bible*
IDB.S	*IDB, Supplement Volume*
i.e.	id est (that is)
IKaZ	*Internationale katholische Zeitschrift*
Interp.	*Interpretation*
IThQ	*Irish Theological Quarterly*
JAAR	*Journal of the American Academy of Religion*
JBL	*Journal of Biblical Literature*
JBR	*Journal of Bible and Religion*
JETS	*Journal of the Evangelical Theological Society*
JQR	*Jewish Quarterly Review*
JR	*Journal of Religion*
JSNT	*Journal for the Study of the New Testament*
JSNT.S	Journal for the Study of the New Testament, Supplement series
JThS	*Journal of Theological Studies*
LXX	Septuagint
MSSNTS	Monograph series. Society for New Testament Studies
MT	Masoretic Text

n.	footnote number
Neotest.	*Neotestamentica*
NIC	New International Commentary (on the New Testament)
NIGTC	New International Greek Testament Commentary
NRTh	*Nouvelle revue théologique*
n.s.	new series/nouvelle série
NT	New Testament
NT	*Novum Testamentum*
NT.S	Novum Testamentum, Supplements
NTA	Neutestamentliche Abhandlungen
NTD	Das Neue Testament Deutsch
NTS	*New Testament Studies*
OBO	Orbis Biblicus et Orientalis
OT	Old Testament
p./pp.	page/pages
par.	parallel/parallels
PSV	*Parola spirito e vita*
QD	Quaestiones Disputatae
RAC	*Reallexikon für Antike und Christentum*
RdT	*Rassegna di teologia*
RExp	*Review and Expositor*
rhs	*Religionsunterricht an höheren Schulen*
RNT	Regensburger Neues Testament
RSV	Revised Standard Version
SBL.DS	Society of Biblical Literature, Dissertation Series
SBM	Stuttgarter biblische Monographien
SBT	Studies in Biblical Theology
sec.	section
SJTh	*Scottish Journal of Theology*
SQE	Synopsis Quattuor Evangeliorum
StANT	Studien zum Alten und Neuen Testament
StBi	Studi biblici
StEb	*Studi Eblaiti*
StNT	Studien zum Neuen Testament
Str-B	H. STRACK – P. BILLERBECK, *Kommentar zum Neuen Testament aus Talmud und Midrasch*, I-VI, München [4]1965.
SubBi	Subsidia biblica
TDNT	*Theological Dictionary of the New Testament*
TDOT	*Theological Dictionary of the Old Testament*
ThHK	Theologischer Handkommentar zum Neuen Testament
ThLZ	*Theologische Literaturzeitung*
ThPQ	*Theologisch-praktische Quartalschrift*

ThZ	*Theologische Zeitschrift*
tr.	translator
trans.	translation
TThZ	*Trierer theologische Zeitschrift*
USQR	*Union Seminary Quarterly Review*
v./vv.	verse/verses
VD	*Verbum Domini*
VT	*Vetus Testament*
WBC	Word Biblical Commentary
WUNT	Wissenschaftliche Untersuchungen zum Neuen Testament
x	symbol for «times»
ZKTh	*Zeitschrift für katholische Theologie*
ZNW	*Zeitschrift für die neutestamentliche Wissenschaft*
ZThK	*Zeitschrift für Theologie und Kirche*

BIBLIOGRAPHY

1. Commentaries

ANDERSON, H., *The Gospel of Mark*, Grand Rapids 1984.

BOCK, D.L., *Luke 1:1-9:50*, Grand Rapids 1994.

BRANSCOMB, B.H., *The Gospel of Mark*, London 1964[7].

BROWN, R.E., *The Gospel According to John I-XII*, AncB 29; New York 1966.

CARRINGTON, P., *According to Mark*, Cambridge 1960.

CARROLL, R.P., *Jeremiah: A Commentary*, Philadelphia 1986.

CRANFIELD, C.E.B., *The Gospel according to St. Mark*, CGTC; Cambridge 1977[5].

DAVIES, W.D. - ALLISON, D.C., *A Critical and Exegetical Commentary on The Gospel According to Saint Matthew*, I-III, Edinburgh 1988-1997.

ERNST, J., *Das Evangelium nach Markus* RNT, Regensburg 1981.

FITZMYER, J.A., *The Gospel According to Luke I-IX*, AncB 28, New York 1970.

————, *The Gospel According to Luke X-XXIV*, AncB 28A, New York 1985.

GNILKA, J., *Das Evangelium nach Markus*, EKK II/1,2, Zürich 1978-1979.

GOULD, E.P., *A Critical and Exegetical Commentary on the Gospel according to St. Mark*, ICC, Edinburgh 1907[4].

GREEN, J.B., *The Gospel of Luke*, NIC, Grand Rapids – Cambridge 1997.

GRUNDMANN, W., *Das Evangelium nach Markus*, ThHK, Berlin 1977[7].

GUELICH, R.A., *Mark 1-8:26*, WBC 34A, Dallas 1989.

GUNDRY, R.H., *Mark: A Commentary on His Apology for the Cross*, Grand Rapids 1993.

————, *Matthew: A Commentary on His Handbook for a Mixed Church under Persecution*, Grand Rapids 1994[2].

HAGNER, D.A., *Matthew 1-13*, WBC 33A, Dallas 1993.

HARRINGTON, W., *Mark*, Wilmington 1979.

HEIL, J.P., *The Gospel of Mark as Model for Action. A Reader-Response Commentary*, Mahwah NJ 1992.

HENDRIKSEN, W., *The Gospel of Mark*, Edinburgh 1987.

HOOKER, M.D., *The Gospel According to Saint Mark* London 1991.

HURTADO, L.W., *Mark*, Peabody 1989[2].

JOHNSON, S.E., *A Commentary on the Gospel According to St. Mark*, London 1960.

KEENAN, J.P., *The Gospel of Mark. A Mahāyāna Reading*, New York 1995.

KERTELGE, K., *Markusevangelium*, Würzburg 1994.

KLEIST, J.A., *The Gospel of Saint Mark*, Milwaukee 1936.

KLOSTERMANN, E., *Das Markusevangelium*, HNT 3, Tübingen 1936[3].

LAGRANGE, M.-J., *Évangile selon Saint Marc*, EtB, Paris 1929[4].

LAMARCHE, P., *Evangile de Marc*, EtB n.s. 33, Paris 1996.

LANE, W.L., *The Gospel According to Mark*, NIC, Grand Rapids 1974.

LÉGASSE, S., *L'évangile de Marc*, I-II, LD Commentaires 5, Paris 1997.

LIGHTFOOT, R.H., *The Gospel Message of St. Mark*, Oxford 1950.

LOHMEYER, E., *Das Evangelium des Markus*, Göttingen 1967[17].

LÜHRMANN, D., *Das Markusevangelium*, HNT 3, Tübingen 1987.

MANN, C.S., *Mark*, AncB 27, Garden City 1986.

MARSHALL, I.H., *The Gospel of Luke. A Commentary on the Greek Text*, NIGTC, Grand Rapids 1989.

MORRIS, L., *The Gospel According to Matthew*, Grand Rapids 1992.

NINEHAM, D.E., *Saint Mark*, Middlesex 1963.

NOLLAND, J., *Luke 1-9:20*, WBC 35A, Dallas 1989.

PAINTER, J., *Mark's Gospel*, London/New York 1997.

PESCH, R., *Das Markusevangelium*, HThK II/1,2, Freiburg 1976-1977.

PLUMMER, A., *The Gospel according to St. Mark*, Cambridge 1914.

RAWLINSON, A.E.J., *St. Mark*, London 1949[7].

SADLER, M.F., *The Gospel According to Mark*, London 1889[3].

SCHNIEWIND, J., *Das Evangelium nach Markus*, Göttingen 1952[6].

SCHWEIZER, E., *Das Evangelium nach Markus*, NTD 1, Göttingen 1983[6].

STOCK, A., *The Method and Message of Mark*, Wilmington 1989.

————, *The Method and Message of Matthew*, Collegeville 1994.

SWETE, H.B., *The Gospel according to St. Mark*, London 1908[2].

TAYLOR, V., *The Gospel According to St. Mark*, London 1987[2].

VAN IERSEL, B., *Reading Mark*, Edinburgh 1989.

VAN IERSEL, B.M.F., *Mark. A Reader-Response Commentary*, tr. W.H. Bisscheroux, JSNT.S 164, Sheffield 1998.

WEISS, B., *Die Evangelien des Markus und Lukas*, Göttingen 1901⁶.

WELLHAUSEN, J., *Das Evangelium Marci*, Berlin 1909².

WESTERMANN, C., *Isaiah 40-66: A Commentary*, Philadelphia 1969.

WILLIAMSON, L., *Mark. Interpretation. A Bible Commentary for Teaching and Preaching*, Atlanta 1983.

2. Books and Articles

ABRAMS, M.H., *The Mirror and the Lamp: Romantic Theory and the Critical Tradition*, New York 1958.

ABRAMS, M.H., *A Glossary of Literary Terms*, New York 1981.

ACHTEMEIER, P.J., «"He Taught Them Many Things". Reflections on Marcan Christology», *CBQ* 42 (1980) 465-481.

————, «The Ministry of Jesus in the Synoptic Gospels», *Interp* 35 (1981) 157-169.

AHARONI, Y., *The Land of the Bible. A Historical Geography*, tr. A.F.Rainey, London 1979.

ALAND, K., *Synopsis Quattuor Evangeliorum*, Stuttgart 1990¹³.

ALLAN, G., «He shall be called - a Nazirite?», *ET* 95 (1983) 81-82.

ALTER, R., *The Art of Biblical Narrative*, New York 1981.

AMBROZIC, A.M., *The Hidden Kingdom: A Redaction Critical Study of the Reference to the Kingdom in Mark's Gospel*, CBQ.MS 2, Washington 1972.

————, «New Teaching with Power (Mk 1,27)», in *Word and Spirit*, Fs. D.M. Stanley, Willowdale 1975, 113-149.

ANDERSON, H., «Jesus: Aspects of the Question of His Authority», in *The Social World of Formative Christianity and Judaism*, Fs. H.C. Kee, Philadelphia 1988, 290-310.

ARENS, E., *The ΗΛΘΟΝ-Sayings in the Synoptic Tradition. A Historico-Critical Investigation*, OBO 10, Freiburg 1976.

ARGYLE, A.W., «"Outward" and "Inward" in Biblical Thought», *ET* 68 (1957) 196-199.

————, «The Meaning of ἐξουσία in Mark 1:22,27», *ET* 80 (1969) 343.

ARNOLD, G., «Mk 1,1 und Eröffnungswendungen in griechischen und lateinischen Schriften», *ZNW* 68 (1977) 123-127.

BÄCHLI, O., «"Was habe ich mit Dir zu schaffen?" Eine formelhafte Frage im A.T und N.T», *ThZ* 33 (1977) 69-80.

BAILEY, K.E., *Through Peasant Eyes*, Grand Rapids 1980.

BALZ, H., «φοβέομαι», *EDNT* III, 429-432.

BALZ, H. – SCHNEIDER, G., ed., *Exegetical Dictionary of the New Testament*, I-III, Grand Rapids 1990-1993.

BARRETT, C.K., *The Holy Spirit and the Gospel Tradition*, London 1947.

————, «The Background of Mark 10:45», in *New Testament Essays*, Fs. T.W. Manson, Manchester 1959, 1-18.

————, *New Testament Essays*, London 1972.

BARTON, G.A., «The Use of ἐπιτιμᾶν in Mark 8:30 and 3:12», *JBL* 41 (1922) 233-236.

BAUER, D., *The Structure of Matthew's Gospel: A Study in Literary Design*, JSNT.S 31, Sheffield 1988.

BAUER, W. – GRINGRICH, F.W. – DANKER, F., *A Greek-English Lexicon of the New Testament and Other Early Christian Literature*, Chicago – London 1979 [2].

BAUERNFEIND, O., *Die Worte der Dämonen im Markusevangelium*, Stuttgart 1927.

BAUMGARTEN, J., «καινός», *EDNT* II, 229-232.

BECKER-WIRTH, S., «Jesus treibt Dämonen aus (Mk 1,21-28)», *rhs* 28 (1985) 181-186.

BEHM, J., «καινός», *TDNT* III, 447-450.

BERGER, K., «Jesus als Nasoräer/Nasiräer», *NT* 38 (1996) 323-335.

BERKEY, R.F., «ΕΓΓΙΖΕΙΝ, ΦΘΑΝΕΙΝ, and Realized Eschatology», *JBL* 82 (1963) 177-187.

BERTRAM, G., «θάμβος, θαμβέω, ἔκθαμβος, ἔκθαμβέομαι», *TDNT* III, 4-7.

BEST, E., *The Temptation and the Passion: the Markan Soteriology*, MSSNTS 2, Cambridge 1965.

————, *Following Jesus: Discipleship in the Gospel of Mark*, JSNT.S 4, Sheffield 1981.

BETZ, O., «φωνή, φωνέω», *TDNT* IX, 301-303.

BEYER, H.W., «βλασφημία», *TDNT* I, 621-625.

————, «διακονέω», *TDNT* II, 81-86.

BIANCHI, E., «Esci da costui! (Mc 1,21-28)», *PSV* 19 (1989) 109-137.

BIELER, L., ΘΕΙΟΣ ΑΝΗΡ. *Das Bild des «göttlichen Menschen» in Spätantike und Christentum*, I, Wien 1935.

BISHOP, E.F.F., «Jesus and Capernaum», *CBQ* 15 (1953) 427-437.

BJÖRCK, G., Ἦν διδάσκων. *Die Periphrastischen Konstruktionen im Griechischen*, Uppsala 1940.

BLACK, M., «The Kingdom of God Has Come», *ET* 63 (1951/52) 289-290.

————, *An Aramaic Approach to the Gospels and Acts*, Oxford 1954.

————, «Scribe (γραμματεύς)», *IDB* IV, 246-248.

BLASS, F. - DEBRUNNER, A. - FUNK, R.W., *A Greek Grammar of the New Testament and Other Early Christian Literature*, Chicago - London 1961.

BLIGH, P.H., «A Note on Huios Theou in Mark 15:39», *ET* 80 (1968/69) 52-53.

BÖCHER, O., *Dämonenfurcht und Dämonenabwehr. Ein Beitrag zur Vorgeschichte der christlichen Taufe*, BWANT 90, Stuttgart 1970.

————, *Christus Exorcista. Dämonismus und Taufe im Neuen Testament*, BWANT96, Stuttgart 1972.

BONNER, C., «The Technique of Exorcism», *HThR* 36 (1943) 39-49.

BOTTERWECK, J. - RINGGREN, H., ed., *Theological Dictionary of the Old Testament*, I-VIII, Grand Rapids 1974-1997.

BOUCHER, M., *The Mysterious Parable: A Literary Study*, CBQ.MS 6, Washington 1977.

BRATCHER, R.G. - NIDA, E.A., *A Translator's Handbook on the Gospel of Mark*, Leiden 1961.

BRIÈRE, J., «Le cri et le secret. Signification d'un exorcisme. Mc 1,21-28», *ASeign* II/35 (1973) 34-46.

BROADHEAD, E.K., *Teaching with Authority: Miracles and Christology in the Gospel of Mark*, JSNT.S 74, Sheffield 1992.

————, «Jesus the Nazarene: Narrative Strategy and Christlogical Imagery in the Gospel of Mark», *JSNT* 52 (1993) 3-18.

BÜCHSEL, F., «ἀντί», *TDNT* I, 372-373.

————, «δίδωμι», *TDNT* II, 166.

————, «λύτρον», *TDNT* IV, 340-349.

BUDESHEIM, T.L., «Jesus and the Disciples in Conflict with Judaism», *ZNW* 62 (1971) 190-209.

BUNDY, W.E., *Jesus and the First Three Gospels. A Introduction to the Synoptic Tradition*, Cambridge/Massachusetts 1955.

BULTMANN, R., *History of the Synoptic Tradition*, tr. J. Marsh, Oxford – Peabody 1963.

BURKILL, T.A., *Mysterious Revelation: An Examination of the Philosophy of St Mark's Gospel*, New York 1963.

BURKITT, F.C., *The Syriac Forms of the NT Proper Names*, London 1912.

————, «Capernaum, Capharnaum», *JThS* 34 (1933) 385-389.

BUTTRICK, G.A., *The Interpreter's Dictionary of the Bible*, I-IV, Nashville 1962.

BYWATER, I., «Poetics, Chapter II», in *The Complete Works of Aristotle*, II, ed. J. Barnes, Princeton, New Jersey 1984, 2316-2340.

CAMPBELL, J.Y., «The Kingdom of God Has Come», *ET* 48 (1936/37) 91-94.

CAQUOT, A., «נער», *TDOT* III, 49-53.

CARLSTON, C.E., «The Things That Defile (Mark vii.14) and the Law in Matthew and Mark», *NTS* 15 (1968/69) 75-96.

————, *The Parable of the Triple Tradition*, Philadelphia 1975.

CARTER, W., «Jesus' "I have come" Statements in Matthew's Gospel», *CBQ* 60 (1998) 44-62.

CHATMAN, S., *Story and Discourse: Narrative Structure in Fiction and Film*, Ithaca 1978.

CHILTON, B.D., «Exorcism and History. Mark 1,21-28», in *Gospel Perspectives. The Miracles of Jesus*, VI, ed., D. Wenham – C. Blomberg, Sheffield 1986, 253-271.

CITRON, B., «The Multitude in the Synoptic Gospels», *SJTh* 7 (1954) 408-418.

CLARK, K.W., «Realized Eschatology», *JBL* 59 (1940) 376-383.

————, «Galilee», *IDB* II, 344-347.

COLWELL, E.C., «A Definite Rule for the Use of the Article in the Greek New Testament», *JBL* 52 (1933) 12-21.

COOK, J.G., *The Structure and Persuasive Power of Mark. A Linguistic Approach*, Atlanta, Georgia 1995.

CORBO, V.C., «Capernaum», *ABD* I, 866-869.

COUTTS, J., «The Authority of Jesus and of the Twelve in St. Mark's Gospel», *JThS* 8 (1957) 111-118.

CRIM, K., *The Interpreter's Dictionary of the Bible*, Sup. Vol., Nashville 1976.

CROSSAN, J.D., «The Seed Parables of Jesus», *JBL* 92 (1973) 244-266.

————, «Parable», *ABD* V, 146-152.

DAUBE, D., «ἐξουσία in Mark 1,22 and 27», *JThS* 39 (1938) 45-59.

————, *The New Testament and Rabbinic Judaism*, Salem, New Hampshire 1984.

DAVIS, P.G., «Mark's Christological Paradox», *JSNT* 35 (1989) 3-18.

DE JONGE, M., *Christology in Context: the earliest Christian response to Jesus*, Philadelphia 1988.

DE LA POTTERIE, I., «De Compositione evangelii Marci», *VD* 44 (1966) 135-141.

DELORME, J., «Aspects doctrinaux du second Évangile. Études récentes de la rédaction de Marc», *EThL* 43 (1967) 74-99.

DETWEILER, R., ed., *Reader-Response Approaches to Biblical and Secular Texts. Semeia* 31 (1985).

DIDEBERG, D. – BEERNAERT, P.M., «"Jésus vint en Galilée". Essai sur la Structure de Marc 1,21-45», *NRTh* 98 (1976) 306-323.

DILLON, R.J., «"As One Having Authority" (Mark 1:22): The Controversial Distinction of Jesus' Teaching», *CBQ* 57 (1995) 92-113.

DODD, C.H., *The Parables of the Kingdom*, London 1948.

DOMERIS, W.R., «The Holy One of God as a Title for Jesus (1,24)», *Neotest.* 19 (1985) 9-17.

DONAHUE, J.R., «Tax Collectors and Sinners: An Attempt at Identification», *CBQ* 33 (1971) 39-61.

DOUGHTY, D.J., «The Authority of the Son of Man (Mk 2:1-3:6)», *ZNW* 74 (1983) 161-181.

DRURY, J., «The Sower, the Vineyard, and the Place of Allegory in the interpretation of Mark's Parables», *JThS* n.s. 24 (1973) 367-379.

DUNN, J.D.G., *Jesus, Paul, and the Law. Studies in Mark and Galatians*, Louisville 1990.

DWYER, T., «The Motif of Wonder in the Gospel of Mark», *JSNT* 57 (1995) 49-59.

————, *The Motif of Wonder in the Gospel of Mark*, JSNT.S 128, Sheffield 1996.

EDWARDS, J.R., «The Authority of Jesus in the Gospel of Mark», *JETS* 37 (1994) 217-233.

EGGER, W., *Frohbotschaft und Lehre. Die Sammelberichte des Wirkens Jesu im Markusevangelium*, FTS 19, Frankfurt/M 1976.

————, *Methodenlehre zum Neuen Testament. Einführung in linguistische und historisch-kritische Methoden*, Freiburg 1987.

EMDEN, C.S., «St. Mark's Use of the Imperfect Tense», *ET* 65 (1954) 146-149.

EVANS, C.F., *The Beginning of the Gospel... Four Lectures on St. Mark's Gospel*, London 1968.

EVANS, O.E., «The Unforgivable Sin», *ET* 68 (1957) 240-244.

FENDRICH, H., «κράζω», *EDNT* II, 313-314.

FISH, S., «Interpreting the *Variorum*», in *Reader-Response Criticism: From Formation to Post-Structuralism*, ed. J.P.Tompkins, Baltimore – London 1980, 164-184.

————, «Literature in the Reader: Affective Stylistics», in *Reader-Response Criticism: From Formation to Post-Structuralism*, ed. J.P. Tompkins, Baltimore – London 1980, 70-100.

————, *Is There a Text in This Class? The Authority of Interpretive Communities,* Cambridge – London 1980.

FLENDER, H., «Lehren und Verkündigung in den synoptischen Evangelien», *EvTh* 25 (1965) 701-714.

FLOWERS, H.J., «'Ως ἐξουσίαν ἔχων (1,22)», *ET* 66 (1954-55) 254.

FOERSTER, W., «ἔξεστιν, ἐξουσία, ...», *TDNT* II, 560-574.

————, «δαίμων, δαιμόνιον», *TDNT* II, 1-19.

FOWLER, R.M., *Loaves and Fishes: The Function of the Feeding Stories in the Gospel of Mark*, SBL.DS 54, Chico, Calif. 1981.

————, «Who is "the Reader" in Reader Response Criticism?», *Semeia* 31 (1985) 5-23.

————, *Let the Reader Understand. Reader-Response Criticism and the Gospel of Mark*, Minneapolis 1991.

FORSTER, E.M., *Aspects of the Novel*, New York 1927.

FRANCE, R.T., «Mark and the Teaching of Jesus», in *Gospel Perspectives. Studies of History and Tradition in the Four Gospels*, I, ed. R.T. France – D. Wenham, Sheffield 1980, 101-136.

FRANKEL, R., «Galilee (Prehellenistic)», *ABD* II, 879-895.

FRANKEMÖLLE, H., «συναγωγή», *EDNT* III, 293-296.

FREEDMAN, D.N., ed., *The Anchor Bible Dictionary*, I-VI, New York 1992.

FREYNE, S., *The Twelve: Disciples and Apostles. A Study in the theology of the first three gospels*, London 1968.

————, *Galilee, Jesus and the Gospels. Literary Approaches and Historical Investigations*, Dublin 1988.

————, «Galilee (Hellenistic/Roman)», *ABD* II, 895-899.

FRIDRICHSEN, A., «The Conflict of Jesus with the Unclean Spirits», *Theology* 22 (1931) 122-135.

FRIEDRICH, G., «κηρύσσω», *TDNT* III, 697-714.

FULLER, R.H., *The Mission and Achievement of Jesus*, SBT 12, London 1963.

FUSCO, V., *Parola e regno: La sezione delle parabole (4,1-34) nella prospettiva marciana*, Aloisiana 13, Brescia 1980.

GARLAND, D.E., «"I am the Lord your Healer" Mark 1:21-2:12», *RExp* 85 (1988) 327-343.

GENETTE, G., *Narrative Discourse: An Essay in Method*, tr. J.E. Lewin, Ithaca 1980.

GLASSON, T.F., «Mk 15:39: the Son of God», *ET* 80 (1968/69) 286.

GOPPELT, L., *Theology of the New Testament*, I, tr. J.E. Alsup, Grand Rapids 1981.

GRÄSSER, E., «Jesus in Nazareth (Mk VI:1-6a): Notes on the Redaction and Theology of St. Mark», *NTS* 16 (1969/70) 1-23.

————, *Jesus in Nazareth (Mc 6:1-6a): Bemerkungen zur Redaktion und Theologie des Markus*, BZNW 40, Berlin 1972.

GRILLI, M., *Comunità e Missione: le direttive di Matteo. Indagine esegetica su Mt 9,35-11,1*, EHS.T, 458, Frankfurt am Main – Berlin – Bern – New York – Paris – Wien 1992.

GRIMM, W., «ἐπιτάσσω», *EDNT* II, 41.

————, «θαμβέω, θάμβος», *EDNT* II, 128-129.

GRUENTHANER, M.L., «The Demonology of the Old Testament», *CBQ* 6 (1944) 6-27.

GRUNDMANN, W., *Der Begriff der Kraft in der neutestamentlichen Gedankenwelt*, Stuttgart 1932.

————, «κράζω, ἀνακράζω», *TDNT* III, 898-903.

GUILLEMETTE, P., «Mc 1,24 est-il une formule de défense magique?», *StEb* 30 (1978) 81-96.

————, «Un enseignement nouveau, plein d'autorité. Étude de Mc 1:21-28», *NT* 22 (1980) 222-247.

HAHN, F., «Das Gleichnis von der ausgestreuten Saat und seine Deutung (Mk iv.3-8, 14-20)», in *Text and Interpretation: Studies in the New Testament Presented to Matthew Black*, ed. E. Best – R. McL. Wilson, New York – London 1979, 133-142.

HARGREAVES, J., *A Guide to St. Mark's Gospel*, Valley Forge PA 1965.

HARRISVILLE, R.A., «The Concept of Newness in the New Testament», *JBL* 74 (1955) 69-79.

HASEL, G.F., «Sabbath», *ABD* V, 849-856.

HATCH, E. – REDPATH, H.A., *A Concordance to the Septuagint and Other Greek Versions of the Old Testament*, I-III, Oxford, Grand Rapids 1897, 1987.

HAUCK, F., «ἐκβάλλω», *TDNT* I, 527-528.

————, «παραβολή», *TDNT* V, 744-761.

HAWKINS, J.C., *Horae Synopticae. Contributions to the Study of the Synoptic Problem*, Oxford 1899.

HAYES, J.H. – HOLLADAY, C.R., *Biblical Exegesis: A Beginner's Handbook*, London 1988².

HEAD, P.M., *Christology and the Synoptic problem. An argument for Markan priority*, MSSNTS 94, Cambridge 1997.

HEDRICK, C.W., «The Role of "Summary Statement" in the Composition of the Gospel of Mark: A Dialog with Karl Schmidt and Norman Perrin», *NT* 26 (1984) 289-311.

HENGEL, M., «The Son of God», in ID., *The Cross of the Son of God*, London 1986, 1-90.

HERRENBRÜCK, F., «Wer waren die "Zöllner"?», *ZNW* 72 (1981) 178-194.

HOLLENBACH, P.W., «Jesus, Demoniacs, and Public Authorities», *JAAR* 49 (1981) 567-588.

HUDSON, D.F., «῾Ως ἐξουσίαν ἔχων», *ET* 67 (1955-56) 17.

HULTGREN, A.J., *Jesus and His Adversaries: The Form and Function of the Conflict Stories in the Synoptic Tradition*, Minneapolis 1979.

HUNZINGER, C.-H., «σίναπι», *TDNT* VII, 287-291.

ISER, W., *The Implied Reader: Patterns of Communication in Prose Fiction from Bunyan to Beckett*, Baltimore – London 1974.

————, *The Act of Reading: A Theory of Aesthetic Response*, Baltimore – London 1978.

JACOBS, M.M., «Mark's Jesus through the eyes ot twentienth century New Testament scholars», *Neotest.* 28 (1994) 53-85.

JAY, E.G., *New Testament Greek: An Introductory Grammar*, London 1987.

JEREMIAS, J., «Zöllner und Sünder», *ZNW* 30 (1931) 293-300.

————, *Jesus' Promise to the Nations*, SBT 14, London 1958.

————, «γραμματεύς», *TDNT* I, 740-742.

JEREMIAS, J., «Palästinakundiches zum Gleichnis vom Sämann», *NTS* 13 (1966/67) 48-53.

——, «πολλοί», *TDNT* VI, 543-545.

——, *Jerusalem in the Time of Jesus. An Investigation into Economic and Social Conditions during the New Testament Period*, London 1969.

——, *New Testament Theology*, London 1971.

——, *The Parables of Jesus*, London 1972.

——, *Neutestamentliche Theologie* I. *Die Verkündigung Jesu*, Gütersloh 1973.

——, *The Eucharistic Words of Jesus*, Philadelphia 1977.

JOHNSON,JR, E.S., «Is Mark 15,39 the Key to Mark's Christology?», *JSNT* 31 (1987) 3-22.

JOSEPHUS, F., *The Works of Josephus: New Updated Edition. Complete and Unabridged in One Volume*, tr. W. Whiston, Peabody 1987.

KALIN, E.R., «"That I May See": Christology and Ecclesiology in Mark», *CThMi* 20 (1993) 445-454.

KALLAS, J., *The Significance of the Synoptic Miracles*, London 1961.

KAMPLING, R., «Dämonismus und Exorzismus in der Jesusüberlieferung», *Diakonia* 21 (1990) 306-314.

KATO, Z., *Die Völkermission im Markusevangelium Eine redaktions-geschichtliche Untersuchung*, EHS.T, 252, Bern – Frankfurt am Main – New York 1986.

KAZMIERSKI, C.R., *Jesus, the Son of God. A Study of the Marcan Tradition and its Redaction by the Evangelist*, FzB 33, Würzburg 1979.

KEE, H.C., «The Terminology of Mark's Exorcism Stories», *NTS* 14 (1967-68) 232-246.

KELBER, W., *The Kingdom in Mark: A New Place and a New Time*, Philadelphia 1974.

KENNARD JR., J.S., «Was Capernaum the Home of Jesus?», *JBL* 65 (1946) 131-141.

KENNEDY, J.M., «The Root G'R in the Light of Semantic Analysis», *JBL* 106 (1987) 47-64.

KERTELGE, K., *Die Wunder Jesu im Markusevangelium. Eine redaktions-geschichtliche Untersuchung*, StANT 23, München 1970.

KIM, T.H., «The Anarthrous υἱὸς θεοῦ in Mark 15,39 and the Roman Imperial Cult», *Bib* 79 (1998) 221-241.

KINGSBURY, J.D., *The Christology of Mark's Gospel*, Philadelphia 1983.

KINGSBURY, J.D., *Conflict in Mark: Jesus, Authorities, Disciples*, Minneapolis 1989.

————, «The Religious Authorities in the Gospel of Mark», *NTS* 36 (1990) 42-65.

————, «The Figure of Jesus in Matthew's Story: A Literary Critical Probe», *JSNT* 21 (1984) 3-36.

KITTEL, G., «ὑπακούω», *TDNT* I, 223-224.

————, «ἀκοή», *TDNT* I, 221-222.

KITTEL, G. – FRIEDRICH, G. ed., *Theological Dictionary of the New Testament*, I-X, Grand Rapids 1964-1976.

KLAUCK, H.-J., *Allegorie und Allegorese in synoptischen Gleichnistexten*, NTA 13, Münster 1978.

KLAUSER, T., «Akklamation», *RAC* I, 216-233.

KLAUSER, T. – DASSMANN, E., *Reallexikon für Antike und Christentum. Sachwörterbuch zur Auseinandersetzung des Christentums mit der Antiken Welt*, I-XVII, Stuttgart 1950-1996.

KLEINKNECHT, H., «πνεῦμα, πνευματικός», *TDNT* VI, 332-359.

KOCH, D.-A., *Die Bedeutung der Wundererzählungen für die Christologie des Markusevangeliums*, BZNW 42, Berlin 1975.

KOLLMANN, B., «Jesu Schweigegebote an die Dämonen», *ZNW* 82 (1991) 267-273.

KREMER, J., «Jesu Antwort auf die Frage nach seiner Vollmacht. Eine Auslegung von Mk 11,27-33», *BiLe* 9 (1968) 128-136.

————, «πνεῦμα», *EDNT* III, 117-122.

KÜMMEL, W.G., *Promise and Fulfillment*, SBT 23, London 1961.

KRUSE, H., «Die "dialektische Negation" als semitisches Idiom», *VT* 4 (1954) 385-400.

————, «Das Reich Satans», *Bib* 58 (1977) 39-41.

KUTHIRAKKATTEL, S., *The Beginning of Jesus' Ministry according to Mark's Gospel (1:14-3:6): A Redaction Critical Study*, AnBib 123, Rome 1990.

LAGRAND, J., «The First of the Miracle Stories According to Mark (1:21-28)», *CThMi* 20 (1993) 479-484.

LAMBRECHT, J., «The Christology of Mark», *BTB* 3 (1973) 256-273.

————, «ἐξίστημι», *EDNT* II, 7-8.

LANG, F., «Kompositionsanalyse des Markusevangeliums», *ZThK* 74 (1977) 1-24.

LARSSON, E., «συζητέω», *EDNT* III, 284.

LEE, M.Y.-H., *Jesus und die jüdische Autorität: Eine exegetische Untersuchung zu Mk 11,27-12,12*, FzB 56, Würzburg 1986.

LESKY, E. – WASZINK, J.H., «Epilepsie», *RAC* V, 819-831.

LIDDELL, H.G. – SCOTT, R. – JONES, H.S., *A Greek-English Lexicon*, Oxford 1992[9].

LIEW, T.-S. B., «Tyranny, Boundary and Might: Colonial Mimicry in Mark's Gospel», *JSNT* 73 (1999) 7-31.

LINNEMANN, E., *Gleichnisse Jesu: Einführung und Auslegung*, Göttingen 1978.

LOHSE, E., «σάββατον», *TDNT* VII, 1-35.

———, *The New Testament Environment*, London 1989.

LÜHRMANN, D., «Die Pharisäer und die Schriftgelehrten im Markus- evangelium», *ZNW* 78 (1987) 169-185.

MALBON, E.S., «Galilee and Jerusalem: History and Literature in Marcan Interpretation», *CBQ* 44 (1983) 242-255.

———, «The Jesus of Mark and the Sea of Galilee», *JBL* 103 (1984) 363-377.

———, «Τῇ οἰκίᾳ αὐτοῦ: Mark 2:15 in Context», *NTS* 31 (1985) 282-292.

———, *Narrative Space and Mythic Meaning in Mark*, New York – San Francisco 1986.

———, «Disciples/Crowds/Whoever: Markan Characters and Readers», *NT* 28 (1986) 104-130.

———, «The Jewish Leaders in the Gospel of Mark: A Literary Study of Markan Characterization», *JBL* 108 (1989) 259-281.

MALONEY, E.C., *Semitic Interference in Marcan Syntax*, SBL.DS 51, Chico, CA 1981.

MANICARDI, E., *Il Cammino di Gesù nel Vangelo di Marco*, AnBib 96, Roma 1981.

MARCUS, J., *The Mystery of the Kingdom of God*, SBL.DS 90, Atlanta 1986.

———, «Mark 14:61: "Are You the Messiah-Son-of-God?"», *NT* 31 (1989) 125-141.

MARSH, J., «Authority», *IDB* I, 319-320.

MARTIN, R.P., *Mark: Evangelist and Theologian*, Exeter 1972.

MARUCCI, C., «Die Implizite Christologie in der sogenannten Vollmachtsfrage (Mk 11,27-33)», *ZKTh* 108 (1986) 292-300.

MAYNARD, A.M., «τί ἐμοὶ καὶ σοί», *NTS* 31 (1985) 582-586.

MCARTHUR, H.K., «The Parable of the Mustard Seed», *CBQ* 33 (1971) 198-210.

MCCASLAND, S.V., «The Demonic "Confessions" of Jesus», *JR* 24 (1944) 33-36.

MEISER, M., *Die Reaktion des Volkes auf Jesus. Eine redaktionskritische Untersuchung zu den synoptischen Evangelien*, BZNW 96, Berlin 1998.

METZGER, B.M., *A Textual Commentary on the Greek New Testament*, Stuttgart 1975.

MEYE, R.P., *Jesus and the Twelve. Discipleship and Revelation in Mark's Gospel*, Grand Rapids 1968.

MICHEL, O., «κύων, κυνάριον», *TDNT* III, 1101-1104.

MOULTON, W.F. – GEDEN, A.S. – MOULTON, H.S., *A Concordance to the Greek Testament*, Edinburgh 1989[5].

MOULTON, J.H. – HOWARD, W.F., *A Grammar of the New Testament Greek*, II, Accidence and Word Formation, Edinburgh 1963.

MOULTON, J.H. – MILLIGAN, G., *Vocabulary of the Greek Testament*, London 1929.

MOULTON, J.H. – TURNER, N.A., *A Grammar of the New Testament Greek*, III, Syntax, Edinburgh 1963.

————, *A Grammar of the New Testament Greek*, IV, Style, Edinburgh 1976.

MURPHY, C.M., «Discipleship in Mark as Movement with Christ», *BiTod* 53 (1971) 305-308.

MUSSNER, F., «Ein Wortspiel in Mk 1,24?», *BZ* 4 (1960) 285-286.

NEIRYNCK, F., *Duality in Mark. Contributions to the Study of the Markan Redaction*, BEThL 31, Leuven (1972) 1988.

————, «Duality in Mark», *EThL* 47 (1971) 394-463.

NEUSNER, J., «First Cleanse the Inside», *NTS* 22 (1975/76) 486-495.

NEYREY, J.H., «The Idea of Purity in Mark's Gospel», *Semeia* 35 (1986) 91-128.

OEPKE, A., «ἀπόλλυμι», *TDNT* I, 394-396.

OKOYE, J.C., «Mark 1:21-28 in African Perspective», *BiTod* 34 (1996) 240-245.

OSBORNE, G.R., «Structure and Christology in Mark 1:21-45», in *Jesus of Nazareth: Lord and Christ. Essays on the Historical Jesus and New Testament Christology*, Grand Rapids 1994, 147-163.

PAGE, S.H.T., *Powers of Evil. A Biblical Study of Satan and Demons*, Grand Rapids – Leicester 1995.

PAYNE, P.B., «The Order of Sowing and Ploughing in the Parable of the Sower», *NTS* 25 (1978/79) 123-129.

PESCH, R., «"Eine neue Lehre aus Macht", Eine Studie zu Mk 1,21-28», in *Evangelienforschung: Ausgewählte Aufsätze deutscher Exegeten*, ed. J.B. Bauer, Graz – Wien 1968, 241-276.

————, «Ein Tag vollmächtigen Wirkens Jesu in Kapharnaum (Mk 1,21-34.35-39)», *BiLe* 9 (1968) 114-128, 177-195, 261-277.

————, «Levi-Matthäus (Mc 2,14/Mt 9,9; 10,3): Ein Beitrag zur Lösung eines alten Problems», *ZNW* 59 (1968) 40-56.

————, «Das Zöllnergastmahl (Mk 2,15-17)», in *Fs. B. Rigaux*, Gembloux 1970, 63-87.

PETERSEN, N.R., «"Point of View" in Mark's Narrative», *Semeia* 12 (1978) 97-121.

PFISTER, F., «Beschwörung», *RAC* II, 169-176.

PIMENTEL, P., «The "unclean spirits" of St. Mark's Gospel», *ET* 99 (1987) 173-175.

PINTO, E., «Jesus as the Son of God in the Gospels», *BTB* 4 (1974) 75-93.

PÖHLMANN, W., «εὐθύς, εὐθέως», *EDNT* II, 77-78.

POWELL, M.A., *What is Narrative Criticism? A New Approach to the Bible*, London 1993.

PROCKSCH, O., «ἄγιος», *TDNT* I, 88-97; 100-110.

PRYKE, E.J., *Redactional Style in the Marcan Gospel. A Study of Syntax and Vocabulary as guides to Redaction in Mark*, MSSNTS 33, Cambridge – London 1978.

QUESNELL, Q., *The Mind of Mark: Interpretation and Method Through the Exegesis of Mark 6:52*, AnBib 38, Rome 1969.

REISER, M., *Syntax und Stil des Markusevangeliums*, WUNT 2/11, Tübingen 1984.

RENGSTORF, K.H., «ἀπόστολος», *TDNT* I, 407-445.

————, «διδαχή», *TDNT* II, 163-165.

————, «μαθητής», *TDNT* IV, 415-460.

REPLOH, K.-G., *Markus - Lehrer der Gemeinde. Eine redaktionsgeschichtliche Studie zu den Jüngerperikopen des Markus-Evangeliums*, SBM 9, Stuttgart 1969.

RESSEGUIE, J.L., «Reader-Response Criticism and the Synoptic Gospels», *JAAR* 52 (1984) 307-324.

RHOADS, D., «Narrative Criticism and the Gospel of Mark», *JAAR* 50 (1982) 411-434.

————, «Mission in the Gospel of Mark», *CThMi* 22 (1995) 340-355.

RHOADS, D. – MICHIE, D., *Mark as Story: An Introduction to the Narrative of a Gospel*, Philadelphia 1982.

RIVKIN, E., «Scribes, Pharisees, Lawyers, Hypocrites: A Study in Synonymity», *HUCA* 49 (1978) 135-142.

ROBBINS, V.K., *Jesus the Teacher: A Socio-Rhetorical Interpretation of Mark*, Philadelphia 1984.

ROBINSON, J.M., *The Problem of History in Mark and other Marcan Studies*, Philadelphia 1982.

ROHDE, E., *Psyche, Seelencult und Unsterblichkeitsglaube der Griechen*, II, Tübingen 1907.

SABOURIN, L., «The Miracles of Jesus (II). Jesus and the Evil Powers», *BTB* 4 (1974) 115-175.

SALDARINI, A.J., *Pharisees, Scribes and Sadducees in Palestinian Society*, Edinburgh 1989.

————, «Scribe», *ABD* V, 1012-1016.

SANDERS, E.P., *Jesus and Judaism*, London 1985.

————, «Sin, Sinners (NT)», *ABD* VI, 40-47.

SCHAEDER, H.H., «Ναζαρηνός, Ναζωραῖος», *TDNT* IV, 874-879.

SCHENKE, L., *Die Wundererzählungen des Markusevangeliums*, Stuttgart 1975.

SCHLIER, H., «ἀμήν», *TDNT* I, 335-338.

SCHNACKENBURG, R., *God's Rule and Kingdom*, Montreal 1963.

SCHNEIDER, C., «κάθημαι», *TDNT* III, 440-444.

SCHNEIDER, G., «ἀκοή», *EDNT* I, 52-54.

————, «νέος», *EDNT* II, 462-463.

————, «ὑπακούω», *EDNT* III, 394-395.

SCHNEIDER, J., «ἐξέρχομαι», *TDNT* II, 678-680.

————, «συζητέω», *TDNT* VII, 747-748.

SCHOLTISSEK, K., «Nachfolge und Autorität nach dem Markusevangelium», *TthZ* 100 (1991) 56-74.

SCHOLTISSEK, K., *Die Vollmacht Jesu: Traditions- und redaktionsgeschichtliche Analysen zu einem Leitmotiv markinischer Christologie*, NTA 25, Münster 1992.

SCHMIDT, K.L., *Der Rahmen der Geschichte Jesu: Literarkritische Untersuchung zur ältesten Jesuüberlieferung*, Berlin 1919.

SCHÜRER, E., *The History of the Jewish People in the Age of Jesus Christ*, I-III, Revised and Edited by G. Vermes – F. Millar – M. Black, Edinburgh 1973-1987.

SCHWEIZER, E., «"Er wird Nazoräer heissen" (zu Mc 1,24; Mt 2,23)», in *Judentum, Urchristentum, Kirche*, Fs. J. Jeremias, BZNW 26, Berlin 1960, 90-93.

————, «Anmerkungen zur Theologie des Markus», *Neotestamentica*, Zürich – Stuttgart 1963, 93-104.

————, «Die theologische Leistung des Markus», *EvTh* 24 (1964) 340-355.

————, «πνεῦμα, πνευματικός», *TDNT* VI, 389-451.

SELWYN, E.G., «The Authority of Christ in the New Testament», *NTS* 3 (1956/57) 83-92.

SHAE, G.S., «The Question on the Authority of Jesus», *NT* 16 (1974) 1-29.

SKA, J.L., *«Our Fathers Have Told Us»: Introduction to the Analysis of Hebrew Narratives*, SubBi 13, Roma 1990.

————, «Sincronia: L'analisi narrativa», in *Metodologia dell'Antico Testamento*, ed. H. Simian-Yofre, StBi 25, Bologna 1995, 139-170.

SMITH, S.H., «A Divine Tragedy: Some Observations on the Dramatic Structure of Mark's Gospel», *NT* 37 (1995) 209-231.

STARR, J., «The Meaning of "Authority" in Mark 1,22», *HThR* 23 (1930) 302-305.

STAUFFER, E., «ἐπιτιμάω», *TDNT* II, 623-626.

STEIN, R.H., *The Proper Methodology for Ascertaining a Marcan Redaktionsgeschichte*, Ann Arbor 1969.

————, «The "Redaktionsgeschichtlich" Investigation of a Markan Seam (Mc 1,21f)», *ZNW* 61 (1970) 70-94.

STERNBERG, M., *Expositional Modes and Temporal Ordering in Fiction*, Baltimore 1978.

————, *The Poetics of Biblical Narrative: Ideological Literature and the Drama of Reading*, Bloomington 1987.

STOCK, K., *Boten aus dem Mit-Ihm-Sein. Das Verhältnis zwischen Jesus und den Zwölf nach Markus*, AnBib 70, Rome 1975.

STOCK, K., «Gesù è il Cristo, il Figlio di Dio, nel Vangelo di Marco», *RdT* 17 (1976) 242-253.

————, «Das Bekenntnis des Centurio, Mk 15,39 im Rahmen des Markus-evangeliums», *ZKTh* 100 (1978) 289-301.

————, «Gliederung und Zusammenhang in Mk 11-12», *Bib* 59 (1978) 481-515.

————, «Theologie der Mission bei Markus», in *Mission im Neuen Testament*, ed. K. Kertelge, QD 93, Freiburg – Basel – Wien 1982, 130-144.

————, *Jesus die Frohe Botschaft: Meditationen zu Markus*, Innsbruck – Wien 1983.

————, «La conoscenza dei demoni (Mc 1,34)», *PSV* 18 (1988) 93-112.

————, «Die Machttaten Jesu. Ihr Zeugnis in den synoptischen Evangelien», *IKaZ/Communio* 18 (1989) 195-206.

STRACK, H.L. – BILLERBECK, P., *Kommentar zum Neuen Testament aus Talmud und Midrasch*, I-VI, München 1965[4].

SUHL, A., «Überlegungen zur Hermeneutik an Hand von Mk 1,21-28», *Kairos* 26 (1984) 28-38.

SWAIN, L., «The Divine Face of Man: Mark's Christology», *Clergy Review* 58 (1973) 696-708.

SWETNAM, J., «On the Identity of Jesus», *Bib* 65 (1984) 412-416.

————, Review of: V.K. ROBBINS, *Jesus the Teacher, Bib* 66 (1985) 136-139.

————, *An Introduction to the Study of New Testament Greek*, Part I: Morphology, SubBi 16/I, Roma 1998[2].

TAGAWA, K., *Miracles et Évangile. La pensée personnelle de l'evangéliste Marc*, EHPhR 62, Paris 1966.

TANNEHILL, R.C., «The Gospel of Mark as Narrative Christology», *Semeia* 16 (1979) 57-95.

TATE, W.R., *Reading Mark From the Outside. Eco and Iser Leave Their Marks*, San Francisco 1995.

TAYLOR, D.B., «Jesus - of Nazareth?», *ET* 92 (1980) 336-337.

TAYLOR, V., *Jesus and His Sacrifice. A Study of the Passion-Sayings in the Gospels*, London 1955.

THEISSEN, G., *The Miracle Stories of Early Christian Tradition*, tr. F. McDonagh, Philadelphia 1983.

THRAEDE, K., «Exorzismus», *RAC* VII, 44-117.

TÖDT, T., *The Son of Man in the Synoptic Tradition*, Philadelphia 1965.

TOMPKINS, J.P., «An Introduction to Reader-Response Criticism», in *Reader-Response Criticism: From Formation to Post-Structuralism*, ed., J.P. Tompkins, Baltimore – London 1980, ix-xxvi.

TOOLEY, W., «The Shepherd Image in the Teaching of Jesus», *NT* 7 (1964) 15-25.

TROCMÉ, E., «L'expulsion des marchands du Temple», *NTS* 15 (1968/69) 1-22.

TRUNK, D., *Der messianische Heiler. Eine redaktions- und religionsgeschichtliche Studie zu den Exorzismen im Matthäusevangelium*, Freiburg 1994.

———, «Jesus, der Exorzist», *ThPQ* 145 (1997) 3-13.

TURNER, C.H., «Marcan Usage: Notes, Critical and Exegetical, on the Second Gospel», *JThS* 25 (1923-24) 377-386; 26 (1924-25) 12-20, 145-156, 225-240, 337-345; 27 (1925-26) 58-62; 28 (1926-27) 9-30, 349-362; 29 (1927-28) 275-289, 346-361.

———, «Text of Mark 1», *JThS* 28 (1926-27) 150-158.

TWELFTREE, G.H., «ΕΙ ΔΕ … ΕΓΩ ΕΚΒΑΛΛΩ ΤΑ ΔΑΙΜΟΝΙΑ…», in *Gospel Perspectives. The Miracles of Jesus*, VI, ed. D. Wenham – C. Blomberg, Sheffield 1986, 361-400.

———, *Jesus the Exorcist. A Contribution to the Study of the Historical Jesus*, WUNT 2/54, Tübingen 1993.

USPENSKY, B., *A Poetics of Composition; The Structure of the Artistic Text and Typology of a Compositional Form*, tr. V. Zararin – S. Wittig, London 1973.

VAN DER LOOS, H., *The Miracles of Jesus*, NT.S 8; Leiden 1965.

WASZINK, J.H., «Besessenheit», *RAC* II, 183-185.

WEBER, J.C., «Jesus' Opponents in the Gospel of Mark», *JBR* 34 (1966) 214-222.

WEISS, J., «ΕΥΘΥΣ bei Markus», *ZNW* 11 (1910) 124-133.

WEISS, W., «*Eine neue Lehre in Vollmacht*»: die Streit-und Schulgespräche des *Markus-Evangeliums*, BZNW 52, Berlin 1989.

WILDER, A.N., «The Parable of the Sower: Naiveté and Method in Interpretation», *Semeia* 2 (1974) 134-151.

WREDE, W., *Das Messiasgeheimnis in den Evangelien. Zugleich ein Beitrag zum Verständnis des Markusevangeliums*, Göttingen 1901.

YATES, R., «Jesus and the Demonic in the Synoptic Gospels», *IThQ* 44 (1977) 39-57.

ZERWICK, M., *Untersuchungen zum Markus-Stil. Ein Beitrag zur stilistischen Durcharbeitung des Neuen Testaments*, Roma 1937.

————, *Biblical Greek*, adapted by J. Smith, Roma 1990.

ZERWICK, M. – GROSVENOR, M., *A Grammatical Analysis of the Greek New Testament*, Roma 1988[3].

INDEX OF AUTHORS

TABLE OF CONTENTS

TESI GREGORIANA

Since 1995, the series «Tesi Gregoriana» has made available to the general public some of the best doctoral theses done at the Pontifical Gregorian University. The typesetting is done by the authors themselves following norms established and controlled by the University.

Published Volumes [Series: Theology]

1. NELLO FIGA, Antonio, *Teorema de la opción fundamental. Bases para su adecuada utilización en teología moral*, 1995, pp. 380.

2. BENTOGLIO, Gabriele, *Apertura e disponibilità. L'accoglienza nell'epistolario paolino*, 1995, pp. 376.

3. PISO, Alfeu, *Igreja e sacramentos. Renovação da Teologia Sacramentária na América Latina*, 1995, pp. 260.

4. PALAKEEL, Joseph, *The Use of Analogy in Theological Discourse. An Investigation in Ecumenical Perspective*, 1995, pp. 392.

5. KIZHAKKEPARAMPIL, Isaac, *The Invocation of the Holy Spirit as Constitutive of the Sacraments according to Cardinal Yves Congar*, 1995, pp. 200.

6. MROSO, Agapit J., *The Church in Africa and the New Evangelisation. A Theologico-Pastoral Study of the Orientations of John Paul II*, 1995, pp. 456.

7. NANGELIMALIL, Jacob, *The Relationship between the Eucharistic Liturgy, the Interior Life and the Social Witness of the Church according to Joseph Cardinal Parecattil*, 1996, pp. 224.

8. GIBBS, Philip, *The Word in the Third World. Divine Revelation in the Theology of Jen-Marc Éla, Aloysius Pieris and Gustavo Gutiérrez*, 1996, pp. 448.

9. DELL'ORO, Roberto, *Esperienza morale e persona. Per una reinterpretazione dell'etica fenomenologica di Dietrich von Hildebrand*, 1996, pp. 240.

10. BELLANDI, Andrea, *Fede cristiana come «stare e comprendere». La giustificazione dei fondamenti della fede in Joseph Ratzinger*, 1996, pp. 416.

11. BEDRIÑAN, Claudio, *La dimensión socio-política del mensaje teológico del Apocalipsis*, 1996, pp. 364.

12. GWYNNE, Paul, *Special Divine Action. Key Issues in the Contemporary Debate (1965-1995)*, 1996, pp. 376.

13. NIÑO, Francisco, *La Iglesia en la ciudad. El fenómeno de las grandes ciudades en América Latina, como problema teológico y como desafío pastoral*, 1996, pp. 492.

14. BRODEUR, Scott, *The Holy Spirit's Agency in the Resurrection of the Dead. An Exegetico-Theological Study of 1 Corinthians 15,44b-49 and Romans 8,9-13*, 1996, pp. 300.

15. ZAMBON, Gaudenzio, *Laicato e tipologie ecclesiali. Ricerca storica sulla «Teologia del laicato» in Italia alla luce del Concilio Vaticano II (1950-1980)*, 1996, pp. 548.

16. ALVES DE MELO, Antonio, *A Evangelização no Brasil. Dimensões teológicas e desafios pastorais. O debate teológico e eclesial (1952-1995)*, 1996, pp. 428.

17. APARICIO VALLS, María del Carmen, *La plenitud del ser humano en Cristo. La Revelación en la «Gaudium et Spes»*, 1997, pp. 308.

18. MARTIN, Seán Charles, *«Pauli Testamentum». 2 Timothy and the Last Words of Moses*, 1997, pp. 312.

19. RUSH, Ormond, *The Reception of Doctrine. An Appropriation of Hans Robert Jauss' Reception Aesthetics and Literary Hermeneutics*, 1997, pp. 424.

20. MIMEAULT, Jules, *La sotériologie de François-Xavier Durrwell. Exposé et réflexions critiques*, 1997, pp. 476.

21. CAPIZZI, Nunzio, *L'uso di Fil 2,6-11 nella cristologia contemporanea (1965-1993)*, 1997, pp. 528.

22. NANDKISORE, Robert, *Hoffnung auf Erlösung. Die Eschatologie im Werk Hans Urs von Balthasars*, 1997, pp. 304.

23. PERKOVIĆ, Marinko, *«Il cammino a Dio» e «La direzione alla vita»: L'ordine morale nelle opere di Jordan Kuničić, O.P. (1908-1974)*, 1997, pp. 336.

24. DOMERGUE, Benoît, *La réincarnation et la divinisation de l'homme dans les religions. Approche phénomenologique et théologique*, 1997, pp. 300.

25. FARKAŠ, Pavol, *La «donna» di Apocalisse 12. Storia, bilancio, nuove prospettive*, 1997, pp. 276.

26. OLIVER, Robert W., *The Vocation of the Laity to Evangelization. An Ecclesiological Inquiry into the Synod on the Laity (1987), Christifideles laici (1989) and Documents of the NCCB (1987-1996)*, 1997, pp. 364.

27. SPATAFORA, Andrea, *From the «Temple of God» to God as the Temple. A Biblical Theological Study of the Temple in the Book of Revelation*, 1997, pp. 340.

28. IACOBONE, Pasquale, *Mysterium Trinitatis. Dogma e Iconografia nell'Italia medievale*, 1997, pp. 512.

29. CASTAÑO FONSECA, Adolfo M., Δικαιοσύνη en Mateo. Una interpretación teológica a partir de 3,15 y 21,32, 1997, pp. 344.

30. CABRIA ORTEGA, José Luis, Relación teología-filosofía en el pensamiento de Xavier Zubiri, 1997, pp. 580.

31. SCHERRER, Thierry, La gloire de Dieu dans l'oeuvre de saint Irénée, 1997, pp. 328.

32. PASCUZZI, Maria, Ethics, Ecclesiology and Church Discipline. A Rhetorical Analysis of 1 Cor 5,1-13, 1997, pp. 240.

33. LOPES GONÇALVES, Paulo Sérgio, Liberationis mysterium. O projeto sistemático da teologia da libertação. Um estudo teológico na perspectiva da regula fidei, 1997, pp. 464.

34. KOLACINSKI, Mariusz, Dio fonte del diritto naturale, 1997, pp. 296.

35. LIMA CORRÊA, Maria de Lourdes, Salvação entre juízo, conversão e graça. A perspectiva escatológica de Os 14,2-9, 1998, pp. 360.

36. MEIATTINI, Giulio, «Sentire cum Christo». La teologia dell'esperienza cristiana nell'opera di H.U. von Balthasar, 1998, pp. 432.

37. KESSLER, Thomas W., Peter as the First Witness of the Risen Lord. An Historical and Theological Investigation, 1998, pp. 240.

38. BIORD CASTILLO Raúl, La Resurrección de Cristo como Revelación. Análisis del tema en la teología fundamental a partir de la Dei Verbum, 1998, pp. 308.

39. LÓPEZ, Javier, La figura de la bestia entre historia y profecía. Investigación teológico-bíblica de Apocalipsis 13,1-8, 1998, pp. 308.

40. SCARAFONI, Paolo, Amore salvifico. Una lettura del mistero della salvezza. Uno studio comparativo di alcune soteriologie cattoliche postconciliari, 1998, pp. 240.

41. BARRIOS PRIETO, Manuel Enrique, Antropologia teologica. Temi principali di antropologia teologica usando un metodo di «correlazione» a partire dalle opere di John Macquarrie, 1998, pp. 416.

42. LEWIS, Scott M., «So That God May Be All in All». The Apocalyptic Message of 1 Corinthians 15,12-34, 1998, pp. 252.

43. ROSSETTI, Carlo Lorenzo, «Sei diventato Tempio di Dio». Il mistero del Tempio e dell'abitazione divina negli scritti di Origene, 1998, pp. 232.

44. CERVERA BARRANCO, Pablo, La incorporación en la Iglesia mediante el bautismo y la profesión de la fe según el Concilio Vaticano II, 1998, pp. 372.

45. NETO, Laudelino, Fé cristã e cultura latino-americana. Uma análise a partir das Conferências de Puebla e Santo Domingo, 1998, pp. 340.

46. BRITO GUIMARÃES, Pedro, *Os sacramentos como atos eclesiais e proféticos. Um contributo ao conceito dogmático de sacramento à luz da exegese contemporânea,* 1998, pp. 448.

47. CALABRETTA, Rose B., *Baptism and Confirmation. The Vocation and Mission of the Laity in the Writings of Virgil Michel, O.S.B.,* 1998, pp. 320.

48. OTERO LÁZARO, Tomás, *Col 1,15-20 en el contexto de la carta,* 1999, pp.312.

49. KOWALCZYK, Dariusz, *La personalità in Dio. Dal metodo trascendentale di Karl Rahner verso un orientamento dialogico in Heinrich Ott,* 1999, pp. 484.

50. PRIOR, Joseph G., *The Historical-Critical Method in Catholic Exegesis,* 1999, pp. 352.

51. CAHILL, Brendan J, *The Renewal of Revelation Theology (1960-1962). The Development and Responses to the Fourth Chapter of the Preparatory Schema* De deposito Fidei, 1999, pp. 348.

52. TIEZZI, Ida, *Il rapporto tra la pneumatologia e l'ecclesiologia nella teologia italiana post-conciliare,* 1999, pp. 364.

53. HOLC, Paweł, *Un ampio consenso sulla dottrina della giustificazione. Studio sul dialogo teologico cattolico luterano,* 1999, pp. 452.

54. GAINO, Andrea, *Esistenza cristiana. Il pensiero teologico di J. Alfaro e la sua rilevanza morale,* 1999, pp. 344.

55. NERI, Francesco, *«Cur Verbum capax hominis». Le ragioni dell'incarnazione della seconda Persona della Trinità fra teologia scolastica e teologia contemporanea,* 1999, pp. 404.

56. MUÑOZ CÁRDABA, Luis-Miguel, *Principios eclesiológicos de la «Pastor Bonus»,* 1999, pp. 344.

57. IWE, John Chijioke, *Jesus in the Synagogue of Capernaum: the Pericope and Its Programmatic Character for the Gospel of Mark. An Exegetico-Theological Study of Mk 1:21-28,* 1999, pp. 364.